God's Action in the World

Also available from Bloomsbury

Contemporary Arguments in Natural Theology, edited by Colin Ruloff
and Peter Horban
Four Views on the Axiology of Theism, edited by Kirk Lougheed
Free Will and Epistemology, by Robert Lockie
Free Will and God's Universal Causality, by W. Matthews Grant
Human Dignity in the Judaeo-Christian Tradition, edited by John Loughlin

God's Action in the World

A New Philosophical Analysis

Marek Słomka

BLOOMSBURY ACADEMIC
LONDON • NEW YORK • OXFORD • NEW DELHI • SYDNEY

BLOOMSBURY ACADEMIC
Bloomsbury Publishing Plc
50 Bedford Square, London, WC1B 3DP, UK
1385 Broadway, New York, NY 10018, USA
29 Earlsfort Terrace, Dublin 2, Ireland

BLOOMSBURY, BLOOMSBURY ACADEMIC and the Diana logo are trademarks of
Bloomsbury Publishing Plc

First published in Great Britain 2021
This paperback edition published in 2022

Copyright © Marek Słomka, 2021

Marek Słomka has asserted his right under the Copyright, Designs and Patents Act,
1988, to be identified as Author of this work.

For legal purposes the Acknowledgments on p. viii constitute an extension
of this copyright page.

Cover image: Winter sunset by the Oslofjord at Botnerbaugen in
Larkollen, Rygge kommune, Østfold fylke, Norway.
© Oyvind Martinsen / Alamy Stock Photo

All rights reserved. No part of this publication may be reproduced or transmitted
in any form or by any means, electronic or mechanical, including photocopying,
recording, or any information storage or retrieval system, without prior
permission in writing from the publishers.

Bloomsbury Publishing Plc does not have any control over, or responsibility for, any
third-party websites referred to or in this book. All internet addresses given in this
book were correct at the time of going to press. The author and publisher regret
any inconvenience caused if addresses have changed or sites have ceased to
exist, but can accept no responsibility for any such changes.

A catalogue record for this book is available from the British Library.

Library of Congress Cataloging-in-Publication Data

Names: Słomka, Marek, author.
Title: God's action in the world : a new philosophical analysis / Marek Slomka.
Description: New York : Bloomsbury Academic, 2021. |
Includes bibliographical references and index. |
Identifiers: LCCN 2020054501 (print) | LCCN 2020054502 (ebook) |
ISBN 9781350180383 (hardback) | ISBN 9781350180390 (ebook) |
ISBN 9781350180406 (epub)
Subjects: LCSH: Providence and government of god. | God. | Theism. |
Religion and science.
Classification: LCC BD541 .S56 2021 (print) | LCC BD541 (ebook) | DDC 212—dc23
LC record available at https://lccn.loc.gov/2020054501
LC ebook record available at https://lccn.loc.gov/2020054502

ISBN: HB: 978-1-3501-8038-3
       PB: 978-1-3502-3678-3
       ePDF: 978-1-3501-8039-0
       eBook: 978-1-3501-8040-6

Typeset by RefineCatch Limited, Bungay, Suffolk

To find out more about our authors and books visit www.bloomsbury.com
and sign up for our newsletters.

*To my parents
and in memory of archbishop prof. Józef Życiński (1948–2011)*

Contents

Preface and Acknowledgments		viii
Abbreviations		ix
Introduction		1
1	On the Action	9
2	On God	21
3	On the World	77
4	Threats and Challenges	123
Conclusion		167
Notes		175
Select Bibliography		213
Index		221

Preface and Acknowledgments

In 2018, the John Paul II Catholic University of Lublin published the Polish edition of my book devoted to the problem of divine action in the world. Encouraged by the positive reviews it received and the interesting feedback it was given, I continued my analyses of this fascinating question. I have reworked the original text and submitted the new manuscript to Bloomsbury. I am truly happy that my work will now be available in English.

I would like to express my thanks to all the academics that have helped me notice many significant aspects of the discussed problem. I would also like to express my gratitude to the employees of Bloomsbury Publishing that have provided their professional assistance at the various stages of the book being prepared for print. I would like to give additional thanks to the people involved in helping me with the English text of the book: Tomasz Pałkowski, Brian Panasiak, and especially to Monika Metlerska-Colerick, whose contribution to the realization of the project cannot be overestimated. Finally, I would like to wish all those who supported me in the process of preparing this book to personally experience God's action in their lives.

* * *

The project is funded by the Minister of Science and Higher Education within the program under the name "Regional Initiative of Excellence" in 2019–2022, project number: 028/RID/2018/19, the amount of funding: 11 742 500 PLN.

Abbreviations

CC   *Chaos and Complexity. Scientific Perspectives on Divine Action.* 2nd ed. Edited by Robert J. Russell, Nancey Murphy, and Arthur R. Peacocke. Vatican City State: Vatican Observatory Publications; Berkeley, CA: The Center for Theology and the Natural Sciences, 2000.

EMB   *Evolutionary and Molecular Biology. Scientific Perspectives on Divine Action.* Edited by Robert J. Russell, William R. Stoeger, Francisco J. Ayala. Vatican City State: Vatican Observatory Publications; Berkeley, CA: The Center for Theology and the Natural Sciences, 1998.

NAP   *Neuroscience and the Person. Scientific Perspectives on Divine Action.* Edited by Robert J. Russell, Nancey Murphy, Theo C. Meyering, and Michael A. Arbib. Vatican City State: Vatican Observatory Publications; Berkeley, CA: The Center for Theology and the Natural Sciences, 1999.

QC   *Quantum Cosmology and the Laws of Nature. Scientific Perspectives on Divine Action.* 2nd ed. Edited by Robert J. Russell, Nancey Murphy, and Chris J. Isham, Vatican City State: Vatican Observatory Publications; Berkeley, CA: The Center for Theology and the Natural Sciences, 1999.

QM   *Quantum Mechanics. Scientific Perspectives on Divine Action.* Edited by Robert J. Russell, Philip Clayton, Kirk Wegter-McNelly, and John Polkinghorne. Vatican City State: Vatican Observatory Publications; Berkeley, CA: The Center for Theology and the Natural Sciences, 2001.

SPDA   *Scientific Perspectives on Divine Action. Twenty Years of Challenge and Progress.* Edited by Robert J. Russell, Nancey Murphy, and William R. Stoeger. Vatican City State: Vatican Observatory Publications; Berkeley, CA: The Center for Theology and the Natural Sciences; Notre Dame, IN: University of Notre Dame Press, 2008

ATR   *Anglican Theological Review*

JETS   *Journal of the Evangelical Theological Society*

JR   *Journal of Religion*

RelS   *Religious Studies*

TS   *Theological Studies*

Introduction

A God who no longer plays an active role in the world is in the final analysis a dead God.[1]

The concept of divine providence (in its non-homogenous varieties) can be found in the doctrines of all major monotheistic religions. This weighty idea cannot be limited to mere acknowledgement of an unspecified relationship between "heaven and earth," but should rather highlight the real and tangible influence of the Creator on the fate of creation. A detailed elaboration on the theory of God's interaction with the world, and most importantly with the human being, remains a significant goal of theology. However, a crucial input in this field can also be provided by philosophers: a) introducing the already available viewpoints, b) clarifying the meaning of employed terminology, and c) analyzing the suggested solutions from the perspective of their internal coherence and compatibility with the current state of research in the areas of philosophy, theology, or even natural sciences.

In undertaking my research in the scope outlined above I make the assumption that theism is a valuable (albeit subject to modifications) constituent of academic thought and the entirety of human culture. However, it is not my immediate goal to account for the value of theism. The main aim of this book is to analyze the problem posed in the title, which in itself determines and organizes the substantive framework of the totality of this study as well as the constituent parts thereof. Thus, chapter 1 discusses the question of action (in the context of God's interaction with the world). In chapter 2 I reflect on the nature of God (as revealed in relation to the world). Chapter 3 is devoted to reflection on the world (in light of the world's relation to God). Finally, the last chapter presents the threats and challenges which cannot be overlooked while examining the issue of the Creator's influence on creation.

Through analyzing each of the above-mentioned points I strive to take into account the most varied range of approaches and theories concerning theism. Nevertheless, on the conceptual and argumentative level I mostly resort to the studies conducted in the broadly understood area of analytic philosophy. It has recently managed to identify enormously valuable elements from the many varieties of theism, starting with traditional Thomistic concepts, moving through their modified forms (e.g., Molinism), to types of theism which have emerged in recent decades, particularly open theism[2] (also called free will theism) and probabilistic theism.[3]

An equally significant aim of this book is to demonstrate that the question of divine action is of a markedly interdisciplinary and intersystemic character. This is why the research undertaken had to embrace the diversified philosophical discourse, the numerous approaches present in theistic thought, the close relation of philosophy and theology, as well as the connection between philosophy and the natural sciences. I would also like to note that the solving of the problems which emerged in the course of my analysis called for a particular mindset, that is one that, while respecting academic rigor, remains open to the most individual and subjective aspects of human existence.

The last half-century has brought a prodigious development of research concerning theism. It was over fifty years ago when prolific and distinguished publications in the fields of the philosophy of God and the philosophy of religion appeared (e.g., by R. G. Swinburne), with these works continuing to serve as an important reference in theistic discussions. Since the 1970s we have also been observing a revival of the above-mentioned disciplines in the analytic milieu (e.g., A. C. Plantinga, P. van Inwagen). Simultaneously, essential transformations have taken place in the field of natural sciences, with the most notable breakthrough being the 1960s discovery of microwave background radiation, with this providing a strong empirical argument for the evolutionary view of the universe. More so, the year 1966, at least in the United States, can be considered as the beginning of the constructive contemporary debate concerning the relation between religion and science. The release of *Issues in Science and Religion* by I. G. Barbour,[4] and the foundation of the *Zygon: Journal of Religion and Science* provided a landmark position for the symbolic manifestation of a new phase of an interdisciplinary dialogue that was actively carried on in the following years.

The evidence that the current achievements of the natural sciences are taken into account in the studies of divine action in the world comes with the publications authored by the participants of the many debates being part of the Divine Action Project (DAP), organized by the Vatican Observatory and The Center for Theology and the Natural Sciences with a seat in Berkeley, California (whose publications include volumes issued after five international conferences,[5] as well as other research outcomes of their participants). The DAP has been the biggest endeavor in this field in recent years.

Such intensely led discussions were inspired by a conference organized on the initiative of John Paul II at Castel Gandolfo between September 21 and 26, 1987 (on the occasion of the 300th anniversary of the publication of Newton's *Principia*). The pope's message, addressed several months later to the director of the Vatican Observatory,[6] was deemed groundbreaking for the dialogue between religion and science. Since the theologians, philosophers, and natural scientists participating in successive DAP conferences can be treated as proponents of the essential aspects of the problems discussed in my own work, I often draw from their output. One of the signs of such references is the terminology used in the present monograph. The phrase "divine action in the world" has become deeply embedded in theistic discourse.[7]

In recent decades, many acknowledged philosophers and theologians (e.g., P. Clayton, W. B. Drees, N. Murphy, J. F. Haught, N. H. Gregersen, D. Edwards, K. Ward, D. R. Griffin, T. F. Tracy, and M. J. Dodds) have noticed and expressed the need for a more thorough discussion of the question of divine action in the world. Philosophically-oriented natural scientists (e.g., P. C. Davies and G. F. Ellis) have also entered a debate covering the area. We must also note the body of scholars educated in both the humanities and natural sciences who take an active part in this discussion (I. G. Barbour, A. R. Peacocke, J. C. Polkinghorne, W. R. Stoeger, F. J. Ayala, G. V. Coyne, and R. J. Russell). The wide circle of intellectuals conducting studies on divine action in the world proves what an important and cognitively appealing constituent of academic culture this issue is.

Taking into account the output of the scholars mentioned above I also draw on texts authored by other representatives of contemporary theism, with this being significant for my analyses. Studies that I find personally of great importance and value are those written by my fellow Polish philosophers, including publications by M. Heller, S. Judycki, P. Gutowski, J. Wojtysiak, R. Mordarski, and J. Życiński. The last philosopher, despite his sudden death while still an engaged and creative scholar, left us with a remarkable and widely recognized academic output[8] which included a reflection on divine action in the world. The way of reasoning demonstrated by this professor and Great Chancellor of the John Paul II Catholic University of Lublin provided significant inspiration for me during the many detailed deliberations included in the present monograph. This fact stems from my former position as an assistant lecturer in the Department of the Relationship between Science and Faith which was directed by Życiński, as well as my experience of being his personal secretary accompanying him in his everyday work as the Archbishop of Lublin. This experience has allowed me to get acquainted with the mindset of the man who authored two volumes devoted to theism and analytic philosophy[9] as well as several hundred other publications.

Among works that were published in Polish, the book released in 2014 by D. Łukasiewicz stands out in particular.[10] Its chapters are devoted to the main varieties of theism which take into consideration the reflection on divine providence. The fundamental point of reference for the outline of my study, however, is provided by particular subject components of the area I focus on. By assuming such a scheme, I wish to emphasize that the seeds of truth, which is polyphonic in nature, are embedded in many intellectual traditions. From this perspective, it is of secondary importance who indeed is right: be it the Molinists, open theists, probabilists, or the proponents of the most traditional approaches.

Theistic thought assumes different forms for various reasons. The approach presented by Plantinga or Swinburne is essentially divergent from the one proposed by Peacocke or Haught. The two latter scholars may at times seem to be authors of a purely theological discourse. Their work, however, can be a rich source of many crucial strands of the kind of theism which belongs to the field of natural theology or philosophy of God. In the past several decades many insightful studies have been published in the area called philosophical theology, with this being usually recognized as a subfield of philosophy.[11]

Acknowledging the merits of many of the developing contemporary trends of theistic thought, I underline the significance of those taking into account the challenges posed by the natural sciences. They emerge as an efficient instrument for discovering the truth about the workings of the world. I regard the fundamental elements of the scientific worldview to be an important point of reference for many elaborate questions covering the field of theism (e.g., for the question of creation). I deem irrational the treatment of antiscientific hypotheses as equal to hypotheses which are widely accepted by scientists. The concept of scientific theories, in its most crucial aspects, is one which I share with K. R. Popper,[12] whose model suggests that there is a fundamental difference between science and pseudoscience,[13] all the while stressing the limits of science and the importance of its being open to new solutions.

It is by no means my aim to absolutize the current state of scientific achievements. The presently prevalent naturalistic paradigm is justifiably censured when the boundary between methodological and ontological naturalism is radically crossed. The future state of science may significantly differ from the present one, not only as far as the data provided by experimental research is concerned, but also in terms of theory and employed models: on the level of methodology, terminology, and subject matter. The limits of rationality do not overlap with the boundaries of a generally accepted scientific method. Even programs designed to search for unified theories in physics, which often reveal the reductionist mindset of their founders, indirectly certify that the partial solutions available at the present stage of scientific achievement cannot be dogmatized.[14]

In light of the above, philosophy plays a particularly significant role, because it can serve as a bridge between science and theology on the path to truth concerning the interaction of the Creator with creation. On the one hand, philosophy provides protection from those scientific tendencies which lead to the conclusion that the empirical research method has a monopoly on valuable analysis of different phenomena, including religious experience. On the other hand, the specificity of disciplines like the philosophy of God, the philosophy of religion, or even the philosophy of nature allows for the placing of the elements of the God–world relationship outside the sphere accessible only to people who embrace Christian revelation.

In the analysis of questions familiar to both philosophy and theology I judge it necessary to define a principal framework. I hold that this is unsurpassable while thinking about the issue of divine action in the world. Such clarification stems from my conviction that there are canons of rationality. This is why I am very critical of a broadly-understood doctrinal fundamentalism in the light of which certain philosophical concepts (incorporated into the predominant interpretations of religious theories) are practically not subject to modifications assessed as the programmatic weakening of theism. But it also needs to be stressed that there are no essential grounds on which religious doctrines and beliefs should be denied any value and deemed to inhibit the development of humans who, in the most extreme case, are argued to be delusional about God.[15]

In presenting the main problems which emerge in my investigations, I do not confine myself merely to rejecting the above-mentioned extremes. By demonstrating the value of different elaborate approaches, I argue for the need of further, open debate and a well-disposed, receptive reflection on the reservations that arise from various critical circles. Taking these objections into consideration enables a development of theistic thought that does not destroy its very foundations, even when significant modifications are introduced. Theism should not be practiced from merely one cognitive perspective, for example, drawing solely on conceptual analyses. We need to take into consideration new challenges, particularly those brought about by the natural sciences.[16]

The scientific context of the issues I discuss motivates me to delineate a wide potential area of the Creator's influence on creation. It is for this reason that I include the processes of nature, laws of nature, regularities and chance, boundary conditions, chaotic systems, the self-organization of structures, and human choices.[17] I recognize divine action in the world as real and objective if only in the sense that this action is not limited to subjective human impressions or those convictions alone which are not subject to any form of rational verification or falsification. I perceive the necessity of placing the concept of divine action between the idea of God's omnipotence as absolutely unlimited, and a deism which excludes the providential engagement of the Creator in the development of creation.

I knowingly highlight those domains of divine action in the world question that seem to be of the utmost importance. An additional reason for the choices I make is the conviction that finding a potential solution to one of the problems analyzed has a substantial impact on determining the answers regarding other aspects of the issue at hand. Therefore, I revisit certain trains of thought several times. I do not consider this action as unnecessary reiteration, but rather as purposeful emphasis done for the demand for a broader perspective. The advantage of such a perspective is the possibility of avoiding a merely fragmentary view of the question and instead striving to demonstrate coherently how multidimensional this issue truly is. The problem is complex to such a degree that to comprehend some of its nuances calls for drawing on additional sources, which I refer to at each given stage of the analysis.

Among the publications I quote, one can find studies of the history of theistic thought. After all, during the analysis of the present subject it is impossible to ignore the intellectual achievements of the most renowned personages of the history of theism. However, the fact that I take into account the output of people like Augustine of Hippo, Anselm of Canterbury (or Aosta), Thomas Aquinas, and other outstanding representatives of the reflection on the nature of God and His interaction with the world, does not mean that my study will have the characteristics of a historical-critical analysis. Since such an approach is beyond the scope of the present publication, I draw on high-quality studies. It is not my essential aim to delve into the original works by these authors, who have left permanent traces of their genius in the many various stages of the development of Christian thought.

Bearing in mind the content framework delineated above, I address the following specific issues. Chapter 1 is a presentation of the main assumptions and concepts that refer to divine action in the world. This part of my reflection embraces various types of Creator–creation relationships, models of divine action in the world, the philosophical-scientific typology of causality and its implications for theism. I argue that apart from having the traditional distinction between primary cause and secondary causes, it is useful to elaborate on approaches that consider the current scientific worldview. The types of causality enumerated in the light of science will be treated as a context for formulating a theory of the non-interventionist influence of the Creator on His creation.

Chapter 2, devoted to the idea of God, begins with a presentation of the principles of the philosophical approach to the absolute being and the pluralism of theisms.

Despite their diversity, several crucial components of the concept of God can be distinguished that frequently form the subject of elaborate theistic reflection. The theme of my study forces me to concentrate on those elements of God's nature that are most significant for determining His interaction with the world. This is why I focus on the idea of God as a creator and person and the analysis of the following attributes: simplicity, omnipotence, and omniscience. I also discuss issues regarding God's immutability and His relationship to time. This section of my book is designed to be an attempt at presenting the origins of the difficulty of formulating a coherent theory of God being active in the world. I strive to discern the reasons that lead many theists to a partial reconsideration of the concept of God, while not having to overturn the fundamental assumptions of the Christian message. Instead finding contradictions between the particular theistic trends, I identify the substantive reasons for their development and make use of the valuable intuitions they convey.

Chapter 3 reflects on the nature of the world and explores whether and in what way God is actively present in it. From the philosophical perspective it is not an easy task to demonstrate that the Creator participates in the history of creation, and especially in the history of human beings. It seems that the more the autonomy of the world in relation to God is accentuated, the more strenuous the attempts at justifying God's influence on the course of world history.[18] Striving to find the potential manifestations of the Creator's presence in creation, many theists argue that providence is manifested through the laws of nature, the origins and character of which cannot be fully explained by the empirical sciences. A particularly complicated task is to argue for the immanence of God in the world with regard to the workings of evil, its extreme symptom being the suffering of innocent human beings. It is in this context that the idea of God's *kenosis* is formulated and the following question is raised: How does one bring together the autonomous character of the world and its dependence on the Creator? Such a dependence is revealed in an original manner by the panentheists. I show here that even while being critical of panentheism it is worth understanding at least some of the assumptions on which the reasoning of the proponents of this current is grounded. However, the most crucial points discussed in this chapter are those of the autonomy and the evil present in the world. My argument is that the world develops autonomously thanks to a complex network of the laws of nature which are simultaneously a manifestation of the Creator's imaginative presence in His creation. The ontic and moral imperfection of contingent beings does not appear to be evidence of the inexistence (or the inactivity) of God. This is more of a consequence that both the world and humans are not "puppets in the hand of the Creator." His actions are more difficult to detect in part because many theistic views (at least *implicite*) adopt an idea of God whose omnipotence relies mainly on the suspension or overturning of the laws of nature. The present study, by contrast, emphasizes the role of God's noninterventionist action in the world.

The final chapter points out the contemporary threats and challenges that pertain to the issue of divine action in the world. Some of them are already signaled earlier in my study. However, I want to highlight the questions which are, to my profound conviction, particularly relevant today. Thus, I am critical of the "God of the gaps" concept and the recurring attempts to draw upon naive forms of teleology. Nevertheless, the latter can assume a rational form, thus allowing the complementary use of teleological and deterministic interpretations in the discussion of divine action in the world. This is an example of such a development of theism, the practicing of which does not have to be based on copying formulaic philosophical conclusions. The creative evolution of certain ideas, theistic systems and the concepts used by them leads to the revival of theism. Such refreshment is also strengthened by taking into account the worldview presented by the natural sciences, the consequence being the reinterpretation of events estimated as random, as well as a greater emphasis on the unity present in the different "levels" of nature and in its entirety. This, in turn, in the process of defining the potential ways in which the Creator influences creation, can be expressed by introducing new terminology including metaphors and analogies.

A book on divine action in the world could well begin with a presentation of the details of the scientific worldview to show the basic elements of contemporary natural sciences, and subsequently move towards an investigation of the rational models of the Creator's participation in the (specifically defined) creation. I understand such a cognitive strategy, but my intention is to discuss a feasibly open outlook concerning the three successive components of the issue delineated in the title of my book. The main arguments and premises inclining me towards specific solutions are included in each of the first three chapters. Remarks presented in their final sections are not of a definitive summary nature which would take the form of an unambiguous resolution. Some crucial statements are included in the last chapter, and particularly in the conclusion of the book. These statements also take the form of postulates which accentuate my standpoint as viewed from a broadly historical and scientific perspective.

Given the context referred to above it is easier to justify why my study does not begin with a chapter on the nature of God, even if such a choice could give priority to reflections on the absolute being and correspond with the meaning of the Latin principle *agere sequitur esse*. It is true that by becoming familiar with God we are able to comprehend His actions better. On the other hand, a starting point for further research may also come in the form of analysis and interpretation of the potential ways of the Creator's actions. Therefore, there are no obstacles that would prevent me from addressing the theories on God's interaction with the world already in the first chapter of my book, especially when admitting this section of my study is in many places introductory and does not refer only to the questions of divine agency, but also to the models of causality present in the natural sciences. The nature of God is discovered in the process of reflecting upon the possible "paths" of his actions and the functioning of the world, not exclusively by means of logical-conceptual speculations on the necessary being. Such reasoning remains a significant component of a trend in theism which stresses the fact that creation bears traces of the Creator and that the human person is indeed the *imago Dei*.[19]

This logic of the reflection on God does not concern merely determining the potential manifestations of His activity. In the light of the analysis of the world and its history it sometimes seems that in certain situations Providence does not work.[20] I discuss this issue within my reflection on the nature of God as respecting the autonomy of creation, with all of its inherent rules, even when as a consequence of their unpredictability thousands of people die in an earthquake. This question additionally refers to human freedom which is not suspended by God even if the lives of millions are at risk due to the perpetrator's insane schemes of war crimes. Irrespective of whether we relate the distinctive silence of God to the idea of *kenosis* or to the concept of His steadfastness (or faithfulness) towards the world, we still have an invariable desire to search for and discover the nature of THE ONE WHO IS.[21]

1

On the Action

This chapter is of an introductory and framing character, marking out the crucial areas of reflection on divine action in the world.[1] Thus, I present the main assumptions and principal models constructed in order to grasp the possible ways of the Creator's interaction with His creation. This part of the book has also the important role of delineating the philosophical-scientific typology of causality, in the light of which innovative theories concerning divine action are being formulated.[2] Since such theories are still insufficiently present in the literature, I devote more attention to them.

The functioning of nature is one of the significant points of reference for the demonstration of the potential paths in which the Creator influences creation. For this reason, apart from the classically invoked claim that God is the first cause and affects the world by means of secondary causes, contemporary theists introduce categories of causality appropriate for depicting the interactions present in the universe. It is underlined that in the functioning of nature one can discover a wealth of interactions taking place between the particular levels of the world's structure, for example, causal conditionings that make the behavior of a given system difficult to predict. Such a character highlights both the openness of the examined system and its susceptibility to the smallest of hardly detectable external influences. This gives an opportunity to develop concepts of divine action which do not have to be confined to distinctions that are already well-established in the philosophical tradition. The character of the course that natural processes take makes it possible to determine the ways in which God can affect the world while not acting *contra naturam*.[3]

Basic assumptions

Assuming the possibility of God's interaction with the world, deism is a minimalist approach. Deists hold that the role of the Creator is limited to the primary act of creation as understood as giving existence to the world. Within this approach it is stressed that God acts only "at the beginning," when He creates the world with its laws. Based on them, the universe is supposed to further evolve without any divine influence whatsoever. Deism met with diverse instances of criticism, both from the internal perspective of theism and thanks to inspiration drawn from the natural sciences. There are no reasons (a statement I justify later in the book) to identify God only as the Prime Mover. Moreover, there is still an open question as to whether the world was created in time or *ab aeterno*, that is to say whether the world has an eternal, albeit created, nature.[4] In the context of such problems, many theists draw our attention mainly to the ontic dependence found within the God–world relationship: a necessary being is the reason behind the existence of contingent beings.

Thus, the world's coming into being calls for an explanation that refers to an adequate cause. This also concerns the sustaining of the world in existence (*conservatio mundi*). Without a relationship with God, the universe could not remain in existence since matter itself does not contain a sufficient foundation (reason) for its own existence. Taking into account the creative character of physical processes does not substantially modify the theistic conviction that God is the ultimate foundation of causality in the world of nature.[5]

In this perspective, resolving the question of whether the laws of nature determine or merely describe the regularities present in the functioning of nature is of secondary importance. Similarly, it is not that essential whether the efficient cause of phenomena is contained in the laws of nature or in nature itself. However, it is crucial to emphasize the continuous action of God (*creatio continua*). In classical theism, God is presented both as the primary cause of all phenomena in the universe, and as a foundation of natural (secondary) causality. In a sense, no natural event should be treated as an expression of an extraordinary act of God since He uniformly influences the entire history of the world.[6]

Nonetheless, some theists claim that certain events taking place in the world are a manifestation of God's special action. The adherents of this option usually unreservedly accept the statement of the Creator's incessant presence in His creation, but they additionally maintain that it is not sufficient for a comprehensive description of divine activity. This approach is endorsed by two diverse groups. The first one underlines that what matters is solely the subjective sense of God's special actions, that is, they are seen as special even though, in reality, God acts through them in the same way as He does through all other events. An example of God's special action in the subjective sense would be the emergence of essential novelty at selected stages of the development of the universe, for example, biogenesis.

The second group asserting God's extraordinary engagement in the history of the world includes those thinkers who claim that at least some special acts of creative action should be allowed an objective meaning. God creates such events by means of direct intervention and/or through the suspension of the laws of nature. Such a standpoint is usually called interventionist,[7] although some of its proponents avoid this terminology by stressing their distance from associating the special and objective actions of God with volitional actions or the suspension of the laws of nature.[8]

The propagators of the idea of special and at the same time objective manifestations of divine action often differentiate direct acts from indirect ones. It is assumed that through indirect acts God can objectively cause a special event to happen by means of secondary causes. Nevertheless, we need to recognize at this point the necessity of God's direct act as initiating the chain of secondary causes. This seems to be indispensable for logical consistency: if the efficient cause brings something about indirectly, *ipso facto* direct involvement is required at the original stage, being a *sine qua non* condition for a causal chain to exist. In this context the problem of the so-called *causal joint* arises.[9]

D. Łukasiewicz distinguishes several principal philosophical (metaphysical) assumptions concerning God's action in the world: (a) there is a personal God who is omnipotent, omniscient, and good; (b) God is the Creator of the world and acts in it; (c) science provides the best (available to us) description and explanation of the functioning of nature; (d) the world is created by God in an evolutionary way; and (e) when creating the world in this way, and in no other, God had specific goals to achieve. The fourth of the above assumptions follows from the first three, whereas the last point is a consequence of all the others. After all, if God is an acting person, He has reasons and aims for his actions. As a (maximally) rational agent, God chooses the best means to realize His plans.[10] The above statements are thoroughly analyzed further on. They call for an analysis which draws on both different varieties of theism as well as the natural sciences.

The models of interaction

The concept of the Creator-creation interaction has had many diverse forms.[11] However, nowadays it is formulated in light of the most important theistic currents and expressive models, often in the form of metaphors and parallels. On the basis of analyses published in the anthology edited by Owen C. Thomas,[12] the essential distinction introduced is the one between the model of God's uniform action and the model of personal agency.[13]

According to the model of God's uniform action, God acts in every event occurring in the world. The only problem is man's limited knowledge about this and the multitude of interpretations that contribute to the divergence in demonstrating the meaning and sense of the Creator's interaction with His creation. This model of God's uniform action is promoted in studies by G. Kaufman and M. Wiles.[14]

These models of personal agency have non-homogenous specific solutions. The first model views God's action in a literal sense. Here, it is accentuated that God operates in a real way, whether the world is causally closed or not. W. Alston undermines the view that causal determinism makes it impossible to discuss God as a personal factor that brings about the existence of specific states of affairs in the physical world. There are also no sufficient arguments to assume the stance of a strictly naturalistic causal determinism. Moreover, deterministic laws are applicable to closed systems, which are not subject to any external influence, and yet we have no grounds to claim that all systems in the world share such characteristics.[15]

Another group of personal agency models refer to the category of embodiment and immanence. On the one hand, God's interaction with the world is compared to the way in which the human mind affects the human body. This idea is developed in the form of biological and feminist analogies used to describe divine action in the world. On the other hand, an image of a dynamic universe with God's immanent presence is proposed, which is intended to emphasize the closeness of the Creator to His creation. Highlighting the immanence of God in the world is characteristic of panentheism,[16] the nature of which is presented in the third chapter of this book.

The universe seen as the body of God is depicted in studies by G. Jantzen. She believes that God can act in the world universally, as well as causing individual events.

Nevertheless, regardless of the manner of acting, all divine acts relating to the world are performed in a direct manner, being analogous to the way in which people control their bodily movements. Such an approach makes it possible to resolve the question of God's omniscience in a maximalist way, but at the same time this strongly generates the problem of evil, the interpretation of the laws of nature, and God's relationship to time. Each of these issues is analyzed by Jantzen, who makes cognitively interesting attempts at overcoming all of the specific types of difficulty.[17] A similar standpoint is taken by S. McFague, who while promoting the model of embodiment, notices its weaknesses, specifically with regard to God's susceptibility to suffering in the world.[18]

Among the models of agency there are also those without embodiment. Criticizing the model of embodiment, T. F. Tracy does not accept the view of the universe as an organism. He rejects the claim that the personal efficient cause requires embodiment. God acts in the world while not being embodied in it. Such an approach is an attempt at synthesizing classical theism with processualism.[19]

The last group of the models of agency is made up of those models which accentuate the role of interaction the most. Russell underlines that criticism of embodiment models comes mainly from the supporters of a particular version of the interaction model. The classic scholar in this field is Polkinghorne. He notices the possibility of a better comprehension of divine action thanks to insightful analyses concerning the interaction between the human and nature which employ findings from the domains of quantum mechanics and chaos theory. Polkinghorne claims that: "The combination of lawlike behavior with openness and flexibility in nature makes human and, in some preliminary way, divine agency conceivable."[20]

The philosophical-scientific typology of causality

Bottom-up causality

The principal way of nature's functioning is usually thought of as a "bottom-up causality" ("bottom-up causation"). We assume *implicite* that the parameters of a given system at a specific stage of its development are essential for establishing its possible future. This is how the causation between the particular levels of complex structures of nature is interpreted: the components of an organism determine the way it behaves in such a manner that they are deemed necessary in explaining the course that processes take. This does not only imply the perspective of evolution in time, but also the relationship between elements which constitute a greater whole. The classic examples of bottom–up causality are provided by research on reactions (to stimuli) of the organism of humans whose brain serves as the foundation for mental and psychic processes. On the basis of experiments scholars assume a causal connection between the administering of chemical substances and the improvement of human mood. This concerns both headache alleviation and coping with depressive states.[21]

Bottom–up causality is a fundamental property of the "hierarchic" structure of the physical world. What happens at each higher level of organization is based on causal functioning at the lower level. With such assumptions, the specific character of chemical processes is explained by reference to physics, and material tests consist in analyzing the impact of the chemical and physical structure of materials on their particular properties. In such research sometimes a mechanistic concept of nature is adopted, according to which, if we knew the physical states of the human brain "in all its recesses," we could possess a knowledge of someone's thoughts and intentions. In this case, the only problem would be epistemic boundaries, alien to Laplace's demon.[22]

The extreme expression of emphasizing the role of bottom-up causation is the program of strong reductionism. This approach assumes that the entirety of a system (its structure and functioning) is only a sum of its constituent parts, their properties, and behaviors. The emergent characteristics of a given structure appear at a certain stage of its development as an apparent novelty. In the strict sense, all parameters of a system are a simple consequence of the properties of this system's components.[23] Such an approach leads to an altogether deterministic interpretation of natural phenomena, illustrated by the idea known as *petty reductionism*. In the final years of the past century, this position characterized the concepts of many physicists who had been striving to discover a single unitary theory. For this reason, basic formulas were being sought that would enable a deductive acquisition of information concerning the later stages of the evolving world. S. Weinberg claimed that one of the goals humans have is to persistently strive to find a few simple laws which might explain why nature, with its complexity and richness of forms, is what it is.[24] Strong reductionism has been the subject of many critical studies. One such major challenge for mechanical-reductionist philosophy was quantum theory, which (at least in its Copenhagen interpretation[25]) stresses that the physical world has an open structure and the scenario of the development of nature can be predicted only with a certain degree of probability.

Quantum providence

The indeterminacies of quantum mechanics were treated by some theists as the grounds for formulating a concept of God's acting in the world, without violating the laws that govern the universe. According to Pollard, if we assume that every event taking place in nature can be scientifically explained, the theory of God's influence on the world's history can be rationally constructed only by reference to quantum indeterminacies. To achieve His aims (not acting *contra naturam*), God exerts influence on quantum probabilities.[26]

On the quantum level there are certain indeterminacies (that occur within mathematically set limits). This enables events that are not unambiguously determined by the laws proper to the quantum world. Being familiar with those laws does not change the fact that a full prediction of such events remains impossible. Places of indeterminacy are viewed by the proponents of the quantum providence theory as providing for the possibility of God's causal actions. This is directly undetectable to us, even though it can reveal its consequences in the macroscopic world. Thus, by means of quanta, God is able to direct both cosmic and biological evolution, as well as the history of individuals and the entirety of humankind. In this way, God can causally affect the elementary level of the physical world, indirectly determining the properties of all physical beings.[27]

The question of divine action taken by means of quantum indeterminacies has become the subject of lively discussion among DAP participants. This was most conspicuously visible during a conference devoted to the problem of chaos and complexity, which was organized in 1993 in Berkeley, California. The greatest supporters of the theory of God's action on the quantum level were G. Ellis and N. Murphy, who, in specifying the criteria which the concept of divine action in the world should meet, underlined that what needs to be found is a sphere between deism (divine indifference) and occasionalism (here: God's special influence on the course of every event). According to Murphy, the option which manages to avoid these threats comes with an idea of God as making use of the laws of quantum physics in creative interaction with nature. In accordance with those laws, quantum objects have a wide spectrum of potential behaviors in the future.[28] Using scenarios that are implied by the distribution of probability, God can make one of them happen, not another. This would be an example of God affecting the course of the world on the quantum level, hence bottom-up causality.[29]

The concept of acting through quantum indeterminacies is sometimes regarded as a sophisticated return to the discredited idea of the *God of the gaps*, this being a topic of detailed reflection in the fourth chapter of this book. Polkinghorne points to the fact that Murphy sanctions the probabilistic interpretation of quantum mechanics.[30] There are no reasons for making theological conclusions so strongly dependent on the state of natural sciences at their present stage of development. Quantum mechanics is not an ultimate theory since it does not take into account quantum gravitational effects. The unification of quantum mechanics and general relativity expected by many scientists can enforce an essential reinterpretation of both of these theories. Already, the existing state of knowledge of quantum mechanics demonstrates diverse possibilities of interpretation. Contrary to the conclusions formulated by Bohr, Bohm argues that quantum mechanics is of a deterministic character.[31] Such an approach would not leave any room for divine action through quantum indeterminacies. Heller adds that entering the formalism of quantum mechanics allows academics to pose numerous objections, irrespective of these interpretations. In addition, it seems more rational to stress that God does not act selectively but is continuously engaged in the entire history of the world, and for this reason His action is difficult to detect.[32]

Apart from these reasons for criticism, the concept of quantum providence generates the problem of God's direct responsibility for the suffering present in the world and constitutes a form of so-called epistemic deism. Can anything be claimed about divine action if it happens in spheres inaccessible to human experience? Why would God act only on the quantum level? Epistemic deism does not provide answers to such questions.[33]

Top-down and whole-part causality

By rejecting strong reductionism, which derives the causal source of all changes in a given system from its lowest levels, what is often highlighted is the role of "top-down causality," also named "downward causality" or "downward causation."[34] A question posed in this context is to what extent a system as a whole affects its constituent parts, or to what extent the phenomena taking place on a higher level of organization influence phenomena on a lower level. It is assumed that the higher level (or the entirety of a given structure) has an inherent causality and can affect a lower level thereof. Based on such assumptions, the theory of "whole–part causality," or "whole–part causation," was elaborated,[35] usually presented in combination with the concept of top-down causality.[36]

A moderate type of top-down causality does not allow higher-grade phenomena to have a direct influence on the laws governing the lower grade. On the other hand, this option eludes vitalism, which entails the existence of creative forces that do not come under scientific description.[37] Manifestations of the vitalistic approach can be found in dualistic concepts from the domain of psychology and the philosophy of man (e.g., the theory of causal relationship between the immaterial soul and the body). Treating such approaches with reservation, many authors of studies on downward causation demonstrate the way in which this causation functions, starting with simple physical examples. Neither the single molecules making up a wheel going down an inclined plane nor the force of gravity affecting it is sufficient to explain the wheel's rotary movement. We need to take into account the higher level of the structure's organization—the shape of the wheel.[38]

Demonstration of the character of top-down causality was significantly influenced by analysis of nonlinear dissipative systems. Changes in the parameters of the constituent parts of these systems on a micro-level are induced by the state of the entire system, which has an impact on the individual elements. These elements would manifest a different behavior if isolated. This is why it is underlined that the whole is greater than the sum of its parts. Such a view of causality does not exclude the bottom-up influence but claims that this position is insufficient to grasp certain natural phenomena. A relevant example is provided by the so-called Bénard convection: at a certain stage of heating a fluid its single "cells" manifest a coordinated behavior. In biology, this is exemplified by the way a cell controls the behavior of its single constituent molecules.[39]

In order to clarify the functioning of whole–part type causality, it is crucial to refer to the so-called boundary conditions of the system. With complex physical phenomena it is usually assumed that boundary conditions limit a series of initial conditions, some of which being essential properties. Boundary conditions are understood as selecting and delimiting the different options of a system's development. The realization of one of the possible scenarios implies that a certain option was chosen, as in the case of the environment in which a system is developed (two bean seeds of similar biological parameters will develop differently because of the diverse environmental conditions in which they grow). The series of initial conditions (called *constraining conditions*) which affect choice possibilities is treated as a type of boundary condition.[40]

The theistic interpretation of top-down causality entails that a specific event in the world is perceived as an indirect action of God who acts "downwards." Divine action would then proceed from higher to lower levels of nature (analogous to the way the mind affects the brain). Another example of this kind of action would be God influencing the initial conditions or the environment of a given physical system (analogous to the way convective whirls form in a container filled with a heated fluid). A special example of whole–part causality is divine impact on the initial conditions of the evolution of the entire universe. It is assumed, for instance, that these conditions were selected by the Creator in such a manner as to allow, at a certain stage of cosmic development, the emergence of life and, subsequently, the arrival of a species endowed with consciousness.[41]

Making use of the idea of top-down causality, Polkinghorne notices the possibility for a theistic interpretation of chaos theory and the increase of complexity. Since nonlinear chaotic systems are internally unpredictable, it is reasonable to formulate an ontological hypothesis that the physical world is open to a great extent.[42] This creates an opportunity for the development of a concept of divine action which is not performed *contra naturam*.[43] This approach was elaborated by Peacocke, who believes that top-down action is a kind of "constraint" imposed upon the world. Divine action thus influences the course of world history, but at the same time does not violate the world's laws and regularities. This manner of holistic influence on the world as a whole is inherent in God. These specific constraints shape the course of events in such a way that the crucial divine aims designed for the world will be attained. Such an action can be performed without upsetting the natural relations and autonomy of nature, including those at the lowest levels of its structure.[44]

Lateral causality

With the decline of naive mechanical philosophy, previously unknown possibilities for interpreting natural phenomena have emerged. This has found expression in the concept of "lateral causality" ("lateral causation"), which is not focused exclusively on analyzing quantum processes, but also on the specific nature of the many systems examined within the framework of classical physics. A new direction of research was introduced by the discovery of the subtleties found within the functioning of complex dynamic systems whose state is far from equilibrium. Already at the turn of the twentieth century, it was observed that systems operating like a predictable and reliable clock constitute only exceptional cases of dynamic behaviors. Typical examples used in the formulation of innovative approaches were systems sensitive to the minutest alterations in the environment, the consequence being an almost infinite diversity of possible states.

Lateral causality is physically exemplified by the way billiard balls behave in a game. It would seem this serves as a classic example of a movement that is possible to predict and described by Newton's laws. However, it transpires that the state of the system after each consecutive collision depends on minute changes in the momentum and position of individual balls. Marginal differences in the collision angles are mutually superimposed, thus generating changes at an exponential rate. Gas molecules behave in a similar way. In a brief time interval, shorter than one microsecond, each collides with another over fifty times. As a result of even relatively few collisions, the final state of the system depends on unpredicted modifications. The final outcome can be influenced by, for instance, a change in the gravitational field, caused by the presence of an additional electron in a remote part of the universe, "the weakest force due to the smallest particle the furthest distance away."[45]

Lateral causality is disclosed both in the subtle nature of chaotic and complex systems in physics, as well as in biological processes and meteorological phenomena. (I discuss this in more detail while describing the laws of nature.) The impossibility of predicting precisely a development scenario is not only a cognitive problem, but also reveals an integral and important trait of nature which is flexible, whereas deterministic models provide only an approximate picture of reality. As a result of analyses concerning the specific character of many complex systems, we can discern in the world signs of structural openness, which also refer to the functioning of man and his relative, and at the same time real, freedom. Governed by the laws of nature, we are not entirely conditioned by the previous states of our development. A complicated network of causal connections renders us susceptible to the influence similar to that in the butterfly effect. Everyday experience teaches us that a seemingly trivial component of the "existential jigsaw" can significantly transform many important elements of human biography.

The ontic openness of the world is at times treated by theists as a property that makes "room" for divine action. This is not, or at least does not have to be, a return to placing God's presence in ontic gaps. The flexibility of nature is not special, but its integral dimension. The closed world of determinism facilitated a deistic interpretation of the Creator–creation interaction or enforced strong interventionist approaches. On the other hand, divine action in nature which does not evolve according to a fixed plan and is prone to modifications that are difficult to predict, can be presented as a creative interaction that is more similar to a delicate breeze (incidentally, treated in the Old Testament as a manifestation of God's presence in the world[46]) than an imposition of one possible scenario.[47]

The primary cause and secondary causes

Apart from the approaches drawing on the natural sciences, many authors stress the value of the classical distinction between primary cause and secondary causes.[48] This is already present in the philosophical-theological system elaborated by St. Thomas Aquinas. The complicated structure of the world, the functioning of which entails a great number of interconnected events, allows us to speak of cause-and-effect chains. Together, these make up the entirety of natural history. Each and every physical cause, which is an integral part of the evolutionary process, both in terms of inanimate as well as animate nature, can be called a secondary cause. These secondary causes are distinguished from the primary cause, God, who has not only created the world and sustains it in existence, but also viably affects its history by means of secondary causes. Neither of these causes would be able to exist and serve its function without the first cause. In giving existence to secondary causes, God is present in them and acts through them.[49]

Aquinas assumes that God is a self-existent being (*ipsum esse subsistens*), hence existence "belongs" to His nature. This situation is different in creation. Creation does not have the source of existence in itself. All creatures depend on God for their existence and functioning. Their fundamental dependence on the Creator explains and justifies the distinction between the primary cause and secondary causes. God is the first cause because He enables all creatures to exist and acts providentially through them.[50] All causes discovered in the behavior of nature remain secondary causes.[51]

It is worth taking notice of the arguments introduced by St. Thomas which justify that God acts through secondary causes and not directly. What Aquinas clearly underlines is that the autonomy of the created world is respected by the Creator who does not violate the natural order of cause and effect that He Himself established. In a real way, God affects the course of world history, but not through interventionism. Aquinas writes that "there are certain intermediaries of God's providence; for He governs things inferior by superior, not on account of any defect in His power, but by reason of the abundance of His goodness; so that the dignity of causality is imparted even to creatures."[52]

It is not that the laws of nature are merely seemingly autonomous, while God remains the only cause of the processes and events in the world. The Creator consciously shares His efficient power with creation, being constantly present in the whole history of the universe and in every place within it. Within a scenario of this kind, Aquinas recognizes God's free choice. Even though He would be able to act without any mediation, He does not do that for two reasons:

> First, because the order of cause and effect would be taken away from created things: and this would imply lack of power in the Creator: for it is due to the power of the cause, that it bestows active power on its effect. Secondly, because the active powers which are seen to exist in things, would be bestowed on things to no purpose, if these wrought nothing through them. Indeed, all things created would seem, in a way, to be purposeless, if they lacked an operation proper to them; since the purpose of everything is its operation.[53]

Thus, the functioning of secondary causes and the primary cause requires a proper understanding. This chiefly regards the question of two different causes leading to the same effect. As a primary cause, God acts in sustaining the existence of His creation. The Creator acts also through secondary causes, without determining their behavior but triggering specific effects in the physical world. What is needed for the world to function are secondary causes as well as the primary cause, with both of them complementarily being the condition for and the explanation of natural phenomena. This can be exemplified by means of double causality found in the human experience of action. By shaking a pear tree, we cause its fruit to fall. We realize, however, that a similarly important cause of this phenomenon is the force of gravity, without which the predicted effect would not occur.[54]

The essential issue is to find a solution to the problem of whether God as the first cause is a sufficient condition for the occurrence of a given phenomenon. Stoeger gives a negative answer to this question, treating secondary causes as equally important for the occurrence of cause-and-effect relations in nature. The omnipotent God suspended His power to be the only sufficient condition for phenomena in the world. This is connected with the concept of divine "self-emptying." The *kenosis* of the Creator is based, among other things, on His voluntary renunciation of being the only cause of events in the world. This is why God is not a sufficient reason for the existence of the individual human being. Secondary causes are also necessary, as exemplified by the action of parents and the biological reproductive processes. The American Jesuit observes that in Christian doctrine this remains true even "with respect to an event like the Incarnation. God invites it but does not force it. That *fiat* of Mary was essential to the concrete realization of the Incarnation."[55]

The concept of double causality stands out in relation to the types of causality that are underpinned by contemporary scientific knowledge. In some sense (which is alien to processualists), an interpretation concerning the functioning of the world on the basis of the co-presence of secondary causes and the primary cause can be introduced together with an analysis of the phenomena characterized by top-down, bottom-up, and lateral causality. The last three are different varieties of causality described independently by the natural sciences which can serve as an inspiration for reflection on divine action in the world. The distinction between secondary causes and the primary cause takes place only on the grounds of theism. Such a proposition continues to be intellectually appealing since it highlights the real presence of cause-and-effect relationships in nature and the dependence of creation on its Creator. What remains problematic is the dualism postulated by this approach.

* * *

In light of the above analyses, it is worth stressing that theism, in undertaking reflection on God's interaction with the world, is presently under a pressure of some kind. On the one hand, scholars recognize the need for taking into account naturalistic explanations of the functioning of the world while simultaneously maintaining distance from the presentations of divine action found in the categories of interventionism.[56] The existential consequences of interventionism come in the form of crucial questions, for example: Why does God react to one particular situation whereas His presence would be more desirable in another? It is for this reason that scholars make a more intense use of inspiration drawn from the scientific theories of causality, which enable them to develop a concept of the Creator influencing His creation in a way which complies with the laws of nature. On the other hand, particular approaches need to be formulated in a way that "guarantees God" the possibility of His most real and detectable influence on world history. Otherwise, we would move away from the principal elements of Christian doctrine. In a sense, this problem was already noticed in the Middle Ages, when scholars attempted to solve it by introducing the concept of *creatio continua*, which put emphasis on the fact that creation is an ongoing act of God. Thanks to Him, individual entities exist and function in accordance with the natural order, being able to serve as actual causes of other entities and states of affairs. In the twentieth century another distinction was added: between categorical causes (which produce effects that are consistent with their proper category of causality) and the Transcendental Cause, that is, God. He is directly present in the world and in each causal relation occurring in it, not only by giving existence to categorical causes, but also by making the emergence of a causal relationship possible. Therefore, God is creatively immanent in all natural processes without violating their integrity and autonomy.[57]

Presenting God as the immanent cause of the development of the world is characteristic of circles which stress a theistic interpretation of the laws of nature.[58] This question is elaborated upon in the third chapter of my book. Even at this stage it is worth pointing out that with such an understanding of non-interventionist divine action, the boundary between action's natural and supernatural dimensions becomes blurred. However, this is not done by eliminating the Creator's supernatural influence on creation, but by means of noticing His active presence in what was deemed natural (in other words, in nature). Such an approach avoids dualism and interventionism, while not posing the threat of eliminating God from the image of the world. On the contrary, this position ensures that the Creator is present both in the entire world system and in the slightest manifestations of its working.[59]

2

On God

An analysis of the issues pertaining to divine action in the world calls for an insightful study of the character of the efficient agent. Hence, this chapter of my book is devoted to reflection on the idea of God specific to monotheistic religions, with particular emphasis given to Christianity. The wealth of thought in this area can be seen in the plurality of theistic systems that attempt to approach the crucial elements of this issue.

We can highlight the several essential components of the idea of an absolute being that are treated by leading philosophical schools as necessary to consider. The subject matter of this book calls for attention focused on those aspects of God's nature that are the most significant in determining His interaction with the world. For this reason, I address the question of God as a Creator and a Person, as well as analyze His attributes of simplicity, omnipotence, and omniscience. The topics that recur in this section also include divine immutability, God's relationship to time, and impassibility.

The idea of God and the ways of its presentation

The foundations of theism

God is usually understood as a personal, omnipotent, eternal, and perfect being (ontically and morally). He is the object of human worship as the creator of the universe and guarantor of the fulfillment of the ultimate human aspiration for happiness. Irrespective of more detailed proposals that I present in the latter part of this book, this concept of God is shared by followers of the main monotheistic religions. What makes Jews, Muslims, and Christians differ is primarily their assessment of Jesus Christ. Since the present study is of a philosophical nature, this question I put aside, even though some authors, especially those of Protestant provenance, engage in theistic discussion without such strict methodological rigidity.[1]

I also apply methodological rigor to the aspects of the discussed problem that are characteristic of a specific Christian denomination. The question of sacraments or other doctrinal elements of a particular denomination are not an object of my consideration, even though some of them may inspire a renewed interest in certain themes from the field of the philosophy of God. The character of this discipline also prevents me from providing arguments based on data pertaining to revelation.[2]

In some cases, however, this does provide a significant context for my reflection, and allows me to acknowledge the difficulty of creating such an image of God in which theological aspects are consistent with philosophical ones. The Trinitarian doctrine challenges the model of God's simplicity, and treating love as the basic dimension of His action poses many problems if a maximalist view of omnipotence is assumed.

On the other hand, many doctrinal solutions fundamentally depend on the kind of philosophy which we (at least implicitly) adopt. Drawing upon philosophical concepts to explain complex theological questions is, after all, a natural and valuable component of the mutual relationship thereof. Problems arise when uncritical adherence to one specific interpretative model stalls the development of approaches that would have otherwise creatively evolved together with other philosophical trends. An equally important question is of the worldview behind particular theistic proposals. Adopting a specific, and at times naive, worldview can result, and often results, in scholars becoming confined, either consciously or not, to ideas that at a later stage of history came to contradict scientific data.[3]

Obviously, while reflecting on the issue of divine action in the world, philosophy should carry out research which is autonomous in regard to both the empirical sciences and theology. The care taken to respect these crucial distinctions does not change the fact that the main point of reference for my analyses is the concept of God as rooted in Christian culture. This stems not only from the conviction that the other two main monotheistic religions share with Christianity the fundamental (essential) attributes of God,[4] but more importantly, from the standpoint taken by the theists listed in the introduction. Even if these theists do not adhere to the Christian worldview, they still treat it as the main setting for the reflection. The depth of this thought gives reason to perceive Christian doctrine as a cognitively attractive object of philosophical reflection. This, in turn, makes it possible to reveal the variety of nuances that make up the colorful mosaic of theism.[5]

The Christian idea of God presupposes His action in a world with which He maintains a continuous relationship.[6] Deism takes a stance which is incompatible with the Christian image of the Creator whose role is not merely limited to bringing contingent beings into existence. The nature of God's interaction with the world is dynamic and ends in the final and ultimate union that all believers hope for.[7] Divine action in the world affects both man and "the rest of nature." Some contemporary approaches put more emphasis on the fact that the Creator influences the entire world, and hence it would be a mistake to divide particular beings, space, or time into separate divine acts.[8]

In classical theism it is assumed that God is a conscious and active being, who is also the ultimate source of existence for contingent beings. God is comprehended as a disembodied spirit, which makes a more precise presentation of His relationship with the physical world harder. The Creator is essentially different from creation, with this hindering the formulation of a precise theory of His action in the world governed by autonomous laws. It can be claimed that the omnipotent God is not constrained by the laws of nature and can act beyond them or *contra naturam*. Nevertheless, such an approach generates further problems in providing a rational depiction of the nature of God and His interaction with the world.[9]

The attributes of God

A coherent presentation of God's attributes is especially difficult. It is assumed in philosophical theology that we cannot ascribe to God traits that are mutually contradictory. Therefore, studies conducted in this area focus on the internal unity of God's individual attributes and their mutual coherence. In this light the following question can be posed: Which attributes are necessary and which ones are contingent?[10] T. V. Morris points out that the attributes that are related to the God–world relationship (e.g., omnipresence) should be regarded as contingent, since they refer to the contingency of creation.[11] In the second half of the twentieth century, problems with a detailed characterization of the divine being resulted in skepticism about the cognitive accessibility of God's nature, or even doubts whether He possesses any nature at all.[12]

D. Blumenfeld deemed the Christian view of God as intrinsically inconsistent, claiming that an absolutely perfect being cannot be simultaneously omnipotent, omniscient, and entirely good.[13] N. Kretzmann pointed out that immutability is incompatible with omniscience and N. Pike was critical of combining omnipotence with perfect goodness.[14] Some attributes cause serious problems when portraying God's interaction with the world, particularly with man. God's benevolence was often demonstrated as inconsistent with the presence of evil in the world, particularly when considering extreme manifestations of suffering. Divine omniscience, in turn, seemed to be incompatible with the libertarian concept of freedom.[15] A further problem was posed by the eternalist understanding of time found in reflection on God's eternity,[16] with this implying a strong concept of His omniscience and omnipotence. Likewise, it was difficult to demonstrate the necessity of God's existence in the face of all that is contingent.[17]

In discussions regarding the nature of God, such as were being conducted in the last several decades, numerous doubts were highlighted. Scholars were well aware that the acceptance of one attribute usually implies the necessity of accepting others (e.g., by acknowledging God's simplicity we should also recognize God's aseity, immutability, and infinity). Essential questions arise mainly in the context of attributes which seem to contradict one another. Can we rationally claim that a simple God is a creator, a person, and life? Can we reconcile God's simplicity with His freedom? Many participants of the presently on-going debate give a negative reply to the last question. In assuming that God is free we cannot simultaneously state His simplicity, as claim the critics of traditional theism.[18]

Setting aside the many specific controversies, we need to note that the list of attributes studied by contemporary theists does not generally differ from the collection determined by classical philosophy. Apart from the attributes that are typically given priority in acknowledged companions to philosophy of religion—simplicity, necessity, immutability, eternity, omniscience, omnipotence, and perfect goodness—others are added, namely omnipresence, providence, foreknowledge, aseity, disembodiment, impassibility, freedom, or even sovereignty and beauty. Editors of these publications usually allow authors to analyze individual attributes separately, without trying to solve the problem of assembling them into one coherent whole.[19] This task, however, is undertaken by the authors of monographs concerning the question of God's nature and attributes.[20]

In contemporary times many theists adopt the Anselmian approach to God's attributes and present them as a set of perfections. Paradoxically, such an approach results in the weakening of certain attributes, so that their presentation as a whole could provide a coherent portrayal of God's nature. In place of eternalism, presentism is introduced, thus enforcing the rejection of the idea of immutability and attenuation of omnipotence and omniscience, at least in respect of God's knowing future human actions. This stems both from the awareness of problems created by the existence of evil in the world and scholarly attempts at defending the free will of sapient beings. These two areas are an essential (and in the opinion of some, insurmountable) challenge to classical theism. Attempts at reconciling the phenomenon of freedom and evil with the strong concept of God's eternity, immutability, and omniscience are undertaken by analytical Thomists who underline the value of other important attributes, namely: simplicity, infinity, omnipotence, will, impassibility, and moral perfection.[21]

The modification of classical theism as far as reflection on divine attributes is concerned has taken various forms in the course of history.[22] This is represented by Thomists, Ockhamists, and proponents of the above mentioned Anselmianism. A way to tackle the problems identified by the critics of a narrowly understood version of theism was provided by Molinism. The mail goal of Molinism is to disprove the allegations that the omniscient God appears to be responsible for the existence of evil or even its author. After all, theism should not become a form of fatalism or philosophical Calvinism.[23]

In the subsequent part of this book I refer to the above concepts while discussing some nuances of Creator-creation interaction. At this stage of my investigations, however, it is important to classify the specific attributes of God. One way would be to distinguish between God's essence—embracing simplicity, perfection, infinity, immutability, eternity, and goodness—and His action which calls for reflection on intellect (knowledge), will, omnipotence, and providence. By another approach, a distinction is assumed between the "positive" attributes (i.e., wisdom, goodness, justice) and the "negative" attributes (i.e., immutability, disembodiment, infinity, timelessness).[24]

Considering the fundamental significance of some attributes for the issue of the Creator's interaction with His creation, I devote to them separate sections of this chapter. Other attributes (though not all) are the subject of analysis in various places of the present study. After all, it is difficult to ponder the concept of God's simplicity or omniscience without referring to His immutability, freedom, and relationship to time. On the other hand, the problem of God's immanence in the world raises fundamental questions concerning the existence of evil, especially in evil's most extreme manifestations. The problem of evil and suffering, in turn, is related to the issue of God's goodness.

The cultural and philosophical sources of Christian thought

In order to understand the determinants of the particular solutions arrived at in the course of reflection on the attributes of God and His nature, we must outline the cultural context which, to a great extent, has molded Christian doctrine. The latter evolved in the milieu of two great intellectual and spiritual traditions. On the one hand, the natural ground for the expression of the truths of the faith was provided by Judaism and its characteristic manner of conveying messages, using colorful language and many symbols. The Creator was presented as dynamically interacting with His creation, thus revealing His presence and taking care of the work of His own making. At the same time, He was close to human beings, involved in man's fate, and manifested such personal traits as joy, anger, and the ability to forgive. The Old Testament put emphasis on the possibility of encountering God in nature and human history that is a path to salvation. The Creator was a faithful companion to the fate of both man and the world, but it was also within His power to alter decisions once taken, or suspend the laws of nature.

On the other hand, Christian thought of the first centuries remained under the strong influence of Greek intellectual heritage. Greek philosophy was born in a polytheistic context (gods existed in the world and were distinguished from other beings),[25] but with time this philosophy evolved to build a specific image of the only God. He was now seen as distant to contingent beings, for interacting with them might undermine His greatness. Any kind of change would disclose the weakness of the Absolute. Revering Him was conditioned by His ontic distinctness from creation. God appeared above all else as the rational *Logos*, designing the order of the world in a purposeful manner.[26] The static perfection of God as demonstrated in Greek philosophy cannot be blemished by being immersed in time or physical space. A strong dualism marked both God's relationship to the world and the relationship between spirituality and physicality, with this including the structure of man. Matter symbolized the worthlessness of the world and the human body was perceived as a prison of the soul which strives for liberation.[27]

The idea of *Logos* helped the Greek Fathers of the Church to solve an extremely important question: How can God be an immutable being and simultaneously influence the world?[28] God's relationship to the world was explained as a downward action. As a consequence, thinkers were convinced that the only way to comprehend the Creator is through enlightenment following from faith, rather than a "bottom-up" search for the secrets of creation that contains traces of God. St. Augustine wrote: "For understanding is the reward of faith. Therefore, do not seek to understand in order to believe, but believe that you may understand."[29]

The "top-down" strategy was later applied by St. Anselm of Canterbury when presenting God *a priori* (in terms of necessity). Thus, He was defined as a being beyond which no greater thing can be conceived. Anselm claimed that God is the most perfect among all existing beings. From a concept formulated in this way, it transpires that the properties attributed to God make up one perfect whole. The attributes of the absolute being are perfect to the highest degree: God has to possess all perfections at the maximum level, that is, the highest possible. Properties understood in this way are derived from the very essence of God, with Him possessing them in a necessary manner, so there is no possibility, either logical or existential, for Him to lose any of them. The idea of a being than which a greater cannot be thought permits specific attributes to be inferred: immutability, aseity, eternity, omniscience, omnipotence, goodness, and omnipresence. These attributes are necessary and belong to the essence of God.[30]

Since the attributes enumerated above pertain to God's perfections, it is difficult to indicate one principle behind this collection. None of these attributes can be distinguished as formally ordering the nature of God or of being primary in the logical sense. A given attribute reveals itself in an adequate manner, depending on a particular manifestation of divine activity. It can be stated, however, that for Anselm it is of utmost priority to underline the necessity of the most perfect being's existence. Human language is insufficient to express the transcendent character of God's attributes, but the best method to comprehend the divine nature is to maximize individual traits *ad infinitum*, in a qualitative rather than quantitative manner.[31] The Anselmian approach is based on philosophical analysis of the concept of God and on the logical deduction of all the individual attributes that emerge from the idea of the necessary being. Thus, one who understands philosophy and is familiar with logic must come to acknowledge the existence of God as an *a priori* necessary truth. The most Perfect Being is the abstract "God of the philosophers" and it is of no major significance how this relates to God's image present in the religious message.[32]

A different—"bottom-up"—strategy of reflection was put forward by Aquinas. He formulated a doctrine which refers to the phenomena of the world and is not based only on logical analysis, a characteristic of the Anselmian approach. The philosophy behind Aquinas's concept was the Aristotelian system, which generated some considerable problems.[33] After all, the Stagirite accepted the immutable and eternal nature of beings, which was compatible with the teleological structure of the world. Thanks to that order each thing attains its proper end. Aware of such difficulties, Aquinas effectively modified and applied Aristotelian philosophy to his innovative presentation of God's relationship to the world. This later prevailed in the teaching of the Church for many centuries.

The doctrine introduced by Aquinas presents God *a posteriori*, from the perspective of the effects His action has on the world. The analysis of the world suggests that all beings are of a contingent character. This calls for the acknowledgement of the first cause—the ultimate source of all existence. In the divine being the essence and existence are identical. God is *Actus Purus* and hence a simple being. From within, as it were, this simplicity organizes the essence of God and ensures the coherence of His other attributes: perfection, infinity, immutability, timelessness, goodness, omniscience, and omnipotence. Within a simple being, individual attributes are identified as different only in formal terms.[34]

On the Creator–creation interaction, Aquinas remained to a great degree influenced by the thought of St. Augustine. According to both thinkers, God, directly or indirectly, by means of a chain of secondary causes, predetermines everything that happens in the world. He holds complete power and control over each and every being and event. Irrespective of time, the power of God presumes His full awareness of everything: past, present, and future events. God knows everything because He causes everything.[35]

Despite the different ways of adopted reasoning, the Thomistic approach to the nature of God and His attributes shares many elements with the Anselmian one. The two schools make up one tradition of classical theism. What distinguishes them is the point of departure for the argumentation concerning the existence of God and determination of the fundamental attribute: while Anselm emphasizes the role of necessity, Aquinas underscores simplicity. Mordarski points out that contemporary analytic philosophy, which prefers the method of logical analysis, favors the *a priori* approach to studying the nature of God and His attributes. In contrast, Thomistic aposteriorism is followed by analytical Thomists. However, the conclusions they formulate are often compatible with the *a priori* tradition. The theory of Aquinas appears to be much more intuitive in many of its details and the simplicity of God organizes remaining attributes in a coherent manner. The attributes of God are only formally different from divine nature, and do not constitute a mere collection of the perfect qualities of the supreme being.[36]

Contemporary currents of theism

From the moment the Aristotelian-Thomistic system was created, its impact on the development of specific solutions elaborated upon within Christian theism has been systematically growing. Nonetheless, in the course of time, this philosophy has been subject to many modifications introduced in response to criticism that revealed some problematic areas: divine omnipotence and omniscience, human freedom, physical and moral evil, and the autonomy of nature.

A special attempt at a renewed understanding of both the nature of God and His action in the world came with Neo-Thomistic approaches.[37] The distinction between the primary and the secondary cause, which was characteristic of the Christian tradition, was modified in the light of ideas introduced by Kant. One of the main problems that called for examination was how to coherently explain the presence of God's action and the simultaneous operation of created factors in one event. In the late twentieth century, some original solutions in this respect were proposed by W. N. Clarke, E. McMullin, and W. Stoeger.[38]

However, the entire twentieth-century history of Neo-Thomism clearly shows that there are many ways to develop the Aristotelian-Thomistic heritage in its many aspects. Apart from the most traditional school, that is, Neo-Thomism (sometimes also referred to as conservative theism), at least three other and equally important forms of evolved Thomism can be distinguished: existential Thomism, transcendental Thomism, and Louvain Thomism. The last one originated in D. Mercier's intellectual environment and stemmed from the conviction that philosophy needs to be practiced in light of the natural sciences. In Poland, this thinking was present in publications by I. Radziszewski (the founder of the Catholic University of Lublin), and then by S. Mazierski and K. Kłósak. At KU Leuven the same philosophical current was promoted by J. van der Veken, who became involved in the development of processual thought.

Inspired by the intellectual output of A. N. Whitehead, processualism accounts for a scientific worldview while formulating a program of theism. Questioning many assumptions of classical approaches, both processual philosophy and theology offer a new concept of God. He is considered to be the ontic source of the so-called "initial aim," around which every actual being is created. In presenting God as the foundation of rationality and the ontic reason for cosmic order, Whitehead introduced the idea of the "primordial" nature of God. As far as contemplation of God's interaction with actual beings is concerned, this pertains to the "consequent" nature of God.[39]

The crucial part of the Creator's influence on His creation is played by "persuasion" and "lure." They give rise to a fascination with patterns revealed by the "Divine Poet of the World." However, this enchantment does not determine us. Through His interaction with the world of actual beings, the sempiternal and infinite God changes along with the evolution of the world. Hence, to some extent, He depends on the world. By realizing His own aim which is unknown to us, God remains transcendent in relation to the world of actual beings, although He is also immanently present in them.

In respect of many crucial issues, processual theology and philosophy are approaches that are essentially different than the Aristotelian-Thomistic concept, the former rejecting the classical idea of God acting by means of secondary causes. Processual scholars point out that God does not fully determine the course of a particular event but acts by means of making the realization of a specific aim attractive. Apart from being predetermined by the past states of a given process, the irreducible elements of novelty appear at subsequent stages of an event's course. Representatives of this approach include C. Hartshorne, J. Cobb Jr., and D. R. Griffin.

Hartshorne regarded as entirely wrong the concept of God understood in an abstract and static way. The origin of this concept should be traced in Greek philosophy (which considers change to be a manifestation of imperfection), and in systems that attribute to God particular qualities to an absolute degree. Difficulties with reconciling God's omnipotence and omniscience with the freedom of creation were a direct consequence of the classical approach. Another problem was how to link the idea of God's immutability to the conviction that He is alive and reacts to what occurs in the world, engaging in real dialogue with creation.

Processual theism puts emphasis on the fact that God is a changeable and dynamic being, even if equipped with a certain degree of immutability. In the case of God, change is never an act of regression, but always a progress. God's interaction with the world is sometimes compared to the way a human mind affects the body. This is one of the metaphors frequently used in panentheism, according to which the world exists in God. This interpretation is treated as an elaboration of the stance taken by the Apostle Paul on the Athenian Areopagus: in God "we live and move and have our being."[40]

Analytic philosophy has a distinctly autonomous history with regards to reflecting on theistic issues. For many decades, this philosophical school, created at the turn of the twentieth century, gave little consideration to questions concerning the existence or nature of God. Attempts at reflecting on chosen aspects of religion undertaken by some representatives of this intellectual system did not produce any substantial effect. In the 1970s, this tendency took a different turn in Anglo-Saxon circles. Studies published by A. C. Plantinga, R. M. Adams, W. P. Alston, P. van Inwagen, and other acknowledged authors resulted in an increased creative interest in the issues of the philosophy of God among many academics, including successors of the intellectual legacy of Aquinas.[41]

The confrontation of analytic philosophy with classical theism has borne numerous intellectual fruits in the last several decades. These results are even more discernible because many contemporary continental philosophers distance themselves from philosophical theology, especially when concerning such questions as the Creator–creation interaction. Among other reasons, this stems from the fact that the above philosophers put an exceptionally strong emphasis on God's transcendence, hence rendering Him distant from the world and unattainable for any cognition in human categories. Other representatives of this group, in turn, tend to combine theistic reflection with cultural transformations of the concept of God and an increasingly religious secularization. In this context, the intense development of theism, recently observable in the English-speaking countries, has provided the grounds for creative discourse which addresses significant religious questions in a philosophically meaningful manner.[42] It can be stated that great progress has been made in the way God's attributes and nature are being explicated.[43]

Analytic philosophical theology has its own distinct character, based, among other things, on logical analysis of theistic problems. Among the many intellectual links of analytic philosophy, its relationship with Neo-Thomism is worth noting. This is significant both in terms of the subject and the adopted approach characterized by a very precise use of religious terminology. The far-reaching application of the analytic apparatus to the discussion of the questions of classical theism resulted in many successful attempts at translating difficult issues into the language of analytic philosophy. This frequently involved introducing partial modifications to the particular solutions put forward by Aquinas. Analytic philosophical theology is an example of how a traditional theistic system can be revived by means of contemporary philosophical tools.[44]

The problem of language

The question of language has been posing a constant problem for the specific variants of theism, a fact that is especially visible if we attempt to describe God's attributes in light of His relationship to the world and especially to human beings. Within the framework of classical Thomism, the question of terminology might be formulated in the following way: How can we apply language—which is used to describe created, finite, spatial, and temporal beings—in reference to God who is not created, non-spatial, and timeless? After all, the terminology normally used in this context includes categories that seem to have no proper application to God. Verbs such as "to love," "to act," "to think," "to consider," "to reflect," and "to know" all contain the idea of time. God, however, is so radically different from us that the words which describe Him cannot possess the same meaning as the ones with which we denote objects present in the physical world.[45] Is it indeed enough to elevate the meaning of these terms to the highest degree?

Aquinas was already aware of these dilemmas, but he rejected the suggestion that God cannot be spoken of in affirmative sentences at all. The Angelic Doctor's detachment from apophatic theology was combined with his conviction of the existence of a both specific and positive language which can be used in reference to God. Aquinas especially highlights the language of analogy and metaphor. The latter seems to be a natural component of Christian theism, which frequently uses figurative language to convey the nature of God. However, different types of analogy called for more clarification. Under the analogy of attribution, God possesses everything that is necessary for creating particular beings as good. Under the analogy of proportion, God is good in a way inherent in Himself by being perfectly who He is supposed to be. Such clarification is not a solution to all linguistic problems, and Aquinas did not hesitate to accentuate human limitations on the way to knowing God and His nature. We do not possess sufficient cognitive abilities to fully explain what it means for the Creator to exist, create, or love.[46]

Irrespective of the different epochs shaping the image of theism, in the linguistic context there is a recurring relationship between the choice of terminology and the approach which, to a greater or lesser extent, underlines God's transcendence in relation to the world. The more we emphasize that God, as a simple being, exists outside of time and space, the less can be said about Him in affirmative language. *Via negativa* becomes the natural path for those scholars who significantly reduce or even eliminate God's immanence in nature, making Him distant from man and the world. In the extreme form, such an approach can result in deism, which excludes the Creator–creation interaction, including providence understood as God's attention to the fate of human beings and the entire universe. On the other hand, blurring the difference between God and the world leads frequently to the anthropomorphization of language and pantheistic approaches. That is why clarification of the concept of creation is of the utmost importance. Since this constitutes one of the essential components of Christian theism, below I focus my analyses on God who manifests His creative power in the world.

The creative power

Platonism vs. Aristotelianism

The history of the Christian doctrine of creation has been remarkably influenced by the medieval rivalry between Aristotelianism and Platonism. Many elements of Plato's philosophy, elaborated by the Church Fathers, became part of Christian teaching. Platonic concepts seemed to resonate well within the fundamental intuitions of religious faith. After all, the material world, which is subject to change, is but a shadow of what corresponds to the unchangeable reality of ideas. In the anthropological context, Platonism appeared to harmonize with the distinction—deeply rooted in the intellectual tradition—between the immortal soul and its opposite, the body, which is subject to decay. The sophisticated and poetic language of Plato matched the bold ideas which he advanced in his own creative manner. The authority of Plato was so great that as late as in the thirteenth century his *Timaeus* still inspired many with its reflection on God and nature. In the latter domain, however, various manifestations of fantasy and speculation could be found, which were closer to mythology than to a reliable elucidation of physical phenomena.[47]

For a long time, circumstances were favorable to the development of Platonism, also because the Aristotelian approach seemed to contrast sharply with the Christian view of the Creator–creation relationship.[48] If the natures of beings are eternal, then it is impossible to assume the world's beginning. Thus, it should come as no surprise that when the Stagirite's works were brought to Europe by the Arabs, Church representatives watched their spread with a great deal of suspicion.[49] Numerous cases were documented of interventions held by Church hierarchs who—being concerned for the integrity of the long-held teaching on creation—compiled long lists of the errors allegedly committed by Aristotle. This affair grew to serious proportions when in 1229 Pope Innocent IV issued an official ban on studying Aristotle's works.[50]

Nonetheless, the impact of the Aristotelian worldview was very intense. In the second half of the thirteenth century, European academic centers were already permeated with Aristotelian ideas. This process was vividly emphasized by A. Koyré who wrote that Aristotelianism was disseminated at universities and appealed to knowledge-hungry people. Koyré also claimed that the power of Aristotelian reflection sprang from its academic value.[51] Hence, it is no wonder that in a little while, in order to meet the needs of the times, efforts were made to reconcile Aristotelian thought with the doctrine of the Church. This was possible thanks to the creative mind of Aquinas who—instead of artificially bending the widely spreading philosophy to conform with the commonly accepted reflection on God the Creator—introduced a conceptual distinction between the creation of the world and its beginning. In such a way conclusions drawn about the existential dependence of creation on the Creator did not refer to the temporal order and encouraged favorable attitudes to the scientific search for the genesis of the universe. For the Christian thought on creation, it was no longer crucial whether there was a "first moment," and what it looked like.[52]

It needs to be underlined that neither the Platonic Demiurge, nor the Aristotelian Prime Mover was the creator of the world in the classical sense, even though both possess some traits of a creator. The former was not involved in the process of creation but rather in the ordering of primary chaos, which (being the building material used to impose order) was not conceived as the constituent matter of the created entities, but as an intermediate state between what already exists and what will exist. The Demiurge could not create things, because for Him this would mean becoming inevitably defiled with the imperfection of the material world. This was unacceptable in the Greek philosophical tradition. Aristotle's Absolute, in turn, is a spiritual being, a pure form which is not subject to any change. The Unmoved Mover is the purpose of the world, attracting it to Himself by being the ultimate end of everything.[53]

Christian doctrine

In his creative application of Aristotelian thought to theism, Aquinas presented the act of creation as imparting existence to the world, which can either have a beginning in time or be eternal.[54] Thus, God is the efficient cause that precedes the world in the logical sense. In the twelfth century, Maimonides presented a similar idea, but it was Aquinas who applied this theory to solve problems connected with the incorporation of Aristotelian philosophy in Christian doctrine. Thomistic metaphysics stresses that the world is made up of contingent beings (their existence is not necessary), so they acquire their existence from God, who cannot *not* exist because existence is His essence. The act of creation implies granting existence, and this allows the question of a beginning in time to be left open. Thanks to this interpretation, Aquinas did not see any major threats in the Aristotelian idea of the world's sempiternality, and viewed God's creative action as producing the entire substance of being.[55]

Stating that God created the entire substance of being is crucial to understanding the *creatio ex nihilo* category. Nothingness is in no way a being precedent (either in the temporal or logical sense) in relation to created things. The essence of the act of creation lies in the fact that no "material" precedes it. In reference to St. Anselm's thought, the author of *De aeternitate mundi* explains that

> "all things, except the Supreme Being, are made by him out of nothing in the sense that they are not made out of anything, and no absurdity results." On this understanding of the phrase "out of nothing," therefore, no temporal priority of non-being to being is posited, as there would be if there were first nothing and then later something.[56]

Natural and finite causes result in alteration to an already existing substance, while God is the one who makes this substance come into being. According to Aquinas's concept, the result induced in the act of creation is instantaneous and does not happen through change. Thus, in this context, there is no temporal interval between a cause and its effect. Only God is a cause which does not have to precede the effect in the temporal order. This argument, under the visible influence of the Stagirite's thought, culminates in the logical conclusion that

> if, granted a cause, its effect does not immediately exist as well, this can only be because something complementary to that cause is lacking: the complete cause and the thing caused are simultaneous. God, however, never lacks any kind of complementary cause in order to produce an effect. Therefore, at any instant at which God exists, so too can his effects, and thus God need not precede his effects in time.[57]

Time-independent imparting of existence to beings provided good grounds for the introduction of the concept of *creatio continua*. This was already expressed by St. Augustine, who claimed that the act of creation covers the entire duration of all that is created. Should the Creator suspend His protection of the world, it could not remain in existence even for an instant: "God is working until now in such a way that if his working were to be withheld from the things he has set up, they would simply collapse."[58] A clear echo of this view can be found in the above-mentioned study by Aquinas. In its final section, the author even recalls the example used in *De civitate Dei*, which captures the idea of creation as a sempiternal causal dependence, leaving out the solution to the problem of the world's origin in time. Much as Augustine, Aquinas deemed as crucial the conclusion regarding the continuous dependence of creation on the Creator: "if the creature were left to itself, it would be nothing."[59]

Referring to the classifications presented in the first chapter of this book, it needs to be underscored that the creation of the world (*creatio ex nihilo*) and the sustaining in existence of all that has already been created (*creatio continua*) are usually treated in Christian theism as manifestations of God's ordinary action. This is distinguished from special divine action, both in its noninterventionist form (action which does not violate the laws of nature) and in the interventionist one (in which God acts by suspending the laws of nature, or against them). Given scholastic thought, the above distinction is, nonetheless, incomplete since it does not account for God's causal cooperation with natural causes, an idea propounded in the Middle Ages. This type of Creator–creation interaction can be treated as the third kind of ordinary divine action.[60]

The time of revision

The Christian doctrine of creation, which evolved for many centuries, had to face new challenges in the age of scientific revolution. At that time, it might appear that since Newtonian mechanics implied a causal closure of nature, there is no "space" for *creatio continua*.[61] Apart from the initial act of creation, divine action might, at its utmost, be based on an interventionist violation of the laws of nature. These laws were not treated as a "place" where God's presence was manifested, but as a peculiar causal competition with the Creator. The seventeenth-century deistic trends supported such an approach.[62]

Additional difficulties arose under the influence of D. Hume and I. Kant, who denied the value of natural theology and metaphysical speculation on causality. In undermining the possibility of uncovering divine design present in creation, some philosophers suggested reducing religion solely to the sphere of morality. However, the transformations of the Christian doctrine concerning God's creative action were affected not only by external criticism.[63] The nineteenth century brought about renewed reflection on the appropriate interpretation of biblical texts, accentuating the need for adequate historical and critical studies in this area. F. Schleiermacher, one of the fathers of modern hermeneutics, understood the Creator–creation relationship as God's universal immanence in the world. In this context, miracles were thought to be all those natural phenomena which could be theologically interpreted.[64]

Despite many valuable instances of reflection on the genesis of the world and divine action, in conservative milieus, until the late nineteenth century it was believed that the act of creation was a relatively recent individual event. Pursuant to this view, God created something external to Himself within an already existing space. The fact that this was actually a deistic idea was frequently overlooked. The Creator appeared as radically distant from nature, and by definition could not blend with creation. God's transcendence in relation to the world was emphasized so strongly that the idea of immanence seemed impossible to uphold.

Such an image underwent essential modifications as a consequence of scientific discoveries. The origin of the world, previously dated (by the Anglican bishop J. Ussher) by adding up the life spans of all Biblical prophets to 4004 BC,[65] was proven, thanks to geological research, to have been a much earlier process. The view holding the external character of divine action clashed with modern cosmology and the theory of evolution which demonstrated the dynamics of the natural world and explained the presumable mechanism of changes occurring in living organisms. The phenomenon of the internal vitality of nature supports a proper understanding the continuous process of creation.[66]

Nowadays, many authors stress that God's action in the world does not merely involve sustaining existence. It is often emphasized that the Creator operates by means of widely understood laws of nature. Their comprehension and description, however, are only a part of what constitutes divine action in the world. The entirety of creation is, in a sense, a manifestation of the uniqueness of the Creator's nature and the manner in which He interacts with the world. God acts through secondary causes in many different ways. Regularities, bonds, and relationships in nature exist in a particular way thanks to His assent or choice. The Creator participates in the history of creation at each stage of its development.[67]

The above assertions can be reconciled with classic theistic terminology. On the one hand, God's action continues to be creative, and allows beings to be fulfilled. At the same time, the primary cause of the world's existence and development differs essentially from all other causes since this primary cause forms the ultimate foundation of reality. The continuous chain of secondary causes calls for a primary cause as the basis of all forms of being. Only primary causality provides an adequate explanation for the existence and efficiency of the chain of secondary causes.[68]

God is the ultimate source of necessity and contingency present in the physical processes. The interaction between necessity and contingency gives rise to the world's fertility, which consists in continuous emergence of novelty. According to Stoeger, the answer to the question of why the world behaves in this particular way can exclusively be found in relation to the Creator. Only in this way can we explain the (relative) order existing in the world. The process of God "giving Himself" to the world can occur eternally, which, in light of some interpretations, ensues from the uniqueness of the Creator's nature. If we understand this nature as *bonum diffusivum sui*, then the divine benevolence that spreads to creation can be everlasting. From this perspective, creation is a "consequence" of God's nature, and the order that exists in the world appears to be the principal manifestation of His presence.[69]

New proposals and old problems

Creation is also sometimes understood as a self-limitation of God who "within His life makes space" for what is ontically different from Him. This view, inspired by the Cabbalistic Tradition, is suggested by J. Moltmann, who writes about cosmogenesis as a unique "withdrawal of God for the sake of 'giving room' to the world."[70] At successive stages of development, creation manifests fertility rooted in the life of God. While elaborating on these ideas, E. Johnson introduces an analogy between the act of creation and the experience of a woman giving space inside her body for a new human being.[71] D. Edwards claims that the metaphor of a person who makes room within themselves for a new life can be a tremendously rich and evocative image of the divine fertility through which the universe is born in God.[72]

Answering the question concerning the character of the creative act, however, is more important than the use of parallels and metaphors. If it is in God's nature to share existence with other beings, then perhaps, contrary to classical approaches, He must have created the world. Does not His very essence impose a necessity of this kind? When attempting to solve this problem, scholars introduce the concept of God's dual transcendence in relation to the world. The transcendence of power underlines the fact that God with His omnipotence transcends all creation. The transcendence of freedom, on the other hand, means that creation occurs through a free divine act that is not subject to any ontic necessity. Accepting the thesis that "naturally good God had to create the world" calls for consideration of the fact that His action goes beyond the human comprehension of necessity, possibility, and freedom.[73]

Another frequently debated issue is the extent of divine creation. Theists claim that God is not the Maker of His own self. Problems arise if we attempt to answer the following question: Did God create mathematical entities, or logical relations? According to Swinburne, beings existing by the power of a logical relationship do not exist in as real a manner as physical objects, but they arise from the content of the sentences which express them. There exists "an omnipresent spirit," writes the author of *The Coherence of Theism*, "who is the creator of all substances that exist, the existence of which is not entailed by his own existence."[74]

In light of the above formulation, considerable difficulties arise both in the context of the functioning of nature and, above all else, the creative activity of human beings. Is it not people who make schools and factories real? Is it not the Sun and rain that make grass grow? To solve all these problems, an additional proposition is introduced to emphasize the fact that, directly or indirectly, all contingent beings are a result of divine action. In the case of beings not endowed with free will, God causes them to give rise to other entities. In the case of beings in possession of free will, it is God who allows them to act so as to make things come into existence.[75]

One of the greatest intellectual challenges is finding the answer to the question concerning the creation of the human soul. Despite Swinburne's assertion that this problem does not seem to be central to theistic reflection, the question of the genesis of the soul has become one of the main objects of contemporary debate, especially when the scientific perspective of our species' evolution is taken into consideration. Grasping the creative action of God in the *creatio continua* terms provides only a partial solution to the problem since the central dilemma is related to a distinction between the concepts of continuity and discontinuity when interpreting natural processes. How can physical continuity be reconciled with ontological discontinuity that appears during the genesis of the soul (or the human spirit)? A lot depends on defining concepts and giving preference to one solution of the *mind–body problem*. Irrespective of individually elaborated options, the presentation of which lies beyond the scope of this book, I do not think it necessary to adopt an interventionist view of God's action while creating man both in the context of phylogenesis and ontogenesis.[76]

The origin of the world and man is a crucial aspect of the question of God's creative power. Another significant challenge in this respect is the reconciliation of the creative act with the uniqueness of God who, in the main current of theism, is presented as a simple being. This doctrine assumes that God does not possess any accidental traits. Can we say, then, that creation is not a necessary act and stems from the Creator's free act? My following investigations of divine simplicity are an attempt at answering this question.

Simplicity

Sources of the idea

From the very first centuries of the Christian philosophical tradition, its main current generally upheld that God is a simple and unchanging being. Time does not pass for Him and He cannot transform into a different state of existence. Simple God is an immutable unity, the cognition of which evades human understanding. Such cognitive difficulties notwithstanding, many theists are of the opinion that it is impossible to create one coherent concept of God without adopting the teaching of His simplicity since this is a particular attribute that actually integrates the entirety of reflection in the discussed area.[77]

One of the first Christian authors to undertake an insightful study of the question of God's simplicity was Origen. Arguing with Epicureanism and Stoicism, deemed as a threat to the Christian view of divine transcendence, Origen emphasized the actual proposition that one should philosophically comprehend God as an indestructible, non-composite, simple, and indivisible being. According to his *Contra Celsum*, the notion of a being's absolute non-complexity can be fully realized thanks to Christian revelation, especially the idea of God's immutability as depicted in Holy Scripture.[78]

Taking a philosophical approach to simplicity, Origen claimed that God has a simple spiritual nature in which there are no additional attributes. To the highest degree, God is a Monad, Oneness, a Source, and absolutely unlimited Reason. Composite material beings are limited by their own inherent qualities. God/Reason is not subject to such limitations and that is why He is to the highest degree active and operating. Accounting for divine simplicity, Origen does not restrict his argumentation to merely denying God's corporeality but suggests that God be viewed as a fundamental principle of being.[79] All other entities derive from the *principium*, which is the absolute origin of reality. Entities that have their source in God are built of parts, but the *principium* cannot be composite. The complexity within the *principium* would have called for the pre-existence of parts, with this ruling out the fundamental trait of the *principium*—being an absolute beginning.[80]

Many of the nuances regarding the concept of divine simplicity were clarified by St. Augustine, who was also the one to notice the implications of tackling these issues in understanding the Creator–creation relationship, as well as in the language of religion. God and all that He possesses are one. Both substance and attributes are the same in Him.[81] God is what he possesses, hence in the strictest sense He does not possess wisdom, but is wisdom; He does not possess justice, He is justice, etc. God's simplicity is additionally based on the appropriate relationship between all His attributes, with greatness, goodness, truth, and other attributes all being identical.[82]

The simplicity of God is not an impoverishment but indestructible possession of the fullness of being. The perfections attributed to God are real and at the same time identical to Him. The consequence of the lack of difference between God and His attributes[83] is an absolute immutability, which has a special place in St. Augustine's reflection. God cannot lose anything or achieve anything new. He constitutes a perfect unity with Himself, thus being an actual whole. Only God can be said to exist in the full sense of the word.[84]

The above statement gives St. Augustine the space to grasp the essence of the difference between God and the world. Creation is compound and changeable whereas the perfectly simple Creator is immutable. The strong emphasis put on God's transcendence in relation to the world is a result of such an understanding of God's simplicity. However, is the Creator–creation interaction at all plausible under such conditions? How can we imagine the participation of an immutable God in the history of a changeable being? Answering these questions was all the more difficult, since the Bible presents God as intensely involved in the fate of humankind and the world.[85]

St. Augustine points out that the creation of the world did not in any way contribute to enriching God's being. There are eternal ideas of things in God which are simple and identical to Him. The participation of created entities in ideas does not render the latter more divine, nor does the existence of the world make God more perfect. It is His perfection that refines creation. The situation is analogical as far as God's knowledge is concerned. God does not discover new things by coming to know creation. Knowing the world does not in any way expand God's knowledge. The world would not have come into being had God not known of this beforehand. The absolute simplicity and immutability of God does not "interfere" with the interaction He has with creation, because God's transcendence does not mean being indifferent to the world. *De Trinitate* contains a metaphor illustrating the nature of God whose action can be experienced: "light is troublesome to weak eyes, pleasant to those that are strong; (…) by their change, not its own."[86]

Reconciling the philosophical concept of God's immutable simplicity with Revelation posed a significant intellectual challenge for the bishop of Hippo. He was aware of the fact that in the Christian religion there are many notions that refer to God's association with change. It is exactly for this reason that, in Augustine's opinion, the names given for God, especially in Holy Scripture, can be understood correctly only when the specificity of so-called relative expressions is taken into account. In saying that God has become a Father to somebody, we do not mean that a new quality has emerged in Him. We are simply stating that someone has recognized God as their Father. This is a creation that changes under God's influence, whereas He remains immutable.[87]

Anselm of Canterbury, as compared to his great predecessors, analyzed the attribute of simplicity in a truly original manner. When asked to write a treatise on the essence of God, without referring to the data of revelation, Anselm designed his reasoning in a very characteristic way in the successive parts of the *Monologion*. As in Augustine's thought, for Anselm immutability is strictly connected to simplicity, but the latter needs to be, above all else, treated like a demand of reason which acknowledges the existence of a supreme being. God cannot be thought of in the categories of composition since this would mean denying the truth of Him as a supreme being beyond that which no greater thing can be conceived.[88]

According to Anselm, simplicity is contrary to any form of multiplicity in God. All perfections are one and the same in Him. God's wisdom is identical to love and all other perfections. Speaking of God in the categories of perfection, we formulate statements concerning His essence and not His quality or greatness. The essence of God is non-composite and indivisible; thus, terms like "just" or "merciful" do not denote one of His aspects but rather His entire essence. By saying that God is good we are stating that He is pure goodness. Augustine had already written about this, but Anselm provided a philosophical foundation for such an understanding of God's simplicity. God is who He is thanks to Himself; He is who He is by Himself.[89]

In his *Proslogion*, Anselm proves a faithful disciple of St. Augustine in the sense that he combines the ideas of God's simplicity and immutability. Nonetheless, some new terminological nuances emerge in Anselm's reasoning, as well as a different manner of argumentation. Anselm distinguishes between qualities that affect the subject they are applied to, and relationships that do not cause any change. The simplicity of God rules out the occurrence of accidental qualities which generate mutability. The immutability does not contradict God entering into relationships since they do not cause any change in Him. God's immutability results from His simplicity which gains a philosophical explanation thanks to the assumption of the absolute perfection of the supreme being and the *aseity* of His nature.[90]

The doctrine of God's simplicity, as formulated by St. Thomas Aquinas, was influenced to a greater degree by the thought of Boethius.[91] Among the axioms presented in *De hebdomadibus*, two seem to be crucial for grasping God's simplicity: (a) in each simple entity the existence thereof and what it is now are one single thing, and (b) in each composite entity existence is different from what the entity is. In Boethius's concept of God's simplicity what comes to the fore is the idea of form, which is pure being and decides on the existence of every being. The way to comprehend God's simplicity lies in the negation of being composed of form and matter. God is a being in the strongest sense of the word.[92]

The analysis conducted by Boethius was significant to the extent that his presentation of simplicity became a point of reference for understanding the remaining attributes of God. Simplicity was treated as a metaphysical basis for Boethius's discourse. As a consequence of this insightful analysis of the question, other attributes of God gain a solid foundation.[93] Przanowski claims that in this particular way of reasoning one can find the cause for Aquinas's decision to include the doctrine of God's simplicity at the beginning of *Summa Theologiae*.[94]

In making use of the numerous valuable elements of the reflection on the simplicity of God, as well as enriching his view with the context of everyday experience, Aquinas noticed that reality is composite on many levels. The simplicity of one being, stemming from its lack of composition of one kind, is not identical to the simplicity of another being, which can be devoid of composition of a different kind. The simplicity of the most fundamental constituent of the material world appears to be different from that of a point in a geometrical system; the simplicity of the human soul or a universal is yet altogether different. However, we can determine the common properties of simple beings. This happens because simplicity (next to composition) is the essential way of actualization of an entity that one of the transcendentals, Oneness (*unum*), refers to.[95]

Both the simple and the composite being are unities in the sense of their internal indivisibility into being and non-being. Nevertheless, simple beings can be ascribed certain characteristic traits that differentiate them from those beings the unity of which is the unity of composition. The simpler a thing is, the more power and nobility it possesses. Simple beings are less vulnerable to destruction. An elaborate theory of simplicity does not serve Aquinas merely as a tool for examining the nature of God (who remains the only absolutely simple being), but it is also an integral part of the entirety of his thought, including his logic, *philosophia naturalis*, and even ethics.[96]

Aquinas's presentation of God's simplicity is not solely a lecture on the non-composite nature of God. There are also two other fundamental elements of his doctrine: the problem of religious language and God's relationship with the world. Working on the structure of *De potentia*, Aquinas leads the reader into the depths of teaching on God in keeping with the questions that emerge on this path. If the Creator is simple and absolutely transcendent, can we have any cognitive access to Him and state anything reasonable about Him? Can such a God, and in what form, enter into a creative relationship with the world? Other works in which Aquinas attempts to provide an answer to these questions include: *The Power of God*, *Summa Theologiae*, and *Summa contra Gentiles*.[97]

Striving to disclose the specificity of God's simplicity, Aquinas drew on the output of Aristotle. Aquinas's reference to the category of act and potency, thus enabling a hierarchical presentation of reality, is of particular significance. On the basic level of reality there is raw, chaotic matter, devoid of structure or shape, characterized by pure potency, without any form of realization. On the next level, there are substances that exist in the universe (actual beings endowed with potency). On the highest level presides God, i.e., a being without any potency. Having any form of potency would indicate imperfection. God is the only one who does not possess potency; He is pure act. God exists outside of time and does not have a body because He is not made up of parts.[98]

In this theistic system, the simplicity of God does not signify any lack at all. The Thomistic-Aristotelian tradition does not associate simplicity with a negative expression of a structure existing without parts, but with perfection. Divine *simplicitas* is incomparable both to the simplicity of any known physical object or to any idealized product of reason, for instance a point not equipped with any spatial dimension.[99]

Accounting for the simplicity of God's nature, Aquinas pointed to God's lack of imperfections and the compositions typical of matter. More so, Aquinas stressed the fact that God is not contracted to any generic or specific nature. There are no accidental qualities in Him since each of them is an act for a substance and this therefore suggests composition. Thus, God's attributes have an ontic status which is different from accidental qualities. God's attributes do not violate God's simplicity since they differ, in relation to His nature and one another, only conceptually. This richness of the divine nature makes us reach for diverse terminology in order to describe it.[100]

The identity of the individual being and its nature, which constitutes simplicity, was also a point of departure for stating the Oneness of God (*unicitas*). This is an attribute which not only defines ontic unity, but also uniqueness in nature and the impossibility of divinity to be reduplicated. The existence of only one unique Absolute is possible because it is in Him that a complete identity of nature and individuality "takes place." It is also for this reason that He is God and this very God exactly.[101]

For classical theism, the absolute simplicity of God is an attribute which forms a sufficient condition for many other qualities of the Creator such as: disembodiment (not being composed of parts), non-spatiality (lack of location), atemporally understood eternity (no "before" and "after"), immutability (lack of properties or states), internal non-conditioning (lack of internally conditioning parts), and aseity (absolute independence—existing "by itself," not being composed of essence and existence). Assuming that aseity implies a mathematically immeasurable infinity and modal necessity, simplicity becomes a sufficient condition for these qualities as well.[102]

The discussions of the last centuries

The concept of divine simplicity was strongly criticized by D. Hume. He suggested that a serious treatment of simplicity rules out the formulation of any statements regarding

God, and even leads to atheism. At first, the author of the *Dialogues Concerning Natural Religion* gave a thorough presentation of the idea of simplicity, and subsequently accused its proponents of doublespeak as well as of depriving the entirety of religious discourse of any sense whatsoever.[103] G. W. Leibniz emphasized that God is the first simple substance that eminently contains all of the other perfections. Achievements in the area of classical metaphysics, within the scope discussed here, were undermined by G. Hegel and W. James. The latter criticized the scholastic way of formulating statements concerning God in categories of metaphysical attributes as being nonsensical from the point of view of practical religion.[104]

In contemporary times, we can distinguish two major areas of reflection on the simplicity of God. The first one is mainly situated in the field of systematic theology which takes into consideration data from Christian revelation. This area analyzes not so much the attribute of simplicity itself but its significance for the model of God's immutability. Rejection or essential reinterpretation of the concept of the immutability of God leads to an undermining of the doctrine of His simplicity. Many authors point out that the image of God who is loving, co-suffering, open to human pleas, and participating in the transformations which affect human beings and the world, cannot be reconciled with the philosophical idea of simplicity. Not being composed of act and potency, God remains unsusceptible to any external influence. Therefore, He is not capable of entering into dialogue with human beings.[105]

On philosophical grounds, on the other hand, there is an ongoing discussion which invokes classical arguments in support of God's simplicity, with this also being the object of criticism expressed by many contemporary theists. Authors defending the discussed doctrine point out that God is a pure act and there is nothing potential about Him. The basis for this philosophical cognition of the nature of God is formed on the grounds of the consequences stemming from the confirmation of the existence of a perfect being. God is not a composite being—within Him there is no difference between what He is and His very existence. An *Actus Purus* is not composed of substance (understood as a substrate) and accidental qualities. Should God possess properties which differ from His being, He would have lost His absoluteness, ontic sovereignty, and necessity.[106]

The immutable being is eternal (either timeless or everlasting), hence no properties or temporal parts can be distinguished in Him. The perfection of God's existence and His ontic simplicity form the basis for the cognition and proper understanding of His other attributes. Simplicity is a formal attribute and a foundation both for ruling out all literal presentations of God, as well as for the hierarchy among the stated qualities. After all, attributes are applicable to God to different degrees.[107]

The fullness of actuality and the fact that the *Actus Purus* is not a substrate of any accidental qualities generate identity between God and His attributes. Also, there is no real difference among individual attributes. Such an assertion (referred to as the thesis of identity) is one of the hot spots of debate concerning God's simplicity, because it is difficult to say anything about particular attributes in this context. Adopting this model of simplicity gives rise to substantial problems as regards the value of knowing God's nature and the meaning of metaphysical propositions concerning God. On the other hand, comprehension of human cognition of God's nature has to be non-contradictory and connected to the doctrine of God's ontic and epistemic transcendence, the justification thereof being made exactly by the doctrine of simplicity.[108]

In the last half-century, reflection on the simplicity of God has gained a different dimension altogether, especially in the Anglo-Saxon countries. This discussion became lively in the very same intellectual milieu which produced a strong criticism of the model of God's simplicity, as particularly expressed by Hume. In rejecting many of the theses put forward by classical theism, processualists questioned the doctrine of God's simplicity. Hartshorne presents God as a "compound individual." In this view, God is not a single, atemporal actual being, but rather a continuity or a sequence of temporally successive actual beings.[109]

The disputable approach

However, the greatest impact on the revival of analysis of the doctrine of God's simplicity came with the publications by A. Plantinga,[110] as well as by N. Kretzmann and E. Stump.[111] Troubles with the model of simplicity emerge specifically as a consequence of negating the multitude of attributes of God, and negating the differences between these attributes and God. According to Plantinga, this produces absurd consequences for understanding the language and manner of discussing God, and additionally leads to rejecting His personal character. Denying all forms of composition in God results in problems which are very difficult to solve. If God is identical to his properties, which are also mutually identical, then "technically" God is one property. Thus, God possesses only one property: Himself. This fact cannot be reconciled with the distinguishing of such qualities as goodness and omnipotence. Hence, an essential question arises: can such God be presented as a personal, omniscient, and loving Creator? God, being His own property, appears to be more of an abstract entity than a person as characteristic of Christian theism.[112]

Contemporary supporters of the doctrine of God's simplicity claim that Plantinga understood it incorrectly. According to B. Leftow, Plantinga thinks that when he states that there is no difference between God and His nature, it is simultaneously assumed that He possesses all of the attributes usually connected with divine nature, and thus lacks the attributes associated with the word "God," which are inconsistent with the attributes normally ascribed to Him. Nonetheless, this seems to be a mistake because the statement "God=God's nature" signifies only that what is identical to divine nature is not an example of attributes usually associated with the nature of God. Thus, the invoked thesis of identity does not imply the conclusion that God is an abstract being and possesses only the traits of such a being.[113]

When formulating statements on the attributes of God we have to realize that the content of the phrase, for example, "God is wise" conveys a different meaning than "God is good." In this and only in this sense can we say that God has different properties. At the same time, it can be rationally stated that divine wisdom does not differ from God's goodness. Analogically, "the wisdom of God" does not signify something completely different from what is conveyed by the name "God."[114] The doctrine of simplicity stresses that words used to refer to God differ in their meaning, but nonetheless signify one indivisible object.[115]

According to B. Davies, the attribute of simplicity refers to what God is not rather than to what He is. Hence, Plantinga did not understand the negative character of the doctrine of simplicity sufficiently. In this context, Aquinas argued that there is a group of statements which should be excluded when we formulate declarations concerning God. Thus, we should not associate Him with someone who possesses properties distinct from one another and, at the same time, different from Him as their subject.[116] K. Rogers, in turn, reproaches Plantinga for omitting the connection between the simplicity of God and the treating of Him as *Actus Purus*, which was essential for Aquinas. According to Rogers, simplicity does not generate an abstract image of God in which He cannot be a person. The specificity of God viewed by Christian theists is based on the fact that He acts in a rational way, being at the same time His own action.[117]

Leading questions

Important points were introduced to the discussion on God's simplicity by Stump and Kretzmann. For them, the main problem is the reconciliation of simplicity with the freedom of God's will in relation to the world, starting with the act of creation. Does God as a simple being, and hence necessary and immutable, remain free in His actions? Answering a question posed like this is a condition for the consistency of the concept of God as formulated by classical theism.[118] However, the reconciliation of the image of God who has unchanging power and will with the idea of human freedom is of equal importance.[119]

Stump points out that the philosophers and theologians of the three great monotheistic religions (Judaism, Christianity, and Islam) perceive the attribute of simplicity as essential for understanding God's nature. God is an absolutely perfect being, with this calling for simplicity. The following theses remain crucial in this context: (a) God cannot have any spatial or temporal parts (He is not a physical being); (b) God cannot have any intrinsic properties which would be of an accidental nature; and (c) in the nature of God there cannot exist any real difference among His own essential properties, as well as between His essence and existence.[120]

All of God's properties are either intrinsic essential properties or accidental extrinsic properties (e.g., being an object of reflection or adoration) which do not compose Him. Thus, it has to be stated that all of God's intrinsic attributes are identical to His simple essence and maintain identity both with one another and with divine existence. Because of the problem caused by this multitude of attributes, some theists defending the doctrine of God's simplicity make use of a distinction between *intrinsic properties* and *extrinsic properties*. Each potential change within the former would result in a simultaneous change of the very being possessing such properties. On the other hand, the modification of extrinsic properties is not a real change that takes place in a given subject.[121]

In a simple and immutable God there is one indivisible act of the will, through which He wills both Himself as a necessary object as well as the freely created world. Clarification of the character of the act of creation reveals problems with the *simplicitas Dei* doctrine. Within the main trend of Christian theism, a view was held that creation is not a necessary act and results from God's freedom. Such action is not necessary in an absolute sense. God, who is free to act (in the libertarian sense), can act differently from how He does. If the act of creation is contingent, can it be assumed that God does not create? It seems that it cannot be consistently stated that God does not possess intrinsic accidental qualities (in accordance with the doctrine of simplicity) and that at the same time it is possible that there is a God who does not decide to create the world.[122]

Doubts also arise when we state that God wills Himself and the created world through one indivisible act of will, simultaneously assuming that "willing Himself" is an absolutely necessary act of His will and that willing creation is a contingent act of His will. Przanowski underlines that "God without a decision to create" would differ to some extent from "God with a decision to create." In the light of the above, it is difficult to defend the thesis that God does not possess any accidental qualities and that all of the attributes that are ascribed to him constitute His essence and are a unity. The weight of the above-delineated problems, as well as the essential questions regarding the integrity of classical theism, reverberate in the on-going discussion conducted by many known representatives of theism.[123]

T. O'Connor points out that it is not easy to reconcile God's simplicity with the possibility of Him creating another world or not creating a world at all. In some specific cases, the reason for God's action would lie in a difference of His will or decision. The latter two would clash, and hence God, in two different possible worlds, would also differ in terms of His nature. Accepting this difference would have to be understood as an introduction of an intrinsic accidental quality. Otherwise, it remains to be stated that the creation of a concrete world by God has to be necessarily referred to His nature and He is not free in regards of this action. If God's action is not comprehended in a determinist way, the model of simplicity itself is threatened since it posits a correlation between God's internal state (His reasons for action and His recognition of the conditions necessary to realize a goal) and an action's intention, which is generated by the Creator. The supposed requirement of such a correlation is that in the case of a different contingent order of the world, the internal states corresponding to God should be different too. Thus, the actual intention behind the creation of the world remains contingent.[124]

T. O'Connor attempts to solve the above problem by means of eliminating the causally intermediating intention of creating the world. From this perspective, God creates a contingent order directly. In a wider model of action, such a view is not constituted by a certain internal state but by a particular "execution" of power which efficiently produces a given state of affairs. Thus, no internal states are presupposed as existing in God apart from the reasons that stand behind creating this or that possible world. However, the will to create a given world is not an internal state distinct from God; therefore, the contingency of various world orders does not have to imply the existence of different intrinsic properties of an accidental character in God.[125]

The conducted analyses demonstrate the magnitude of problems which, despite their unquestionable philosophical appeal, the concept of God's simplicity can cause. It is difficult to prove this concept's consistency with the idea of God's existence as a Creator who is free to act. The simple and entirely immutable God is seen more as an abstract being rather than a person as characteristic of Christian theism. It is not easy to include the attribute of simplicity in an image of God who is full of life and love, remains open to human pleas, and participates in human history as well as in the transformations which affect the world. Declarations uttered by theists defending simplicity, who claim that the aforementioned does not make God abstract and static, are not accompanied by sufficiently convincing arguments. On the other hand, moving away from the idea of simplicity and immutability results in equally serious consequences for theism. These consequences are revealed in processualism which rules out the attribute of God's simplicity and stresses the fact that, in some respects, God is a changing being. The concept of God's dual nature seems to be counterintuitive from a philosophical perspective even though it undoubtedly highlights the dynamics of the God–creation interaction. One way to avoid the conclusion concerning God's two natures is to adopt an aspectual approach to the question. Nonetheless, bipolar suggestions on how to explain the specificity of God's existence and action should be given more meticulous analytical attention.

The concept of a simple and immutable God has crucial significance for many strands of theism. It concerns, among other things, the above-mentioned question of God as a person, as well as His impassibility. The last problem is analyzed at the end of the next section of this book, since only in having understood the character of the personal existence of God can one address the question of whether God is susceptible to suffering or any other "external" influence. Attempting to find an answer to the above will yet again invoke the issue of God's immutability.

Personal existence

The Christian God is a person

In the history of theism, profoundly varied concepts of God have emerged that identify Him with the entirety of existence, view Him as energy, and ascribe to Him life or a certain degree of psyche. German idealists interpreted the all-pervading whole as a spirit, reason, will, or idea that evolved from the multitude of moments. In some sense it can be said that the existence of God is also accepted by pantheists and even materialists. However, should not theism be confined only to the acceptance of the existence of God as a person? Is not the word "God" exclusively set aside for the personal creator?[126]

Christian theism is commonly identified with a personalistic approach which stresses the fact that the fundamental object of interest is a being who can be named a person. Thus, this highlights that what is meant by God is a being that is self-aware, intelligent, free, good, omnipotent, omniscient, and at the same time present in the history of the world and mankind. Others add that when analyzing a person the following traits should be taken into account: consciousness, the possessing of beliefs, desires, values, and being capable of abstract thinking. In the most straightforward religious sense, these traits describe a being who can be personally addressed, who can be called "you" (or "thou").[127]

Proving that such a being really exists is a task for personalistic theists. They should rationally demonstrate which of the fundamental attributes ascribed to God by them (usually including simplicity, omnipotence, omniscience, and omnipresence) correspond to the idea of a person. A problem equally significant to that of the very existence of a person like God is the attempt to answer the question of whether the notion of a personal God is consistent.[128]

The pluralism of arguments

Wojtysiak presents several basic areas in which the arguments for the existence of a personal God are formulated. On the ontological level, he mentions mainly the philosophical thought of St. Anselm of Canterbury and Descartes, both of whom begin with the commonly used idea of God. We identify this idea with the most supreme being (absolutely perfect). A conceptual analysis thereof leads to the conclusion that such a being can be exemplified. Otherwise, an empty notion of the supreme being would not fulfill its essential conditions. Irrespective of the controversies which have arisen in the context of the ontological argument, the widely accepted statement is that being a person is more perfect than "being-not-a-person."[129]

In formulating his argument, Anselm claims that God possesses the best personal attributes. God is: "just, truthful, blessed, and whatever it is better to be than not to be. For it is better to be just than not just; better to be blessed than not blessed."[130] Descartes, in turn, highlights the ideas of omniscience and omnipotence, and especially the personal epistemic-moral quality of: "not-being-a-deceiver."[131] Thus rendering the classic ontological argument more modern, Plantinga underlines that the supreme being has to be a person and as such He is in possession of omniscience, omnipotence, and a moral perfection in every world.[132]

The influence of Aristotelian-Thomistic philosophy affects cosmological arguments which lead from analysis of the causes of phenomena in the world to the conclusion of the personal Creator. Advocates of this view demonstrate that contingent beings do not find the source of their existence in themselves. Thus, it needs to be assumed that there is a necessary being who constitutes the ultimate cause of the coming about of other beings. Since the acceptance of such argumentation does not directly lead to asserting the existence of a personal God, the above train of thought was gradually developed. The most significant personalistic theories emerged as a result of the following ways of reasoning: (a) the ultimate cause of existence has to be a person; (b) the ultimate and perfect cause of contingent beings has to be personal; (c) the efficiency of the ultimate cause of all physical beings can be grasped only by analogy with the action of a personal being who distinguishes himself by means of the will and/or intellect.[133]

The last of the above-mentioned argumentation strategies can be found in the medieval Arabic natural philosophy which negates the thesis of the world's sempiternal nature. The so-called *kalam* argument for the existence of God stems not from the contingency of particular beings, but from the contingency of the world as a whole. In accordance with this philosophical position, the cause behind the existence of the world had not been operating eternally, but rather chose a specific moment for the act of creation. This leads to the conclusion that the Creator, who is the cause behind creation, has the traits of a person, at least as concerning the will and cognitive abilities.[134] This tradition of thought is familiar to A. B. Stępień who claims that while analyzing the essence of the Absolute as the ultimate reason behind contingent beings, one comes to the conclusion that He could not have been the cause of their existence out of necessity. God was able to beget contingent beings only by an act of free decision. Thus, the Creator possesses the following "traits": a personal life, a will, and an intellect. Perhaps divine action is similar to the activity of the human consciousness which, by thinking, creates purely intentional beings—thus concludes Stępień.[135]

Reflecting upon the problem of God's personal existence, Swinburne distinguishes two arguments: the scientific and the personal one. The first refers to the physical causes of phenomena and the laws of nature. The latter refers to people, their intentions, and ability to act. Science clarifies the course of events in the world but does not answer the question: why does the world exist at all? Also, the genesis of the laws of nature remains outside the reach of scientific explanation. Taking into account the principle which favors the simplest possible explanation, it is assumed that the omnipotent God/Creator exists, viz. a person who makes free choices and intentional actions.[136]

The next group of arguments for the existence of God as a person is given the name of anthropological arguments. Irrespective of debates concerning the conclusiveness of their character, it is worth emphasizing that these arguments follow from specifically personal data, and employ people's experience of absolute moral obligations, their need for sense in life, and their desire for complete happiness. If such experiences are interpreted through the appreciation of their values, e.g., cognitive values (and not in a reductionist or subjective manner), then it can be rationally assumed that enumerated experiences are guaranteed by a personal being. Other explanations seem to omit the personal character of specifically human experiences. Only a perfect Person (having the right and the power to) can make demands of us and satisfy our most profound needs.[137]

Wojtysiak points out that various manners of argumentation supporting the existence of a personal God are at times used jointly. A telling example of such an instance can be found in *Theodicy* by G. W. Leibniz. In his opinion, the necessary and ultimate cause behind the existence of the world has to be:

> intelligent: for this existing world being contingent and an infinity of other worlds being equally possible, and holding ... equal claim to existence with it, the cause of the world must need have had regard or reference to all these possible worlds in order to fix upon one of them. This regard or relation of an existent substance to simple possibilities can be nothing other than the *understanding* which has the ideas of them, while to fix upon one of them can be nothing other than the act of the *will* which chooses. It is the *power* of this substance that renders its will efficacious. Power relates to *being*, wisdom or understanding to *truth*, and will to *good*. And this intelligent cause ought to be ... absolutely perfect in *power*, in *wisdom* and in *goodness*, since it relates to all that which is possible. ... Now this supreme wisdom, united to a goodness that is no less infinite, cannot but have chosen the best.[138]

Among the numerous attempts at demonstrating God as a person, teleological argumentation has a particularly long history. The specificity of this approach is based on detecting the indicators of order in nature, which are treated as a result of an intentional design on the part of an intelligent being. The agent behind the order perceived in the world is supposed to be the personal God who acts according to a well thought out plan. From the time perspective, however, it seems that this type of argumentation is a relatively weak form of support for the thesis of God as a person. The critics of teleological explanations point out that the manifestations of harmony in the world can be either apparent or local. Even more, science formulates naturalistic explanations for the "project" of nature (e.g., evolutionary mechanisms). This problem is taken into consideration in the last chapter of this book.

Today it is often stressed that the various arguments for the existence of God do not directly imply His personal character. The impossibility of the existence of an infinite chain of causes or the requirement of the existence of a necessary being on account of the contingency of the world, as well as other ways of deduction in this field, leave us, at most, with the conclusion that there must be a supra-individual reason which pervades everything in existence—a peculiar soul of the world, or the Platonic Demiurge. This problem emerges currently also in the context of reflection upon the teleological version of the anthropic principle. Contrary to frequently formulated theses, philosophical-theological interpretations of the coordinations of the physical parameters enabling (human) life to arise do not directly enforce the acceptance of the existence of the personal God.[139] There are no decisive reasons for the designer of cosmic coordinations to be treated *ipso facto* as a personal, transcendent, and infinitely perfect being. In a sense, the pantheistic deity of Heraclitus might be able to meet the demands of such a perception of the world.[140] There are authors who refer in this context to the impersonal *Logos*, with this being a form of energy which introduces orderly structure to physical processes.[141]

According to Judycki, some hope in solving the problems of substantiating the thesis of a personal God can be found in arguments which draw on Anselmian intuitions. The ways of reasoning which start with the idea of the supreme being remain valuable since they attempt to demonstrate that we can not only think of such an idea, but also that this very idea necessarily implies such a being's existence. A being of this kind would not be supreme if it did not possess a personal character. Thus, if we assume that such a being's existence stems from its very idea, then this being must be a person. Judycki calls this way of reasoning *causa totalis*, i.e., deducing from the entirety of attributes. This reasoning embraces a concept of God wherein He is not only the efficient cause, but is also complete perfection, thus including the attribute of being a person.[142]

It is of fundamental significance to discern the difference between the cognitive perspectives of the philosophy of God and the philosophy of religion. Christian theism characterizes God as an entity who—being the fullness of existence—has to be a person. However, on the level of the philosophy of God, problems emerge concerning a conclusive demonstration that the Supreme Being respects our most fundamental axiological convictions. A full answer to the question "Is God good?" is eventually brought by the philosophy of religion, which assumes the existence of a personal Creator.[143] This approach is close to many of the authors participating in the *Divine Action in the World* project.[144]

The question of the personal existence of God is also undertaken from the perspective of reflection on the rationality of the world, which is subject to the various analyses that humankind is capable of, including the most abstract formulas. Explanation of this fact is facilitated by the assumption that the traits typical to the rationality of humans are to the highest degree characteristic of the source of each being's existence. Since in the world the human being is the uppermost manifestation of the unification of the physical, the mental and the spiritual, then it seems rational to suggest that the Creator who endows His creation with existence should be personal. There are no visible reasons to limit the source of existence to some unclear force, or even reason. As Peacocke stresses, this Ultimate Reality "*must be the self-existent Ground of Being; one, but a diversity-in-unity, a Being of unfathomable richness; supremely and unsurpassedly rational; omniscient; omnipotent; omnipresent and eternal; and at least personal or supra-personal.*"[145]

The eternal problem of time

A crucial context for the problem of God as a person is His relationship to time. J. Lucas claims that being a person implies having a consciousness, a trait of which is sensing the passage of time. God, as seen in Christian theism, acts in time and history, interacting with creation. Negating the Creator's reference to the passage of time would be, according to Lucas, to deny His personal character.[146]

In the Christian theory of creation it is assumed that God surpasses the temporal-spatial order remaining its intentional cause. However, this does not have to mean that the Creator exists entirely outside of time and space. After all, it is stressed that God is omnipresent and continuously sustains everything in existence. Peters does not see any problem with assuming God's existence in time.[147] Ascertaining His omnipresence implies a relation to the past, the present, and the future. God is present in each moment of the world's development. In each of these moments the following thesis can be formulated: "God exists now." Such an understanding of the question of God's relationship to time modifies the theory that the absolute being's insusceptibility to alterations excludes any real reference to reality which is subject to change and development.[148]

Many authors see the genesis of the static image of God as being rooted in Hellenistic culture and Greek philosophy. Being embedded in time was seen as one of the signs of imperfection. God, on the other hand, did not enter into a relationship with His creation and remained timeless. The problem was presented differently in the Judeo-Christian religious tradition. The Creator is viewed as eternal while also interacting with creation. God's transcendence in relation to the world is described as complementary to His presence in nature and human history. God's continuous immanence and action stem from His personal and relational nature.[149]

God as presented in the Christian tradition is not viewed as timeless in the sense of lacking any relationship to time. The eternal and time-surpassing Maker interacts with His creation in a personal manner, referring to the events of human lives which occur in time, as well as the decisions that result from our freedom. Such an understanding of God's relationship to time can seem to be a better means of explaining His personal interactions with individual people than the model presented by Boethius. Elaborating on the thought of St. Augustine, Boethius demonstrated God's eternity as a complete, concurrent, and perfect possession of an infinite life.[150] God, as if "from the top," has one continuous view of what we see as the past, the present, and the future.[151] The eternity of God perceived in this manner signifies: (a) atemporality (not having extension and not lasting in time; a lack of temporal sequences), (b) life (possessing a mental life and the ability to act, yet without the sequences of intellectual states and the succession of events), (c) boundlessness (not having a beginning or end in the sense of being unlimited as regards scope, contrary to an existence spanning the past, the present, and the future), and (d) lasting (the fullness of continuity, i.e. possessing entirety as an unlimited and infinitely stretching life lacking temporal sequences).[152]

The traits enumerated above are characteristic of the existence of God who is a living and personal being but remains outside of time. According to some interpretations, the existence of such a being is only seemingly characterized with static immobility. The followers of Boethius argue that he means the entirety of activity based on such an atemporal existence which can under no circumstance be reduced to time and consists of lasting while lacking successive temporal sequences. Boethius places this in opposition to the extension of temporal life which cannot be available instantaneously as a whole.[153]

The view held by classical theism states that—contrary to beings existing in time—God, who possesses the entirety of life instantly, has to be timeless and atemporal. God's infinite existence is the fullness of lasting and existing which is inaccessible to entities subject to the passage of time and mutability. The being who owns the entirety of life and exists in eternity understood in this vein can be said to be, in some way, existing in the present. The presence of the eternal being is the lasting of a simple being, the existence of whom is identified with essence, with all attributes remaining identical. The eternal present is an infinitely extended lasting in which the past and the future are indistinguishable. In this way, the entirety of the life of the divine being coexists with the temporal being in each moment of its existence. Nonetheless, such a coexistence of God with the world does not have the character of an immobile *nunc stans*, but rather of a personal dynamism.[154]

The concept of eternity introduced by Boethius, including its many contemporary elaborations, has led to many debates concerning God's transcendence and immanence in the world. Striving to take both of these categories into account in a complementary way, Peacocke objects to presenting God as a completely atemporal being claiming that:

> *God is not timeless*; God is temporal in the sense that the divine life is successive in its relation to us—*God is temporally (and so personally) related to us; there is a dipolarity in God's relation to time—God is transcendent, but also experiences succession* in relation to events and persons; *God creates each segment of time in the created world; God transcends past and present created time; God is eternal* in the sense that there is no time at which God does not exist nor will there be a future time at which God does not exist; *God is omnipresent—is present to all past events and will be to all future events.*[155]

The question of God's relationship to time is later discussed in the section on omniscience. However, it should be stressed here that analysis of the problem of the

Creator-creation interaction helps one to grasp those aspects which enable the assumption that God's involvement is personal. Ascertaining that God has a real influence on the events taking place in the world calls for ascribing Him with the predicates of having goals and the intention to act. For this reason Peacocke states that from the perspective of top-down influence on the world, God emerges as "at least personal."[156]

Divine immutability and impassibility

Those who emphasize a strong contrast between the attributes of an absolute being and the traits of a human being often highlight the idea of divine impassibility. This originated on the grounds of the Greek philosophy which influenced Christian theism.[157] The concept of a static and impassible God as presented in the philosophy of Plato effectively downgraded the model of the Biblical God who is active and susceptible to suffering. Significant impact in this field should be ascribed to Philo of Alexandria who, in attempting to reconcile Judaic thought with Platonism, incorporated an image of the God of Israel into the framework of Greek philosophy in which immutability was treated as the most fundamental attribute of the Absolute.[158]

For Platonic and neo-Platonic reflection, it was fundamental to present God as a completely self-sufficient, perfect, and transcendent substance which is not susceptible to any changes. God cannot be affected by anything from the outside. Hence, His attribute must be impassibility since otherwise something might rule over Him.[159] This would reveal divine weakness—a form of naturally changeable emotionality, or susceptibility to suffering.[160]

Being a self-determining and independent entity, the God of the Greek tradition could not suffer. Showing fear would be a sign of imperfection, which would reveal vulnerability to external influences. God has to be devoid of all feelings, including the negative ones. Suffering and compassion would mean that God is becoming an object of pain or emotion while He cannot be an object of anything. No form of emotionality can be reconciled with the nature of God who never becomes but eternally is.[161]

The idea of God as being impassible and insusceptible to any change was included in the reflection of the Fathers of the Church. In the Middle Ages, arguments in support of divine immutability were given additional enhancement by the Scholastics. This concept appeared to leave no room for demonstrating the Creator's freedom and spontaneity while acting in creation. In the God–human relationship, really new and creative elements can appear only on the part of humans. The absolute being does not have any potentiality or receptiveness.[162]

The above standpoint had dominated Christian theism for many centuries. The revival of discussion concerning this problem came in the first half of the twentieth century. However, it was not academic debate, but humanity's existential experience that most affected attempts at revising the image of God. The disappearance of nineteenth-century optimism, as well as the drama of two consecutive world conflicts, resulted in an intense emergence of fundamental religious questions. It seemed that to defend theism in the context of manifestations of extreme suffering was only possible by means of adopting an image of God who is present amidst the dramas of the world.

God should share human pain and participate in it. Otherwise He would be of little significance to man.[163]

Extreme experiences, their symbol being Auschwitz, motivated some theists to reinterpret the doctrine of divine immutability. Can it be accepted—assuming that the personal God is full of love and compassion—that His immutability is of an ethical value, and not an ontic one? Can God—being in a living relationship with humans—change not only the inner life of man but also, to some extent, Himself? This concept was elaborated upon especially by processualists and is manifested in the distinction between the primordial (immutable) and the consequent (subject to change) dimensions of divine nature.

Process philosophers attempted to answer the questions of how and why God is capable of suffering. Within this approach, God "takes into himself all that has happened within the world, and so is not only affected but is also actually constituted by it. Thus, all of the joy, pain and suffering which occurs within the world and the lives of human beings become the tangible experiences of God."[164] God emerges as a personal entity, being simultaneously subject to change.

Summing up this part of the book, it needs to be underlined that for philosophical reflection on the nature of God neither historical events, nor biblical messages and religious doctrines should be of straightforward consequence. On the other hand, it seems that the concept of God formulated on philosophical grounds has been too strongly dominated by certain elements of ancient Greek culture for far too long. This is rooted in mythological presentations which are essentially different from the personal image of God present in Christian thought, with the latter being born in the context of reflection on the theological truth of the Holy Trinity and the character of the mutual relations found between divine persons. On the basis of these analyses, scholars had elaborated a conceptual foundation for personalism which was later to become an important part of philosophical anthropology. Such lessons of history can serve as a valuable inspiration during contemporary attempts at developing a theory of God as a person. Instead of anthropomorphically creating an image of God that resembles that of man, it is worth specifying the conditions under which the absolute being can be treated as a person. In this regard, philosophical research should be continued, especially if we wish to reconcile the concept of a personal God with such attributes as simplicity or immutability. Serious challenges also emerge while discussing the problem of divine omnipotence.

Omnipotence

Classic questions and classical answers

The beginning of an organized reflection on God's omnipotence can be found in the thought of St. Augustine. Addressing the question of whether Christ might have stopped Judas from betraying Him, the author of *De natura et gratia* stated that God could have done many things, but did not want to (*potuit, sed noluit*). St. Augustine's contribution to subsequent doctrinal solutions is also revealed in his statement concerning the particular attributes of God. God was able to do something because of His power but could not do it on account of His justice (*poterat per potentiam, sed non poterat per iustitiam*). The above issues were discussed several centuries later by St. Anselm, who stressed the fact that words like "good" or "just" have a fixed content that is connected to the nature of God by no accident. This content is not "external" in relation to God whose actions would have to be consistent with the content of the terms. Individual expressions related to the attributes of God convey meanings which originate in His nature and are founded in it.[165]

The above approach was an inspiration for Pietro Damiani, who claims that the power of God surpasses His actions.[166] During Damiani's famous discussion with the abbot of Monte Cassino, the question arose of whether God can change or cancel the past of the world. Desiderio assumed that God's peculiar powerlessness is a result of His own choice. According to Damiani, if God does not do certain things here and now (does not heal the sick or oppose the unjust) then it means that He simply cannot do these things. God's power and will are interdependent, with power being limited by the will.[167]

These eleventh-century debates resulted in the subsequent formulation of the distinction between the absolute and the ordained power of God. *Potentia absoluta* is an area concerning all the possibilities that God could choose from, while *potentia ordinata* points to those things which He actually does choose. Absolute power is only limited by what is absolutely impossible. Thus, divine omnipotence is confined by the principle of non-contradiction and God's specific nature.[168] Both of them delimit the entire will of God. Medieval deliberations regarding God's power also gave origin to other terminological propositions, the most well-known of which remains *potentia extraordinaria*. God's extraordinary power is disclosed during His direct interventions in the world, usually defined as miracles.[169]

The distinction between absolute and ordained power was discussed with reserve by St. Thomas Aquinas. This did not entirely correspond to Aquinas's view on rationality which is revealed in the world created by God. The author of *Quaestiones disputate de potentia Dei* was closer to the statement formulated by Augustine, namely that God was able to do something as a result of His power, but could not do this on account of justice. However, the latter should not be understood as an attribute of God but as being faithful to the order imposed in the world. For Aquinas, the boundary of divine power was also set by the principle of non-contradiction.[170] God cannot be the cause of any inconsistency. This belief was a reason behind the statement that on the basis of divine actions, performed *de potentia ordinata*, one cannot assume that God would be able to cancel or change everything.[171]

According to Aquinas, the omnipotent God cannot do certain things. In *Summa contra gentiles*, Aquinas explicitly expresses the idea that not even God can make a thing exist and not exist simultaneously. Divine omnipotence does not embrace actions which violate the laws of logic or mathematics, nor certain logically probable activities, which God would not be able to do. For instance, God cannot acquire any flaws since this belongs to the sphere of so-called passive potency. Moreover, God remains faithful to his vows, and hence he cannot do what He decided not to do or abandon doing what He promised to perform.[172]

The omnipotent being, as presented by Aquinas, remains free from metaphysical inconsistency. God cannot sin, desire evil, or lean towards them. In *Summa contra gentiles*, we can read the following words:

Every act of God is an act of virtue, since His virtue is His essence (Chap. XCII). The will cannot will evil except by some error coming to be in the reason, at least in the matter of the particular choice there and then made. For as the object of the will is good, apprehended as such, the will cannot tend to evil unless evil be somehow proposed to it as good; and that cannot be without error. But in the divine cognition there can be no error (Chap. LXI). God is the sovereign good, admitting no intermixture of evil (Chap. LXI). Evil cannot befall the will except by its being turned away from its end. But the divine will cannot be turned away from its end, being unable to will except by willing itself (Chap. LXXV). It cannot therefore will evil; and thus free will in it is naturally established in good.[173]

In the strict sense, not performing actions which are morally wrong does not limit omnipotence[174]. Aquinas enumerates many of the activities that God cannot perform, starting with things that regard His existence. In this view, God is simple and immutable; thus, He cannot, for instance, become angry.[175]

The Subtle Doctor

Divine omnipotence was understood differently by John Duns Scotus. To him, *potentia absoluta* was not only a sphere of possibilities from the free selection of which God created the world and its laws. Absolute power is also the ability to act outside the once imposed order, or even against this order. In developing his ideas, Duns Scotus used the legal terminology of his time and employed it in demonstrating the different types of God's power. By doing so, Scotus moved beyond earlier interpretations. A manifestation of the innovative approach taken by Scotus is, among other things, the application of the same definition of free choice to both God and man. If we act according to the law or the requirements of reason, we do this because of our voluntary choice, and not as a consequence of absolute necessity.[176]

To a great extent, Duns Scotus drew on the Anselmian tradition, while combining omnipotence with God's creative activity. Emphasizing that the category of omnipotence cannot refer to the intrinsic actions of God (in relation to Himself), the Scottish Franciscan friar employed the principle of non-contradiction. The concept of omnipotence as founded on such grounds was understood as the active power to create everything that is possible and, at the same time, not necessary by itself, and lacking contradictions. This active creative power can act directly or indirectly, which is essential in the context of distinguishing between the philosophical and the theological perspective of deduction. Natural reflection can lead us to the conclusion that there is a first (active) efficient cause that provides specific effects in an indirect or direct manner. Should the first cause not operate, no other one would be able to be the cause. The natural order of efficient causes is only possible when it is anchored in a first efficient cause.[177]

Aristotelian statements concerning essential relationships in the chain of causes are not sufficient for a theological characterization of the Creator–creation interaction. God, as presented in the Christian tradition, can act as an active cause without cooperating with other causes. Duns Scotus thinks that in this sense the omnipotence of God cannot be proven by natural reasoning. Proof can only be provided on the basis of the order of causes, and this would be excluded in the case of God's direct action. The argument for introducing this idea lies in the conviction that an entity which is more perfect in causal action has the power to act directly in creating a direct result of secondary causes, even though this is not obvious to natural reason.[178]

It should be noted that the theological presentation of God's omnipotence does not enforce occasionalism in reflection on His action. After all, God can, but does not have to, take advantage of "occasions" for direct action which would nullify the efficiency of secondary causes. For Duns Scotus, the omnipotence of God is an active power to create in a direct manner, without having to cooperate with secondary causes, everything that can be created. The scope of such action covers all that is possible, i.e. all that which does not exist by itself in a necessary way and does not contain contradictions.[179] Duns Scotus is aware that God's omnipotence understood in this vein remains the object of faith, but he claims that this concept can be assessed as very credible.[180]

While demonstrating omnipotence as the power to make everything that can be made, Duns Scotus presents the potential boundaries of divine possibilities. The fundamental reason for God's impossibility to make something is the intrinsic incompatibility of the particular parts of a given entity. In an impossible thing, its constitutive parts are by the very essence mutually exclusive and cannot make up a composition together. Thus, it is not the lack of God's power that limits His action, but rather the substantial mutual exclusion of the individual parts of an entity. Even if every single element was of a non-contradictory character, their coexistence would be impossible. God cannot make such parts which do not constitute a coherent whole, with these parts being formally exclusive. If we treat omnipotence as an active creative power that is realized in what is possible to create, then some beings will remain pure fiction. The reason for such a state of things should be searched for mainly in God's care for the intelligibility of the world.[181]

In reference to divine creative power, Duns Scotus is not a proponent of strong voluntarism or universal possibilism.[182] At first, a potential being has the status of an object to which God refers intellectually. If such an object is of a rational character, it becomes created through an act of God's will. The sphere of possibility is connected with the activity of the divine intellect and the sphere of reality with the activity of God's will. Assuming that creation becomes realized in an act of God's will, Duns Scotus avoids problems regarding the limits of omnipotence since this concerns God's active (that is efficient power) rather than God's power to know.[183]

In some respects, Duns Scotus sets very wide boundaries for divine omnipotence. If it was God's wish, not only the physical and the metaphysical worlds could have been different, but also the scope of moral norms. Being free, God can act within the framework of an already imposed law (in accordance with ordained power), or outside of it (in accordance with absolute power). In this respect, the world can be arranged in many non-contradictory ways. God can change both the legal and moral order in this way, thus organizing the world anew. The omnipotent God can dispense from each commandment, apart from situations implicating contradiction. Therefore, what remains irrevocable, even by means of absolute power, are the commandments which refer to God Himself; for instance, loving Him as a perfectly good being who should be loved to the highest degree.[184]

Does this scope of divine omnipotence not undermine human trust in the stability of world order? Does it not generate fear that God might deceive us like a demon creating worlds with no fixed norms? In addressing such questions, one should remember that according to the theory elaborated upon by Duns Scotus, not even the omnipotent God can produce such states of things which would be inconsistent with His goodness, wisdom, and justice. God's action has to be orderly and compatible with His essence. A new world order introduced by God would have to be consistent with the one previously established.[185] The power which selects a specific scenario and imposes laws is the will of God, but such action is preceded by His intellect, which always submits intelligible content to be realized. In divine action there are no exceptions to the rule of rationality.[186]

Increasing doubts

Reflecting on the demon hypothesis from the perspective characteristic of his philosophical thought, Descartes defended the strong version of God's omnipotence to which even those states of things are subject which we treat as necessary.[187] However, it seems that this thesis was of an epistemological character: we do not know what the scope of God's omnipotence is because our mind is finite.[188] Thus, perhaps what we perceive as necessary is not such to God. To some extent, Descartes leaves open the ultimate solutions to the question of the scope of God's omnipotence.[189]

Elaborating a particular theistic system, Leibniz adopts the thesis "God is omnipotent" as one of the main assumptions. In the context appropriate to theodicy, Leibniz raises the problem of God predicting evil and allowing it to happen, even though He could prevent a given evil thanks to His omnipotence. Referring to the fundamental question of whether we live in the best possible world, in the last essay included in his most famous work, Leibniz puts forward the following statement: "Whoever does not choose the best course is lacking either in power, or knowledge, or goodness. God did not choose the best course in creating this world. Therefore, God was lacking in power, or knowledge, or goodness."[190]

Leibniz challenges all three components of the above conclusion. In undermining stipulations concerning God's lack of any power whatsoever, the German philosopher proves that the Maker might have created everything and hence is omnipotent. What remains notable is the attempt at reconciling God's omnipotence with His omniscience and goodness. Published for the first time in 1710, *Theodicy* draws on the solutions to the problem of omnipotence formulated by St. Augustine and St. Thomas Aquinas, and contains an original approach to the question presented by the exponent of the idea of the best world possible.[191]

Undertaking the topic of theodicy, D. Hume was aware that the question of omnipotence lies at the foundation of many debates concerning theism. In *Dialogues Concerning Natural Religion*, Hume puts arguments in the mouths of fictional debaters. Criticizing the rationality of belief in divine power, Philo recalls a classical dilemma: "Is he willing to prevent evil, but not able? then is he impotent. Is he able, but not willing?

then is he malevolent. Is he both able and willing? whence then is evil?"[192] The infinite power, wisdom, and goodness of God seem to be irreconcilable with evil and suffering. If evil exists, at least one of the above-mentioned attributes should be rejected.[193]

Nonetheless, Philo points out that such reasoning can be undermined since it is not certain whether settling arguments on divine attributes is a competence of the human mind. The answer given to the question "Why is there any misery at all in the world?" is accompanied with an epistemological deduction:

> Not by chance surely. From some cause then. Is it from the intention of the Deity? But he is perfectly benevolent. Is it contrary to his intention? But he is almighty. Nothing can shake the solidity of this reasoning, so short, so clear, so decisive; except we assert, that these subjects exceed all human capacity, and that our common measures of truth and falsehood are not applicable to them.[194]

Irrespective of ongoing discussion concerning Hume's religious beliefs, cognitive skepticism is a characteristic trait of his many studies. It is uncertain if we are at all capable of comprehending what divine omnipotence means. It is probable that this simply remains outside of human reach.[195]

In subsequent periods of the history of philosophy, it was often claimed that adopting the strong version of God's omnipotence leads to a deterministic approach which negates the autonomy of nature's processes, as well as human freedom. This danger was particularly and clearly stressed by processualists, for whom divine action has an inspiring dimension to the nature, and not a tyrannical one. A world exposed to the violence of the Creator would be worthless and ultimately "degrade" God Himself. The creative power embedded in creation is conditioned by its factual autonomy. Hartshorne has gone as far as to state that the introduction of the traditional concept of omnipotence was a fundamental mistake because it sentenced God to a world without life and development, and hence devoid of sense.[196]

Discerning the numerous problems connected with the presentation of divine omnipotence, many critics of classical theism underlined that certain questions are difficult to ultimately resolve. Can the actions of the omnipotent God be based on a peculiar withdrawal of freedom from creation? Can the omnipotent being create entities which He is not able to later control? J. Mackie claims that there is no satisfactory answer to the second question. Should it be answered in a negative way, we would state *ipso facto* that there are things which God cannot do. If, however, God creates rules which constrain Him, or things that are outside of His subsequent control, He cannot be treated as omnipotent. As a result, the paradox of omnipotence emerges.[197]

Problems with a consistent presentation of God's nature arise also in the context of His freedom in relation to Himself. What happens to divine freedom if certain actions, even logically possible ones, cannot be performed by God (for instance, God is not able to sin)?[198] It is worth noticing that in reference to human beings, it is assumed that our capability of doing evil is connected with a greater dose of freedom as compared to the state in which we would have been "programmed" only to do good deeds. Not being able to do evil would also signify a lack of freedom in the sense of having the possibility to decide among alternative moral options. Is not the situation the same for God? Does not the fact that He cannot perform certain actions deprive Him of freedom?[199]

Contemporary classics

In the face of such problems, Swinburne draws on the notion of the perfectly free person. The freedom of human beings, in a metaphysical sense, can be spoken of when no external causes induce a human being to act. We assume that God's actions have to be no less free than human actions. The absolute being cannot be determined by the various factors which influence our choices and which we have no control over. In the case of God, there are no such external determinants, therefore He can be regarded as a perfectly free person. God does not perform actions which He knows would be morally worse to perform, rather He withholds himself from performing them. The divine being's decision to forsake morally wrong actions is not arbitrary because it is resolved by having adequate reason. Refraining from doing evil is not a sign of a lack of freedom, but of the rationality of God who never ventures to do things incompatible with His nature. God's actions always aim towards a goal and He must "see his action as in some way a good thing. Hence it is not logically possible that God should do what he does not believe to be in some way a good thing."[200]

Noticing the difficulties regarding the interpretation of omnipotence, P. Geach introduced distinctions that enabled the perception of many of the frequently omitted nuances of omnipotence. In Geach's opinion, one needs to discern the essential difference between the notions of "almightiness" and "omnipotence". Geach stresses that in relation to God it is better, especially in the religious approach, to use the term "almighty" because—in contrast to the word "omnipotent"—this word remains closer to the Biblical context. The first of the above-mentioned terms is characteristic of a confessing religious faith and the latter of theoretical reflection which focuses on detailed theistic questions. The adjective "almighty" should be used to signify divine power over things and the word "omnipotent" to highlight God's ability to do everything. However, the problem remains that, despite age-long debates and advancement in philosophical thought, it is impossible to ascribe the statement that God can do everything with sense that is free of all internal contradictions and the possibility of being unconditionally accepted as part of Christian theism.[201]

The polysemic understanding of omnipotence is also identified by G. van den Brink, who distinguishes between three basic options in this regard. In the first sense, God's power can be explained as His universal dominion and authority. The unique Pantocrator rules over everything, being an absolutely sovereign Master of all and holding full power over what happens in the world. The second solution puts stress on the fact that the power of God is revealed in His creation and sustains the world in existence. Such an understanding interprets divine omnipotence as fully actualized and closely combined with each and every particle of the universe. The first option, however, is not excluded here, although it focuses not so much on God's domination over everything, but on the *conservatio mundi*. The third understanding of omnipotence is the most controversial one as it underlines God's ability to realize all possible states of things. This type of power is not actual but "virtual" and belongs to God's theoretical potentialities and not to His sovereign reign or function of sustaining the world. Since God's power is infinite, there are no things which are outside His ability to achieve. Nevertheless, the assumption that God can make logical contradictions true at any given time causes fundamental objections in milieus which accentuate the idea of the Creator's faithfulness towards His creation.[202]

The exclusion of things which are logically impossible does not end philosophical debate on divine omnipotence. Swinburne points to the fact that should we isolate a set of logically possible actions, we will find such actions which can be performed only by specific persons. For instance, in the strict sense, only a physically capable man can climb to the top of a high mountain. The omnipotent God cannot perform this particular action because He is not a corporal being and remains immutable.[203] Thus, in a modified definition, stress would be put on the fact that the omnipotent being is capable of causing every state of things available to it and logically possible. Nonetheless, in this case also new problems arise concerning God's relationship to time: can God modify earlier states of things?[204]

The answer to the above question concerns both the more general issue of the possibility of doing something which is a past state of things and the problem of whether a potential change in the past would generate a contradiction. The latter could be avoided with the assumption that a change in the past is connected to a simultaneous change in knowledge of the past. In this context, we raise the problem of the status of the postulate of exclusion causing earlier states of things. Some scholars claim that the postulate of limiting omnipotence based on exclusion causing earlier states of affairs is of a supralogical character.[205] Thinkers who are of the opposite opinion, but at the same time agree that past states cannot be created, formulate the following definition: An omnipotent being is an entity who during time t has the ability to create everything available to this being and to create any logically possible state of things, at the time after t.[206]

The definition presented above can be completed with the statement that states of things occurring after time t should be logically consistent with what took place before time t. Swinburne thus points to the existence of logically necessary states of things, for instance: a triangle is a geometric figure and a square block lying on a table is a physical object.[207] In this perspective, a question arises of whether the omnipotent God should be capable of creating such logically necessary states of things. If we assume that triangles are geometric figures independent of anyone's action, we arrive at the conclusion that the omnipotent being, acting at time t, is able to create everything available to this being and logically possible contingent states of things after t.[208]

Between extremes

Referring to the classical view of God's nature discussed in the first part of this section, the concept of omnipotence should meet both the requirements of logic, and some supralogical criteria, for example that God cannot do things which are morally wrong. It needs to be emphasized that an understanding of omnipotence formulated in this manner is still intellectually appealing since it conveys a way of thinking which is characteristic of the main trends of the Christian tradition and does not "remove from

God" anything necessary for Him to be seen as the object of religious worship. Modification of the maximalist definition of omnipotence, thus restricting itself to some extent, is the dominant contemporary outlook on omnipotence found in analytic philosophy of religion,[209] and protects against many difficulties, including the paradox of the stone.[210]

God, devoid of logical and metaphysical contradictions, is seen as a rational being. He is definitely not a being less deserving of reverence than God with an unlimited omnipotence. Acceding to irrational actions would be something that would "disparage God" and negate His divine nature. An omnipotent being can perform all logically consistent actions, as well as those which have no visible reasons not to perform. The fact that God's will cannot be realized with the interference of causal factors does not deny God the power to act. Even more, God is not any the less due to the fact that His power cannot be used in a way which is perceived as senseless from the perspective of a perfect being.[211]

What appears to be internally inconsistent is the standpoint presented by universal possibilism. The claim "God has a power referring to all truths" leads to the biggest controversy when we relate to God Himself. If this sentence is not subject to God's power, it is false because there is a truth in reference to which God does not have power. Should we state that divine omnipotence refers to this truth, it is possible that the sentence is false, which, in turn, undermines the absolute power of God. It seems that the following two sentences cannot be simultaneously treated as true: "God has power referring to all truths" and "Maybe God does not have power referring to all truths." Universal possibilism cannot be falsified by means of classical logical argumentation when its necessary character is being questioned. Thus, paradoxically, it is probable that the theory of universal possibilism remains true despite its inconsistency.[212]

An essentially different point of view concerning God's omnipotence is presented by universal creationism, which proclaims that the Creator is not capable of changing the modal status of sentences, even though He could have done so during the process of creation. When creating, God had a free choice, both in terms of determining the modal status of judgments, and their truth value. On the other hand, theistic activism stresses that abstract objects and necessary truths are causally dependent on God but are not under His control. God was not capable of not creating abstract objects and necessary truths, and He could not have created them in a different way. In this approach, among the abstract objects created by God, there are properties which constitute His nature. Does God also create Himself then? Avoiding such absurd consequences, the proponents of theistic activism claim that God cannot be identified with His nature. Hence, in creating His own nature, God does not create Himself.[213]

The independence of abstract objects and the necessary states of things from the power of God is accepted in Platonically oriented forms of theism. The followers thereof claim that abstract beings exist objectively and necessarily. Thus, they are not controlled by God, and not even created by Him or dependent on Him. In some sense it can be said that they exist in a way similar to Him because their existence is necessary. Such a stance essentially limits the omnipotence of God who acts in the sphere of independent necessities within the framework that depends on what already exists.

Thus, it comes as no surprise that many representatives of Christian theism have expressed diverse views stressing that abstract objects and all kinds of necessities do not exist independently of God but are ideas in His mind. In this context, it becomes pointless to wonder whether God might change His non-contradictory way of thinking, because He Himself is the measure of rationality.[214] However, God possesses His properties essentially and does not create them, being subject to these properties in the sense that they are not external to Him. This standpoint has become the reason why the critics of classical theism ask whether God is a prisoner of His own nature.[215]

The return to Christian roots

Insightful and sophisticated analyses conducted by contemporary theists demonstrate that the problem of God's omnipotence is continuously and vividly present in philosophical debates. As extreme ideas can be treated: the concept of unlimited power, and the minimalist option that finds many followers among processualists. The Christian image of God "suggests" one more solution which is called revisionist. This focuses not so much on conceptual discussions as on emphasizing the type of power that is paradoxically revealed in humility, weakness, and the ability to sacrifice oneself for others. This approach accords with the common conviction that effective action does not have to be based on enforcing specific states of things or by demonstrating the might of strength. A more valuable way of demonstrating power lies in maintaining dignity and internal freedom, and rejecting violence. This is visible especially in extreme situations, both on the human and divine levels. A distinguishing example of such a situation for Christians is the victory of goodness over evil achieved by the power of love to which violence is entirely alien. Thus, discussions on omnipotence should not concentrate on the image of an omnipotent God who violates the laws of nature, disrespects human freedom, and intervenes to demonstrate His power in particular situations.[216]

The image of the omnipotent God as presented by Christian theism should take into account the specificity of religion. Christianity's fundamental elements are not only events such as incarnation or resurrection, but also the figure of a suffering Savior who "made himself nothing, taking the very nature of a servant"[217] and "humbled himself and became obedient to death—even death on a cross!"[218] Reflection on these issues does not belong to the domain of philosophy. Nevertheless, on Christian grounds, a concept of omnipotence should be constructed which is alien to tyrannical action. The manner in which God reveals His omnipotence essentially changes one's interpretative focus and eliminates associations with forced courses of events. Understanding creation as an act of the Maker's love calls for adopting an idea of the world's autonomy and human freedom at each stage of history. Thus, the omnipotence of the Creator should be viewed in light of God's ability to enter a relationship with His creation—with all of the potential consequences thereof. God, bonding with His creation, becomes to some extent "vulnerable to hurt" when He respects the integrity of nature with its laws. The Creator can never act in a way that would be contrary to His nature. In the Christian understanding, love remains God's fundamental property and this excludes acting by means of violence.[219]

The idea of *kenosis*, presented in detail in the next chapter of this book, has gained diverse elaborations in the twentieth century, including the thesis of God's powerlessness or helplessness. Promoting the latter category, E. Schillebeeckx stresses that omnipotent God is susceptible to being hurt, but at the same time does not exclude the divine's real influence on the history of the world and human fate. The power of God is seen as the possibility of overcoming evil and introducing effective changes, especially in the sphere of our existential engagement for the sake of goodness.[220]

Reflection on the kenotic aspect of God's nature gained a particular dimension in light of historical events which enforced an intellectual revision caused by the tragedy of wars, human suffering, and the increasing exploitation and destruction of the natural environment. An extreme manifestation of such reflection on the traumatic experiences of humans can be seen in the question why God did not prevent evil during the cruel annihilation of millions of innocent beings. In this context, scholars point to the dimension (frequently marginalized in the past) of the humble presence of God who respects human freedom and the autonomy of His creation.

Whitehead stated that the Christian view of God is too often closer to Caesar's model rather than to the standards of the Gospels. Even more, the despotic concept of the Creator's omnipotence in relation to His creation did not leave room for the image of the world brought about by post-Darwinian science. After all, evolutionary sciences can form a valuable inspiration for formulations of theism which take into account the autonomous activity of the forces of nature across long periods of time.[221]

The autonomy of nature as God's self-limitation

In the theistic tradition, deeply rooted in Western culture, the power of God was frequently presented in the categories of domination. In debates concerning God and evolution, attention is often given to questions of how to reconcile His action with the autonomous, impersonal, and partially accidental character of the laws of nature. As a result, at least *implicite*, divine power is presented as a domination. Reflection on the functioning of nature from the perspective of God's interaction with the world and His susceptibility to suffering is often moved to the background of discussion. In many elaborate debates triggered by the problem of "evolutionism–creationism," theists often adopt an idea of God equipped with the traits of patriarchal hegemony. By favoring a view of God who is might and strength, scholars undermine (or ignore) scientific outcomes and distance themselves from the idea of God's *kenosis*. At times, such situations take place even in the case of the proponents of theistic evolutionism who are satisfied with claiming that evolution is God's way of creating. Meanwhile, thinkers should not overlook the pain, the elimination of the weaker, the immensity of the struggle for existence, and losses which accompany the process of evolution.[222]

Many representatives of theism distance themselves from the theory of evolution, fearing that the image of the functioning of nature provides too little room for the activity of the omnipotent God. Needless to say, a serious understanding of religious faith calls for the Creator to be actively engaged in the processes of nature. However, God is often presented rather as a God of war, nations, or a peculiar patron of culture.[223] As a result, it was claimed that to ensure sufficiently strong foundations for religious belief, we need the idea of divine impassibility. Nonetheless, Haught's attempts to convince that the functioning of the world—the autonomy of the processes of nature, the creativity of natural selection, the randomness of mutations, and even the immense losses and pain embedded in the operation of evolution in the course of time—is easier to comprehend from the perspective of the image of the Creator accompanying the development of His creation and to some extent susceptible to suffering. Irrespective of the specific solution to this problem, the crucial task of Christian theism is to demonstrate such divine action in the world which is not carried out by means of violence.[224]

The thesis of the self-limited omnipotence of God is formulated both in the context of the specificity of Christian doctrine and in light of contemporary scientific findings. On the one hand, God can only do things which stem from His nature. If love belongs to the essence of God, He cannot put such pressure on the activities of human beings that it would take away their freedom. On the other hand, God's omnipotence is limited in regard to the physical world. This does not only refer to the issue of refraining from acting *contra naturam*. It should also be taken into account that the outcomes of an event's measurement are probabilistic on the quantum level. To have power over such events, God would have to predict with precision what is going to happen should He act in a specific way. This seems impossible in relation to events on the quantum level (which is the object of my detailed analysis in the section devoted to the problem of random events). Thus, the structure of the universe implies an image of God whose omnipotence and omniscience are limited.[225]

Omniscience

Why is it so important to us?

Omnipotence is often combined with its epistemic dimension: omniscience. Religious people usually claim that God knows everything: He is omnipresent and nothing can be hidden from Him. Considering the many difficulties and strong consequences of such a standpoint, already at the beginning of this part of my book it needs to be said how much depends on adopting or rejecting the concept of God's simplicity, and on answering the question of God's relationship to time. The simple and timeless God has a simultaneous view of events located along the timescale in the physical world. From such a divine perspective, time does not elapse. Each event that has ever taken place or will take place in the future is simultaneously present to God. The timeless God knows everything because for Him there is no division into past, present, and future. On the other hand, the Creator knows which stage the history of creation is occupying. God knows the course of events in detail.[226]

In discussions on God's omniscience, essential controversies arise regarding the question of human freedom. How can we be free if God knows the future? Perhaps life is entirely predetermined, and would this leave us with an illusion of freedom? Can the Creator's goodness be reconciled with His deciding on the future fate of creation? The last of the above-posed questions suggests that God is the cause of future events. However, Christian theism proposed a different solution: when something happens,

God "perforce" knows about it. In light of that, God's knowledge is not causal. God can timelessly see our future actions, but they follow from man's free choice. Thus, such a concept does not signify predestination.[227]

For Aquinas, God's knowledge is the cause of events in the world. According to him, God is not a being endowed with qualities. All of His attributes are identical. The simple and timeless God does not depend on the world in any way. God's knowledge of a particular event is the cause of its happening. Therefore, it can be said that Aquinas's view in this respect leads to a deterministic view of world history.[228]

This statement should not come as a surprise since Aquinas was aware of the consequences of renouncing the maximalist concept of God's knowledge. Accepting the position arguing for God's dependence on specific human choices leaves the crucial problem of reconciling this outlook with God's simplicity. An entirely simple God cannot gain knowledge from His creation. In this context, one solution would be to negate God's simplicity and state that He exists in time.[229]

Assuming that God is everlasting and exists in time does not generate problems with His knowledge about the past and the present. Problems arise in case of knowledge regarding the future.[230] It can be claimed that God knows all possible options of events and is able to predict in detail those events which are entirely dependent on the present state of the universe. But does God—understood in this vein—know the future which is the result of man's free choice? The answer seems to be negative if we assume that human freedom is based on a real choice between different ways of acting. In accordance with this view, our choices, albeit conditioned by many factors, are authentically free. Human beings are free to choose from among particular options of action, with this not entirely being determined by the nature of an action's agent and/ or circumstances.[231]

In some sense, the presented proposition does not, however, exclude the omniscience of God, who knows everything that can be known from a logical point of view. God is familiar with all true statements concerning the past and the present. Since the future is open, we can say that it is not yet in existence. This is why being unfamiliar with future human actions would not limit God's knowledge. The future is full of possibilities that will not become realized until man makes a free choice. This standpoint is inscribed in the program of open theism, even though, at least in some aspects, it is shared by representatives of various currents in reflection upon divine nature.[232]

God always knows more

Elaborating on this thought from the perspective of the natural sciences, J. Polkinghorne claims that the image of an eternal God familiar with the future functions well within the framework of a static and deterministically closed world of being. On the other hand, contemporary science presents a world of incessant becoming in which events of a random course constitute an integral part of the whole. Chaos theory and quantum mechanics convey the truth of the openness of natural processes, the future of which cannot be predicted on the basis of Newton's equations. Knowledge of God who acts in a world of this kind embraces all possible configurations of events. Nevertheless, God does not know the future in its entirety before it happens. Thus, He does not possess absolute knowledge. This can be deemed to be one of the elements of God's *kenosis*, which is the consequence of creating a genuinely open world. The intrinsic and authentic creativity of nature is realized both through generating novelty in physical or biological structures, and also in the free choices made by beings bestowed with consciousness.[233]

Resolving the problem of God's knowledge looks completely different when human freedom is viewed exclusively as the possibility of acting in keeping with our nature. We fulfill our desires, but they are determined by broadly understood nature: not only by genes, but also by education and social conditioning. We think that we are free but in fact we are confined to a choice between options which become realized in the specific, strictly determined environment of our lives. When we adopt such an assumption, God can indeed know the future.[234]

In discussing the question of providence and evil in the world, P. Geach uses the metaphor of a chess grandmaster. When playing chess against this grandmaster, we are free to make rationally planned moves with particular chess pieces. The final result of the game, however, would be prejudged in favor of the grandmaster. In treating God as the "absolute grandmaster," we can assume that He will realize His scenario. His intentions cannot be thwarted. God can effectively carry out His plan of action, even though He communicated his plan to humanity beforehand.[235]

Geach's proposition includes a strong version of knowledge of a grandmaster who can predict every move of his opponent. It seems that this is not necessary for demonstrating the concept of the sempiternal God who realizes His aims. After all, it can be assumed that God is familiar with all the options of action available to us, even not knowing what particular choices we are going to make. People are not capable of preventing God's designs by upsetting his long-term intentions. Vardy prefers an approach within which God cannot predict each of our actions with absolute precision. Nonetheless, God knows that He is going to "win the match" and that His ultimate goals are going to be achieved irrespective of man's particular moves.[236]

The above image of God can, for many reasons, appear as intellectually appealing. It accentuates the personality of God whose unawareness of our future choices does not result in creation slipping out of the Creator's control. There is some dynamic interaction between God and the world that presupposes human freedom. The critics of this concept point to its anthropomorphic character.[237] God has to act in such a way as to "ensure that the free actions of men and women do not undermine his purposes."[238]

Can God predict what cannot be predicted?

From an equally important (for the issue of God's omniscience) perspective of reflection on time, P. Davies points to the fact that in everyday experience we do not doubt the passage of time. We make use of the distinction between the past, present, and future. However, the more profoundly these notions are examined, the more intense the conviction that they are ambiguous. The physical theory of relativity excluded the universal presence common to all observers. In light of the foregoing, how can we look at the passage of time from the God's perspective? What does it mean that He is eternal?

If we understand the concept of God's eternity as His existence without beginning or end for an infinite amount of time, numerous controversies are born. God existing in time would be prone to changes. Moreover, time is an element of the physical universe and can be extended or shortened in accordance with the laws expressed in the language of mathematics. Time is also strictly connected to space and, just like matter, "takes part" in physical processes. If we assumed that God had not created time, He would also not have created space. Even more, if there had been a primary space-time, then the matter and order of the universe could have emerged automatically by means of entirely natural processes. Thus, God existing in time falls into a peculiar trap of the physical universe—He would not be able to be omnipotent in a maximalist (thus embracing the epistemic aspect) understanding of the word.[239]

An alternative option is to assume that God exists entirely outside of time and space. An atemporally existing Creator of space-time does not become entangled in the problems presented above. Nevertheless, according to Davies, such a Creator cannot be thought of as a personal God who thinks, plans, sympathizes, and enters into relationships with human beings. It is difficult to understand how a timeless God can act in time. Contemporary science concerning time generates many consequences for such a concept of God's omniscience.[240] Can a timeless being possess knowledge? After all, gaining knowledge requires time even though knowledge itself does not, with the assumption that what we know is not subject to change. If we assume that God knows the position of every atom at a given stage of evolution, will His knowledge in this respect change in the future? Atemporal knowledge implies being familiar with all events in time.[241]

The key to understanding timelessness is providing an answer to the question concerning the nature of time. This has always been one of the most serious philosophical problems, but the last several decades have brought forth new approaches to the problem, especially from the perspective of natural science. As I mentioned previously, contemporary physics challenges both the idea of absolute temporal simultaneity, as well as the conviction that "one and the same" absolute time can serve as the measure of events in the systems of two different observers. The theory of relativity has refuted the theory of privileged observers and the absolute simultaneity of events. Simultaneous events, as perceived by an observer at rest, take place at a different time from the perspective of a moving observer. Since no reference frame can be treated as an absolute cognitive point of reference, a sequence of events is subject to relativization. This is not dependent on a more or less insightful adherence to the procedures that ensure precise observation. It means that there is no distinguished horizon from which one can objectively state whether occurrences are simultaneous or not. Thus, a sequence of events cannot be identified with the entirely "external" and stable relationships between these events. Differences result from the state of an observer's movement as well as from the fact of the finitude and stability of the propagation of light in a vacuum. Since the speed of light is an invariant of motion in every system, the pace of time must change in different systems. There is no one universal time that could be regarded as an absolute measure for the sequence of occurrences.[242]

Special complications arise if we try to find a definite resolution to the question of whether events distant from one another take place simultaneously. Since the perspective of individual observers is always arbitrary and any other vantage point may be equally valid for measurement procedures, any participant of the experiment can provide a specific sequence of events that take place in his surroundings with time proper to this situation. From the point of view of another observer, this sequence of the same events can change, especially when the second observer views these shared events while moving at a very high speed (approximate to the speed of light). Hence, every reference system is relative and thus does not guarantee a fully objective observation of a certain sequence of events.[243]

Contemporary science affirms that the course of certain processes of nature can be known only to a lesser or greater degree of probability. Regularities in relations between events taking place on the subatomic and quantum levels are of a statistical character. Irrespective of the measured interval, we know, at most, what part of the atomic nuclei of radium will decay. What will happen to a single atomic nucleus cannot be precisely predicted. Physicists argue for the inherent unpredictability of measurement outcomes in the microworld. It cannot be precisely determined which atom of radium will decay in the shortest possible interval of time.[244]

Thus, if we assume that omniscience is the ability to know everything that is logically possible to be known, even God cannot possess ultimate knowledge of the future. As far as the outcomes of certain events are concerned, God has a probabilistic knowledge thereof.[245] This does not only regard the microworld because, if a quantum event takes place in a system in which its effect can be enhanced to a macroscopic level, then the events can also turn out to be unpredictable. However, the concept of God's limited knowledge does not regard so-called chaotic processes. These processes remain unpredictable to us, most of all due to our imprecise knowledge of the initial conditions which can change the course of a process to a substantial extent. The omniscient God has full knowledge of these conditions and can predict their effects in the future.[246]

The open world of processualists

This view of God's knowledge in light of contemporary science is close to the position held by processualists. Proponents of processualism reject both the strong concept of omniscience and divine omnipotence as, in their opinion, this would mean that the world is devoid of autonomy. If we are free, our acts cannot be predicted in detail. In this context, we need to characterize God's relationship with a creation whose freedom of development signifies a delimiting of divine knowledge.[247] Understanding the world as a collection of free and feeling beings, Hartshorne redefines the classical understanding of God's omniscience and omnipotence.[248]

The process of divine cognition is understood as occurring in relation with an object. From such a perspective, God's knowledge is defined as an infinite class of relationships, not all of which are real. Here we speak of subject–object relations. Within these relations, the subject is always in an internal relation with the object, with the latter being in an external relation with the subject which comes to know the object. The subject, recognizing an object understood as the mind, shows receptiveness. The subject is open to an action of the object. Coming to know something is based on being under the influence of something, whereas being recognized means exerting an influence. Hartshorne claims that only those entities which are actualized can be known.[249]

For processualists, contrary to Aquinas's approach, divine cognition is not an exception and requires a real, and not only mental, relationship between the subject and the object. Since the subject forms an internal relation with the object, likewise God, in the process of knowing the world, has to form an internal relation with the world. Knowing the world is not limited only to the divine intellect. This cognition is part of the experience of God that changes and constitutes Him.[250] The world is changeable, hence God as He comes to know it is changeable, too. In rejecting the Thomistic conviction that an object exists in a subject in the way that a subject does, Hartshorne claims that an object shapes a subject. Thus, cognition is identified with an object's coming to being. In coming to know the world, one participates in its mutability, thus adjusting cognition to the existence of an object.[251]

The concepts of time and eternity are some of the main constituents of processual metaphysics. Timelessness is treated in this system as nonsensical. An atemporal God would not be able to come to know entities which exist in time and, by their nature, are subject to mutability. The assertion that God would know without changing is irreconcilable with the principal assumptions of Hartshorne's system. Paradoxically, a smaller existential change takes place in the human subject who comes to know the world. This is because man's cognition is defective and God's is adequate to the object of His cognition that causes an ontic change in the divine subject.[252]

According to processualists, unlimited divine omniscience would entail determinism. God fully knowing the future would signify a delimiting of the spontaneity of beings, with this ultimately boiling down to determinism. It is not the case that in knowing a cause, we also know an effect. For Aquinas, God—perfectly knowing Himself and being the cause of all things—is familiar with all results, regardless of the time of their realization. Hartshorne opposes such an approach. He claims that (assuming that created beings are free) a cause does not entirely predefine an effect.[253]

Contemporary science ascertains that the laws of nature are not of an entirely deterministic character. Process philosophy adds that the future is authentically open. Otherwise, it would be identical to other moments in time, with this possibly resulting in the futility of any becoming whatsoever; everything would exist simultaneously. Within the processual view, the associated limitation of God's knowledge stems from the spontaneity of actual beings, but this does not mean that God appears to be deprived of perfection. His lack of detailed knowledge concerning the future is not a limitation for God since the future is not yet in existence. However, God can foresee a future which is not yet fully determined. To assure the freedom of beings, God does not know everything, but only what has already taken place and is actually becoming. All the same, God knows the most of all beings.[254]

God knows the actual as actual and the potential as potential. If a given being is subject to indeterministic development, God does not know all of this being's future details until they become realized. Divine knowledge embraces all possible scenarios of the future. Such an approach leads to the formulation of a thesis concerning the continuous growth of the knowledge of God who comes to know what is actually to be known. Potential states do not exist as detailed beings at the present stage. God knows the possibilities of development in a general manner and this allows Him to know the kind to which a possible concrete entity will belong.[255]

For processualists, future events do not exist beforehand in God's mind. Since the future is not yet in existence, God does not possess adequate knowledge of it. The critics of this concept stress that even humans have some idea of the future. Hartshorne does not deny this but claims that what is unknown is the exact future course of world history. For this reason, God does not possess detailed knowledge of the world, the nature of which entails the freedom of beings and their creativity. Today, the only thing we can speak of is a certain plan for the future, not of the complete determination of the future. The result is only partially dependent on a cause.[256]

Among all individual beings, God has the greatest influence on the fate of the world. This does not mean that God knows and can do everything. Since the world has an intrinsic autonomy in its development, God can attract or encourage actualizing individuals to realize His aims and not fully decide on their future. In rejecting the traditional concepts of divine omniscience and omnipotence, processualists deem these concepts erroneous and inadequate with regard to religious intuitions. A God who fully determines the future might appear as a cosmic tyrant and despot who should be charged with being responsible for evil. Such a God would not be able to become the object of the religious practices which are characteristic of Christians.[257]

Analytical Thomism vs. open theism

Contemporary scientific knowledge concerning the problem of time is also used by analytical Thomists who examine the question of God's nature. The conclusions they formulate differ from the ones put forward by processual philosophers but are an ambitious attempt at including the output of relativistic physics. In undertaking the task of confronting Boethius's understanding of eternity with the theory of relativity, E. Stump and N. Kretzmann present a coherent concept of timeless existence. From this viewpoint, eternity is comprehended as the complete and perfect possession of an infinite life, within which there is no distinction between the past and the future, nor does time as viewed therein have any sequential order. From God's perspective, no temporal events are earlier or later because this would entangle Him in a series of consecutive events. Eternal presence is an infinitely stretched lasting for which there is no "before" or "after." It can be said that a being existing in eternity as defined in this way, and possessing the fullness of life, has a present existence, even though this existing is a type of lasting which has no aftermath. Thus, it cannot be reasonably stated that an eternal being has existed and will exist because it simply exists timelessly. True lasting is fully realized, and nothing ceases to exist within this lasting. Being a stable and immutable guarantee of lasting and of the foundation of the existence of entities situated in time, God has to possess such a manner of existence in which everything is actual and unchangeable. Eternity is a timeless presence.[258]

The above approach demonstrates that the classical doctrine of divine eternity viewed as timelessness can be consistently presented in light of actual scientific knowledge. It seems that there is no correct way to solve the problem of the simultaneity of actions between the timeless being and temporal beings. Nevertheless, the analytical

Thomists present eternity as the atemporal way of the absolute being's existence and a specific system of reference in which there is no succession of events. An event taking place in eternity is eternally simultaneous with every other event. The existence of a timeless being for whom all events in time are eternally simultaneous does not settle the question of the simultaneity of events in the physical world.[259]

The omniscient and eternal God has a simultaneous awareness of all the details of a human life, but at the same time He knows that individual events take place in temporal sequences, with Him knowing the time of their realization. For the eternal being, all events which take place in the world are present "straightaway." The assumption that a given event is in the future for us but in the present for God does not entail the acknowledgement of the existence of two objective realities. In this first one, my death would be in the future; in the second one, my death would be present within my entire life. The concept of timeless eternity emphasizes that there is one reality but that this reality is composed of two ways of being, two ways of real existence, and two diverse kinds of lasting and their perception through measures that cannot be reduced to themselves: time and eternity. When my death refers to the actual time then—being situated on a temporal continuum—my death is not simultaneous in relation to the present but rather is a future event.[260]

Numerous questions arise in this context. Can the eternal (in the above sense) being act in time? How can He cause events in time? Can an effect of God's action in the world be temporally posterior to His eternal action? Does such a concept of the eternal being remove Him too much from temporal beings? Is it not obvious that for the agent of action to be directly aware of temporal events, He has to have some awareness in time? Perhaps the timeless God's knowledge concerning temporal events is intermediated? In what way are two beings of a radically different existential status (temporal and eternal) present and at the same time current to one another? From a temporal frame of reference, the acting God seems to be present in time (even though He is not), and from an eternal perspective, temporal beings appear to be present in eternity (while being in temporality). Is divine knowledge of temporal events real if it does not view them as they are but as what they seem to be from the horizon of eternity? Does this mean that the absolute being has incomplete knowledge of temporal events? When assuming that God's knowledge is a particular indirect presentation of temporal events, do we at the same time prejudge that God's perspective does not view these events but rather their atemporal representation, even while presuming a completely faithful projection? In discerning such difficulties, Hasker states that an absolute being who indirectly experiences events at various moments cannot be timeless but exists in time and experiences temporal sequences.[261]

The position of open theists, which will be thoroughly presented in the next part of this section, remains strongly critical of the idea of simultaneity as formulated in the milieu of analytical Thomists. Nevertheless, the latter cannot be accused of a lack of insightful analyses pertaining to both the question of eternity and God's knowledge. Analytical Thomists think that for an omniscient being existing in timeless eternity and conscious of all temporal events (as also future ones from the temporal perspective), these temporal events must be present. What we think is past, present, or future, is always present to God conceived in this way. In this light, the question of whether a being like this knows what time it is now should be answered affirmatively. The timeless and omniscient God knows in His eternal presence what time it is now in the temporal presence.²⁶²

Is the omniscient and eternal God an immutable being? Stump and Kretzmann stress that it is not the content of divine knowledge that changes, but rather this knowledge's reference to temporal or eternal actuality. In this way it can also be consistently demonstrated that God's knowledge of actual temporal events is also a knowing of when these events actually take place, as well as the timeless knowledge that these events take place actually. The authors of this solution claim that to understand it correctly, we need an accurate concept of a non-temporal cause that eternally causes temporal effects. It would be a mistake to ask whether the absolute being today knows what is going to happen tomorrow. The timeless God cannot be located in a local reference frame since this is an unjustified reduction of the eternal to the temporal. No local perspective confines the eternal being to whom the entire course of time is available timelessly. God has a simultaneous view of temporal reality from infinitely many systems of simultaneous reference. What is important is the fact that in simultaneously perceiving temporal events from infinitely many cognitive perspectives, God does not exhaust His being and existence. This is because God does not exist ontically in these systems of reference, but epistemically chooses a viewing perspective for a given temporal event. In the latter regard, the concept of analytical Thomists is essentially different from the standpoint of open theists. The global cognitive orientation of God goes beyond local reference frames. Thus, we can speak of the metaphysical transcendence of the absolute being in relation to all time perspectives, with this being the key to grasping timeless eternity.²⁶³

When the question of eternity as timelessness is examined, the pros and cons of the presented solution are pointed out. This lets us defend the strong concept of omniscience that is characteristic of Thomist circles. In timeless eternity, God can possess all possible knowledge—even of the future events caused by people—without encroaching on the freedom of choice. The atemporal idea of eternity also provides a consistent view of immutability and the omnipotence of the absolute being. Nonetheless, problems remain with rendering the other attributes consistent. After all, the question arises regarding how a timeless being can be endowed with a life that entails conscious processes, and therefore activity or even change. How can personal existence be possible in which everything is actual, immutable, and not subject to the passage of time, while having a real reference to the changeable world? It is also not easy to grasp the essence of existence in constant presence and in experiencing the fullness of existence. What is also visible is the difficulty in clarifying the nature of the relationship between the eternal agent and the temporal effect of this agent's action. Can it be stated that eternity is a component of temporal events? Can the eternal God be a participant of temporal events without depriving Himself of eternal existence?²⁶⁴

The defenders of the atemporal concept of eternity strive to provide detailed answers to these questions. However, this is not the main point of reference for contemporary philosophical discussions of God's knowledge. As I have already stressed in the beginning of this section, these discussions are dominated by—and specifically in light of the scientific worldview—thought invested in human freedom. In this regard, several fundamental standpoints emerge whose essential details have to be examined.²⁶⁵

Human freedom

Hard determinism acknowledges that all actions are ultimately determined by events which are external in relation to human power. Thus, in essence, we do not have any causal control over our actions. Such an approach satisfies both the theistic views stressing the fact that God predefines everything that happens in the world, as well as scientific statements that all natural processes (sooner or later) can be explained on the level of physical interpretations. Therefore, in this sense, human actions do not differ from any natural processes. In the context of God's knowledge, this concerns mainly the decisions which man makes, with their effects appearing to be of secondary significance.[266]

A different standpoint is compatibilism. Its proponents claim that for human freedom it is most important that the subject decides and acts the way it wants. The freedom to want is essential here. Thus, it is irrelevant whether the intentions of actions and truly made decisions are an effect of the physical causal chains which precede them. Even if human choices are derivative in relation to the processes which take place in the human brain, what is crucial is that man can do what he wants.[267] Compatibilism as proclaimed in the theistic context accentuates that God is not only the first cause of all events and processes, but is also man's ultimate determining factor. However, this does not destroy human freedom because God also determines whether certain events are free or not. Theistic compatibilists profess that without God's action, all of our decisions would be merely consequences of physical causal chains. Nevertheless, God co-determines each free act of human freedom. As a result, God who exists out of time is aware of everything that happens in time.[268]

Libertarianism proclaims that free actions are real and that no action can be determined by something situated outside of the causal control of the decision-making man. Such a stance gives rise to difficulty given scientific knowledge, since, in some sense, this position undermines the explanatory powers of physics, and assumes that there can be human actions that do not stem from physical causes and cannot be scientifically explicated. Theistic libertarianism is usually identified with Molinism, which stresses that God has a three-fold kind of knowledge at His disposal: natural knowledge (concerning necessary truths out of His control), free knowledge (concerning contingent truths He fully controls), and middle knowledge (*scientia media*), referring to counterfactual statements which describe the free actions of all people.[269] Before deciding to create particular people, God knows what each of them—while remaining free—will do in specific circumstances. However, these circumstances do not determine the decisions man will make. Counterfactual statements are out of God's control because man is free in his actions. God has middle knowledge before he decides to create. However, what we mean is logical precedence, not temporal precedence, since Molinists share the view held by classical theists that God does not exist in time. *Scientia media* ascertains that God—in choosing between various scenarios of creation—will reach His intended goals.[270]

Libertarian revisionism is a stance that originates in theism. Its proponents adopt the concept of freedom in the libertarian sense, but in discerning the difficulties in reconciling this stance with the concept of providence, they strive to modify the traditional concept of God. The object of particular criticism is Molinism. Contrary to Molinism's assumptions, God cannot possess knowledge of the truth of counterfactual conditions because He would have to know the facts and these do not exist before free humans make specific decisions.[271] It is the agents behind actions that provide meaning to counterfactual conditions, rendering them true. God can only with a certain degree of probability know how free beings will act. Revisionists claim that this solution seems to be more valuable than classical theism which puts too much emphasis on God's full control of everything that happens in the world. God, who has probable knowledge at His disposal, has sufficient possibilities of predicting and does not remove the real freedom of choice from man. Authentically interpersonal relationships are possible only when we assume the freedom of the persons who form them.[272]

The debate on God's knowledge has given rise to various outlooks. The basis for main solutions was either to accept or reject the thesis that the anticipative knowledge of God of a specific event is of necessary character. The representatives of classical theism, in adopting the theory of simple foreknowledge, have to acknowledge the authenticity of the conclusion that future events are necessary. The continuators of L. de Molina's thought state that God possesses unlimited knowledge of the future, but this does not entail necessity and can be reconciled with human freedom. God's foreknowledge of future contingent events is counterfactually dependent on these events. If God knew beforehand that Judas would betray Him, then this betrayal was sure to happen. If Judas had not betrayed God, then God would have always known that. Thus, God has an unlimited knowledge of the future and man has a freedom undetermined by God. In possessing an antecedent and complete knowledge of everything from all possible beings and situations in the world, God chose those events which He deemed worthy of creation. Acknowledging that Molinism is a sophisticated attempt at solving the problem of omniscience, Łukasiewicz notices serious difficulties in this position and gives attention to the essential issue of weakening God's omnipotence. After all, scholars would have to accordingly accept that there is something which is different from God and was also not created by God, namely, the statements and counterfactual truths all possible beings and situations which these beings could find themselves in. God, on the basis of these mutually independent truths and His knowledge of His own intentions, would decide on whether to create everything that exists. However, this is a huge constraint imposed on divine omnipotence because these situational and counterfactual truths (freedom truths) are situated outside the reach of God's power.[273]

The concept formulated in the sixteenth century by the Spanish Jesuit is being developed nowadays among the representatives of open theism (also called neo-Molinism or free will theism).[274] One of the main theses of this position is accepting that there are assertions concerning future contingent events that are neither true nor false. This is mainly aimed at overcoming the theological fatalism expressed in the following statement: if God infallibly knew that a given human deed would take place, then it cannot be free in the libertarian sense. Open theism rejects the assumption of the infallibility of divine foreknowledge and claims that God does not have knowledge of future contingent events. This does not imply that God does not possess any knowledge of the future whatsoever. This also does not have to lead to the statement that God necessarily does not have knowledge of the future in a certain respect.[275]

One of the most significant arguments for weakening the concept of divine omniscience is the problem of the evil that results from human action. It seems that only when the omniscient God does not know how people endowed with free will act, He bears no responsibility for evil. Critics of this argumentation underline that if God, according to open theism, has a complete and detailed knowledge of all past and present states of the world and has the power to act in the world, He can cause some events to occur and others not. The answer to such objections comes with the statement that God cannot cause anyone who freely plans evil to simultaneously not want to commit an evil act in a free manner.[276]

The assumption that God has limited knowledge concerning the future is the principal component of W. Hasker's approach. Drawing on the famous evidential argument from pointless evil, Hasker rejects the second premise of W. Rowe's reasoning which states that an omniscient, absolutely good being would prevent pointless evil in the world.[277] In one of the five reasons formulated in support of this view, Hasker stresses that God does not have sempiternal knowledge (neither in advance nor indirectly) of what free people will do, and does not know how much pointless evil is necessary for man to morally improve.[278]

Hasker's proposition does not seem convincing, especially in terms of the insufficiently justified (or perhaps even false) assumption concerning human morality. The advantage of open theism is its firm emphasis on human freedom. In the context of God's knowledge, this current of theism points to the incompatibility of perfection and "strong" (i.e., unlimited) omniscience, the limiting of omniscience (the greater knowledge, the less God's omniscience), and the more personalized character of the God–human relationship.[279]

In detailed discussions concerning the problem of divine omniscience, the fundamental question concerns the way in which God knows the future, including human choices. Proponents of the concept of simple foreknowledge think that the only adequate answer is to state that God simply knows what is going to happen. Among the solutions characteristic of open theism, there is a distinction between two types of future events. The first one speaks of events which God has no prior knowledge of. God has antecedent knowledge of all possibilities but does not know which one will be realized, while man simultaneously is indeterministically free (an essential precept in open theism) in relation to planned actions. This would not be the case if God had prior knowledge of free human actions. The second type of events concerns those which God knows in advance. Such knowledge can be based either on the divine decision that an event is going to happen (God has predetermined man to act according to specific circumstances),[280] or on divine deduction that an event is going to happen (with this based on God's complete and infallible knowledge of the past and the present, e.g., concerning the character of the acting agent).[281] Open theism assumes that it is within God's power to determine everything, but in an act of self-limitation He renounces full control over the world. Only in this way can the autonomy of nature and the authentic freedom of human action be assured.[282]

Essentially different to the above standpoint is the one rooted in the Augustinian theory of predestination and presented by the Calvinists. Future contingent events are necessary from the perspective of God's antecedent knowledge, which, however, as supporters of this view claim, does not rule out human freedom.[283] For the followers of

Calvinism the key concept is that of the efficacy of God's grace. Each person who receives it will do good. Having the foreknowledge of His own intentions concerning a recipient of his grace, God knows how he or she will behave. In this context, the problem arises whether God knows the behaviors of people deprived of grace, i.e., those not destined by Him to do good. If this is the case, then: Does God not determine sin by being ultimately its originator? In response to this objection, it is usually claimed that God does not want sin and does not cause it, but only allows it to happen. Knowing of all the cause-and-effect chains in the world and His own intentions, God has antecedent knowledge of a given sin happening. It seems, however, that—if we treat God as the ultimate cause of all cause-and-effect chains—the question of responsibility for evil remains insufficiently resolved.[284]

In attempts at reconciling divine omniscience with human freedom, the views expressed at the various stages of theism's development have been considerably influenced by the concept elaborated by Boethius. He claimed that divine knowledge of the future is not prior to but simultaneous with the future. For God existing beyond time (or "outside of time") all events (past, present, and future from our perspective) are given in one, timeless "now." Hence God knows the future in a way analogous to the human perception of the present. Divine knowledge of the future is not foreknowledge since it does not belong to the past. Thus, this is not necessary in the sense of historical necessity, and neither are the acts of will and human choice that are known to God as part of His foreknowledge. Divine knowledge of the future and (indeterministically understood) human freedom are not mutually exclusive.[285]

Boethius's thought faced extensive criticism which still has many proponents. Theists have frequently underlined that Boethius downplays the providential action of God, thus reducing Him to the role of an observer who watches world history from afar. When creating the world, God did not know what it would be like. But, with the world already existing, God cannot change anything any more. Noticing such problems, many followers of Aquinas stress the role of the distinction between the temporal and the logical order. Although God comes to know the world from the perspective of timeless eternity and His knowledge of temporal events is always simultaneous with them, then logically speaking, God's knowledge is antecedent.[286] After all, the Creator of the world (as the absolute sovereign and the first cause of all existence) knows the world in the process of knowing Himself. The philosophers who joined the discussion of this subject have often emphasized that timeless eternity is—in a way similar to the past—immutable and causally closed and hence necessary. This leads to fatalism, which to this very day is frequently a moot point in debates inspired by Boethius's concept.[287]

As can be seen on the basis of these analyses, resolutions concerning divine knowledge are of crucial significance to many of the approaches from other spheres of philosophical theology, especially when considering the questions of predestination, providence, and the problem of evil. None of the presented standpoints provide a definite solution to the most essential question: How does one reconcile divine omniscience with human freedom? Open theism has not yet developed a uniform semantic framework for sentences on future contingent events. Molinism does not provide grounds for the truthfulness of counterfactual conditionals. The theory of simple foreknowledge is sometimes treated as a variety of Calvinist determinism which is close to theological fatalism in reducing man to a submissive puppet and God to the role of the originator of evil.[288]

Problems also arise with regard to the question of God's knowledge of the subsequent stages of the development of nature which, in light of science, is seen as open to various scenarios in the future. It is true that adopting the idea of the atemporal existence of God is in this context a solution encouraging a maximalist approach to His omniscience. The atemporal concept of eternity enables a consistent view of the immutability and omniscience of the absolute being. On the other hand, however, such a theory brings problems in demonstrating the Creator's interaction with creation. It is difficult to view an atemporal necessary being as a person endowed with the fullness of life and activity as directed at contingent beings. The omniscient Absolute "observing" events occurring in the physical world from a timeless perspective seems to be a rather emotionless witness to the fate of creation. This view does not match the image of God present in the Christian tradition.

* * *

I started the chapter on God, seen as the agent and cause of action in the world, by outlining the principal components of the idea of an absolute being, God's unique nature, and the ways in which these questions are approached in contemporary analytic philosophy. Christian theism stresses that the existence of God implies His action in the world. Providence constitutes an inseparable component of the Creator–creation relationship. Such a conclusion requires going beyond deistic approaches to these issues. Nonetheless, it is not enough to stress that God sustains the world in existence, but it is essential to strive for a more precise definition of the *creatio continua* formula and analyze those divine attributes which seem to be particularly important for the characterization of God's interaction with the world. Therefore, I discuss questions concerning divine creative power, simplicity, personal existence, omnipotence, and omniscience. This, in turn, made me reflect on God's relationship to time, His immutability, and several other issues often discussed in contemporary theistic circles, e.g. divine impassibility.

At the end of each section of this chapter, I formulated certain conclusions which are sometimes more like antinomies rather than unequivocal conclusions. My explorations demonstrate that theists have so far been unable to present a consistent concept of the absolute being that meets all the criteria essential to a comprehensive approach to the question of God's interaction with the world. The attributes enumerated above have been the object of thorough reflection within various currents of theism. None provides a sufficient reference point for the formulation of a theory of divine action and in each of them one can identify areas that are difficult to resolve definitely. This does not signify that contemporary philosophical theology is essentially indisposed to address such questions. In many aspects progress is readily noticeable, for example, regarding the question of God the Creator. Even though important details concerning reflection on God's action in the world have been elaborated upon in theistic debate, some issues are still the object of fundamental controversies that reflect a substantial difference of opinions (e.g., with regard to God's omnipotence, His relationship to time and knowledge of the future).

3

On the World

This part of the book is devoted to reflection on the nature of the world and the question concerning whether (and how) God is present in the world. From the perspective of philosophy, it is not easy to demonstrate that the Creator participates in the history of the creation, and particularly in the history of humankind. The more the world's autonomy in relation to God is accentuated, the harder it becomes to justify that He influences the course of world history. Many contemporary theists deem the laws of nature to be the main manifestation of divine action, and underline that their genesis and specificity cannot be fully explained on the grounds of natural sciences.

A particularly complicated task—to which I give most thought—is to argue in support of God's immanence in a world prone to the influence of evil. The most extremely painful manifestation thereof is the suffering of innocent human beings, and the prompting of the subsequent question: Is God an emotionless observer of the dramas which affect the world and man? Some theists, who give a negative response to this question, formulate a theory of God's *kenosis*, which is presented at the beginning of the third section of this chapter. However, this aforementioned section is mainly devoted to panentheism, which moves beyond the classical interpretation of the creation–Creator relationship. Authors who elaborate on the concept of *kenosis* put a strong emphasis on God being present in the world, whereas panentheists highlight the world as existing in God. The common denominator of these two groups is their stress on the closeness between the Creator and His creation.

Autonomy

Between autonomy and independence

Creation is always somehow related to the Creator, but detailed presentations of this relationship are very diverse. It seems that the fact of being created by God does not determine the entire evolution of the world. In some sense, the world can shape itself and develop on its own. Our intuition suggests that the more independent an individual being is from another being, the greater its worth. The specificity of processes in nature leads to the conviction that God does not interfere in the world by means of withdrawing the autonomy of its development. This is highlighted particularly in reference to beings endowed with consciousness who, albeit dependent on God in existence, are to a certain degree independent from Him in their action. Christian theism often stresses that we possess freedom thanks to the Creator and this enables us to make genuine choices as well as to become responsible for our actions.[1]

Emphasizing the world's autonomy does not *ipso facto* mean that God's influence on the world's fate is negated, but it invokes various questions, especially the problem of evil. Did the evolutionary history which led to the genesis of sentient beings have to entail the annihilation of so many creatures? Why did the omnipotent and infinitely good God introduce a mechanism that brings so much pain? Could not God have made people free in a way which would not result in so many seemingly unnecessary costs? I attempt to answer these questions in a subsequent section. Here, I focus on an analysis of the problem of creation's distinctness from the Creator.

While formulating a detailed concept of the world's autonomy, one needs to avoid anthropomorphizing nature. It would be erroneous to claim that at individual stages of nature's development its components chose such coincidences of chemical or biological parameters to lead to the genesis of man.[2] The world as such does not possess the agency that is appropriate for planning its own future.[3] Refraining from anthropomorphizing approaches does not mean, however, that creation is not ascribed any creative properties. On the contrary, multiple solutions appear nowadays which accentuate that the Creator does not only sustain the world in existence (*conservatio*), but also makes it capable of autonomous development (*concursus*). Rahner undertakes reflection on this problem as a theologian, but many of his intuitions can be used on the grounds of philosophical theism. The German Jesuit introduces the notion of creation's active self-transcendence, underlining that—thanks to the creative power of God—there is an internal dynamism in the world, which is an intrinsic trait of the world. The idea of self-transcendence allows the nature's processes (even those that reveal ontological discontinuity) to be interpreted without reference to special divine intervention. God remains immanently present in the world, enabling nature to shape itself and function in a creative way. The Creator "puts pressure"[4] on creation to continually develop. In this context, *creatio continua* means that God enables the constant emergence of new forms thanks to the autonomous processes, relations, and cause-and-effect connections which exist in nature.[5]

According to Rahner, creation's self-transcendence constitutes one of the two ways in which God acts in the world. The first way concerns the self-bestowal of God who enables the universe to evolve and takes an active part in its development. These complementary and fundamental traits of God's presence in the world provide the foundation for the Christian model of the Creator–creation interaction. The concept of the top-down and bottom-up divine action (in the sense characteristic of this approach) allow one to engage in reflection both from the theological perspective (with the Incarnation at its center), as well as in reference to contemporary science (the canvass of which being the evolutionary character of nature's development).[6]

Contrary to many appearances, the stressing of creation's autonomy does not generate essential problems in maintaining the thesis of the world's dependence on God. Admittedly, commonsense experience suggests that dependence implies the stripping away freedom. However, in the case of understanding the relationship between creation and the Creator, this intuition calls for a revision. The world is autonomous and internally creative thanks to the constant dependence on God. Rahner underlines that the closer creation is to the Creator, the more it "can be itself." This point becomes more comprehensible with the use of theological inspirations which stress that the more God attracts us, the freer we become. In receiving grace, we experience an internal freedom which comes from God and is directed towards Him.[7]

The paradox of having autonomy and being simultaneously dependent on the Creator seems particularly significant in the context of human action. Man deems himself free when he himself is the cause of action. God, however, is not just one of the world's beings whose role is to affect human actions from the outside as in the case of a person being forced by someone else to undertake an action. God enables man to act and makes him a free agent of particular choices. We experience such agency in relation to other human beings who—in expressing love or regard—respect our individuality and do not subjugate us. It can be said that to love others means to give them a "space" in which they can be themselves, develop, and grow.[8]

The process of creation is understood as an expression of love and "endowing the world with its own existence." The world's development takes place according to the nature specific to physical beings. This does not mean that the Creator retreats from creation for He can act in the world through a series of secondary causes.[9] God conditions and enables the nature's development and the realization of human freedom, "patiently waiting" for events to unfold. Nonetheless, this is not passive expectation but an active form of accompanying creation in the process of *autopoiesis*.[10] God does not abandon the world even though He accepts limitations in interacting with nature. Even during the most critical periods of history, God does not violate the laws of nature and does not take freedom away from man. The Creator consistently allows history to realize itself, even when the events composing it seem to radically oppose His will.[11]

The concept of God's "restraint" in terms of interventions is more comprehensible thanks to contemporary science which sheds new light on many aspects of Christian doctrine, for instance the truth concerning man as the crown of creation. Today we know that for more than ten billion years processes took place which relatively recently led to the emergence of our species. Stage by stage, nature generated gradually newer structures: from the synthesis of elements, such as carbon, through the emergence of life (starting with its most basic forms), and finally reaching the appearance of human consciousness. Stating, after one of the first Christian theologians, that man is the glory of God (*Gloria enim Dei vivens homo, vita autem hominis visio Dei*[12]), we can simultaneously assert from the evolutionary perspective that God's intentions have a long-term span of realization. The love of the Creator is combined with His ability to respect the autonomy of creation, thus acting with patience within it, and leading to ultimate fulfillment, notwithstanding a detailed course of events.[13]

The status of the laws of nature

A particular manifestation of nature's autonomy is the laws which are the foundation of the world's stability. The laws of nature are treated by many theists as a sign of the "constancy and faithfulness" of God who providentially takes care of the world and is present in it.[14] In this context, the question of the ontological status of the laws of nature remains relevant.[15] This does not merely concern general statements drawn mainly from the Platonic philosophy. The specificity of the functioning of the world, which is not chaotic, allows one to justify the above theses and to refer to God as the source of cosmic order.

The origins of the contemporary debates concerning the laws of nature date back to the times of Hume, who opposed the necessitarian interpretation, accusing it of maintaining a metaphysically charged notion of cause. The proponents of the theory of regularity claim that the laws of nature are merely a description of reoccurring natural phenomena. Formulas like *(x) (Fx=>Gx)* only state the stable relationship of the co-occurrence of particular F and G phenomena. According to a radical interpretation of Hume's thesis, the conviction of the stability of the laws of nature, as well as the classical idea of cause and effect, are metaphysical anachronisms and should be definitively eradicated from the natural sciences.[16]

The necessitarian interpretation of the laws of nature emphasizes that they cannot be reduced to the regularities present in the physical processes. Given these regularities, scholars need to assume the existence of hidden relationships (which constitute the order of nature), even if in a given situation no empirical research confirms it. Identifying the laws of nature with observed regularities does not solve fundamental problems. On the one hand, regularity does not seem to be a sufficient condition for detecting a law of nature. Many regularities cannot be treated as the laws of nature.[17] On the other hand, regularity is not a necessary condition for a law of nature. There are probability laws which allow for local irregularities. Additionally, in certain processes regularities are only detectable on the macro scale.[18]

The above attempt at characterizing the specificity of the laws of nature gives rise to important questions. Which physical connections are denoted by the operator of implication "=>", if a law of nature is presented in the following formula: *(x) (Fx=>Gx)*? How can we interpret the relation of physical necessity between F and G? Maybe it would be easier to imagine the universe in the shape of a chaos devoid of necessary dependencies between individual elements, devoid of order and universal laws? Positivistically minded scientists consider the above problems to be lacking sense. Nonetheless, many philosophy-oriented physicists move beyond the level of empirically confirmed theories, and address questions outside the narrow scope of science. Why do the laws of nature exist at all? Could not all physical processes be unique? Why does a set of laws familiar to us become realized in the world? Are these laws absolute in the sense that no alternative laws should be able to become realized? Why is it possible to describe complex physical processes by means of simple mathematical formulas?[19]

Such questions do not have their proper answers in the natural sciences and lead toward philosophical or theological reflection. Discussions on the necessity of natural phenomena, the laws of nature and the order and purpose of the world belong to classical philosophical topics. The continuators of Hume's thought readily set deterministic interpretations of natural phenomena against teleological ones. The first kind of interpretation is supposed to belong to the domain of science, while the latter is a philosophical relic. Setting these interpretations against one another is now being often questioned in the philosophy of science. It is being stressed that physical determinism does not rule out ontological teleology but takes into account a different aspect of physical reality that requires other explanatory categories. Philosophical interpretations of the complementarity of deterministic and teleological categories calls for elaboration of an appropriate theory of the laws of nature, with this providing a more adequate picture of the specificity of diverse processes and enabling academics to reflect on God's immanence in the world.[20]

Leaving aside (at this stage of analysis) reflection on Paley's approach and theistic theories formulated on the basis of epistemic gaps, one can search for "traces" of God in the laws of nature and in the world's harmony made up by these laws. This thought was developed—in a very characteristic way—by Teilhard de Chardin who wrote about the action of the Creator as being revealed both in the laws of cosmic evolution, as well as in physical and biological processes. A different form of the same tradition is presented by process philosophy, in which God—being immanently present in the universe—was demonstrated by Whitehead to be the poet of the world. In the second half of the last century, the order of the cosmos had inspired many philosophy-oriented physicists to formulate new theistic interpretations of the laws of nature and the phenomenon of their mathematical description.

A considerable contribution to this area was provided at conferences organized by the Vatican Observatory and the *Center for Theology and the Natural Sciences* (Berkeley, CA). These two organizations launched a research program on divine action in the world which examined the current state of scientific knowledge, particularly evolutionary and molecular biology, quantum cosmology, physics, and neurophysiology. As a result of the five conferences, a series of studies was published, in which the participants proposed many innovative solutions to the problem of divine immanence in the world. The laws of nature are usually presented by these thinkers as the principal manifestations of the Creator in creation.[21]

Paul Davies criticizes those scholars which view the laws of nature in the categories of a cultural fabrication. In conferring an ontological status to the laws of physics, Davies stresses that they are discovered in a process of scientific development and receive a mathematical form of expression. The laws we are familiar with, even though they are not final and are an approximation of truth, still reflect the real order of nature. Nonetheless, the laws which underlie physical phenomena are not available to direct observation. These laws have to be meticulously "extracted" from nature by means of experimental procedures and mathematical theories. Discovering the laws of nature is only possible by persistent search since they are encoded in a specific way. Deciphering this code and disclosing the "message" hidden in nature is for many theists synonymous with finding the "traces" of God's action in the world. Nothing points to people as the authors of the cosmic code, even if they manage to break it. Organized research in this respect is the domain of science, thanks to which scholars can decipher the secrets of the universe, thus discovering the laws that govern it.[22]

Nature's creativity

Many contemporary scientists claim that the laws of physics are sufficient not only for explaining the increase of complexity in nature, but even for explaining the initial Big Bang. The genesis of the world as we know it might have taken place according to the laws of quantum physics which allow for the occurrence of such authentically spontaneous events.[23] More so, even though in its first stage the universe's state was very simple, and almost devoid of properties, the diversity of matter and energy had been emerging gradually as a consequence of long and complicated processes of self-organization. "The laws of physics – states the laureate of the 1995 Templeton Prize – not only permit a universe to originate spontaneously, but they encourage it to organize and complexify itself to the point where conscious beings emerge who can look back on the great cosmic drama and reflect on what it all means."[24]

The creativity of the world, as revealed in the emergence of novelties and the organization of physical systems, is a result of the operation of the laws of nature. For physicists who lean towards Platonic ideas, these laws have the status of ageless, unchanging truths which distinguish them from the local states of the universe that change in time. Such an interpretation contributed to the revival of the old philosophical-theological debate concerning the difficulty of combining the eternal with the temporal. The question of time was an important element of such discussions even in the days of St. Augustine. However, he did not see a problem in stating that the world—thanks to the act of creation—came into being together with time (and not in time). The last question to be solved was God's relation to time. What transpired to be useful in this regard was reflection on the specificity of the laws of nature. On the one hand, they govern the processes of the physical world which is subject to constant transformation, and on the other hand, these laws require being referred to the law-maker, who is identified by Christian theism with the eternal divine *Logos*.[25]

Even if we assume the possibility of a naturalistic interpretation of the specificity of physical processes, on the fundamental level there are still problems which cannot be explained scientifically no matter the progress made in science. In this context one of the weightiest questions is: Why do the laws of physics, governing the structures which emerged in the Planck era, in the course of time facilitate the genesis of life and consciousness that subsequently conditioned the origin of culture?[26] Raising this problem makes us aware that the creativity of nature is revealed at each stage of its development. Thus, it is insufficient to focus only on the genesis of the universe. The Big Bang is sometimes identified with the act of divine creation while nature never ceased to be creative. Hence, the "space" of God's creative presence does not have to be sought only in the primary stages of evolution. Nevertheless, God did not have to interfere with the course of the physical processes which led to the emergence of life and intelligent beings. The idea of God as one of the many active forces in nature that compete with one another weakens the value of theism. The image of God becomes much more intellectually appealing when we assume that His interactions with the world are not selective, but that He endows the laws of nature with power, as a consequence of which "complex order emerges from chaos, life from inanimate matter, and consciousness from life."[27]

The question concerning the specificity of the laws of nature which allow for biogenesis and anthropogenesis is so significant insofar as only a narrow set of physical parameters enables the emergence of an environment suitable for the development of life, including its very complex and human forms. Davies stresses that randomly selected laws would lead either to a cosmic disorder or a monotonous simplicity. The universe we inhabit is equipped with the laws of nature which assure a specific kind of harmony between creativity and discipline. The laws of nature introduce limitations to the possible scenarios of evolutionary development, thus preventing cosmic "anarchy." However, these limitations do not restrict physical systems to the extent that only changes of little consequence can take place; on the contrary, the aforementioned limitations stimulate matter and energy to generate authentic novelty. This phenomenon of nature was called the principle of maximum diversity[28] by Dyson, who was led to the conclusion that we live in the most interesting universe possible.[29]

The discovery of the specificity of the laws of nature which facilitate the emergence of life and consciousness is linked to the identification of a state called the edge of chaos.[30] It characterizes living organisms which, in the process of development, are marked with coherence and cooperation. Mathematical studies prove that designing such a state is possible only within a very specific form of laws. Even slight modification thereof would probably lead to chaos or even the complete disintegration of the universe. A minute change in the intensity of fundamental physical interactions would endanger the existence of such systems as the fixed order of stars and, as a consequence, life as we know it. The laws governing the universe we live in give the impression of being selected and attuned with such subtlety that some of the philosophy-oriented natural scientists support the teleological version of the anthropic principle. Irrespective of debate concerning this principle and the difficulties scholars have with proving that states like the edge of chaos are an outcome of design, in many aspects the world can be viewed as ingeniously arranged. One should not underestimate this fact and belittle the significance of the creative "abilities" of the laws of nature, or the intelligibility of nature, as well as deem this phenomenon a peculiar quirk of fate that can be dismissed with a tautological statement like: we live in a world which enabled our genesis. In avoiding indiscriminate versions of teleological reasoning, one can rationally speak of a certain form of blueprint inherent in nature, or at least of a more profound meaning of existence.[31]

Davies distances himself from statements that God designed the world in a "tailor-made" way so as to enable our arrival, as well as from suggestions that human existence is a random result of the activity of undirected forces of nature, or an incidental byproduct of evolutionary mechanisms. Undoubtedly, the physical and mental construction of *Homo sapiens* contains contingent traits of secondary importance. In this regard, the development of the universe could have led to the realization of a different scenario. However, when analyzing the specificity of the laws of nature it seems that—at some stage of cosmic history independent of the place and time of realization—they guarantee the emergence of life and consciousness (or at least render this highly probable[32]). It does not mean that biogenesis or anthropogenesis had taken place *contra naturam*, because they are the effect of the functioning of the laws of nature. Even though we are not situated in the center of cosmos, human existence is the integral component of the creative evolution of the universe. In this sense it can be stated that we have not come to being by coincidence,[33] and that we are a part of a broader plan.[34]

Even if one does not support all of Davies's theses, it needs to be noted that the constantly evolving universe is not subject to one fixed design in which all details would be "imposed in advance."[35] At various stages of nature's development, unpredictable bifurcations of systems occur. These bifurcations cannot be described in the language of algorithmic compressibility since they express the non-linearity of evolution. The future depends not only on "initial conditions" (for theists: the decision of the Divine Designer), but also on the many complex conditionings which emerge in the course of nature's development. Nonetheless, this is ultimately directed at "evolutionary consummation."[36]

God's presence in the world is explained in the categories of the possibilities and dispositions encoded by Him, with this being revealed in the functioning of the laws of nature. In this sphere one can apply the analogy to non-linear thermodynamics. The state to which the non-linear evolution of physical systems tends is called the attractor since it behaves as if it were attracting the individual levels of a system (*attrahere*). In mathematics, the attractor is the collection (or point) which in the course of a given process seems to be attracting the points situated in its surroundings. A significant component of this process is the dynamics of a local orientation towards a physical state which is not yet realized but makes the impression of attracting (at a given stage) the evolution of an entire system towards itself. Despite discontinuities present at various stages of evolution and the lack of clear-cut determination, which with a physical necessity would impose the occurrence of certain states, one can rationally formulate a hypothesis of the local directionality of evolutionary processes as a result of an attractor's activity.[37]

In comparing the action of God in the processes of evolution to the role of a cosmic attractor, it is stressed that He directs the processes of nature towards aims which have not yet been actualized, and includes these goals in His plans by means of attraction. Thus, in this context, one can speak of cosmic directing the world's evolution by God. Nevertheless, this is not an interpretation which is close to Paley's teleology, but much more sophisticated theistic description of the complicated functioning of nature. God, acting in nature, defines new directions of the development of processes which are not subject solely to deterministic conditionings. According to Życiński, such analogies help to overcome the anthropomorphisms present in teleological versions of evolutionism.[38]

The image of God acting as a cosmic attractor alludes to already-mentioned Teilhard de Chardin's idea of the *Omega* Point, towards which the processes of the world's development are directed. Teilhard de Chardin does not explain in great detail the mechanisms that determine such an orientation. In his view, evolution leads, most of all, to cosmic unification, with God being both the principle of this integration as well as the *Omega* Point. The originality of this concept is manifested in the way it moves beyond the classically posed question concerning the ontological principle of the world's development (the *Alpha* Point), while focusing on the eschatological aspects of nature's processes (the *Omega* Point). Theistic evolutionism structured in this way enables reconstruction of earlier periods of evolution, but also search for answers to questions about future of the world.[39]

Many theistic studies emphasizing the role of teleology in the world's development have long portrayed God as the designer of a unique cosmic program. Evolution had to attain a goal which God had intended for it, progressing in accordance with minutely defined deterministic laws of nature. Its functioning, as described by contemporary science, leads to different conclusions. Discontinuities and bifurcations randomly modify the scenario of development that was deemed the most likely at its previous stage. The character of stochastic processes does not allow precise orientation towards an unavoidable goal attained at a closely predictable stage of development.[40]

The theistic interpretation of the laws of nature leads to the conclusion that God does not fully determine the future, but rather that He leaves it open.[41] This does not downplay physical necessity but shows that the course of nature's processes exceeds the narrow limits of determinism that would allow a precise determination of the course of a given system in a simple way. The rational structure of the world "rooted" in the divine *Logos* reveals its specific nature both in the ballistic trajectory that is congruent with Newtonian laws and in the behavior of elementary particles, which is difficult to predict with precision.[42]

Thus, certain possibilities remain forever open in nature. Such indeterminacies are a consequence of indeterminism and the unpredictability of physical systems both on the quantum and the macroscopic levels. It is worth underlining in this context that even if someone claims that the laws of nature are ultimately deterministic, there is still "room" for the creativity of the universe to generate unpredictable novelty.[43] The characteristics of non-linear systems, or those which are far from equilibrium, make us realize that slight changes in initial or boundary conditions are essential for the functioning of a given system, and are able to radically change its future behavior or the manner of its organization. Through the exchange of energy, certain factors can cause the modification of initial or boundary conditions, and even affect the genesis of a new system which in other circumstances would never have emerged.[44]

Alston points out that, in circles of academics aware of the significance of quantum theory for the comprehension of the world's functioning, a crucial change has taken place in the way in which the Creator's activity in creation has been interpreted. In the light of (narrowly understood) deterministic interpretations of physical phenomena, even God (acting through the laws of nature) cannot change the state of someone's consciousness or stop the development of a disease. An alternative to this was to suggest the suspension of the natural causes' operation, which leads to an interventionist model of the Creator–creation interaction. Such problems do not appear when we take into account the character of quantum phenomena. The basic laws of quantum mechanics enable us to estimate the probability of the occurrence (under given circumstances) of a particular outcome of an event. A very unlikely state of a system can be realized without violating the statistical laws of nature. This gives some theists an opportunity to explain God's action.[45]

An additional problem to be solved is the transition from the subatomic to the macroscopic level. In this context, Alston puts forward the hypothesis that divine action in the microscopic world can cause effects on the level of the macro-world. Discoveries in the domain of quantum mechanics provided many new opportunities for describing the Creator's interaction with creation. It can be assumed that God designed the universe in such a way as to be able to act according to statistical laws, thus remaining the efficient cause of events. However, this need not lead to the conclusion that quantum mechanics is a necessary point of reference for defending the thesis of the compatibility of God's action with the laws of nature. We also need to consider the fact that the laws of nature known to us operate in a specific way in systems that are not affected by any external stimuli apart from the ones we include in the description of the character of phenomena. Nevertheless, it cannot be entirely ruled out that certain factors are hidden from earthly observers. None of the laws known to us accounts for absolutely all of the possible causes of the course of physical phenomena.[46]

The laws of nature are for many theists the basic *medium* for God's action in the world, thus expressing—in an imperfect manner—His nature.[47] In this way, divine goals are achieved not despite but through indeterminacies which are part of the world's working. God is not understood as one who acts parallel to the laws of nature but through them and hence both through necessity and randomness. The latter characterizes not only the functioning of inanimate beings, but also of biotic systems. This is why, according to Edwards, each adaptation or mutation can be treated as an expression of the divine art of creation.[48]

Stoeger proposes a distinction between scientifically-viewed regularities or relationships that exist in nature and the overall structure of the laws of nature which the earthly observer has no access to. The theories and formalism describing individual laws leave the relationships organizing the world at the elementary level outside our cognition. Such relationships would serve as a link between the personal and the impersonal world. A substitute for such cognition is the discerning of the important elements of physical indeterminacy and the susceptibility thereof to human activity.[49]

Two types of laws of nature are also postulated by Polkinghorne, who formulates theses akin to Stoeger's approach. Taking into account the creative character of the world's development and the phenomenon of its relative order, one needs to notice the existence of comprehensive and elementary laws of nature. Their mutual interaction generates the rich diversity of the world. The character of this interaction can be interpreted by reference to so-called top-down emergence. The increasing complexity of a given system creates an environment of relations in which authentic novelties appear. It remains to clarify how and why complexity leads to the emergence of new entities, and not to their duplication on the same level of a given structure.[50]

The law of emergence embraces both processes characterized by physical continuity and the ontological "leap."[51] This does not mean that there is a certain magical ingredient of the world without which life or consciousness could not emerge from matter. However, it is worth noticing that cognitively interesting processes take place at critical stages of nature's development. An adequate approach to the specificity of qualitative changes calls for moving beyond the confines of conceptual reductionism.[52]

The idea of ontological emergence puts emphasis on the fact that in the description of certain phenomena, one cannot refer solely to constituent components because their behavior is fundamentally affected by the entirety of a given system. Without omitting the classically-understood emergence of novelty at certain stages of a system's development (for example, when we assume that the synthesis of chemical ingredients in proper proportions brings an expected and recurrent effect),[53] we can regard emergence as a bi-directional process. Phenomena of a higher order should be associated with phenomena of a lower order and vice versa. Thus, we aim not only at acknowledging the autonomy of individual strata, but also at noticing their mutual interaction.[54]

God is hardly a watchmaker

While maintaining a distance from all forms of vitalism, Polkinghorne defines his standpoint as contextualism. Its main idea is to notice that the behavior of the component parts of a given system is dependent on the nature of the whole they constitute. Obviously, there are processes which seem to be mechanical and are entirely conceivable by reference to the traits of their elementary components. However, this does not imply that the richness of nature is exhausted in the most familiar processes and laws. Even more, as a result of scientific advancement, and while interpreting the world's functioning, scholars have to—more and more often—refer to the concept of top-down emergence. Recalling a well-known metaphor coined by K. Popper, we can state that there are more clouds in nature than clocks.[55]

Systems whose behavior can be described in terms of classical mechanics seem to belong to a minority in nature. Slight initial disorder results in relatively small changes in the behavior of such systems, hence they are to the great extent predictable and "tame." But most of the physical world does not function like this. It is often the case that a given system (even at a relatively low stage of complexity) is extremely susceptible to slight changes in its environment.[56] Such systems manifest unpredictability, though not completely. The character of these systems cannot be fully captured by the term "chaos theory." There is a cognitively interesting trait of chaos that lies within Newtonian mechanics: it is characterized by "apparently random behavior arising from solutions to deterministic equations."[57]

Chaotic systems are unpredictable by their very essence. In the long-term perspective one cannot predict the behavior of chaotic systems because they are deeply sensitive to changes in their surroundings. The problem is whether this concerns only epistemological statements. Some philosophy-oriented natural scientists suggest moving beyond stating that human cognition has limited possibilities and encourage a bold formulation of hypotheses which are adequate for the contemporary scientific worldview. In this way, the borders of classical physics become an inspiration to search for a new physics. Within it, the unpredictability of processes is treated as an ontological openness.[58] The future is not a repetition of the past, but an authentic becoming.[59]

In the above view the realization of future events should be compared to an outcome of a game of chance. There are deterministic principles that result in the given course of a system, but they are not entirely reduced to the familiar laws of physics which regulate only some ways in which events can proceed. Hence, a space opens up for original presentations of causality which are not adequately depicted within the framework of currently known physical theories. What also emerges is the possibility of discerning "room" for the operation of holistic organizing principles, human intentionality, and God's interaction with the world. These organizing principles can result in the emergence of as yet unrealized possibilities.[60]

Deterministic chaos expresses the existence of subtle and flexible traits in the physical world, the laws of which have not yet been ultimately discovered. The asymptotic approximation of these expected laws are the ones that we are currently familiar with. In this context, one can be tempted to make use of the instruments of quantum mechanics to explain the functioning of systems open to the future. Despite the appeal of such a solution, Polkinghorne distances himself from it by arguing that quantum mechanics has got various interpretations and unresolved problems. Particularly unclear is the explanation of the mutual interactions which occur between the microscopic and macroscopic worlds.[61] Furthermore, something that we experience as "everyday openness should not have to depend on goings-on in the microworld."[62]

The specific character of the complicated network of the laws of nature provides grounds for many concepts of divine action. Some scholars go as far as to claim that interpretation of the laws of nature entails a particular way of presenting the Creator–creation interaction.[63] This takes place thanks to the openness of the structures and processes the autonomy of which is not suspended or annihilated by God. In the act of creation, the world was endowed with the autonomy of existence and development.[64] Only in a universe characterized by authentic openness to the future can beings endowed with freedom emerge. It remains interpretatively problematic to demonstrate the equilibrium between the sphere of God's activity and the space of freedom left by Him in a self-creating world, both on the level of emergent structures, as well as on man's conscious creativity. This problem recalls theological difficulties in clarifying the relationship between grace and nature.[65]

The regularity of nature's processes reflects the "credibility" of God, whose action is rational and creative. The Creator–creation interaction takes place within the framework of processes open to the future. This can be associated with the concept of God filling the gaps present in nature. However, this has nothing to do with the discredited view of a "deity being an antidote" to the deficiencies of the naturalistic interpretation of the world. The hypothesis of God was becoming unnecessary with academic advancement, particularly when more and more questions were receiving scientific answers. New approaches emphasize, however, that the Creator remains in relation to the entirety of creation and not merely its parts. More so, if one understands "gaps" as a space for the possibilities that exist in the ontic structure of the world, then contemporary science confirms that they remain an integral component of nature. In acknowledging the actual operation of top-down causality, we have to assume the existence of intrinsic "gaps" ("envelopes of possibilities") that are revealed in the bottom-up account of nature.[66]

Undertaking reflection on divine action from the perspective of the outcomes of scientific research, one needs to refrain from altogether blurring the boundary between God's activity and the functioning of physical processes. As I have already stressed, God cannot be treated as one of the causes that operate in the world.[67] Otherwise, instead of being the personal Creator, God would have the face of a peculiar Demiurge, or an unspecified invisible efficient cause that operates within physical events. In striving to underline the specificity of divine action, Polkinghorne writes that its character "is not energetic but informational," embracing the entirety of nature and its encoded tendency to generate novelty. The world created by God is governed by regular laws that provide a "sense of cosmic order."[68]

It is usually claimed that theistic statements formulated alongside the analysis of the laws of nature are easier to maintain within their Platonic interpretation. This accentuates that the laws of nature exist independently of their particular exemplification in the form of relations or regularities of phenomena revealed in the world's functioning.

A detailed description of these laws is only a reflection and an approximation of a reality which is ontically independent from the physical world, and prior to it. Nevertheless, it also transpires that theists who are critical of Platonism see no problem in emphasizing that God acts through the laws of nature.

Stoeger does not detect any philosophical-scientific arguments to claim that the laws of nature have an existence independent of their specific manifestations in the world. According to this American scientist, the (detected by the human mind) regularities and relations which occur in the world on all of its various levels and the models thereof constructed with the language of mathematics are of a descriptive value and not a prescriptive one. Thus, it is difficult to suggest that there is a more elementary level of reality which enforces the occurrence of phenomena in a way observable in the physical world. Nonetheless, irrespective of the philosophical declarations formulated in this sphere, Stoeger presents a program of the Creator-creation interaction from the perspective of the uniqueness of a network of laws that are characteristic of the world we live in. In this approach, God acts through the laws which an earthly observer comes to know only partially. Even more, contrary to the capabilities of man, the regularities and relations which occur in the world are "experienced" by God as they are in their entirety, "from the inside."[69]

The analyses conducted in this section of the book put stress on the autonomy of the laws of nature, as well as on the fact of these laws being a manifestation of God's presence in the world. Assuming that the laws of nature are the work of the divine lawmaker, one needs to face questions concerning evil and suffering. On the other hand, highlighting the Creator's immanence in creation enables one to avoid the conclusion that God remains distant from the fate of man and the world. This problem poses a particular challenge for theists who strongly emphasize the absolute being's transcendence in relation to contingent beings.

Evil

Variety of standpoints

Reflecting on the question of divine action in the world, one cannot leave out the problem of evil, both natural and moral. What is even more, Stump is of the opinion that, in the context of striving to provide an answer to the "*unde malum?*" question, a sharp division between moral evil and natural evil distracts our attention from the crux of the matter – the overarching role of suffering. Natural evil would not give rise to any essential doubts in the sphere of religious faith if there were no beings suffering as a result of earthquakes, floods, hurricanes, etc. It is the experience of suffering, not its source in the domain of nature, that generates the question: why does God permit evil to exist?

Thus, the distinction between moral evil and natural evil is not of the greatest importance and oftentimes distracts from the point. Misunderstandings also arise when suffering is identified with pain. After all, it needs to be stressed that pain is neither a necessary, nor a sufficient condition of suffering. The acuteness of suffering does not have to "go hand in hand" with an intensification of pain. On the one hand, there are known cases of painless neurological syndromes that disable a person's autonomous functioning and can even lead to their general unhappiness. On the other hand, a lover of marathons does not think of long-distance running (connected *ipso facto* with pain) in the category of suffering, but rather satisfaction, or even joy.

It is difficult to show decisive correlation between suffering and evil. Even while lacking such forms of suffering as psychic dilemmas or pangs of conscience, people who do great evil to their fellow human beings are usually treated as if their own life also suffered as a consequence thereof. It seems to be a widespread viewpoint that no one would swap their life stories with a person defined as a moral monster, even if they appeared to be someone satisfied with themselves. Bearing in mind such nuances of the discussed problem, in my subsequent analyses I focus on the question of broadly-understood evil, making use of such terms as suffering, pain, moral evil, and sometimes even sin.[70]

Irrespective of the elaborate distinctions present in topic-related studies, what should be identified is the fact that contemporary ways of interpreting the functioning of the physical world to a great extent affect the possible solutions which are centered around answering the fundamental question of theodicy with this *ex definitione* addressing the problem: *Si Deus est, unde malum?* Is it possible (and if so, then how) to reconcile the conviction of the Creator's goodness with the experience of the ontic and existential contamination of creation?[71] The fact that contemporary science discloses previously unknown aspects of the ways of the workings of the laws of nature can paradoxically facilitate the defending of the idea of the providence of God as continuing to care for human beings and for the world.

In adopting an entirely deterministic concept of the functioning of nature, a theist would have to maintain that the manifestation of divine action is, in fact, found in every single event, even those situated at the very end of a long causal chain. An extreme variant of such an approach leads to the conclusion that God not only permits but also creates the evil that is present in the world. Such consequences do not emerge when we adopt structural indeterminism as revealed in the course of nature's development. However, even if we assume this interpretative perspective, dilemmas concerning divine providence appear. Can a perfectly good and omnipotent Creator leave so much to chance? Are not the suffering and losses that result from the course of evolutionary history too big a price to pay for the freedom of creation?[72]

Apart from the straightforward context of the natural sciences, reflection on the problem of evil undertaken on the grounds of analytic philosophy of religion has also been unfolding in two essential spheres in the last several decades. The first sphere includes the logical argument from evil against the existence of God and comes down to an attempt at proving or undermining the following thesis: if evil exists, God does not.[73] The leading representatives of this philosophical debate, Pike and Plantinga, have effectively pointed to the fact that God might have had a logically necessary reason to permit evil.[74] As a result, in the 1990s the topic of on-going discussion changed and academics put at the center of concern the evidential (or probabilistic) argument in its many varieties. This was based on the following assumption: the quantity (or quality) of evil present in the world testifies against the authenticity of theism, thus rendering the hypothesis of God's existence unlikely.[75]

This transformation was also a consequence of other premises. In reaction to arguments concerning the logical possibility of reconciling evil with the existence of God, atheists started to emphasize that it is more important to answer the question of whether, in the face of evil, God's existence is at all probable. Even more, in the context of the theistic hypothesis of the greater good, in demonstrating that God might have had a morally sufficient reason to permit evil, with this even sometimes presented as a condition necessary for the existence of goodness,[76] some manifestations of evil were highlighted which do not seem to result in any goodness whatsoever. As claimed by Rowe, a lot points to the fact that there are such cases of evil in the world which God could have eliminated from creation without losing the greater good or permitting an equally nonsensical, or even worse, kind of evil. Such instances of evil can be presented which seem to be completely pointless. Thus, there is no adequate good that might account for this kind of evil.[77]

A modified version of the probabilistic argument was presented by Paul Draper. According to him, the essence of the problem is not the fact that theism is improbable in the face of evil, but that it provides a much worse explanation of the extent of the evil that exists in the world, as well as its proportion to goodness. This is more easily comprehensible when we assume that God does not exist or when we at least accept that He is indifferent to our suffering.[78]

Even in the circle of theists who have a more traditional attitude and concentrate most of all on stressing the lasting significance of reflection on God's nature, in posing a question concerning evil (especially the authentic one, the occurrence of which renders the world axiologically worse), they more clearly discern that there are essential problems with the classical presentation of divine attributes. After all, it may seem that accepting the simplicity of God leads to the conclusion that He wants evil and causes it Himself. If God is eternal and immutable, His omniscience is also of such a character. As a consequence, omniscience is necessary, that is, an event known to God has to happen. Otherwise, God's knowledge would have to be modified, which is impossible if we assume His immutability. If God is indeed simple, the attributes of omniscience, will, and power are identical (if omniscience is necessary, divine will and omnipotence are also necessary). Since God knows that an event is going to take place, it will necessarily happen (God's knowledge of this event is necessary). If God wants a given event to take place, it will necessarily occur. In other words: if an event happens, it necessarily happens because of a necessity stemming from God.[79]

The above conclusion is difficult to accept for the representatives of Christian theism, even though some of them claim that its classical form leads to such consequences. As part of an attempt at solving this problem, different propositions are put forward: Aristotelian, Spinozian, and Thomistic. The first and the second of these propositions, albeit relieving God of the responsibility for evil, did not produce the desired effects, and moved beyond the theistic paradigm. The Aristotelian concept is based on the assumption that God is not the Creator of the world and that there is no knowledge about Him. The predominant component of the theory elaborated by Baruch Spinoza is necessitarianism: the world stems from God in a necessary way. According to Spinoza, moral categories have no sense in relation to God as they are not also applied to nature.[80]

Among the contemporary approaches which draw on the Thomistic tradition, it is worth recalling the standpoint taken by Eleonore Stump in which all forms of human suffering are treated as conditional (instrumental) goodness. God is the reason behind all good. It is also God who causes, or coordinates, the events which result in things that we perceive as the evil affecting us. Ultimately, however, all forms of pain sustained by us are oriented toward goodness. After all, suffering cleanses us of sin, teaches us humility, and prompts us to love God. True happiness is based on the contemplation of God and not being satisfied with earthly life. The loss of such merits as health, wealth, or fame does not imply unhappiness. In this context, contemporary Thomists move even further in their argumentation: since human nature is so defective that it does not crave God (and is not even able to extricate such a craving from itself), pain is a form of peculiar medication.[81] This is why Stump calls suffering a particular kind of chemotherapy, aimed at fighting the cancer of the soul. Also, evil caused by humans can have healing properties: it cures pride and restores the love of God.[82]

It was St. Thomas Aquinas who had strongly stressed the liberating nature of pain that should be patiently borne on account of it coming from God and being oriented towards goodness. Suffering is not an absolute evil but rather an instrumental good that leads to fulfillment. Aquinas would add that, pursuant to the Christian message, God is not indifferent to the experience of misery but actively partakes in human unhappiness. Despite the many ways of providing insightful argumentation, such an approach is frequently assessed as unsatisfactory intellectually and—all the more so—emotionally (sometimes even being judged as morally repulsive). To confirm the significance of such reactions certain reasons can be formulated.

On the one hand, Aquinas's theodicy seems to be an apologia for suffering (an apogee of Dolorism), remaining—despite attempts at its justification derived from Christian revelation—a manifestation of indifference to evil. One can rationally ask: why fight with evil or attempt to eliminate pain if these both have a positive value? Can human suffering or even social injustice be easily justified by reference to the higher goals set by God? The response to such questions, however, should take into account the fact that only the suffering caused by God can be of a healing quality, whereas we do not know which forms of suffering have such value. Thus, we cannot justify our inactivity in the face of suffering, least of all our inflicting of suffering on our fellows human beings. In itself, suffering is bad, so we should not inflict it on ourselves in the name of an ill-understood ascesis or our own ambition. Pain becomes good only when it attends leads to our eternal happiness.[83]

On the other hand, it seems to be inhumane to portray earthly existence as a road through misery that leads to the longed-for paradise. Is not the "earthly purgatory" too high a price to pay for the eternal reward? Does not the amount of suffering surpass the measure rationally accountable for happiness? In order to solve such problems, Aquinas strongly accentuates theological truths on divine action in human life. God's active presence is based on providing strength and evoking our conviction of God accompanying us in trying times. It is easier to endure pain when we have the awareness of not being alone in our suffering.[84] In appreciating these arguments, it needs to be admitted, however, that on the level of philosophical explanation they are not sufficient for eliminating existential dilemmas which—in their extreme form—become a basis for rejecting God. An unquestionable asset of Aquinas's view on evil is its coherence with the metaphysics of divine simplicity. All the same, for a comprehensive understanding of this concept it is indispensable that we possess religious faith.[85]

Arguments akin to the ones formulated above are also put forward by Hugh McCann. According to him, God wants suffering to exist but also participates in it. There are no events in the world that would evade divine control or providence. The occurrence of evil, including moral evil, is a condition necessary for man to obtain authentic moral subjectivity and eternal happiness. Through the experience of evil and suffering, we can feel the lack of God and the futility of earthly existence. Weakness enables us to comprehend what life without God and against God is. Extreme manifestations of human evil allow us to see the value of believing in God, as well as evoke the desire to return to Him. In this way, moral evil becomes an important instrumental good, and conditions the ultimate victory over evil.[86]

An essential remaining problem for classical theism is the question of finding a balance between the responsibility of God and human beings for evil, especially moral evil. If God wants us (for the sake of the greater good) to sin and suffer, who bears responsibility for evil?[87] A Thomist will usually respond that while God indeed permits me to fail morally, ultimately it is I who commit concrete evil deeds. Hence, the freedom of our actions is founded on the lack of any external causality that would be external to our free will and that would fully determine our acts. No circumstances external to the decision-making agent (including the laws of nature) predetermine us or make us do evil. Even our convictions and motivations—albeit provoking us to make a specific decision—do not ultimately prejudge our actions. What is characteristic of such an approach is the emphasis put on the fact that God's will does not operate in relation to human will as an external factor. God has the possibility of affecting our choices "from the inside" as a creative cause of the existence of freedom and the force sustaining its activity. Such cooperation between God and ourselves does not violate human freedom understood in a libertarian way and is far from causal determinism and causal necessity.[88]

Being embedded in Thomistic thought, McCann's theodicy has a specificity of its own. It expresses the belief that God wants our suffering, which is not an aim in itself, and that suffering has the character of an instrumental good. In contrast to Stump, McCann identifies the ultimate good not so much with happiness as with victory over evil. Conquering evil is the essential goal of the creation. God wants evil to occur, including moral evil, because he desires us to know that it is the enemy of creation and that He made His contribution in vanquishing it. Depending on the type of evil, overcoming it may take different forms. In the case of personal suffering, success is found in being brave and patient. When others suffer, our contribution to victory is based on actively helping our fellow creatures. Suffering is valuable even when it destroys the sufferer (or when it is entirely unnoticed) because it exposes us to moral and religious trials. The world is seen here as a battle between good and evil, and the extent of the latter is supposed to make us realize what life becomes when it is devoid of God who gives us hope for the final victory. Assuming that God is in control of absolutely everything, we can be certain of the ultimate victory over evil.[89]

Łukasiewicz notices that the advantage of McCann's standpoint is depriving the critics of theism of one of their essential arguments. The question "why had the omnipotent God not created a world in which certain important goods could be attained without the presence of evil?" becomes nonsensical. After all, the good that is meant here is the triumph over evil and one can only conquer an opponent who exists. To eliminate evil in the very act of creation would entail a peculiar escape from the battlefield. Nonetheless, the fundamental problem of this approach is the fate of people destined for damnation— that is to say, the greatest (eternal) evil and suffering. It comes as only partial justification to state that the benevolent God does not take away the right to eternal existence even from those who reject Him and thus sentence themselves to the lack of participation in vanquishing evil.[90]

Is Molinism a good solution?

The issue of the presence of evil in the world sometimes appears to be an insurmountable impediment in the way of formulating a coherent concept of the Creator's influence on creation. As a result, within Christian skepticism it is assumed that in the face of the mystery of evil and suffering, we need to put stress on the fundamental difficulty of knowing the nature of God, or even do as much as abandon the introduction of any affirmative statements in this regard. An attempt at overcoming this impasse comes with contemporary alternatives to classical theism, especially open theism and Molinism. The proponents of both viewpoints decidedly "separate" God from evil. Open theism accentuates that evil acts are committed by free persons whose decisions and deeds are not previously known to God. Irrespective of the differences present in many detailed aspects of open theism, its propagators refute the idea of divine immutability and impassibility. Nonetheless, adopting an image of God who is susceptible to suffering does not provide a definitive solution to the problem of evil in the world.[91]

Molinists deliberate on evil in the context of counterfactual modalities of freedom and creation's autonomy in relation to the Creator. The first of the two fundamental pillars of Molinism is the traditional doctrine of providence. God takes care of the world in such a way as to ensure that all events, including the consequences of human decisions, serve the realization of creation's ultimate goal of leading man to reunion with the Creator. The principal attributes of God are omnipotence (He has the power to control reality because He can create everything, actualize any non-contradictory state of affairs) and omniscience (He has full knowledge of the past, present, and future states of affairs). Molinists tried to reconcile the reign of the Creator understood in this way with the conviction of the authentic freedom of creatures including human beings.[92]

The second founding stone of Molinism is a libertarianism which stresses that man's freedom rules out his actions being predetermined by any external factor. Such an idea of free will is supposed to guarantee an agent's responsibility for actions, as well as the crucial theological truth concerning sin, justification, and final judgment. It seems that the postulate of the existence of a free God who is undetermined in His actions is more reconcilable with libertarianism than compatibilism. On the grounds of the latter view, God would appear as determined by an external cause or His own nature, perhaps rendering all His acts necessary. This would also have to include the act of creation and would be contrary to the views held by many theists.[93]

The idea of God's complete control over the world is difficult to accept while simultaneous stress is put on the autonomy of creation. As a result, Molinists introduce, as previously mentioned, a non-classical concept of divine foreknowledge which is aimed at a coherent presentation of providence and libertarianism. Thanks to middle knowledge (*scientia media*) the Creator can also have control over events caused by free (in the libertarian sense) agents. According to de Molina, the traditional division of truths into necessary (i.e., independent of God's will) and contingent (i.e., dependent on His will) does not exhaust the scope of divine knowledge. After all, there is a middle kind of knowledge which covers contingent truths (logically unnecessary) that are at the same time independent of God's will (their logical value is antecedent to all of God's action).[94]

The sphere of middle knowledge most importantly covers all our free decisions that we might make in all possible situations. *Scientia media* refers both to the events that will take place in the actual world as well as counterfactual situations, i.e. all manifestations (undetermined by the Creator) of the freedom of creatures in all possible worlds. Statements appropriate for middle knowledge have a conditional structure and provide information on what an agent who is free to act will do in any possible situation. Thus, these are hypothetical statements (conditionals) that are supposed to solve the problem of providence. Knowing that in a specific situation we are going to behave in a particular way, God can indirectly lead someone to the occurrence of a given state of affairs. It is enough for God to actualize (create) suitable conditions; the rest will be done by an agent in an entirely free way. In this way, the Creator can govern creation without violating human freedom.[95]

God does not influence the logical value of counterfactual statements. Hence, God can bring only some possible worlds into existence. Uncreatable worlds are those which would contain situations that oppose the choices of free human beings. Thus, the act of creation is not based on the choice of the best possible world, but on the actualization of the best creatable one.[96] The idea of Leibniz, regarded by Plantinga as a mistake, is sustainable only with a simultaneous rejection of compatibilism. If, however, among the possible worlds there had been those in which humans were authentically free, then there had been worlds uncreatable for God. The divine act of creation remains limited to the scope of logical possibilities and man's freedom.[97]

God had no possibility to create the best possible world since it was not creatable. If the conditionals of man's morally wrong choices are independent of God's will, He is not responsible for them. It is free beings who are held responsible for their behavior. Plantinga claims that in each of the creatable worlds which contain free agents at least once somebody will choose evil. In this context, worlds without moral evil are uncreatable, though possible. Plantinga gives this trait of creatable worlds the name of *transworld depravity*.[98]

If someone experiences transworld depravity, then God is not able to create a world in which this person would always choose goodness. According to Plantinga, if this is possible in relation to one person, it is also possible in relation to all free agents. After all, it is not certain whether there are people who, if created by God, would never commit evil deeds. Such a view of the issue leads to stating that God is not able to create a world with free beings and, at the same time, devoid of all evil.[99]

At various stages of history, Molinism was an object of controversy and was sometimes the target of many intellectual assaults. Making use of the categories of Christian revelation, and soon after de Molina's most important publications had been issued, Thomists accused him of subordinating God's grace to man's will.[100] It was underlined that divine knowledge and action have to precede human deeds, as salvation is an act of God, not human choice. Thus, it seemed that undermining the achievements of Molinism was based on theological premises. In fact Thomists questioned the idea of middle knowledge which had become the object of criticism on the grounds of analytic philosophy. Twentieth-century analytic philosophy discussed the question of the logical possibility of this kind of knowledge. However, analytic philosophers have been doing this, contrary to classical Thomism, from libertarian positions. The crucial problem seemed to be connected with counterfactual statements that lack logical value. As contingent, such statements are neither true nor false. The logical value of conditionals is not determined by any logical necessity or by God. *Ex definitione*, middle knowledge remains independent of God's will and primary to all of His acts. If it was God who established the value of counterfactual statements, all human choices would be predetermined by Him. Theological fatalism would lead to the most controversial conclusion, that moral evil is a consequence of the divine order, not a result of the activity of free beings.[101]

Problems with the status of middle knowledge, meticulously analyzed by contemporary critics of Molinism,[102] have crucial consequences for the question of evil and free will theodicy. If conditionals lack logical value, the theistic adherents of libertarianism have two main alternatives. Open theism absolutely rejects the concept of God's foreknowledge since He cannot know our choices before they are realized. The Creator can at most predict with a high degree of probability what a given agent will do, but He cannot have definitive knowledge thereof since the counterfactual statement that is appropriate to a certain action lacks logical value before the action is realized. Such an approach entails the necessity of renouncing the traditional understanding of providence. In endowing us with freedom, God would have to risk the history of the world slipping out of His control. In holding fast to the idea of the Creator's effective care of creation, one would have to suggest that, since God cannot plan the history of the world "in advance," He intervenes in the course of history on an ongoing basis, for the sake of eventually attaining His intended goals.[103]

An alternative solution for theistic libertarians would be to reject the concept of God's existence in time and to adopt an atemporal approach in accordance with which God exists outside of time and remains in the same relation to the past, present, and future. Nonetheless, this does not eliminate the problem of providence. If man's actions are antecedent (in a logical order as different from a temporal one) to God's knowledge, He is passive towards our behavior. If man's action is explanationally subsequent to God's decisions, atemporalism would be combined with a theological fatalism that withdraws real freedom from creatures.[104] With a critical attitude towards the idea of middle knowledge, theists have to weaken the notion of providence or abandon libertarianism. Hence, either we assume that God does not have anticipative control over evil in the world or we cannot refer to free will theodicy.[105]

Even if we ignore the controversies concerning the logical value of conditionals, Molinism does not solve the problem of moral evil. If God possesses *scientia media*, He also knows that—when He actualizes a given situation—we will behave in a specific manner: we will choose either good or evil. Thus, the Creator knows that in a given situation the agent will sin. When we assume that God could place people in a situation in which they will succumb to temptation, or in a reality that will prejudge a morally good action, then fundamental uncertainties arise. Why doesn't God only place people in circumstances that lead to good deeds? When confronted with situations that God knows will generate evil, do we take moral responsibility for our sins?[106]

In response to the first question, Plantinga suggests the previously mentioned concept of transworld depravity. If God possesses middle knowledge, we cannot exclude that from among all possibilities available to Him there is not one in which an arbitrary agent might not sin even once. The second difficulty refers to the problem of moral luck[107] since the moral outcome of a situation often does not depend on us but rather on which particular situation we may find ourselves in. Assuming that in given circumstances we would not assist a dying person (because, for instance, we dread the sight of blood), it remains an open question whether we can speak of any guilt when we are not forced to face a choice of this particular kind, and thus, we have no possibility of doing evil. This problem may appear easily solved but, according to Molinism, the fact of whether we are placed in a certain situation or not does not depend on us, but on God.[108] If we had a choice which was given by God to us, we would definitely not want to be placed in a situation involving a moral trial. On the other hand, God might have spared us such extreme experiences. Why then, in having middle knowledge, does He create for some people circumstances that lead them to moral downfall, and does not do this to others? Moreover, for people convinced of the consequences of our deeds for eternal life, moral luck becomes transformed into religious doom. Should a stroke of luck decide our eternal fate, our salvation or damnation?[109]

The doubts enhanced by questions posed in the following manner demonstrate that, despite a declarative rejection of predestination, Molinism has to face the charge of propagating this doctrine. Does God, in actualizing a given situation which He knows will lead the subject of action to the committing of a great evil, predetermine people's eternal damnation? In responding to such an accusation, one might state that divine judgment acknowledges the fact that the history of someone's life (contrary to the existence of other people) is filled with many very difficult moral choices. Does this mean, however, that the sins of someone disadvantaged by fate are ultimately of a smaller gravity than the same acts of evil committed by a person whose path is "strewn with roses"? Would we give a positive answer if we referred to a crime committed with exceptional cruelty by someone who had a "tough life"? It seems that, irrespective of whether we consider the circumstances of a given person's life in the assessment of such a crime, it is the crime that should be of principal significance for divine evaluation. Thus, none of the proposed solutions to the problem fully meet the expectations expressed by Molinists.[110]

Hence, in striving to solve the enigma of evil, Molinists cannot draw only on the category of free will, and stress that people bear direct responsibility for committed evil. Theistic libertarianism aims at "releasing God of responsibility" in this area. However, this goal is attained neither by the Molinist concept of middle knowledge nor by the proposed presentation of providence. The existence of conditional modes causes each evil deed, even though committed by free agents, to be approved of in the divine act of creation. Thus, in justifying evil in the world, one needs to look for additional reasons, which take two essential forms: an axiological one and a functional one. On the one hand, Molinists might claim that the act of free choice is precious to such an extent (at least as an indispensable component of a whole) that its worth is higher than that of a committed evil (understood as the result of a decision). But such an interpretation would not suffice to persuade a mother whose child has been murdered by a plain degenerate. In an alternate option, one might maintain that ultimately sins play a positive role in divine plans and contribute to man's salvation. In religious language this is called blessed guilt. The problem is, however, that doing evil is understood in the principal sense as the cause of our withdrawal from God.[111]

The problem of responsibility for evil also concerns the question of preventing evil's occurrence. After all, if God possesses middle knowledge, He can prevent evil from happening by not actualizing situations connected with those conditionals which cover moral evil. Thus, the omnipotent and omniscient God might control morality in the world not only by means of directing human decisions (which is contrary to libertarianism), but also by actualizing (or refraining from actualizing) an event appropriate for a given counterfactual statement. Why does God fail to do this? The lack of fully satisfactory answers to this question, as well as the objections presented above, demonstrate that even though Molinism is being developed to this very day by Plantinga and many other renowned theists,[112] this position does not succeed in entirely solving the problem of evil, even if we assume a favorable view of the concept of *scientia media*.[113]

The prospect of uniting creation with God

Despite a certain impasse, the "*unde malum?*" question currently remains an important element of reflection influenced by various philosophical schools. The leading exponents of the essential nuances of this issue as viewed from a theistic perspective are Swinburne, Hick, and van Inwagen. The standpoint of the first is founded on defending free will comprehended indeterministically, but this appears different from the ideas characteristic of Molinism. According to Swinburne, Christian theism should not neglect the fact that for creation the most significant good is not so much a passing worth of some kind but becoming united with the Creator. In many leading currents of the philosophy of God it is claimed that the conditions of the physical world are an environment which enables creation to shape and improve itself, whereas the ultimate goal of creation is perceived to be attaining the fullness of existence.[114] The central reference point of the conducted analyses is man, but his relationship with God regards all of creation and it is from this relationship that the goodness of all created beings stems.[115]

The logic of Swinburne's reasoning takes into account reference to the balance between good and evil "from the divine point of view." The infinitely good God can allow for certain evils to occur on four conditions. The first condition is that there authentically exists a kind of good which is logically impossible for God to have created in any otherwise morally acceptable way different from permitting a given evil to occur. For instance, it is not logically possible for God to have created people with a libertarian kind of freedom, allowing us to choose between good and evil despite all of the efficient causes which we are subject to, and to simultaneously induce us to choose only goodness. It seems logically impossible for God to give us such a good as the opportunity to make free choices without simultaneously permitting evil in the shape of the possibility of making a wrong choice, should we want to make it. The second condition is the fact that God really creates good adequate to a given situation. If God creates a world in which there is pain, He also has to endow us with free will for us to be able to really decide whether we want to courageously accept it, or not. Third, we assume that God has the moral right to permit the existence of evil in specific circumstances. Finally, it is stressed that the expected negative worth of evil does not surpass the positive worth of good. What this means is that the expected worth of permitting the occurrence of a given kind of evil—with awareness of the risk taken—has to be positive (assuming that God does everything that is logically possible to actualize a given kind of good). In other words, God might permit a certain evil if it serves the realization of a greater good.[116]

Swinburne is aware of how often people, including those who believe in the existence of God, think that a given amount of evil in the world does not contribute to any greater good. The extremely acute suffering of innocent children poses a serious challenge to theism. In this context, the main task of theodicy is to demonstrate that every kind of evil present in the world indeed serves the occurrence of a greater good, and that this is not a sufficient proof against the existence and the providence of God. The train of thought of this British philosopher is to a large extent pointed to the realization of certain values which emerge only in critical situations. In referring to the above-mentioned classical way of defending free will, it is emphasized that the real choice between good and evil is made when the subject of an activity has the ability to do evil. This also includes being responsible for others and entails the possibility of helping our fellows or harming them. A world in which people are not given the power to harm others would not provide room for any significant responsibility. Should the Creator bestow on people only slight responsibility for others, He would only allow for moral choices of little consequence. Such a God might resemble a father asking his elder son to look after the younger sibling, but at the same time stressing that each deed will be fully controlled and even the smallest sign of neglect will be punished. Taking genuine responsibility in such a situation would become a fact only when the father passes on to the guardian of his smaller child a significant amount of his own possibilities to act in the sphere of significant affairs, as well as leave the elder son with the freedom to independently decide what to do in particular circumstances. Similarly, God passes down responsibility to enable us to authentically participate in creating the world and co-create ourselves, thus allowing us the possibility of harming each other and even partially upset divine plans. In allowing people to hurt one another, God makes way for the greater good which is doing good things for one another as an effect of free decision.[117]

Possessing such a great good as the freedom to think and act allows man to build his character, but also entails the danger of not taking advantage of moral growth. The so-called greater good defense is a viewpoint which stresses that particularly valuable free choices are only possible as a response to evil. We can only show bravery in enduring suffering when we indeed experience this kind of evil. Included among the good deeds which we can do are, for instance, showing compassion and assisting the poor in coming to terms with the situation they find themselves in. Offering help to the needy is logically possible only when we consider suffering to be an evil thing. In such cases, God enables the actualization of a good which can be attained only when a decision-making person is able to choose evil (at least in the form of declining to help). An alternative would be, for example, if God created a deceptive world in which people only made the impression of seriously suffering and, in fact did not feel any pain. In such circumstances, people who feel that they should help others might really endeavor to assist and put great effort into doing this, being at the same time deceived. The morally perfect God does not want to mislead us, and He simultaneously provides us with authentic opportunities for choosing between good and evil. Allowing evil seems to be a condition necessary for freedom.[118]

The above analyses are strictly connected to the question of moral evil. The efforts of competent people to fight illnesses on a scientific level are only possible when we assume that disease is a component of natural processes that can be examined by detecting their causes. A new kind of illness initially seems to come as an inevitable evil. Nevertheless, people can attain great good in combating this illness. This can be done when we are convinced that an illness is an effect of regular processes. The specificity of these processes is discovered on the basis of meticulous research, as conducted on numerous diseased people, which persistently proceeds towards answering the question concerning the conditions conducive to the transmission of the disease in question.[119] In such situations, sacrificing life for the sake of humanity is generally thought to be a highly valuable manifestation of moral involvement.

From the perspective of the attempt at justifying the presence of evil in the world, one more important aspect of the problem is identified. If we allow someone to suffer, we need to be in a close relationship with the suffering person. We do not have the right to allow a stranger to suffer for their own good or for someone else's good. Nonetheless, people have some rights in this respect as far as their own children are concerned. Permitting the pain a child might feel at the dentist's does not give rise to ethical controversies even when parents find out about the potentially threatened tooth only on the basis of X-rays and the little patient does not complain of any pain before their doctor's appointment. Parents have this right because, to a certain degree, they are responsible for the life of their children, including the goods belonging to this. Since in many respects parents are the source of their child's varied goods, they are also entitled, when necessary, to partially take back some of their good or the equivalent thereof. On the other hand, allowing children to have gradually more and more freedom as time passes and thus more occasions to experience the unpleasant aspects of life, is an important component of bringing them up to be mature. With such assumptions, God, being the ultimate source of existence, has in this respect much greater rights than our parents. Christian theism underlines that we are entirely dependent on God at every moment. However, even the laws the Creator established for creation are limited. To balance this, God cannot take away more from us than He has given. *Summa summarum*, God has to be a benefactor.[120]

Taking into account the "gains and losses" which result from the presence of evil in the world, it is worth noticing the good manifested in the form of being useful to others. This refers to deeds that are the consequence of free choice, involuntary deeds, and the things that happen to someone and are connected with suffering. A great good, also for the author of an action, is the voluntary help given to fellow human beings. Useful goods also include giving appropriate jobs to prisoners. Preventing unemployment, not by means of a simple system of benefits but through creating workplaces, stems from the conviction that the feeling of inutility experienced by unemployed people is evil. Without work, people often feel useless or even worthless to society. Among people who care for the welfare of their country, giving one's life for the motherland is treated as valuable even when the situation refers to a nonprofessional soldier being accepted into the army as part of compulsory conscription. When people die in an accident on a badly signposted road, we hope that their tragedy will lead to improvements that prevent such situations in the future. Similar reasoning is manifested by the relatives of the dead whose organs have been donated for transplant. Even though death and suffering are considered an evil thing, it seems that they might be an even greater misfortune if they do not contribute to the attainment of a useful aim. It is a good thing when our life experiences do not go to waste and can be taken advantage of for the sake of others, sometimes being the source of such a benefaction which human beings would not have been able to achieve in any other way. In the question under discussion, it is of no essential significance if we actually know that the costs we had taken in fact served the benefit of other people, even though such an awareness can provide additional motivation to act. When we find out that our suffering brings a positive effect, we are also satisfied because we had anticipatorily discerned good in such a sequence of events.[121]

If being useful is treated as a great good, from a theistic perspective it can be assumed that whenever God permits human suffering, this suffering is not in vain. The final test to the usefulness of this kind of evil is its contribution to the divine design for the world. God permits suffering, but at the same time it becomes an opportunity for doing good things for others and sometimes even for the sufferer themself. In light of the above, it can be supposed that there are reasons for which God has the right to permit the presence of evil in the world. Irrespective of insightful inquiries on whether our life is dominated more by good than by evil, the latter brings the potential good of being useful. Such ruminations become more credible with the assumption of a close personal relationship in which man trusts God but, at the same time, has the right to expect a reward. This is why Swinburne adds that if, despite everything, someone experiences more evil than good in his life, God is obliged to compensate for this situation in their future life so that, in balance, such a person's existence was a good one.[122] This statement moves beyond the field of philosophical reflection. However, such argumentation is not based on the data of revelation but is an attempt at finding a reasonable basis from which we might assume that a morally and metaphysically perfect being can permit the existence of evil.

What are the aims of the existence of the world?

Thus, the genuine development of human life is conditioned by the occurrence of specific components in the relationship between the Creator and His creation. On the one hand, this entails the affinity of persons, and on the other hand, our cognitive distancing from God.[123] Without this distance, we cannot on our own account test his our moral abilities, learn, make mistakes, experience the consequences thereof, and develop on the path of searching for good. Even more, human beings also need to have an authentic freedom of action in order to make morally significant choices that have consequences for them and their surroundings. Otherwise, God would only appear as someone who is "pulling the strings of history" in fear of it taking an adverse turn. Finally, there must be a relatively stable environment in which a person is able to develop morally. This would be impossible in a world continuously adjusting itself to our particular interests, with this being a world devoid of the fixed laws that are subject to human cognition and enable rational activity.[124]

Hence, the question concerning the reason why good coexists with evil is answered in the context of the purpose of the world's existence. If the divine plan concerns providing creation with development-enabling freedom then the world as we know it can be seen as the natural environment for growth. A different concept of creation is often assumed by the critics of theism who use the problem of evil as an argument against the rationality of believing in God. Anti-theists frequently suggest that the aim of a loving God would have been to create the world as a peculiar hedonistic paradise. The discrepancy between this imaginary picture of the world and the reality we live in proves that God is not omnipotent and good. Hick stated that such reasoning portrays the world–God relationship as resembling that of a man building a cage for his favorite pet to live in.[125]

In criticizing this image of the world, many contemporary authors introduce the idea of people being created as immature children who, existing in the world, are supposed to attain personal growth. Certain environmental conditions can be deemed unfriendly from the temporary point of view, but on a long-term basis are beneficial for integral development. The aim God predefines for the world is not our pleasant existence but creating conditions for our integral growth. Evil states of affairs can, in this context, serve specific, positive functions. The ability to come to know the laws of nature, gain knowledge, and the cultural-spiritual development of individuals and society entail the necessity of permitting pain. Struggling with the shortcomings of life, the varied manifestations of physical evil and suffering constitute an important component of our maturation.[126] Such values as altruism, bravery, and dedication become a well-appreciated constituent of human interactions when someone is in pain and awaits the helping hand of a fellow.[127]

No other living structure can successfully emerge without incurring the costs related to its interaction with the environment. Because of the limited span of existence, complicated organisms can survive thanks to employing more elementary chemical structures obtained by means of assimilating substances that come from other living organisms. Complex living organisms were able to emerge only by means of feeding on others. The huge diversity of developed biological structures comes into being through their modification or elaboration by means of nutrition, by incorporating simpler structures. This unique logic of nature is based on generating new forms of life through the incorporation of already existing forms. The condition of the creativity of the evolutionary process is to replace old patterns with new ones. The biological death of the individual is a "prerequisite for the creativity of the biological order, the creativity that eventually led to the emergence of human beings."[128]

So a question arises: does not the extent of suffering surpass that which seems indispensable for the genesis of man and his development? After all, we deem many manifestations of evil as pointless. Elimination of pointless suffering might be surely accomplished without removing evil as such. Do we have to be sentenced to the immensity of the evil we experience if we acknowledge the value of certain manifestations of the imperfection of being? Why did the evolution of our world not adopt a different scenario?[129]

The above doubts are a classical component of theodicy. Arguments given with reserve towards the notion of the greater good usually contain the most existential examples of suffering. We can easily imagine such ways of "improving the world" as removing cancer or the pain suffered by innocent children. Whether we express it or not, we often assume that our existence was the ultimate aim of the entire process of evolution. Nevertheless, the critics of theism emphasize that the human observer has appeared on the face of the world relatively recently and after a dozen or so billion years one might expect a more successful "product" if human beings are to be treated as the crown of creation. Irrespective of the nuances of the discussion on our distinguished place in nature, the objection against the idea of the greater good boils down to the fact that God could have realized valuable goals in a different manner and with a smaller dose of suffering and evil. Since there are examples of pointless evil in the world, it has not been created by an omnipotent and infinitely good Creator.[130]

As part of the discussion of divine action in the world, scholars point out the substantive dubiousness of such an approach in which evil would be permitted only in situations in which it is necessary or serves as the best means of attaining a greater good. In such an interpretation, each natural or moral evil would have to lead to a good greater than the one which could have occurred without suffering.[131] It seems, however, that evil is not always related to good as a means of achieving good. This circumstance is sometimes insufficiently noticed even though, at least implicitly, it is present in the above-mentioned ways or reasoning. Meanwhile, evil can be a kind of by-product or a concurrent effect, as a component unnecessary for good to emerge. Evil can, but does not have to, be the instrument that leads to the realization of a greater good, which, however, always entails a certain cost. If there is no other way to reach this aim, we can justify the creation of a world in which God permits evil.[132]

Focusing on our freedom to an essential extent changes the perspective from which such problems are examined. If the aim of God is to create people who have free will (in the libertarian sense) then, by nature, they will be able to make morally wrong choices. Perceived from this perspective, the evil which results from such choice is neither a condition necessary for the emergence of a greater good, nor is it a means that enables its realization[133] At least some bad choices do not have to be made for the divine plan of creation to be realized. Morally wrong action is not a necessary component of the world's history. Even more, the world would be a significantly better place without our wrong choices. This does not change the fact, however, that our authentic freedom *ipso facto* entails the possibility of doing evil.[134]

Thus, the aims which the Creator embedded in creation may require permission for the existence of pointless evil. Would it not be better, however, if God limited human freedom by means of suspending free will and determining action in specific moments? Should not God allow morally wrong choices to emerge only in a situation in which they are a necessary or the best means to realize a greater good? It seems that this suggested approach, despite its seeming appeal, remains internally inconsistent and undermines the foundation of moral life. The weightiness of moral choices would have definitely lost its significance if doing evil would in fact be a realization of God's design for the world or was impossible due to a selective suspension of human freedom.[135]

What does science tell us?

The phenomenon of the unity of nature, which constitutes an integral whole, inclines one to examine evil both in the context of free choice and the processes of nature that are devoid of consciousness. Natural evil also can be treated as a side effect of evolutionary history that led to the genesis of good in the world. Susceptibility to evil in each of its dimensions is a causal consequence of the coincidence of conditions which are necessary for the emergence of sentient beings.[136] Nevertheless, the imperfection of creation is above all an indispensable component of the autonomy of the world and human freedom. Without this, it is difficult to imagine a real difference between the Creator and the creation that, according to Christian revelation, "has been groaning as in the pains of childbirth right up to the present time,"[137] but is also directed at being liberated from "bondage to decay."[138]

The "*unde malum?*" question, which has been analyzed within theism, most of all requires reference to the image of God as related to the world. Such an approach has to be consistent and should assume that the laws of nature which are a sign of the *Logos* are immutable. Elimination of pointless evil or suffering would "rip apart" the structures which condition the existence of functional pain that allows us to preserve life. If it is God's intention to create a world with stable laws of nature, we need to accept the existential rupture at each level of nature. One cannot stress the value of free choice or the functioning of an organism that feels the pains which enable an efficient medical intervention, without accepting the fact that this same person is vulnerable to the influence of the natural and moral evils which come from the environment, but at the same time remains open to receiving and conveying expressions of freedom which serve the multiplication of good.[139]

In light of the above it is more clearly visible that some investigations lose their argumentative power. A classic example of this is the attempt at answering the previously posed question: could God eradicate the most glaring manifestations of pointless evil in the world? In other words: is there a pointless kind of evil which could be eliminated without violating the order of nature? Presenting the problem in this manner suggests that we can determine the threshold beyond which excessive and unjustified evil occurs. Defining the boundary between entirely pointless evil and those manifestations of evil which we might be willing to accept as the cost of a greater good seems, however, to be an impossible task.[140]

The above doubts are often presented from the "perspective of God's action." Was not God able to create the world in a more efficient way? The unique balance of gains and losses could be measured in the cost of the evil that is necessary to achieve greater goods. Such calculations might be feasible on the assumption (very unlikely to be adopted) that good and evil can be compared on a uniform scale. Nonetheless, the problem again arrives to the boundary beyond which hypothetical solutions do not appear to bring us any closer to a satisfactory resolution. After all, it is not rationally decidable whether, in the previously discussed context, our expectations would be met when predators or the aging of human organisms were removed from the world. It is difficult to compare good and evil on one scale. There are no criteria to allow one to specify with precision the image of the best possible world[141]

We become aware of the essential difficulty of constructing the concept of a better world through relatively simple thought experiments. Let us assume that we managed to point to instances of pointless and excessive evil. To confirm our hypothesis, it would be good to reconstruct the course of history of a world devoid of this particular kind of evil. Nevertheless, this would require not only coming up with a sophisticated theoretical methodology which could be employed to predict the future, but also a rational and detailed delineation of the history of the world in the newly established reality. However, in the face of a task as ambitious as this, we remain helpless. The reason for our helplessness is not only the fact that our knowledge is seriously limited and predicting the final state of the evolution of certain processes in the universe requires being very familiar with many parameters, including the gravitational effects caused by electrons in the galaxy. Paradoxically, this also regards the fact that awareness of the complicated network of the mutually intersecting laws of nature forces us to be extremely careful while formulating possible scenarios of development. Chaos theory makes us realize that some systems that occur in nature are particularly sensitive to the slightest change in the values of initial conditions.[142] Such systems are commonly present in nature and the typical expression of their functioning is the so-called butterfly effect. A small modification of parameters will sometimes result in disproportionate, at least as it seems to us, effects. Hence, it is not possible to reconstruct the history of a world with precision if we assume that at a certain stage of evolutionary development we can "take out one of the elements of the cosmic entirety."[143]

Weighing the arguments in an honest debate

Without straightforward reference to contemporary achievements in natural sciences, similar conclusions are formulated by Peter van Inwagen. He recalled a classical kind of reasoning which would supposedly serve as a motive for claiming that God does not exist. The argument from evil can be presented in the following way: (a) if God exists, He would be omnipotent and morally perfect; (b) an omnipotent and morally perfect being would not permit evil to emerge; (c) we can observe evil; (d) *ergo*: God does not exist. Dissecting such argumentation calls for an intellectual engagement which programmatically excludes a skeptical or fideistic approach and forces one to search for an explanation of the fact that the presented logic of thought is not an irrefutable proof that confirms the truth of atheism. According to van Inwagen, this is a purely theoretical challenge that can be tackled through critical analysis.[144]

Van Inwagen opposes the frequently posed objection that examining the argument of evil is an ignoble venture because it tries to present the tragedy of suffering in the theoretical framework of emotionless investigation. After all, the task of philosophy is not to come up with a mental medication that would console people afflicted with evil but is to refer in a substantive manner to the above-presented deduction. Van Inwagen claims that instead of having a peculiar moral contempt for theists, in the style characteristic of J. S. Mill's famous arguments,[145] one should balance the reasons "for" and "against" the hypothesis of God in the face of the evil in the world. This is best done by means of elaborating a script of a debate held between a theist and an atheist, the audience consisting of intellectually honest agnostics.[146]

In undertaking this task, van Inwagen understands that the omnipotence of God is His power to create everything that is not, by essence, impossible, either logically or metaphysically. What is assumed is God's moral perfection, and that the scope of His knowledge includes evil in the world. During an ideal debate, agnostics are only driven by their desire to know the truth of whether God exists and are trying to reach this goal despite the final verdict. The disputing adversaries, on the other hand, are not interested in "turning their opponents around." What they have in mind is the influence of their arguments on the beliefs of agnostics.[147]

The first important goal to be achieved in the discussion is for the theist to prove that the premise "God wants for evil not to exist and is able to realize His wish" does not lead to the conclusion that evil does not exist. From a purely logical point of view, God might permit the emergence of evil for reasons which, in His opinion, are more significant than His desire to prevent evil. Analogically speaking, a man can have moral reasons to allow his seriously ill mother to be afflicted with intense pain, even though he has a means at his disposal (e.g. medication) that might protect her from such suffering. Nevertheless, does not an atheist have strong enough arguments to deduce that a morally perfect Creator would have made every effort to prevent the suffering of their creatures? Does suffering have to be the means for achieving a specific goal of the omnipotent being? In answering questions posed in this way, one needs to clarify the possible reasons behind God's decision to permit evil. A theist would have to authenticate his conviction that such reasons might actually exist.[148]

The aim of the aforementioned theist is to justify the thesis of the existence of the entirely real possibility of God having a reason to permit evil, just as a mother may have a rational reason to leave her child at home unattended (e.g., to run to the chemist's to fetch medicine that can save her child's life in a dramatic situation). In responding to the argument from evil, a philosopher usually presents a potential situation in which God allows evil to occur while having sufficient reasons behind this action. Such an invented situation ("story") is deemed by van Inwagen to be a form of defense that should be distinguished from theodicy.[149] Both can have the same content, but theodicy is presented as true, whereas the defense is only said to describe a real possibility.[150]

This distinction refers to classical reasoning concerning the question. Usually, the first object of reflection is the logical problem of evil in an attempt at formulating a non-contradictory defense. Having performed this task, one moves to an analysis of the evidential problem of evil. However, van Inwagen does not see a reason for the probabilistic problem of evil to be analyzed only after we have dealt with its logical aspect. Judging such research to be artificial and impractical, he focuses his attention on the probabilistic dimension of the problem of evil instead, drawing on the philosophical achievements elaborated upon in the course of recent debates concerning evil.

A theist's task is not only to prove that God derives some great good from evil, with this good outweighing a specific evil. Additionally, a theist's defense has to include a statement that there is no possible scenario of attaining such a good without permitting the existence of observable evil (or any other possible evil no less acute in form). Creating such a concept does not seem to be a simple task on account of the idea of divine omnipotence. A man can be forgiven for permitting (or even causing) a specific evil to occur, if it was a necessary means (or an inevitable consequence) of attaining a greater good. We would justify a surgeon who, having no anesthetics at his disposal (e.g. before they were invented), inflicted a particularly strong pain on his patient, if this pain was an inevitable consequence of actions necessary to save a patient's life.[151] Does the same logic of reasoning refer to God in His relation to the world?

In a search for answers, one usually reaches for the argument most commonly used by contemporary theists, that of the free will defense. However, its simple version is not sufficient since it does not manage to overcome two essential objections. First of all, the problem of "why so much evil?" remains unresolved. The classical free will defense can, at most, explain the existence of a certain amount of evil, but not its often overwhelming magnitude. Secondly, what about natural evil? The suffering which has emerged as a result of the action of natural forces cannot be explained by human freedom, even if we take some responsibility for nature's specific development. These areas make us realize that the free will defense can be effective only if it is used in its significantly broader version.[152]

Arguments constructed on the basis of the idea of free will would not be effective if we adopted the compatibilistic concept of freedom. However, the author of the 2003 Gifford Lectures is a declared proponent of incompatibilism[153] and claims that the opposite viewpoint is not credible. Each version of the free will defense has to additionally tackle the problem of God's omniscience. After all, it seems that the existence of a being who knows the future is incompatible with free will. Deeming the arguments in support of the incompatibility of omniscience and freedom to be at least quite convincing (or maybe even decisive), van Inwagen presents an image of God who is eternal but exists in time. It would be difficult to describe in both a reasonable and detailed way the knowledge of a timeless being concerning things which (to us) are in the future. In this context, the suggested solution to the problem of human freedom and divine omniscience refers to the view of omnipotence. An omniscient being cannot know things the knowledge of which is essentially impossible. God knows everything He can know. We are not being contradictory when we state that God does not know what somebody's future free actions will be because such knowledge is—by its very essence—impossible.[154]

The above viewpoint on divine omniscience will be difficult to accept by people who interpret certain Biblical descriptions literally. Nonetheless, the perspective of Judeo-Christian revelation helps van Inwagen to construct a broader version of the free will defense. In referring to the first phases of the history of humanity as presented in the Old Testament, van Inwagen thinks it is reasonable to assume that at a certain moment God endowed our evolving primogenitors with sapience, including communicable speech, the ability to think abstractly, to express selfless love and personal freedom. The Creator had directed the course of evolution in such a way so as to arrive at the emergence of free creatures able to realize who the cause of their existence is. Even if we are not able to comprehend all of the reasons why people received free will, one of them being essential, can be understood: God endowed humanity with freedom because it is a necessary condition of love.[155]

People, however, were not able to appreciate the value of free will and made inappropriate use of it. At a certain stage they also stopped showing gratitude to God and broke their bond with Him. God would have acted in a just manner if He had left these people in the state of decay that they had brought upon themselves and the world. God would have showed mercy if he had ended the story of this devastated man, thus cutting his suffering short. Nonetheless, God, who is love, in trying to salvage humanity, decided to give him a helping hand. This could have been realized in many different ways. However, the most important thing is that the divine plan is designed for man to enter the state of happiness again. This can be achieved only on the path of freedom, without which there is no love. People are supposed to decide on their renewed union with God themselves, but they are not able to do so exclusively thanks to their own efforts. To cooperate with God, one has to be aware of the drama of one's situation and be able to see the need for His assistance.

In putting this story "in the mouth" of the debating theist, van Inwagen bears in mind that it is merely a hypothetical form of defense. But this is the whole point since extended argumentation is not a part of theodicy, which states the factual truth of the coexistence of God and evil. It is enough that the delineated scenario can be true. There are no visible convincing reasons to programmatically reject the possibility that events might have taken such a course. Natural sciences do not prove that there is no room for divine action in evolutionary history. Even more, it cannot be scientifically rejected that the genesis of sapience had occurred suddenly within a locally existing population.[156]

It appears that the fundamental problem for the above-presented defense of the existence of evil is the presence of a kind of suffering in the world which is perceived as particularly acute. In this context, the answer of the atheist who aims at the conclusion that an omnipotent and morally perfect being does not exist would contain several premises, among which one is of specific interest. After all, if God was able to eliminate certain atrocities from of the world without it becoming worse for it, the morally perfect and omnipotent Creator would have done so. Such reasoning is demonstrated by Rowe in his well-known argumentation as credible and simultaneously expressing of our fundamental moral intuitions.[157] Van Inwagen, however, undermines this way of thinking by claiming that there is only one moral principle that might authenticate it: if you are able to prevent evil, you should not allow it to emerge unless its occurrence leads to a greater good and prevents the results of another kind of evil that is at least equally acute. Proving that such a rule is not true moves the author of *The Problem of Evil* to the crux of his argumentation.[158]

In constructing an imaginable situation, van Inwagen presents the dilemma of prison authorities in whose power lies the decision to release a murderer at any given time. Assuming that the prisoner had been sentenced to ten years of jail and his sentence has nearly run its full course, one can presume that he has asked to be released home one day in advance. In the light of the principle presented in the previous paragraph, the authorities should accede to such a request. Twenty-four hours spent in jail before the prison term ends does not seem necessary for attaining any sort of good and may even appear as a wrong. To prevent serious crimes in the future, one cannot see an essential difference between ten full years "behind bars" and a period which is one day shorter. Thus, holding a man in prison on the last day of his sentence would not result in any significant kind of good. In accordance with the rule promoted by the atheist, the prisoner should be released one day earlier. This example demonstrates the falsity of the above principle, especially when you can imagine a situation in which the convict will make use of the legal and moral evasion many times, requesting another pardon (even if it is relatively smaller) every time his sentence is shortened. The last chord on the path heading *ad absurdum* would be the cunning murderer's appeal to the appropriate authorities to reconsider his sentence before he is even locked in jail.[159]

The criteria of the penal system employed in our culture, which are not a compromise between purely ethical and practical reasons but a rational principle of legal and judicial proceedings, assume that as far as punishment is concerned one must set a limit. This is arbitrary and there is nothing essentially wrong about it even though one might endlessly debate whether an imposed punishment is fully adequate to a given situation. Analogical reasoning appears in the extended version of the free will defense. God prevents the emergence of many manifestations of evil which are an effect of becoming separated from our Maker. Nevertheless, God cannot prevent all atrocities since this would destroy His plan of uniting people with Him. The question concerning the reason why He prevents specific manifestations of evil should be referred to our conviction of the arbitrariness of choice in these situations. Thus, it is true that should God prevent a given atrocity, the world as a whole would not become (at least) a significantly worse place, and the general level of life awareness in the imperfect world would not be upset. In preventing one type of extreme suffering, the Creator would not have destroyed His design concerning man. However, God had simply decided where to set the boundary between occurring atrocities and the ones that remain in the sphere of possibility. No matter where the demarcation line is set, the world would still be full of dreadful things assuming the divine scenario concerning the most essential form of help given to people. A single victim of fate will always be able to suggest that it would be possible to create a better world, without the dose of suffering that, no one knows why, befell exactly them.

The fact that there is no optimal amount of horrible events indispensable to the realization of God's plan does not console a suffering person. However, such a consolation is not a reason for the construction of a hypothetical situation in which one can clearly see that an arbitrary choice needs to be made. The fact that a medical commission, in examining a difficult to be rationally explained death of a child during a relatively uncomplicated surgery, states that this death happened as a consequence of unforeseeable circumstances is not a consolation for the parents of the deceased, but allows one to determine that doctors were not to blame. In human reality we are frequently faced with moral dilemmas which demonstrate how difficult it is to draw certain important boundaries, e.g. when the government decides how much of the taxpayers' money should be allocated to financing life-saving medicine. Even the most cautiously balanced decision taken by the functionaries of the Ministry of Health would always be arbitrary and can result in the death or survival of a particular man who cannot afford to buy medicine with their own money. However, this does not lead to the straightforward conclusion that the people who establish the rules of financial support are to blame, even if we assume that a state's budget is not on the brink of collapse and that allocating funds to this cause is not going to ruin the entire economy. The people who govern a country have to decide whether to give more money to the development of infrastructure or to healthcare. According to the same interpretative key one should ascertain that the presence of atrocities in the world does not mean that the omnipotent Creator should be held responsible for them.[160]

In conducting his insightful analysis in the framework of an extended version of the free will defense, van Inwagen deems it necessary to continue searching for answers to the question concerning the sufferings which occurred in the world before the genesis of man. After all, in light of the natural sciences it is indubitable that sentient animals had emerged long before the arrival of *animal rationale*. The length of the story of the human struggle against evil is a relatively small part of the history of life in which sentient creatures had already been dying in painful circumstances. In attempting to tackle this problem, one can introduce a manner of argumentation that stresses the unavoidable arbitrariness of divine decision. The question of the potential prevention or permission of the suffering of an individual representative of the animal kingdom should be inscribed in a wider context of God's action. Detailed reflection on this problem can be found in the article entitled *The Problem of Evil, The Problem of Air, and the Problem of Silence*.[161] The essence of the conducted analysis comes in the form of the statement that a possible demarcation line remains arbitrary and the individual instances of animal suffering are not a deciding component of the argument concerning the existence of an omnipotent and morally perfect Creator. For certain important reasons that are also essential for creation, the world can contain both human suffering as well as the pain of other beings experiencing suffering and pain in such a quantity and kind as occurs at the different stages of the evolutionary struggle for survival.[162]

The above concept is an example of the valuable discussion held with the critics of theism who claim that the God hypothesis can be overthrown on account of the evil present in the world. It transpires that the manifestations of suffering, even in its most acute dimension, do not falsify *ipso facto* the thesis of an omnipotent and morally perfect Creator who cares for creation. Paying great attention to disproving strong (though at times simplified) statements put forward by atheists, van Inwagen simultaneously supports theistic arguments while also being aware of the fact that he does not solve the problem of the existential experience of pain. The above-discussed approach is also characterized by openness to the theological scenario of being salvaged from evil, at least in the form of a potential assumption that the situation which introduced the world to the state of susceptibility to suffering could have taken place. In taking such intellectual steps, the Notre Dame University professor simultaneously stresses that attempting to reconstruct the history of evil should be confronted with the actual state of scientific knowledge. Without neglecting or idealizing this, one can strive to propose a rational reconstruction of the course of events in the face of which God continuously appears as a providential protector of the creation.

Futile evil and atrocious evil

The achievements of the natural sciences provide probabilistic theists with a significant context for reflection on evil. Probabilistic theism is to some extent situated in opposition to the most frequent attempts at solving the "*unde malum?*" question because the answer to a question posed in this way is treated as somewhat a-rational or supra-rational. The proponents of the "theology of chance" claim that not every kind of evil has a reason for its existence in the eternal divine design. Thus, one needs to accept the existence of futile evil and atrocious evil, which are not means to realize any aims, either temporal or eternal. Extremely painful life experiences destroy people and do not serve any purpose. Liberation from evil can be achieved not on the road to overcoming evil, but through a complete lack of any sort of suffering. Happiness can be attained only in a reality in which no evil exists.[163]

Probabilistic theism remains critical of employing biblical inspiration to create the possible scenarios of liberation from evil. There are no hermeneutic grounds for asserting that the cause of suffering and death is original sin because this has only a symbolic, albeit profound, meaning. In the history of humankind there was never a state of ontic or moral perfection. The imperfection of human nature and existence was affected by many random conditionings as part of God's design for the world. The Creator's plan, however, does not include a detailed course of events. Thus, God bears responsibility for the general state of the world and the mechanisms according to which it functions, but not for the particular instances of "rupture" which occur in the course of evolution. Hence, God is not obliged to salvage or mend suffering-prone creation.[164]

In putting emphasis on the autonomy of nature, the functioning of which is the effect of the coincidences of deterministic and random components, we move away from reflecting on the problem of whether the world we inhabit is the best possible one. Stating that a world without the Holocaust would be a better one should be embedded in a wider context of reflection. After all, it appears that it was not possible to create a world in which humans are given space for creativity and experiencing an authentic freedom of choice without the existence of events which are random and not designed by God. Suffering is not an effect of God's action, nor an element of His design. Such an approach does not solve the problem of evil, especially its extreme instances, but neither does this approach become entangled in the difficulties which stem from strongly stressing the necessity of the Creator to intervene in the history of creation.[165]

For different reasons (which are sometimes of a methodological nature) many varieties of theism do not provide a satisfactory answer to questions posed in the situation of evil that affects a specific human being experiencing pain. This also refers to the strands of the discussion that are added to the basis of reflection proposed by the author of the concept of the best of all possible worlds. No matter how we elaborate on the arguments in support of the thesis that the existence of evil does not exclude divine providence, this will always be an insufficient and often emotionless message when seen from the perspective of the suffering of people who are faced with particular existential challenges. This problem was aptly expressed by Bergson when he wrote that it would be "easy to add a few paragraphs to the *Théodicée* of Leibniz. But we have not the slightest inclination to do so. The philosopher may indulge in speculations of this kind in the solitude of his study; but what is he going to think about it in the presence of a mother who just watched the passing of her child?"[166] Awareness of the extreme experiences of pain is the reason why many contemporary authors move beyond the mainstream discourse of justifying the existence of evil.

Compassion instead of speculation

Set against the background of many contemporary attempts at solving the problem of evil, Marilyn McCord Adams elaborates an innovative approach to the issue. Her original proposition is based not so much on searching for new answers to previously posed questions, but on trying to thoroughly reformulate the problem of evil. She is not a supporter of such a way of analyzing the question in which an atheist treats evil as a component of his argument against the existence of God (anti-theology), whereas a theist's main task is to defend himself (or maybe even God) from the posed objections. The apologetic mentality expressed in the sense of the formula "*unde malum?*" had been developed for years on the grounds of the Thomistic approach to evil, evolved as a result of Hume's criticism of theism, and is now dominated by logical and probabilistic argumentation. Meanwhile, the problem of evil should not be presented in light of the question "does God exist?" but as an opportunity for a more insightful examination of the relationship between the divine attributes and the evil present in the world. Moving against the current of contemporary trends in analytic philosophy, Adams promotes an aporetic approach to the question of evil.[167]

Adams does not see why one should focus on looking for reasons behind God's permission for evil in the world. Thus, the desired goal is not the creation of a valuable theodicy or the effective formulation of a defense of the idea of the greater good. To tackle the problem of evil, Adams does not deem it necessary to search for the potential reasons for evil's existence and goes as far as to deny the possibility of coming to know them. The crux of the matter is not to attempt to justify the presence of evil in the world. The main task of theism, however, should be to indicate the ways God can solve the problem of the evil experienced by man. Such alteration to the philosophical approach seems to transform the undertaken reflection in a profound manner. Instead of deliberating on why evil emerged in the world, perhaps we should address the question of whether and how evil can endanger the wellbeing of human existence.[168]

The consequence of this is criticism of the global strategy of justifying the possibility of permitting evil, especially in attempts at finding a distinct reason for evil's existence. The mentality of theists whose main point of reference was Leibniz's thought is manifested in striving to demonstrate that the world we inhabit is the best of all possible worlds and remains the object of divine care as a whole. The dogmatization of this thesis led, according to Adams, to ignoring the most serious manifestations of evil. Meanwhile, the appropriate perspective for considering the problem of evil is that of the individual existence of a man experiencing pain, sometimes extremely acute. In the context of individual pain, at times difficult to be borne, justifying the global problem of evil is of no great significance. A generally good world is also a place for people who, on account of extreme suffering, feel that existence lacks meaning.[169]

The biggest challenge for a theist comes in the form of those manifestations of evil which Adams calls horrendous. This includes the kinds of sufferings whose presence can be a reason to doubt whether the life of a person afflicted with such evil is at all good for them.[170] Such states of affairs undermine the value of a person's existence. Thus, the question of evil should be placed at the center of the anthropology which highlights the subjective determination of human views and behaviors. Nonetheless, Adams does not belittle the investigation characteristic for theodicy, but she strongly distinguishes the subjective elements of reflection on the value of life of men affected by evil.[171]

In trying to answer the question of whether there is such a good that could overcome this horrendous evil, theists should not undertake reflection from the perspective of an axiology which is neutral both worldview-wise and religion-wise.[172] Adams, like Hick, thinks that the basis for reflection on the presence of evil in the world has to be grounded in theistic axiology. Otherwise, a situation is created in which a theist tries to explain the relationship between God and evil on the basis of an a-religious (or even anti-religious) axiology. However, Adams goes one step further, and claims that it is worthwhile for reflection on reconciling the existence of evil with divine providence to take into account, at least to some extent, the context of religious belief and Christian revelation.[173] After all, theism elaborated on with certain elements derived from theological doctrine (e.g. the truths about sin, salvation, eternal life) has a greater explanatory power than a theism which is practiced solely on a philosophical basis through focusing on divine attributes. Paying attention to God's nature is the reason for the impasse evident in the contemporary debate on the problem of evil.[174]

Such an impasse in the above-mentioned discussion was partly caused by the tendency showed by many analytic philosophers to underline the role of searching for adequate reasons for justifying God's permission for evil in the world. Adams generally undermines the point of treating God as a moral subject similar to the human person.[175] Moral categories, intensively employed in the strategy of the free will defense, do not describe horrendous evil well enough. This stems from the fact that, among other reasons, the theodicies which justify the existence of evil with free will have not often provided answers to questions posed in the context of natural evil which cannot be neglected during reflection on horrendous evil. McCord Adams discerns the manifestations of such evil both in situations where we speak of the effects of the functioning of nature, as well as in the cases of suffering caused by man's actions. Hence, the sharp division between these areas loses its significance. What is also worth noticing is that in terms of human action, horrendous evil serves as grounds for questioning the sense of life of both parties of the tragedy: the victim and the perpetrator. Invoking the free will of the author of a horrendous evil while justifying its emergence does not satisfy the victim. Moral categories are not sufficient for justifying the fact that someone is affected with an atrocity for no reason at all.[176]

The criticism expressed by Adams embraced many aspects of the so-far elaborated solutions to the problem of evil. In her opinion, we cannot accept the logic of retribution in accordance with which evil affects people in proportion to the sins they have committed.[177] Suffering cannot always be explained with human blame.[178] Moreover, Adams undermines the thesis put forward by Hick, who saw suffering as an important component of individuals' moral growth. Such a standpoint offers no reasons for evil which does not ameliorate but destroys. Even with the assumption of the eternal reward provided by God, one cannot depreciate the meaning of temporal life, let alone treat people as mere means to a given end.[179] Paying attention to moral categories leads to an overestimation of man's ability to make decisions concerning his own life and is an expression of Pelagianism.[180]

What Adams deems the crucial issue is giving insightful thought to the way in which God can overcome horrendous evil and restore the feeling of life's worth to someone who has been exposed to great ordeals, in order that—retrospectively—such a person can acknowledge that their existence makes sense, and they do not regret any of the extremely difficult situations they have had to face. An adequate response to a question thus posed can be given only when we enter into the area of theological explanation. An experience of horrendous evil cannot be compensated for with any created good, nor with the fact of possessing freedom. Restoration of the feeling that there is a meaning to life can only happen on account of one's relationship with God on the road to salvation.[181] A consequence of this approach is the introduction of rich argumentation from the domain of Christology. This, however, lies outside the scope of this study. Nonetheless, in the context of the analyses conducted in the earlier sections of this book, it needs to be stressed that Adams refers to the idea of "passibility" and of the love of God who should not appear to us as a general merely observing a battle, but as a leader who fights at the head of a battalion of soldiers. Thus, the personal God has to be susceptible to suffering and identify with our fate, as well as really participate in the history of mankind.[182]

This concept, despite introducing certain *novum* to the well-worn and somewhat fossilized (in the recent years) patterns of approaching the problem of evil, has become the object of extensive criticism.[183] This refers, among other things, to the application of the idea, taken from Leibniz, of sempiternal, necessary natures, as a result of which even God would not be able to remove from us the susceptibility we have to the suffering present in the world we inhabit. Being susceptible to suffering, however, does not *ipso facto* signify actual suffering.[184] Adams avoids answering the *"unde malum?"* question posed in the field of philosophy on the pretext of man's cognitive imperfection. According to her, God can have reasons to permit evil which people are not and will not be able to conceive of within their earthly existence. Such a statement is burdened with the flaws characteristic of the skeptical solution to the problem of evil. It is difficult to rationally discuss any kind of sense of evil without addressing the issue of the reasons why evil is permitted in the first place.[185]

Adams's proposed solution to the problem of evil is definitely an expression of an original approach. In many respects, this approach demonstrates a train of thought different from the one present in the mainstream of contemporary debates concerning evil. In striving to redefine the core of the problem, she aptly inscribes the drama of horrendous evil into the context of the meaning of human life. This allows theoretical ruminations to move closer to the existential dilemmas that accompany suffering. The postulate of universal salvation pushes the issue of the freedom of choice, including eschatological choice, to the background of discussion. Referring to free will ceases to be necessary since the *"unde malum?"* question is of no significance. A man asking such a question would not receive an answer even in eternity.[186]

Christian theism searches for solutions to the enigma of evil both from the philosophical perspective that reveals the ontic and moral imperfection of creation which is distinct from the Creator, as well as from the scientific perspective that stresses the specificity of the laws of nature. On the verge between philosophy and theology appears the question of God's presence in the world, with this having the character of *kenosis*. This has already been an object of reflection during discussion of divine omnipotence, which is a fundamental point of reference also for questions concerning evil and human suffering. It is emphasized that despite its acute presence in daily experience, God's immanence in the world is no less real. The Creator who approaches His creation does not appear as a master or a cosmic bureaucrat who is impersonal and indifferent to the fate of man, and is thus creating the system of nature from a safe distance, as well as calculating the distribution of good and evil in such a way as to arrive at a positive final outcome. God takes an active part in the history of the world. Being in a relationship with Him—which is the greatest possible good—does not exclude the suffering of creatures but entails God's engagement. This takes the form of self-limitation, the expression of which, as subject to theological reflection, is the Incarnation. However, the problem of God's *kenosis* is also the object of philosophical analysis.[187]

Kenosis and panentheism

God in the world

The question of "God's humility" is an essential component of Christian revelation. It puts emphasis on the fact that the Creator, in a unique way, "leans over" the fate of creation. The problem of *kenosis* is also an aspect of philosophical reflection in those theistic systems which perceive God not as a cosmic tyrant but as a person involved in the history of mankind and the world. The concept of God's providential action towards His creation does not seem to be easily reconcilable with a conviction of nature's autonomy or the transcendence of God who is fundamentally different from the world. Many authors, however, underline the role of God's immanence in the world no less than His transcendence.

As I have already mentioned in the previous chapter of this book, the very act of creation can be interpreted as God's peculiar withdrawal in order to give room to something other than Himself. Such "stepping aside" should not be understood in the physical but in the ontological sense. Moltmann writes that the existence of the universe entails the self-limitation of the Creator who provides creation with "time in his eternity, finitude in his infinity, space in his omnipresence and freedom in his selfless love."[188]

Divine *kenosis* is described in the language of analogies and metaphors, which can convey a lot of important content. The genesis of the world took place by God's free choice; since this choice was made, creation, to a certain degree, becomes necessary for the Creator and He is constantly involved in it. This situation can be compared to a change a child is adopted. When the adoption is finalized, the child becomes an integral part of the family. The well-being of the child is the purpose of the care of the family, which previously functioned as a self-sufficient unit.[189]

Thus, by voluntarily calling the world into being, God is constantly present in it. Stressing the Creator's immanence in creation requires that we notice important nuances of the problem to avoid potential misunderstandings and interpretative absurdities. They arise even independently of the context of *kenosis*, for instance, when the verb "to be"—used to describe God's being and to the being of entities created by Him—is understood in the same way. This is incompatible with the main current of Christian theism, which states that, in the ultimate sense, the verb 'be' can only be applied to God. Creatures exist inasmuch as the Creator imparts His existence to them. The word *be* is analogical. In this context, the being of God is essentially different from the being of creation.[190]

Moreover, God's presence in the world should not be understood as inclusion in the sense used by set theory. God is not a part of the world; however, He is present in His creation in a real way, similarly to the way certain values exist in the world, even though the reality of the latter differs from the reality of physical objects. Both the concrete and the abstract make up the reality that we experience as rational and comprehensible.[191]

Historically, attempts at a detailed presentation of the uniqueness of the Creator-creation relationship have taken various philosophical forms. John Scotus Eriugena, Meister Eckhart, and Nicholas of Cusa demonstrated that all things exist in God who constitutes the essence of these things. This was understood as the *forma omnium*, *essentia omnium*, and *materia omnium*. The last concept was opposed by St. Thomas Aquinas, who claimed that it would be erroneous to state that God is the first matter of all things.[192] A similar objection was raised by the following statement: all beings are identical to the essence of God. This resulted in blurring the boundary between the Creator and creation.[193]

Wanting to prevent the above difficulties, Alexander of Hales wrote that all beings exist in the same divine essence. Much earlier, Dionysius the Areopagite strove to avoid problems in a similar way when he wrote: "the being of all things is the divinity above being."[194] This formula was approved by Aquinas who remarked that the word "above" removes the danger of pantheism, which identifies the Creator with creation.[195] An original thought was presented by Cusanus, who claimed that God both constitutes the *esse omnium*, as well as transcends the world of creatures: *super esse*.[196] The difficulty with combining these two aspects is well conveyed by the most controversial statement made by Cusanus: "Thus, it seems to be the case that God and creation are the same thing – according to the mode of the Giver *God*, according to the mode of the given *the creation*."[197]

When analyzing the relationship between the Creator and creation, Cusanus took his own intellectual path and introduced the notion of contraction. The only being not subject to this is God, whereas all other beings exist in a state of contraction: *omnia alia contracta*.[198] The imprecise examples of contraction and unclear commentaries provided by Cusanus himself gave rise to interpretative pluralism. One such contraction would be based on the individualization of specific actual beings. This is accomplished by extracting a specific being from the area of not yet actualized possibilities. God extracts and develops particular actual beings from the domain of undetermined potentiality, where they appeared as a possibility devoid of specific properties. The first being that is subject to contraction is the created universe.[199]

In Cusanus' view, contraction manifests the subjection of creation to the divine *explicatio*. Irrespective of the individual possibilities offered by the interpretation of the term used initially, thanks to fifteenth-century inspiration we can explain the ontological conditioning of God's immanence in the world and arrive at the foundations necessary to develop a panentheistic concept of nature, in which the boundary between the Creator and creation will not be blurred. The essence of God is not identical with the essence of the beings that abide in the physical world: "it is not the case that God is in the sun sun and in the moon moon; rather, (in them) He is that which is sun and moon without plurality and difference."[200] Drawing on these historical considerations, panentheists stress that it is not so much that God exists in the world as that creation exists in the Creator who conditions all life and development.[201]

Insightful analysis of the wealth of content found in the works of Cusanus does not justify assigning a pantheistic approach to this thinker. Pantheism is not an unavoidable consequence of emphasizing divine omnipresence. However, the proposition put forward by the author of *De possest* requires the adoption of some essential theses concerning the ontology of possible worlds and the nature of God. The wealth of divine nature is not exhausted by the actually existing world of created beings because in God there are also the possibilities of concrete entities coming into being. In Him everything that variously exists or can exist is concealed: "whatever either has been created or will be created is unfolded from Him, in whom it is enfolded."[202]

The approach presented by Cusanus is different to that of Aquinas regarding perception of God as a pure act free from any potentiality. Aquinas based his interpretation of God's immanence in nature on the concept of participation, which uses the image of a chain of beings embedded in the source of all existence. Participation in the being of the omnipresent God explained both creation's dependence on the Creator and His presence in the world.[203]

The presentation of God's immanence in the world has proponents in both the Aristotelian-Thomistic and the Platonic tradition. The latter is characteristic of the exponents of processualism, for whom *be* means "to be a potentiality with respect to the process of becoming."[204] Whitehead discusses the problem of so-called eternal objects in the context of reflection on the potentiality of the universe. This potentiality has to exist since it is significant to those actual beings in which it is still going to be realized.[205] Similar reflection can be found in studies of many philosophy-oriented physicists, who perceive the basic reality as a set of fields, whereas all else is seen as the consequence of the quantum dynamics of these fields. "It is . . . meaningless to ask what fields are made of . . . The current view is that fields are irreducible—they have no parts; they are the simplest things."[206]

The fields of potentiality are determined by means of equations which describe their changes. A reference to a mathematical description, on the other hand, makes it possible to derive realized physical states from an abstract structure which is subject to mathematical formalism. Procedures of this kind are characteristic of ontology, where the elementary level of reality is thought to be formed by potential beings that are the ontic reason for the actualization of the physical world. Authors with a theistic attitude make use of the above intuitions to express the idea of "God's mind." It is mirrored in the world through physical beings, whose observable parameters are a shadow of the primordial mathematical structure. God's mind remains transcendent in relation to any actualizations of the potentialities contained therein.[207]

The world in God?

Process philosophy has inspired many diverse forms of panentheism, which stresses the "immersion" of creation in the Creator. This idea is elaborated on by Peacocke, who assumes that the world exists in God. The Creator transcends creation, even though He pervades each being and exists in every place and time. Nature is a form of God's creative activity in the world. The Creator is active in the processes of nature, as well as in human consciousness, while preserving the autonomy of the creation. Evil in the world appears to be an element of the peculiar risk God takes. Man, endowed with free will, can shape the world in his own way.[208]

Being present in everything that exists, God cooperates with the system of the world as a whole. In influencing the world, the Creator can affect events on every level of the structure of creation, without abolishing the laws characteristic of a particular area of existence, including the physical, biotic, and psychic. Individual events occur autonomously and this happens in accord with God's design for the world. For God to act, no gaps in the ontic structure of the world are needed.[209]

Analogously to the way the whole affects its constituent parts observable in the working of nature, God can holistically influence the state of the entire system of the world. Each such interaction between God and the world originally occurs with the world as a whole. God's action also embraces the individual levels of the world's structure with their specific complexity. By way of a unique intermediating cascade, God can effect particular patterns of events which express His intentions. The realization of specific events would not be possible without God's purposeful action.[210]

The model of the Creator–creation interaction proposed by Peacocke is compatible with the idea of the causal closure of the world system. All levels of the world's structure are composed only of elementary physical units. There are no dualistic, vitalistic, or any other supernatural levels through which God could put pressure on the world. The Creator's interaction with creation does not take place "from the outside" but "from the inside" of the world. Acknowledging that the world "exists in God" makes it possible to combine God's complete distinctness with His ability to act in the world by means of "whole–part" causality. Is it not true that, if God is infinite, He "will probably have to include the universe in one way or another?"[211]

Peacocke's *Paths from Science Towards God. The End of All Our Exploring* contains a graphical presentation of the panentheistic interdependence between God and the world, illustrating ontological relations. The limitation of this diagram lies in its two-dimensionality, which can lead to the conclusion that God is separated from the world. Indeed, God is "more and other" than the world. Nonetheless, this does not rule out the divine omnipresence in and for the world. God has an immanent influence on the fate of the world and man. Augustine had a similar notion: to him creation is like "some sponge, huge, but bounded ... filled with that unmeasurable sea" of God, "environing and penetrating it though every way infinite ... everywhere and on every side."[212]

Though it might appear so, Peacocke's concept is not devoid of precision or reference to the natural sciences. The panentheism of this British biochemist stems from his conviction that philosophy should be practiced in the context of the leading ideas elaborated upon within contemporary science. One of these ideas concerns the phenomenon of the evolutionary emergence of more complex forms in the course of the development of nature. Emergent structures, and their properties, cannot be completely reduced, either ontologically or conceptually. It is not enough to refer to the previous state of a system.[213] There is an existing and active force in nature which continues to render the world a new place. Christian theism identifies this force with God, whose presence in the world can be compared to the role of the composer of a musical piece. This kind of the Creator–creation interaction is one of the possible ontological interpretations of emergentism.[214]

The problem of God's presence in the world gains an original shape in G. F. R. Ellis's interpretation, which develops a pluralistic ontology of nature. In his concept of *kenosis*, Ellis points to God as being concealed in the world's structure. God does not impose His presence but discreetly attracts us to affirm His existence. God's penetration into the world of man enables him to notice the most profound conditionings for rationality and sense, and also brings a sense of beauty while discovering the Creator's relationship to creation. *Kenosis* is understood as the subtle companionship of God who allows himself to be discovered by people who seek the truth about the world and who are open to transcendental values. The Creator's self-limitation is not contrary to His power since it should not be similar to the power of tyrants but the bravery of people of the great heart. Therefore, the mutual opposition of values does not lead to an antinomy but rather to the discovery of a hidden harmony.[215]

The above approach reflects research that is independent of philosophy practiced in the context of science. Despite his mathematical and scientific education, Ellis proposes a concept of the Creator–creation relationship which is closer to aesthetics or even mysticism. A similar intellectual attitude can be found in the work of the forerunners of panentheism. The term "panentheism" itself was introduced to philosophical literature in the 1820s by the German philosopher and mystic Karl Krause.[216]

What is common to many such elaborate propositions is an attempt at delineating an area between classical theism—stressing the "distance" between the perfect Creator and imperfect creation—and pantheism, which blurs the distinction between God and the world. The development of panentheism, including its idealistic forms, took place in two fundamental spheres. On the philosophical plane, scholars gradually moved away from the metaphysics of substance to promote the metaphysics of subjectivity. In theology, on the other hand, a transition took place from the theology of perfection to the theology of infinity. The world started to be viewed as an expression of a developing spirit embedded in the infinity of God. The result of intellectual explorations that were conceptually akin to German idealism would be the following statement: if God is to be truly infinite, He must contain a finite world within His Divinity.[217]

Process philosophy strove to show panentheism as an intermediate solution between classical theism and pantheism. This was possible by making reference to the so-called law of polarity, which offers a complementary presentation of solutions that are usually perceived in terms of disjunction. Panentheism is constructed as a bipolar doctrine that enables, in some way, the merging of eternity and temporality, as well as transcendence and immanence. Processualists claim that unipolar propositions are the evidence of unjustified absolutization of one of the elements of the opposition over the other. Nevertheless, there is no reason why God could not be defined as a self-aware, omniscient being who, in some respects, is both eternal (immutable) and temporal (mutable). In this context, it is emphasized that God contains all of the world's entities while remaining distinct from it.[218]

The peak of Hartshorne's combinatorics comes with the introduction of the concept of God's and world's dual nature. This innovative and equally controversial idea assumes that both the world and God, with regard to their aspects, have both contingent and necessary natures. On the one hand, the world appears to be a contingent entity and God as the necessary one. On the other hand, the existence of a unique relationship between the world and God (meaning that they seem to have a common aspect) makes the contingent world bear a trace of necessity, and the necessary God reveals a trait of contingency (which makes it possible to speak of the dual nature of both of these beings).[219]

In the Polish intellectual world, Życiński, the author of a book on theism and analytic philosophy, promoted panentheism (though not an indiscriminate one) from the very first years of his academic activity. This is understandable as Życiński was influenced by processualism, to which he gave much thought. In referring to the reflection of Whitehead, Życiński claimed that the field of rationality (or potentiality) constituted by timeless objects should be treated as a manifestation of divine nature. The uniqueness of the rationality field lies in the fact that it constitutes the ultimate ontic matrix defining the spectrum of all possible states of the universe and interconnections among them.[220]

This view unquestionably points to Platonically oriented ontology of nature and was further developed in the framework of scientific panentheism. Życiński formulates a concept of the God–world relationship that avoids spatial categories and anthropomorphisms. The God of philosophy is identified with a nomic-mathematical structure that outlines the possibilities of nature's development. The world participates in an abstract structure which can be explored through scientific reflection. The major goal of human research is to decipher the properties of the world's deepest structure. This is perceived as the foundational idea of science.[221]

The concept of the field of rationality as identified with God raises questions concerning His nature. Christian theism presents God as a person who enters into a relationship with creation, and especially with human beings. From this point of view, demonstrating the nomic structure of the world is not sufficient for a comprehensive demonstration of the unique nature of the Creator who continues to give Himself to creation as a personal gift. This more significant aspect of the divine nature appears to be comprehensible only from the ethical-axiological perspective. Nonetheless, the rationality field hypothesis highlights the immanence of God in nature without ruling out His transcendence, and thus enables reflection in the sphere of scientific panentheism.[222]

Życiński admitted that the view of panentheism he formulated did not show the apparently most essential component of classical theism. In some ways, the philosophy practiced in the context of science he feels attracted to makes it methodologically impossible to demonstrate theses that are distinctive for classical theism.²²³ On the other hand, however, this kind of philosophy is not identified either with pantheism or with strong naturalism.²²⁴ This philosophical current enables one to cope with the cognitive limitations and the specific mentality of contemporary man, who by reflecting on the mystery of the world frequently narrows down the horizon of being by ascribing divine traits to ontically indefinite and transient reality.²²⁵

Panentheism is criticized for a number of things, starting with it being a collection of diverse and often vague ideas. A literal understanding of the panentheistic form of expression gives rise to basic problems in defining God's relationship to the world. However, we must admit that many of the objections that panentheists put forward against classical theism aptly convey certain important religious intuitions. After all, the biblical message does not present God as an alien and distant Absolute who is active only in critical situations, but as a companion of the history of humanity and the world. God fills the entire cosmos, with nature being a manifestation of His immanence. The Creator is not a deistic observer who watches the story of creation, but rather remains continuously involved in the process of its development, and above all in the most personal experiences of the human being. From such a perspective, the God–world interaction does not resemble a mechanistic influence exerted from beyond the system (similarly to *deus ex machina*). On the other hand, no set of realized processes can exhaust the richness of His nature, therefore God is a transcendent being.²²⁶

In disagreeing with the fundamental theses of panentheism, Wojtysiak acknowledges the possibility of considering some of its postulates for theism to develop, especially reflection on God's nature, based on which we can speak of a particular trait of His relational or intentional contingency. This trait is of no consequence for the ontically-modal characteristics of God. Another important element of panentheism is that it takes into account the currently dominant way of thinking that is attracted to science-oriented discourse, mistrust of metaphysical speculation, preference for reasoning in spatial categories, anthropocentrism and "naturocentrism." In this context, panentheism can serve as an opportunity to overcome the naturalistic paradigm, within which we can, at best, defend pantheism.²²⁷ I analyze the question of panentheism one more time at the end of the next chapter of the present study because panentheism emphasizes the closeness of God to the world and uses the language of metaphor.

* * *

I started my presentation of the nature of the world with God operating in it by reflecting on the question of autonomy. It is different from independence, in which all signs of divine presence in the world would be treated as violating the rules governing the world. For many theists, these rules are an expression of the Creator's design. God does not manipulate creation but acts as an agent behind the rationality of the world, which is not chaotic. Contemporary reflection on the laws of nature demonstrates the fact that we frequently interpret them narrowly. Another important problem is the ontological status of the laws of nature (including the question of their theistic interpretation), and understanding the specific character of random processes that can be interpreted as the "instrument" of God acting in nature, rather than a breach in the rationality of the world. This particular issue is discussed in detail in the next chapter.

On the other hand, the cosmos does not appear to be a paradise devoid of ontic and moral fractures. This results from the difference between necessary being and contingent being. Evil and suffering in the world are not conclusive evidence that God does not exist or act in the world. This is easier to understand if we assume that divine action does not consist in suspending or abolishing the laws of nature. Instead of highlighting the role of selective intervention in the structure of the world, God's action should be presented as *creatio continua* and in the categories of providing people with a stable environment for moral growth. Such an approach does not bring consolation to man who finds himself struggling with evil. Such moments naturally lead to the question: Is providence real? Although philosophical analyses do not bring a straightforward answer to it, kenosis is definitely helpful in that. Assuming that God is immanently present in the world, we do not doom ourselves to searching for interventionist manifestations of His action. The closeness of the world to God is strongly underscored by panentheism, which, however, should be further elaborated to avoid the blurring of the ontic boundary between the Creator and creation.[228]

4

Threats and Challenges

The analyses carried out thus far produce many conclusions. Some of them have already been formulated. The present chapter is a presentation of the crucial threats and challenges that the theists who undertake the question of divine action in the world have to face. Apart from the areas of interest directly suggested by the very titles of particular sections of this chapter, what is also significant are the more detailed conclusions arrived at in the course of the present discussion. Detection of these conclusions is facilitated by taking into consideration the historical and scientific perspectives, employing the language of postulation, drawing on fragments of selected studies, and placing a more pronounced emphasis on what determines the development of the discussed question. In order to demonstrate the crux of the matter with precision, in some parts of my study I include a context wider than the main problem itself.

"God of the gaps"

From local interventions to God's continuous action

In the Christian milieu a view has been held for years that the theory of God's presence in the world is easier to be formulated and supported on the grounds of "gaps" present in the scientific depiction of the world. Referring to God's action seemed natural in instances when science could not provide sufficient answers to the question of the causes of given phenomena. The critics of such an approach pointed out, however, that this is burdened with the risks brought about by the advances of science and the emergence of successive discoveries which yield new naturalistic explanations of the course of nature's processes. The progress of science fills interpretative blank spaces on a regular basis. The concept of the "gaps" of an epistemic character serving as an occasion to formulate theistic hypotheses was therefore rejected in the light of contemporary philosophy of science.

The character of ontological causal "gaps" is entirely different. In assuming that God acts within history we should as much as expect them to a certain extent. These "gaps" occur when events are not fully determined by what precedes them.[1] Such situations are an integral part of the processes of nature, provided that we do not perceive them in mechanistic categories, which could be more easily eliminated thanks to the

Darwinian revolution in science, additionally offering new possibilities to elaborate upon the theory of divine action. While within the mechanistic worldview the intervention of God is needed only when the "world clock" calls for repair, the theistic interpretation of the "fertility" of nature which develops continuously allows for relating the creativity of particular organisms to the immanent presence of the Creator in creation.

In the second half of the nineteenth century, the representatives of many important academic centers in England and the United States pointed out that the evolutionary explanation of the way nature works conveyed the Christian message of creation and God's presence within it better than biology elaborated on the grounds of Aristotelian thought. A. L. Moore wrote:

> The one absolutely impossible conception of God, in the present day is that which represents Him as an occasional Visitor. Science had pushed the deist's God farther and farther away, and at the moment when it seemed as if He would be thrust out altogether, Darwinism appeared, and, under the disguise of a foe, did the work of a friend. It has conferred upon philosophy and religion an inestimable benefit, by showing us that we must choose between two alternatives. Either God is everywhere present in nature, or He is nowhere.[2]

Moore claimed that a proper intellectual distance should be maintained towards interpretations which stress the role of God's special interventions in the development of nature. The authors of the latter explanation, often unconsciously, remained close to deism, and limited divine action to the genesis of the world at the onset of history. Darwinism, on the other hand, helped to overcome the oversimplifications brought about by deism and interventionism. Moore, an Anglican clergyman and lecturer in plant biology at Oxford, was of the opinion that everything in the world either is or is not the creative work of God. He also called for returning to the Christian view of "the immanence of divine power in nature from end to end, the belief in a God in Whom not only we, but all things have their being."[3]

In another text Moore additionally claimed that God is omnipresent in all creative activity. Therefore, it would be a mistake to separate the dynamics of nature and all of its laws from God. After all, to a Christian theologian every natural phenomenon is evidence of God's action.[4] For this reason, Darwinian reflection on the functioning of nature served as an occasion for the development of natural theology and the revival of the metaphysical doctrine of the Creator's immanence in creation. This doctrine was never openly challenged, but in practice its exponents often manifested inconsistency. While striving to determine the role of God in the processes of nature, theists often referred to miraculous interventions, as if His immanent presence in the world was devoid of agency.[5]

During this same period, an analogical message was conveyed by Henry Drummond, who stressed that by pointing to special moments of divine action in a given place we imply the lack of God's activity at the remaining stages of nature's development. If God appears exclusively in strictly specified events, He remains absent in others. The idea of the immanent God of evolution seems to be much more valuable than the concept of an occasional miracle-worker. By being ever-present in the world, God is the source of the potentiality of nature in which new possibilities actualize continuously.[6]

The change of the scientific paradigm which took place in the second half of the nineteenth century led to a significantly more frequent presentation of God as immanently present in natural processes. Modern sciences highlighted the continuity of evolutionary transformations without excluding the possibility of acknowledging ontological "leaps" at certain stages of the world's development. However, in such cases there is no need to refer to supernatural causes of phenomena since the undergoing processes are of an emergent character. Treating creation as an event belonging to the past resulted in the perception of divine action at the landmark stages of the world's development as a kind of interventionism. The concept of *creatio continua*, on the other hand, allows for comprehending God as continually bringing nature into being in every manifestation of its fertility. Therefore, we do not need to look for the alleged gaps or extraordinary mechanisms which God supposedly uses in the process of creation.[7]

Are there any gaps left for divine action?

In contemporary times, answering the following question is particularly weighty: are there any "gaps" in nature which testify to the very structure of the world? In this context, Polkinghorne stresses that nature has an integral element of openness that results in its development not being based on the copying of the existing states of events but rather on bringing about an authentic novelty. If top-down intentional causality is at work in the world then there must also exist "spaces of potentiality" which can be called "intrinsic gaps."[8]

A critical point in the course of analyzing the discussed issue is interpreting chaos theory. In the light of its specificity, Drees puts forward a critical assessment of the transition from deterministic theories to ontological openness. Drees notes that the theory of chaotic systems does not require a new principle to be introduced. Scientific studies into the workings of certain non-linear systems do not reveal the existence of any gaps that should be filled with actions carried out by an external personal factor. It is true that complex systems function as if guided by external organizing principles or an intentional agent. However, this can be explained without reference to factors derived from outside of a given system. As such, deterministic chaos "is the extension of the bottom-up program to complex systems."[9]

In discerning the fundamental difference between gaps of an ontological character and those of an epistemological one, it needs to be noted that even if we assume the existence of unpredictability within chaotic systems, these systems are all still embedded in a certain theory.[10] Thus, referring to the idea of "gaps" in this context would not entail stating a lack of knowledge but disregarding it. On the macro-level there are no reasons to ascertain physical discontinuity. The outcomes of the analyses of phenomena which are conducted on the quantum level are an entirely different question.[11]

Drees stresses that the predictability of phenomena does not constitute a necessary condition for explaining their course. The chaos theory concerns such processes of nature which are extremely sensitive to alterations within their initial conditions. We cannot accurately predict tomorrow's weather because we are not able to recognize the subtlety of the interactions which play a significant role in the so-called "butterfly effect."[12] *Post factum*, however, we obtain access to a description of the origins of a situation which could have occurred, for instance, as a result of the minute fluctuations in air density.[13]

Many authors working on the realization of the Divine Action Project dissociate themselves from trying to find one special form of God's presence, either within the framework of the openness of deterministic chaos or within quantum processes. Obviously, it cannot be excluded that God acts within the domain of the unpredictability of the events which make up the evolution of a certain system. Nevertheless, we have access to knowledge concerning the physical causes that can lead to a significant change under the influence of as much as a slight impulse which affects the very onset of an evolving system that is part of the macro-world. An entirely different issue is that of quantum indeterminacies, during interpretation of which we can find reasons to exclude the influence of "hidden variables," and these reasons allow us to rule out an explanation of the limited predictability as a result of real, albeit unobservable, physical processes. Nonetheless, in the case of quantum physics we need to be cautious, since this is subject to alterations and continues to be affected by various interpretations.[14]

In light of an analysis of chaotic systems, we can assume that God has absolute knowledge of their course, comprehending not only all of the deterministic laws pertaining to a given system, but also the initial conditions which will determine a system's state at any specific time, as well as any potential sources of external influence. No unpredictability exists for the omnipotent God and He would know even the most minute fluctuations of dissipative systems, the course of which cannot be fully envisaged by humans. However, this does not seem to constitute a rational reason to formulate the thesis of God manipulating initial conditions to arrive at macroscopic results compatible with His will. Such actions might occur within the flexibility of a given process in a manner undetectable by means of human cognition. Even more, such a manifestation of divine action would be compatible with our scientific knowledge.[15]

Despite having the appearances of intellectual attraction, the concept of God's special action in situations we deem unpredictable would not be essentially different from other interventionist approaches. God would still be seen as interfering with the order of nature, the only difference between this particular hypothesis and other approaches which assume divine intervention being that God's actions are always hidden from us. Allowing for unpredictability, flexibility, and openness in the worldview does not facilitate our cognition of the exact "place" of the causal chain in which God acts in the world, even though our understanding of what happens in the world is enriched in such a situation.[16]

The indeterminacy of data obtained on the quantum level is usually treated by philosophizing physicists as an inherent, irremovable, and fundamental trait of nature. As a result of this, gaps on the subatomic level are sometimes treated as a suitable "field" for divine action. In this way, God would influence, in accordance with the laws of nature, the outcomes of events and humans would not be able to detect such an influence. Certain proponents of this approach go as far as to claim that God affects all quantum events, others assume selective action on His part, especially in situations the consequences of which are revealed on a larger scale. The latter proposal can be understood as pointing out the ways in which God influences the course of biological evolution (on the quantum level of DNA mutations), and even human thought (on the level of neuron synapses).[17]

Peacocke notes that the proponents of God's strong engagement in all quantum events implicitly confirm His complete and direct conditioning of all natural processes. In the end, all natural events are grounded in the quantum level. Such an approach can lead to well-known theodical problems, including those of free will and the presence of evil in the world.

Assuming that God intervenes directly in the script of chosen quantum events (particularly those which—after reinforcement—can lead to significant effects on a higher level, e.g., reducing the occurrence of genetic diseases) is an option which can raise at least two serious objections. First of all, each theory of God's direct and occasional influence on a specific measurement result seems to deny the intrinsic creativity of nature. The processes of nature reveal an inherent rationality, coherence, and creativity that result in the emergence of novelty, diversity, and complexity. Claiming that God's action can affect a change on the level of probability or the actual result of a wave function reduction would mean returning to the idea of God manipulating the very processes and laws which were brought into being and are constantly being brought into being by God Himself. It is of no consequence whether any human observer was actually capable of detecting such an involvement on the part of God.[18]

Secondly, if the outcomes of measurements on the quantum level are, ontologically, of a probabilistic character, God—from a logical point of view—cannot know the exact result of a given measurement result. Even more, a potential interference aimed at the modification of a given event could generate an additional problem: to maintain all of the probability relations that govern quantum events many (one might say: ridiculously many) other events would have to change as well.[19] Only then, in accordance with the model assumption, would humans not be able to detect the violation of general statistics. To provide conditioning for microscopic events on an Earth-scale, God would have to predetermine an immense number of quantum processes in immeasurably long periods in the future.[20]

Genuine and spurious gaps

In expressing his criticism of the "God of the gaps" theory, Heller notes that in the world scientifically viewed as a whole, the traditionally understood "gaps" do not exist. As a consequence, in the world there simply are no "special places" of this kind in which God could act. While approaching certain philosophical questions, however, it is substantially justified to refer to gaps which can be assumed to be *genuine gaps*, with these being different from the so-called *spurious gaps*. The latter are of a temporary character since they are dependent on the state of our knowledge at a given time. Such cases are the result of a theory being incomplete.[21]

Heller puts three cases under the category of *genuine gaps*, all of which are treated by him as an actual scientific challenge. The first case belongs to the ontological sphere and can be expressed in the following question: Why does something rather than nothing exist? Therefore, the problem pertains to "sheer existence." Irrespective of the supposedly successful formulation of the so-called theory of everything, the following question still remains open: who or what has breathed fire into the equations and has made a universe for them to describe?[22] The second *genuine gap* refers to an epistemological issue: why is the world comprehensible at all? Science assumes that the world is rational and as such accessible to cognition; however, science does not explain these phenomena. The philosophy of science does as much as to point to the non-trivial character of this issue but remains helpless in the face of the repeatedly posed question of "Why?" The third case, being an axiological gap, refers to the meaning and value of all existence. Assuming that the universe is in some way permeated with sense, we conclude that this problem eludes scientific methods, and remains an unsolvable riddle both for science and the philosophy of science. From the theistic point of view, the above-mentioned "gaps" have common roots because "the sources of existence, rationality, and value are the same."[23]

From among these gaps Stoeger marks out the first in suggesting that in the strict sense we can only discuss very specific ontological gaps.[24] In his opinion, not one factor from outside the sphere of science is needed to explain the gradual appearance of novelty in nature, even at such stages of its development as the origin of life or the genesis of consciousness. Therefore, the introduction of *élan vital* on the level of biogenesis, or *élan spirituel* when abstract thought first appeared, would suggest a denial of the emergent features of nature and a return to already discredited interventionist ideas. The reason for the introduction of interventionist concepts originated in the conviction that nature does not have any intrinsic creative capabilities and that only God's special action can justify interpretation of the critical turning points of the evolution of nature.[25]

However, stating the fact of nature's fertility, as well as explaining all of nature's detailed workings, does not provide answers to the most fundamental metaphysical questions. Why are the laws of nature of a particular character and not any other? Why does the world continue to develop dynamically without showing any tendency to maintain the existing *status quo*? Why is there order rather than chaos? Such issues are a problem for the natural sciences as well as for philosophy. The entirely different kinds of "gaps" found in scientific cognition are those which become regularly filled with new findings.[26]

A broad understanding of the laws of nature

Stoeger analyzes the problem of "gaps" from the perspective of divine action in the world as well as the issue of primary and secondary causality. The goal of science is to look for the causes of phenomena, the finding of which enriches our state of knowledge. It should be assumed that there are no interruptions in the chain of secondary causes. A consequence of withdrawing from the paradigm of natural continuity would be to renounce the presently binding scientific model and to return to the times when *Deus ex machina* explanations were still an acceptable interpretation. Primary causality should be understood in an entirely different manner since it is essentially different from secondary causes discovered in the process of scientific development. The very existence of a chain of secondary causes, as well as its efficiency, calls for primary causality, with this constituting the ultimate fundament of reality. Classical Christian theism identifies this with God who sustains beings in existence and allows for their fulfillment.[27]

To overcome the mentality which finds its expression in the idea of the "God of the gaps," it is crucial to keep stressing that the act of creation is continuous in its nature. Simply stating the fact that God sustains the world in existence is not sufficient since His presence is manifested in the regularities, bonds, and relationships which make up the laws of nature. Over the course of time, as new encoded natural possibilities become realized, God participates in the creation of structures which are increasingly complex. In such a way, actions which transcend the laws of nature, by lifting or weakening them, seem to move to the background, irrespective of discussions on God's omnipotence.[28] Even in the light of the supposition that the Creator enters into interventionist interactions with creation, it needs to be assumed that the laws of nature are the main manifestation of God's action in the world. Discovering the intricacies of the way nature functions leads us closer to grasping the truth concerning God through revealing the most fundamental manner of His non-interventionist activity in created reality.[29]

The logic behind the *God of the gaps* theory acquires a particular shape when we differentiate between the concept of the laws of nature compatible with our state of knowledge regarding the functioning of the world, and the laws of nature that are perceived as the entirety of things which become realized in the world. The theories and the formalism concerning the laws of nature move the basic relationships which organize the world on the most fundamental level out of reach. And it is these relationships that bind the separate levels of the structure of the world together, particularly the impersonal with the personal one. We do not know the exact ways in which the impersonal world is subordinate to us, but at least we manage to discern some of the elements of the proneness of the nature's indeterminacy to human influence. From the perspective of a human observer these elements can be interpreted as working against the laws of nature. The reason for this can be found in the limitations of human cognition which narrow the concept of the laws of nature. We simply know too little to connect the given aspects of reality to one whole. We do not possess a full comprehension of relationships and regularities on the basic natural level; therefore, within the framework of theistic depictions of the functioning of the world, a temptation arises to introduce the hypothesis of God's interventionist action. The "gaps" in cognition provide a possibility to discern such an interaction between the Creator and creation in which we find the suspension, limitation or abolition of the laws of nature. However, God can act in a perfectly "natural" way through relationships and regularities which we cannot yet grasp in a scientific framework in light of our present state of knowledge.[30]

Renouncing the most naive forms of striving to look for a special divine presence in those of the natural processes the functioning of which has not yet been scientifically explained is an expression of far-sighted theistic practice. Scientists regularly remove these doubts which previously seemed to necessarily require the assumption of God's intervention at certain stages of the world's development. This does not mean, however, that the relationship between scientific and theistic theories has the character of an exclusive disjunction in the light of which the following principle can be formed: the more we know from the scientific perspective, the fewer chances there are of formulating statements concerning divine action in the world. Scientific and theistic interpretations can be treated as complementary approaches. It is in such a context that the ongoing development of nature is explained as the result of God's immanent presence in the world. This train of thought will be continued in the next section of the book since similar problems arise during reflection on teleology.

Teleology

Divine harmony

In the light of the long-standing Judeo-Christian and Ancient Greek concept of rationality and sense, all beings have their proper, natural place and the processes of nature always serve a predefined purpose. Until the rise of modern science, it was commonly believed that the universe is a living, orderly organism which functions in a purpose-oriented way. In this context, Kepler gave testimony to a true intellectual openness when at the turn of the seventeenth century he posed the question of whether the universe appears to be a living organism or a perfectly constructed machine. He could not unambiguously choose any of the given options as intellectually valid. The temptation to treat the world as a living organism was to some extent understandable since many scholars made use of simplified and naive observations. Some of them were supposed to confirm that bees, scorpions, and frogs emerge as a result of the decay of non-living matter, and that mud gives birth to worms in sufficiently humid environments. Even the criticism of the theory of spontaneous generation formulated by Pasteur did not result in the introduction of any essential changes to many commonsense remarks. For years emphasis was put on order in nature and it was observed that the course of all natural processes is a manifestation of an evolutionary plan designed in advance and subsequently realized. Theists had no doubt as to the author of this cosmic blueprint.[31]

In teleology-dominated cosmologies it was stressed that the structure and development of the universe were meticulously defined in the plan of the Creator.[32] The perception of the world as a living organism resulted in the tending of particular physical processes towards their appropriate goals being seen as an expression of the rationality behind creation. As late as the nineteenth century, studies of the functioning of nature contained explanations that water reaches its maximum density at the temperature of –4°C in order to enable the living organisms that dwell in the depths to survive harsh winters.[33]

For a long time, reasoning in teleological categories had its manifestation in explanations that concerned the specificity of the functioning of biotic systems. Before the advance of the Darwinian revolution, animate nature was treated as an orderly system of unchanging species governed by the principle of teleology. Since the seventeenth century a one-of-a-kind alliance of science and religion prevailed in the British Isles, where the harmony of natural processes was underlined from various cognitive perspectives. The good intentions of many intellectuals in searching for an interdisciplinary dialogue did not eradicate the practice of naive reflection dominated by uncritical teleology.

In the British milieu many teleological interpretations emerged in the first half of the nineteenth century despite numerous scientific discoveries made during this same time in various disciplines. Even more, it was thought that thanks to the development of science an element uniting all of the varied research outcomes was arrived at in the form of the law of conservation of energy. There were scholars who perceived this as the means by which all natural phenomena could be connected into one whole. Such a conviction led to the formulation of the following thesis: the world governed by God is full of harmony. It was suggestively noted that mechanical, chemical, and biological phenomena alike are based on converting kinetic energy into heat. Joule stated:

> Thus it is that order is maintained in the universe—nothing is deranged, nothing ever lost, but the entire machinery, complicated as it is, works smoothly and harmoniously. And though, as in the awful vision of Ezekiel, "wheel may be in the middle of wheel" and everything may appear complicated and involved in the apparent confusion and intricacy of an almost endless variety of causes, effects, conversions and arrangements, yet is the most perfect regularity preserved—the whole being governed by the sovereign will of God.[34]

Teleological interpretative patterns gave rise to numerous anthropomorphisms and encouraged scholars to search for manifestations of the divine scheme everywhere. The shape of the human nose had to be justified with the ease with which it holds glasses, and the number and position of the fingers with the opportunity they give to hold a pen comfortably. The regularities which occur within the populations of organisms had to be explained in the same vein. The similar number of newborns of both sexes was interpreted as a manifestation of a harmony designed by God so that, upon reaching maturity, every man was able to easily find a life partner.[35] The purpose and order that govern the world were seen as the expression of a divine project, presented in the most detailed and simultaneously literary manner by Paley. At the beginning of the nineteenth century, Paley formulated a classically shaped argument—based on nature's purposiveness—for the existence and action of God.[36] The theory introduced in the *Natural Theology*[37] was enchanting in its simplicity and orderliness. In its light, God was viewed as the equivalent of the highest engineer, personally generating the processes of adaptation. During his university years in Cambridge, Darwin also found such a vision equally fascinating. In the course of time, however, Darwin's delight transformed into skeptical criticism. Discerning purpose in nature's functioning while a rational explanation could be formulated by reference to the efficient causes of phenomena automatically stalled any further insightful study. Having noticed this problem, Darwin was able to commence a more mature stage of his explorations, as done both while traveling around the world, and in the domestic refuge provided by the little village of Downe.[38]

God in a raindrop?

There were diverse reasons for the relatively slow transformations occurring in this field. One of the main causes was due to the general acceptance of the Aristotelian way of thinking in interpreting natural phenomena. Another significant factor was the fact that emerging dilemmas included theological problems which directly touched the sphere of religious belief. This became evident at the various stages of Darwin's life; having rejected Paley's schemata of reasoning, he was still troubled for a long time by indecisions both in the sphere of intellect and belief. On July 12, 1870 Darwin stated:

> My theology is a simple muddle I cannot look at the universe as the result of blind chance, yet I can see no evidence of beneficent design or indeed of design of any kind, in the details. As for each variation that has ever occurred having been preordained for a special end, I can no more believe in it than that the spot on which each drop of rain falls has been specially ordained.[39]

Subsequent years of reflection on the world deepened Darwin's conviction that the traditional view of order in nature within which God intervenes directly calls for considerable modification. On the other hand, however, the stability and order of the universal laws of nature did not appear to Darwin to be the effect of random conditioning. Therefore, Darwin alternated between a general perspective in the light of which the observed natural order originated in the actions of the Creator, and particular concretizations of the course of phenomena which were dependent on local physical conditions. In one of his later letters, Darwin wrote: "I cannot anyhow be contented to view this wonderful universe & especially the nature of man, & to conclude that everything is the result of brute force. I am inclined to look at everything as resulting from designed laws, with the details, whether good or bad, left to the working out of what we may call chance."[40]

Many natural scientists of that epoch for a very long time found it hard to change their reasoning patterns and begin a consequent search for the causes of phenomena, even while discussing problems as specific as the extinction of a given species. As a result, some publications assert that a lost fight for existence should be explained by reference to a species' inherent purpose, as encoded in nature by God. Hugh Miller stressed that the extinction of some species cannot be explained causally. However, he claimed, one can safely employ teleological interpretation in such cases. In the opinion of the Scottish geologist, the evolution of living beings was aimed at the consolidation of the central position mammals held in nature.[41]

In the circle of "conservative" natural scientists active in the second half of the nineteenth century there were many critics of natural selection theory who adduced a teleological argument. Adam Sedgwick, despite acknowledging the independence of Darwin's mind, feared the ethical implications of the theory of natural selection. In his letter addressed to the author of *The Origin of Species* written on December 24, 1859, the geologist from Cambridge argued that the "crown and glory" of organic science is that it links the material sphere to the moral one by means of the final cause. Even more, in words of painful reproach, Sedgwick stated that Darwin ignored this "link" and did his best to destroy it. Sedgwick's expressive letter concludes with his conviction that thanks to God a break with reference to teleology in the area under discussion is not possible, with this protecting humanity from the rise of brutalization and becoming degraded to the lowest level in history.[42]

The intentional action of God was for a long time identified with selective interventionism. However, by the end of the nineteenth century this had changed among scholars who were well-disposed towards the new findings of biology. An increasing number of representatives of theism were taking advantage of the scientific breakthrough to formulate theses that referred to the idea of *creatio continua*. Iverach wrote:

> To me creation is continuous. To me everything is at it is through the continuous power of God; every law, every being, every relation of being are determined by Him, and He is the Power by which all things exist. I believe in the immanence of God in the world, and I do not believe that He comes forth merely at a crisis.[43]

Avoiding interventionist interpretations pertaining to the actions of the Creator provided space for such explanations which allowed for the perception of evolution as a rational continuation of the divine act of creation. In the case of Iverach, this was connected with an intellectual sensitivity to the epistemological principles that separate humanist disciplines from the natural sciences. He often underlined that theology and biology deal with different research aspects, as a consequence of which the view of the world portrayed by them is also different. In maintaining the cognitive competence of these two disciplines, natural scientists cannot refer to the hypothesis that God leads evolution in a purposive manner. However, in areas where biologists methodically restrict themselves solely to the analysis of the synergy between laws and chance, theologians will search for a more profound argumentation that enables the interpretation of evolutionary processes in the categories of God's creative action. In avoiding anthropomorphisms, the theological explanation of how nature functions does not leave us believing that the world is governed by "blind fate," but provides the possibility of finding traces of the *Logos* embedded in the laws of nature and an opportunity for these laws to be recognized.[44]

Complementarity in place of opposition

In many of the contemporary studies that accentuate the role of God's constant presence in nature, the concept of His immediate intervention loses its former significance. The following thesis subsequently comes to the fore: The Creator participates in the whole process of creation. In metaphorical comparisons God is seen not as a cosmic engineer who supervises the functioning of the world machinery, but rather as an artist who utilizes the qualities of the components of a work of art. Such metaphors, which will be developed further in subsequent sections of my study, convey the truth about the Creator's relationship with creation in a better way than does Paley's "designer" vision.[45] This does not mean that God creates the world without any plan whatsoever. This is not, however, a project vividly portrayed by the author of *Natural Theology*.[46]

The most naive manifestations of the concept of a plan to explain the specificity of nature's development are often rooted in a conviction that the evolution of the universe is of an entirely deterministic character. In such instances, God is portrayed as the Creator who when creating the world took such care of its properties as to achieve the realization of a strictly defined script of development. This concept, however, is incompatible both with the image of God presented by highly developed forms of theism, as well as the interpretation of the laws of nature as being a combination of necessity and chance. The latter introduces a component of spontaneity into the activity of nature, the detailed progress of which is not defined in advance.[47] The laws of nature can at most favor certain evolutionary paths directed towards greater complexity, the most particular expression of which is the abundance of living organisms and the complexity of the human brain with its potential for creative thought.[48]

This interpretation of the evolution of nature can be grasped better by analogy with the workings of lottery games. They are not bereft of rules, with these rules being set beforehand in relation to the game itself, independent of any individual solution that affects a greater or smaller probability of winning. Nevertheless, most often it is not the players who set the rules—they merely accept them upon entering a game. Even more, it is assumed that such games are construed in such a way as to enable a scenario that leads to a win. We can understand the coexistence of the deterministic and indeterministic qualities of natural processes in the same way if we inscribe them in the context of theism.[49] The fact that the development of the universe is directed towards the growth of complexity does not imply the idea of God manipulating evolutionary processes in order to guide them to a meticulously coded design. One can assume, however, that from among all of the potential laws of nature, the Creator chose a set which enhances the probability of originating life and consciousness. All the same, a choice of this kind is not identified with a selection carried out in time, at least not by those theists who claim that the laws of nature are of a sempiternal character and, logically, precede the evolution of the universe.[50]

In some branches of contemporary science we can witness the emergence of a distinctive and significant rehabilitation of teleological interpretations (at times named *quasi*-teleological). To show the transformation which occurred in this field we can refer to areas of physics in which both deterministic and teleological approaches result in identical conclusions. Today, differential and integral interpretations of the conservation principles are adopted as equivalent even though the latter was strongly criticized as late as the 1970s. At that time, the integral approach was deemed a mere mathematical curiosity that was irrelevant to valuable scientific research. In the years to come, however, a fundamental change occurred in this respect.[51] This is most particularly visible in the presence of strong teleological statements in the field of contemporary mathematical physics. In their monograph on the anthropic principle, Barrow and Tipler go as far as to claim that extra-teleological formulations do not have the theoretical strength which is provided by the approach that involves the so-called summing over trajectories.[52] This was introduced on the basis of an interpretation of quantum mechanics which draws inspiration from teleological conceptual proposals.[53]

By taking into consideration contemporary studies in the field of theoretical physics, we contribute to overcoming the opposition between deterministic and teleological interpretations of the specificity of natural phenomena. Processes necessary in the physical sense can also be explained as an evolving system's inclination to reach a specific state that can be described in terms both of finality and of determinism. A situation in which we can effectively make use of efficient and final causes alike takes place in the case of the laws of conservation found in physics. The relations revealed in

Noether's theorem[54] disclose a distinctive trait of the world's structure. The universality of mutual conditionings can be interpreted as a cognitively significant component of the teleological structure of the world. Thus, the category of teleology, often subjected to severe criticism, returns in this "as a substantively acceptable form of description of physical phenomena and one that is equivalent to the causal description."[55]

An analogous turn towards complementary explanations of natural phenomena occurred in twentieth-century biology and was manifested, among other things, within the various versions of philosophical evolutionism. In his theory of teleonomy, Monod strived to combine cause and purpose in a way which would not be threatened by the risks of anthropomorphisms. On the one hand, he expressed a clear disengagement from teleological interpretations. On the other, however, he was convinced that the course of everything seems to suggest that living beings form structures, the organization and conditioning of which are subordinate to a specific purpose: the survival of individuals and, most of all, the survival of species.[56]

Today, many authors use the idea of teleonomy to also shed new light on the possibilities given by the theistic explanation of the way nature functions. In this context, it is often stressed that some systems evolve in a manner which suggests their heading towards the realization of a predefined plan. It is for this reason that referring to the concept of structural directionality seems particularly justified. This excludes direct reference to God inscribing His intentions in the plan of nature's development, while simultaneously defining a set of consequences, the character of which resembles the realization of a pre-designed goal. The teleonomic explanation helps one to avoid strong ontological declarations of a markedly anthropomorphizing tone, while at the same time leaving open the question of whether assuming a particular direction results from the self-organization of a system or is a consequence of the actions undertaken by the Divine Programmer.[57]

Examples of more courageously pronounced statements, supported both theoretically and empirically, on the global direction of evolution are provided in Stoeger's publications. These works pertain to the processes, examined in many spheres (biology, chemistry, astronomy, and geophysics), that—as a result of profound analysis—provide substantive reasons for formulating statements concerning "open teleonomic systems." Stoeger gives examples which prove that local determinism does not preordain its global character, and that the fact that a system aims at a specific final state at a certain stage of its development does not signify *ipso facto* a system's teleological character.[58]

Sometimes, instead of the category of structural directionality, the term "quasi-finality" is employed. Independent of the differences in terminology, what remains convergent is the very content of the theories which allow for the introduction of subtle distinctions in areas previously approached by means of the opposition between determinism and teleology. The legitimacy of such oppositions is questioned when taking into account data gathered during scientific observation, with this providing reasons enough to think that an examined set of processes runs its exact course in such a way as if it were subordinate to a future, as of yet unrealized, goal. The cautious character of the quasi-teleological interpretation of nature is justified by the difficulties that arise when we try to prove that a given goal was indeed consciously adopted in the actions of a particular human being or the Divine Creator.[59]

A weak version of the theory of purposiveness is formulated in a similar vein by Philip Clayton. According to him, the organization of biotic systems seems to function in a way that they are heading in a predefined direction. The constituent parts of a cell, organism, or ecosystem seem to "cooperate" for the survival of the whole.[60] Evolution and the reproduction of organisms are governed by the principle of creating a maximal opportunity for leaving behind a genetic legacy. Obviously, it is impossible, without attempting an annihilation of the methodology of biology, to ascertain that animate nature has the quality of purposeful action. Nevertheless, when discerning the emergence and behavior of organisms, a theory of "purposiveness without purpose" can be proposed. Clayton distinguishes this both from chemical emergence, which is devoid of any teleological dimension, and from purposeful actions on the level of human beings.[61]

The introduction of the "quasi-finality" term does not lead directly to the return of the times when the teleological category dominated science. This introduction does, however, play a significant heuristic role. After all, it transpires that a conflict between two contradictory philosophical declarations can be eradicated thanks to effective attempts at expanding the language of philosophical theories. Complementary use of once antagonized terms is a result of these terms pertaining to complex structures whose qualities extend beyond the set of local causal conditioning and embrace a system in its entirety described in teleological categories. The reinstatement of the concept of purpose in empirical sciences is not identical to asserting the action of a conscious agent. For theists, however, this provides grounds from which to formulate the following hypothesis: God can act in the world in a variety of forms without the need to suspend or break the laws of nature.

Creating a decisive opposition between the teleological and causal interpretation of the behavior of a physical system often occurred for historical reasons. The intensive development of the natural sciences enforced the substitution of teleological explanations with the search for the causes of phenomena so characteristic of the naturalistic approach. Nevertheless, this frequently became an excuse for putting forward the hypothesis, not always directly expressed, that teleological categories are of absolutely no assistance when it comes to explaining the functioning of the world. In contemporary times there are no visible substantive reasons for formulating statements of this kind.[62]

The scientific worldview

Scientific revolution as a gift to theists

In the course of the last several decades, natural sciences have gone through exceptionally radical transformations. Quantum physics, relativistic cosmology, paleontology, neurophysiology, genetics, comparative anatomy, biogeography, embryology, biochemistry, and molecular biology are just some of the many examples of disciplines which have revolutionized the way we think about the world. This genuine intellectual revolution, dating back to the time when *De revolutionibus orbium coelestium* was first published, is symbolized by the people who had made a permanent imprint on the history of humanity: Copernicus, Galileo, Newton, Mendel, Darwin, Einstein, Watson, Crick, and many others.

To some of them, the Christian worldview was an entirely alien concept, albeit their attitude was often a consequence of particular existential experiences or a specific phase of life. Nonetheless, the magnitude of scientific findings which they introduced to the repository of culture remains unquestionable. This fact should undoubtedly be taken into consideration while analyzing the crucial issues that concern both science and religion, namely: the creation of the world, God's presence and action in nature, the genesis of life and man, human freedom and responsibility for actions.[63]

The Christian understanding of the character of the Creator–creation interaction depends to a great extent on taking into account the knowledge on the functioning of nature. The accepted (at least implicitly) worldview should be formulated in light of the current state of scientific research. Since present-day cosmology provides a tangible description of the history of the universe, and the biology of the evolution of life, such data should be given serious consideration. Otherwise, consciously or not, we refer to an outdated worldview. When reflecting on the relationship between the Creator and His creation, drawing upon a particular concept of the world is inevitable. It would be naivety to think that we can give thought to the question of divine action in the world without regard for the research outcomes provided by the natural sciences.

Scholars from leading academic centers agree that the universe as we know it has been evolving for approximately 13.8 billion years and accept scientific statements concerning the significance of natural selection on the development of life on Earth. Such a state of research provides an essential point of reference for the formulation of ideas pertaining to God's action in the world. A change in the scientific paradigm, especially a scientific revolution, should spur us to undertake renewed analysis regarding the Creator's interaction with creation.[64] This model of mutual reference remains consistent with the dynamic character of intellectual reflection introduced in the previous section of this book. This does not entail the absolutization of the scientific worldview, which should be kept "in check" so that we do not yield to current intellectual fashions and maintain the distinctiveness of the reflection found in separate fields of knowledge.[65]

The specific elements of the worldview revealed by the natural sciences affect reflection on divine action. This concerns both detailed data (expressed mainly, but not only, in the language of mathematics) as well as more general theses regarding laws, interdependencies, and the particular traits of nature. Stoeger underlines that the universe evolves on all levels, is rational, has its own integrity, and remains directed in a certain way. On the other hand, authors devoted to examining animate nature stress the price organisms pay for their adaptation to the environment. An integral component of such costs is vulnerability to pain and suffering.[66]

From the theistic perspective, the history of the evolving universe can be seen as the story of creation. For theists who take into account the scientific worldview, the emergence of the subsequent components and structures of nature, eventually leading to the birth of consciousness, is nothing else than the creative action of God who operates within the dependencies and laws of nature.[67] In such an interpretative context, the Creator does not only enable the constant development and transformation of the world but also respects the autonomous character of the processes that lead to the formation of systems which are increasingly complex. While formulating a program of theism which includes the ways of nature's functioning as depicted by scientists, it can be stated that one of God's qualities is to create patiently by means of evolution.[68]

The above manner of interpreting scientific data is characteristic for those representatives of Christian thought who perceive the advance of science as a chance for a renewed demonstration of God's relationship with the world. Instead of the often irrational attempts at undermining the achievements of current intellectual culture, scholars consider up-to-date findings concerning the functioning of nature in the process of formulating various strands of contemporary theism.[69] As a result of this, philosophers analyze questions concerning the philosophy of God and the philosophy of religion that need to be reconsidered in the light of the present-day worldview. An innovative project in the theology of science is similarly being created.[70]

For many decades now we have been witnessing the emergence of new and insightful studies concerning the Creator–creation interaction conducted in the light of scientific findings. The works of the French Jesuit Teilhard de Chardin, who starting from the 1950s authored many publications in this field, were also inspired by science. His approach was characterized by being open to disciplines such as paleontology, in which he specialized. On the other hand, however, many of his reviewers pointed out that his thought verged on mysticism.[71] Earlier, similar views were expressed by A. N. Whitehead, who in turn was criticized for an overly speculative approach and for blurring the demarcation line between experimental sciences and metaphysics.

Independent of any of their specific controversies, both Teilhardism and processualism were valuable attempts at practicing theism in the context of the natural sciences. The second half of the twentieth century saw the arrival of followers of this manner of reflection in approaching the aspects of God's nature and His relationship with the world.[72] With time, two main theistic tendencies formed, both of which essentially refer to the discussion of God's omniscience and omnipotence. Open theism highlights the idea of God not knowing the future, which remains indeterminate and brings along authentic novelty. This strand of theism was particularly popular in the search for a solution to the problem of the mutual coexistence of divine knowledge and human freedom. In turn, the strand of theism which used processual intuitions reconsidered the concept of God's omnipotence and stressed that the Christian idea of *kenosis* rules out God's action *contra naturam*. Within this tendency, the laws of nature are treated as a manifestation of the divine presence in the world and for this reason familiarity with these laws draws us closer to grasping the potential manner of interaction between the Creator and creation. These kinds of reflection appear to be more fitting for the image of a loving God conveyed in Christian revelation.

Many authors searched for a possible use of scientific findings in a more tangible way. These authors called for more than just being careful not to contradict the scientific worldview while formulating theistic theses. With time, numerous publications were directly inspired by solutions found in particular fields of scientific research. It was pointed out that developing the relationship between science and religion or theology merely on a methodological level is not sufficient. More often scholars put forward the suggestion that we should reflect on the scope of the challenge which natural selection and the indeterminacy of processes detected on the quantum level pose for Christian theism.

Does science generate atheism?

Another reason why "post-revolution" science became a challenge for portraying God's relationship with the world was that scientific outcomes were used to propagate contemporary forms of atheism. In some intellectual circles it is still being stressed that science remains an effective rival of religion. According to the new atheists, religious reflection was only legitimate at a time when naturalistic explanations of the functioning of nature were unavailable. Irrespective of the potential criticism of many of the theses formulated by Dawkins, Dennett or Sagan it needs to be noted that the question of evolutionism is undoubtedly one of the more controversial issues that promotes a renewed consideration of crucial religious questions, namely: man's place in nature, our relationship with other species, the possibility of correlating the scientific with the theological concept of the prehistory of the human species, and God's influence on the history of the world.[73]

Dennett claims that the theory of evolution is not compatible with religious beliefs. Moving beyond his scientific competence, he additionally puts forward a thesis that neither the intentional nor the causal actions of the Creator had any impact on the emergence of species, including *Homo sapiens*.[74] An entirely incorrect reaction to such statements would be to close theism off from the natural sciences. All the more so, evoking the traditional Christian message concerning divine creative power and it being open to human cognition is simply not enough. On the other hand, a significant component of the answer to various provocations coming from the "horsemen of atheism" is the development of contemporary forms of theism that not merely copy hackneyed ways of reasoning. If the manner in which we perceive the world has indeed become fundamentally modified and contains many nuances that stress the specificity of nature's complexity or the complicated character of its functioning, then a new intellectual effort is needed on the part of philosophers of God and theologians that will enable them to explain why the natural causes of phenomena do not exclude the possibility of divine action. Even more, it is not worth adopting defensive positions. It is much more beneficial for us to create a program which will to some extent "logically anticipate, systematically ground, and render more coherent than otherwise, what evolutionary science is now discovering about the nature of life."[75]

It is not a question of formulating the concept of God's action in the world on the grounds of the debate conducted with new atheists who claim that contemporary science is generating a strong physicalism that falsifies, or even discredits, theistic approaches. These kinds of theses, formulated in the context of the evolutionary sciences, came into being (to a large extent) as a consequence of a distorted image of God and His relationship with nature. Instead of renovating the warped concept of God and His plan for the world, Christian thinkers might strive to specify theistic theories anew and then present arguments in support of the claim that evolution does not rule out the Creator's active participation in creation. What seems necessary is to renounce the image of God as determining the development of the world in each and every one of its minute details. Rather than presenting a model of the Creator who does not leave any freedom to creation, it is worth portraying God as acting without violence and immanently present in the world. Such an image is constructed in light of knowledge concerning the creative traits of nature and remains coherent with the message of Christian revelation.[76]

Haught points to the fact that the idea of God's *kenosis* has recently been gaining importance in theistic circles. The reasons for this are, among others, the traumatic experiences of the twentieth century and the degradation of the biosystem. Both of these aspects have certainly affected scholars to move away from interpreting God's omnipotence as an unlimited possibility to act in the world. On the other hand, the idea of the Creator's relationship with creation was shaped in the context of new scientific findings, which allow for appropriate depiction of the specificity of evolutionary processes. Detailed demonstration thereof has undoubtedly contributed to revising the ways in which God's interaction with nature is portrayed.[77]

Clarifying the concept of God is not only the starting point but one of the crucial aims of practicing theism in the context of science. A phenomenon which is not always noticed today is the fact that both the exponents of new atheism and groups of Christian fundamentalists share a similar understanding of divine omnipotence. The representatives of the first milieu point out that presenting the "blind" forces of nature—mutation and natural selection—as governing the developmental processes of animate nature has denied humanity the belief that God is omnipotent and in control of the world's fate. Hence, God most probably does not exist at all, and even if He does, His existence lacks actual power over creation. On the other hand, there are theists who put forward a tyrannical vision of the might of God, presented as a peculiar "supervisor of the course of history." It is often assumed, at least tacitly, that God has the attributes of patriarchal domination that exclude Him from acting through the laws of nature, especially in the process of evolution which embraces events deemed to be random.[78]

The common denominator of both these approaches is a similar kind of mentality that is manifested in the idea that natural sciences imply atheism. New atheists admit openly that the development of science allows for the disenchantment of religion, while simultaneously releasing us from the superstitions of the past.[79] From the beginning of the twentieth century, the followers of Christian fundamentalism have claimed that evolutionism constitutes a threat to theism. After disseminating views of this kind, in 1925, in the American state of Tennessee, John Scopes was put on trial and fined for propagating Darwin's theory which was presented as a dangerous alternative to religion. The slogan behind the actions of many of the Dayton fundamentalists suggested that only one can prevail, Christianity or the theory of evolution.[80]

Thus, paradoxically, groups of people who place themselves on opposite sides of the argument share the opinion that religion is supposedly threatened by science. Meanwhile, becoming open to science enables theism to purify God's image of attributes which are entirely alien to Him. Rarely do such attributes have anything in common with core Christian doctrine, having emerged mainly in Western culture, for instance as a result of thinkers overly associating Christianity with institutions that identify the power of action with dominance and even violence. Therefore, in reflecting on the Creator-creation relationship in light of current scientific findings, we can arrive at a theological source which emphasizes the self-sacrificial and relational character of God's nature.[81]

A significant context which helps us to understand the relationship between God and the world in a renewed manner is set by certain crucial elements of the evolutionary concept of animate nature which identifies the long-term transformations of organisms as a consequence of the coexistence of the law of natural selection and random mutations. Nature's exceptional fertility remains the manifestation of its emergent specificity. The available list of extant species contains almost two million items, but it is estimated that there have been at least ten million living species. Beginning from the emergence of life on Earth, the number of species inhabiting our planet has exceeded one billion. The interaction between organisms and the environment leads to the continuous emergence of new species whose traits are not merely the result of the multiplication of the features present at previous stages of nature's development. However, there is a price for adjusting to the surrounding world. The cost of evolution is the extinction of organisms that are less adapted to the environment. Approximately 99% of all species that have ever inhabited the Earth are now extinct.[82] In light of such an image of nature, theistic statements should accentuate the autonomy of the world in relation to God. After all, what would be the sense of asserting that God mechanically steers the development of the world if it is a field of continuous struggle for existence and the place of death of so many life forms? In this context, would not the Creator—assuming His omnipotence—appear as an indifferent observer of the history of creation?

Pain is a constituent element of the creative evolution of nature, the fate of which is not directed by God by means of meticulously programming an "unfeeling" machine. Organisms cannot develop without having to fight for their survival. The evolutionary perspective sheds light on the significance of the loss and suffering which can be seen as an integral element of the world's development. On the other hand, evolutionary theism puts emphasis on the fact that the billions of years of nature's creativity and striving for existence can be better comprehended from the perspective of the idea of God's humility.[83]

One of the fundamental reasons for the theistic detachment from the post-Darwinian interpretation of natural phenomena was the fear that the evolutionary sciences implied too little divine power in the world, or even an entire lack thereof. Within Christian doctrine it is assumed that the Creator is actively engaged in the history of the creation. Therefore, the accidental nature of mutations, impersonal creativity, the character of natural selection, and most importantly the extent of loss and suffering that accompanies evolution, were treated as factors that excluded the theistic interpretation of nature. However, the point of reference this was based on was often the idea of God as being unfamiliar with co-suffering.[84]

Haught claims that one of the crucial tasks of the theology of evolution is to "tell the history of nature" from the perspective of faith in the God who renounces the tyrannical use of force. It is God's creative engagement and His care for the world which form the foundation for the changes which occur in nature. God's immanent presence in evolutionary transformations "restores relationship and redeems all the suffering and struggle that the process involves."[85] Philosophical theism practiced in the context of the natural sciences also calls for a revised image of God as cooperating with the world.[86]

Appreciating the significance of contemporary scientific findings, the theistic interpretation of nature should take into account the opportunistic way in which natural selection works as well as the spontaneous creativity of nature. Approaches which put emphasis on the limitless omnipotence of God fail to make sense of the message concerning nature's profligacy and lack of purpose in the many natural processes the costs of which seem to exceed any gain. If one promotes a concept of God as intervening mechanically in each moment of the cosmic process, the magnitude of the suffering that floods the universe can be interpreted as falsifying the idea of providence. The complicated paths of evolution do not match the image of an omnipotent Creator who designs the course of world events in detail and successfully watches over their realization without causing any "greater losses on either side."[87]

In recent years many strands of Christian theism have overlooked the context of current worldviews while formulating their own specific ideas. Even when the object of reflection was the nature of God or His relationship with the world, analyses were mainly conceptual and rooted in a "pre-revolutionary" comprehension of the way nature functions. Scientific thought was not treated as a serious point of reference for constructing theses concerning the Creator–creation interaction. Even more, in some circles the theory of evolution is still being seen as a threat to the doctrine of creation which might degrade the privileged position of our species in the world. Johnston claims that in rejecting evolutionism, biology will be released from mechanistic philosophy, and humans will no longer have to think of themselves as being the accidental outcome of the workings of natural processes and devoid of a proper value.[88]

It then transpires that some theistic circles still refer to an outdated and frequently distorted kind of reflection on nature which is based on the position proposed by Dawkins. This proves how effective the influence of those who manipulate science for immediate ideological purposes can be in the understanding thereof. Contemporary biology is not connected to mechanical philosophy and the dignity of man is measured by our capability for complex abstract thinking and creating culture—factors which are not questioned in light of present-day scientific knowledge as being features which distinguish us from other species.

The situation becomes even more complicated when considering one more aspect of the impact of science on the understanding of God's interaction with the world. If, as a consequence of natural selection operating over a long time, nature can manifest its creative traits, is drawing on any theistic explanation reasonable at all? Some scholars go so far as to claim that the creative force of nature can be interpreted as like an automatic filtering algorithm, with this being a type of natural selection.[89] Do we then need the hypothesis of a personal God? The question is even more legitimate when we bear in mind that analyses of the way inanimate nature functions—particularly the thermodynamics of states far from equilibrium and chaos theory—support the thesis of natural processes being capable of spontaneous self-organization. Why then do we need to refer to an organizing divine intelligence?[90]

Ideological tendencies in science

It is evident that natural sciences should respect the principle of methodological naturalism. This constitutes a fundamental element of the naturalistic research method and has been accepted even by theistically oriented scholars.[91] They follow the justified conviction that a separate Christian methodology does not exist as neither does Marxist biology or religious physics. Attempts at practicing such disciplines would be a clear manifestation of an intellectual pathology that leads straight to pseudoscience. A parallel situation in the field of science would be to allow for the possibility of explaining the emergence of the specific traits of a given physical system, while interpreting the evolution thereof, with the idea of miraculous intervention or a divine plan. Even a single case of trying to explicate the given properties of a physical system by referring to angelic or diabolic powers would result in opening a methodological gate that leads to the formulating of explanations of natural phenomena with non-physical factors. This would simply mean that we have returned to the times preceding the scientific revolution.[92]

Similarly, there are no substantial reasons to undermine the naturalistic interpretations of the rise of biological complexity, the genesis of life, and consciousness. However, these types of scientific description of natural phenomena do not pose any threat to the issue of God's interaction with the world. We do not expect scientists who work within a specific discipline to draw on arguments which Dennett calls "skyhooks."[93] We can go as far as stating that the more secularized science is, the purer it becomes of traces alien to its character and, as a consequence, the more able it is to enter into dialogue with other disciplines of knowledge in a more straightforward way.[94]

Problems arise when excessive care for methodological correctness leads some of the representatives of the natural sciences to the unjustified disqualification of alternative or complementary ways of explaining how the world works. When methodology is converted into metaphysics, the omission of non-physical factors, which is consistent with the internal principles of science, becomes replaced with the axiom that there are *only* physical objects and physical interpretations.[95] Ontological naturalism assumes, at least *implicite*, that only the methodology of empirical sciences allows for mankind to gain credible knowledge of the world. Physical reality comprehended by means of science would thus be the only sphere of objectivity available to human understanding. No doubt, a strong naturalism (sometimes called physicalism or scientism) is incompatible with the theistic interpretation of nature which emphasizes that evolution, taking place according to the laws of nature, can be simultaneously a manifestation of divine action described by the disciplines outside natural sciences.[96] Within the last approach more detailed theories are presented that go beyond the general statement of evolution being God's way to create. Above all else, such a claim has to confront the problem of evil in the world. Evolutionary biology is certainly not exclusively the discipline which enables one to provide meaning to the history of life.[97]

Theism would be incompatible with natural sciences if they conveyed, *ipso facto*, the message of materialism. Biological evolutionism often presents itself as if it were in essence anti-theistic. However, a thesis of this kind remains a manifestation of metaphysics, and frequently is of an ideological tone. Meanwhile, many representatives of contemporary theism discern the possibility of making a creative use of the scientific worldview in their search for the "place" for God perceived as a lawmaker both in reference to moral principles and the order of nature.[98] In evolutionary descriptions scholars notice traces of God's engagement in the world which develops via the cooperation between deterministic and indeterministic laws carried out over a long period of time. The theistic interpretation of the functioning of nature depends on taking into account the kenotic dimension of God's character.[99]

Does the contemporary state of knowledge concerning the workings of animate nature indeed leave space for theistic interpretations? Answering a question posed in this manner seems to be of crucial importance for practicing Christian evolutionism. One might fear that this would entail noticing manifestations of divine action in the blanks left in the scientific description of the world, signifying a return to the discredited strategy of the "God of the gaps." It needs to be underlined that the theistic reflection on the functioning of animate nature is of an entirely different character. Theistic reflection on animate nature is a form of interdisciplinary dialogue in which scholars appreciate the achievements of current biology (which accentuates the significance of the continuity present in nature), while at the same time refraining from perceiving these achievements as the only sphere which enables the comprehension of the phenomenon of life in all of its various dimensions.

Many authors would sincerely like to close off all paths which lead to such interpretations of the phenomenon of life that go beyond natural sciences. Even otherwise valuable publications sometimes include articles on evolution whose authors try to prove that natural selection does not leave any room for divine action.[100] Of course, science should not search for supernatural causes of the development of life, irrespective of how much life itself eludes naturalistic descriptions. The problem remains whether evolutionism leaves space for a religious interpretation of nature. Scientists tackling this issue frequently exceed their cognitive competence by claiming that the concept of God does not have an explanatory value in the field of biotic system analysis.[101]

Theistic interpretation of nature

It is often stated in scientific circles that a full understanding of the workings of animate nature is only possible when we refer to the interaction between the elements of chance, necessity, and time. Such an approach, however, omits many details which concern the development of life on Earth.[102] Even more, the questions of chance, necessity, and time have already been analyzed for a long time within various strands of theism, both on the level of philosophy and on that of theology. Among other elaborate attempts at a valuable reflection we might also distinguish studies on the order of the world, the predictability of nature, and the genesis of the laws of nature. Natural sciences are not able to justify the fact of the world's existence or of the comprehensibility of nature. As mentioned in the previous section of this book, one fundamental metaphysical question calls for substantial consideration, namely: Why does something rather than nothing exist? This question becomes an even greater challenge if we assume God does not exist. Dennett's answer "why not?" seems very unsatisfactory.[103]

Such analyses are performed on a plane different from that of natural sciences. Therefore, there is no threat of the boundaries between separate disciplines being blurred or of the God hypothesis being used to "fill the gaps" of the scientific description of the world. At the same time, the theistic interpretation of the functioning of nature allows one to notice elements of scientism in science and uncover valuable inspirations which would otherwise remain beyond the scope of naturalistic explanations. A good example here is the question of randomness within the processes of life.

The random character of the occurrence of genetic mutations seems to forejudge the lack of their significance for bio-systems. Nevertheless, randomness is a feature without which manifestations of genuine novelty would not emerge in the course of the world's development. Nature does not function as a system that solely recreates past events, with this being the focus of scientists who search for the causes of phenomena. The randomness of the course of a given process can be seen as a sign of the cosmos being open to previously non-existent forms of order. Natural sciences are not capable of engaging in an integral reflection of this kind when they are overly attentive to the relationship between current events and the phenomena of the past, often disregarding the creative potential embedded in nature. The world's openness to the new would not be possible without the unpredictable character of random processes. Thus, randomness in this context is not nonsensical. Evolutionary theism enables the formulation of the thesis that the randomness of events is a result of God granting autonomy to the world which has the trait of auto-creation. A more detailed analysis of this issue is presented in the subsequent section.[104]

A similar challenge for understanding the way in which the world works can be seen in the determinism of natural selection. If the necessity of selection was analyzed in complete detachment from the randomness of mutation, the world might be perceived as an organism the development of which could be directly predicted thanks to the laws of nature. The stability of these laws is often explained in theistic circles as a manifestation of God's rationality in the world.[105] However, the deterministic character of certain laws does not exclude the workings of chance in nature. After all, nature is dominated neither by inflexible necessity, nor by "blind" chance, but is a unique blend of potentially predictable paths and those open to novelty.[106] The universe is a combination of internal coherence and consistency, and the capacity for the emergence of genuinely original properties, all of which complement one another.[107]

When stressing the autonomous character of the world as governed by specific laws we point out that the functioning of nature is based on a long-term trial-and-error method. Evolution that leads to an increased complexity and the emergence of systems which constitute the foundation of intentionality and consciousness demands extremely long periods of time as an integral component of the process thereof. The interaction between deterministic selection and random mutations can give results seen as an expression of ontological discontinuity with the assumption of such a big number of events taking place in the course of historical eons which would enable the freedom of experimentation. On the other hand, the temporal aspect is a frequent argument given by new atheists. In their opinion, the temporal aspect ultimately settles the issue of the lack of rational grounds from which to introduce the hypothesis of God.[108] After all, the intelligent designer of nature would not wander and stray for so long on the path of attaining His goals. Why would an omnipotent Creator need so much time to carry out His plan?[109]

Such doubts can be viewed in an entirely different light not only when we have modified the idea of God's omnipotence, but also when we underline the auto-creativity and freedom of creation. The vastness of evolutionary time intuitively corresponds with cosmic immensity and does not constitute an impediment on the road to a theistic interpretation of the world. Moreover, to a certain extent time remains a mystery for the natural sciences. Their progress is based on the idea of the irreversibility of time in the universe, but natural scientists cannot explain the phenomenon of the existence of this very trait. Within its cognitive competence, biology cannot provide an explanation for the basics of cosmic temporality.[110]

Evolutionists usually accept time as a given fact, and pass over in silence the question of the complex interconnections between time and space.[111] This may be a consequence of methodological purism, but it should not exclude the explorations in those areas outside natural sciences which reach out to the very core of being. The essence of evolution happening on the basis of natural selection cannot be understood without due consideration of time, which remains inseparable from existence and the nature of the universe. The relationship between time and the entirety of space opens up a path to metaphysical interpretations.[112]

A more profound reflection on the role of time in the processes of evolution calls for moving beyond merely stating that it is a crucial aspect of such transformations. It does not suffice to consider the phenomenon of time as an already existing component that is "ready" to interact with natural selection and genetic mutations. What should be reflected on is the conditions that allow a universe with an irreversible temporality to come into being. Such an inquiry leaves room for the evolutionary theism according to which time is a manifestation of the approaching future, with this subsequently introducing novelty into creation. The advance of the future, which from the Christian point of view is related to God, "gives time its irreversibility, allows the cosmos to expand, and eventually arouses the emergent adventure of life and consciousness."[113]

Regardless of the meticulous presentation of the detailed questions of Christian theism, many authors give serious consideration to the challenges posed by the natural sciences. Assuming that God exists and acts in the world, the presentation and comprehension of all of the particulars of the Creator–creation interaction depends to a great extent on an appropriate dialogue with natural sciences which is not about proving the Christian doctrine by references to science.[114] The main aim of such an endeavor is to reformulate philosophical and theological ideas in such a way as to be able to include the scientific worldview more extensively than before.[115]

Random events

The origin of probabilistic theism

The problem of random events is treated as a great challenge for theism. It seems that the actions of the rational, omnipresent, and omnipotent God should not allow for chance in the world. A lot depends on defining randomness and on the view of the Creator-creation interaction. In both spheres there is a multitude of particular concepts, as well as fundamental changes which occur in these domains under the influence of the development of the natural sciences. The conviction—which has been sustained for a long time—that the nature of divine action and the random events which take place in the functioning of the world are mutually exclusive calls for the revision which is currently being undertaken particularly by the representatives of probabilistic theism.

Many of these academics are inspired by process philosophy, but not all support a significant weakening of God's omnipotence.

Bearing in mind the diverse concepts of chance, it can be assumed that random events occur in nature in places where, on a binary scale, the probability of an event happening is smaller than one. Another way to understand chance is in seeing it as a causeless event. Classical theists claim that in this sense random events do not happen and cannot happen if God is treated as the cause of everything that takes place in the world. In the third meaning, a chance event is an unpredictable event, the occurrence of which was not planned nor expected by anyone. Perhaps certain situations cannot be predicted even with the assumption that we know the entire past of the world, all initial conditions, and the totality of the laws governing nature.[116] In this context a question arises: is it possible that God, having created the world, its laws, and all beings that exist therein, can be unfamiliar with His creation in all of its minute details? It seems that omnipotence, understood as the ability to create everything that is possible and that one wants to create, entails the full knowledge of what happens in the world (epistemic omnipotence). It is difficult to conceive of the existence of events unknown to God or impossible to be predicted by Him. According to the fourth possible view, a random event is a pointless event that does not serve any purpose. Can we assume, in light of such a view, that the perfect God creates beings that have no function at all and are devoid of any meaning whatsoever? Are not the events which occur in the world a result of God's meticulously thought-out design? The existence of purposeless events would undermine the claim of a precise divine plan for the world. Either God does not care for the rationality of the world, or He is not omnipotent.[117]

The above questions require an insightful analysis that does not need to have a speculative or deductive character. An alternative way of examining these questions is of a more inductive and empirical nature. We can, to some extent, deduce what is possible for the omnipotent God from the image of the world. It has been created in a way that stemmed from the divine abilities. It is in this manner that probabilistic theism, also known as theology of chance, is constructed. The concept of God's omnipotence elaborated in light of the above derives its premises from knowledge of how the world functions. Coming to know the world's specificity is supposed to lead to an understanding of God's nature.[118]

Probabilistic theism treats scientific knowledge of the world as a point of departure. The fundamental facts which are taken into account are: cosmic and biological evolution, quantum phenomena, the fate of individual people, and the history of mankind. What is stressed in cosmic evolution is the role of the random coincidences of the physical parameters, which enabled the development of the world, including biogenesis. As far as biological evolution is concerned, scholars underline the randomness of genetic mutations, the significance of the random paths of evolution and natural disasters that lead to the mass extinction of different species. In the context of twentieth-century achievements in quantum mechanics, however, attention is drawn to the fact that certain events are inexplicable and that they are essentially unpredictable. Human behaviors are at times also of this nature. The detailed characterization of indeterministic processes is presented further in this section, but already here—on the basis of the above-mentioned panorama of events—one can safely state that the world was not created according to a meticulously predefined plan. Does God "play dice" then?[119] Is He able to control a world in which there is so much room for chance?[120]

The openness of nature to various scenarios of development can paradoxically be proof for the existence of such a "sphere" of God's action that is much more subtle than action based on a precise determination of the course of phenomena. God might be able to affect the course of various physical and historical processes by "making use of opportunities" when alternative paths of development arise. In this way, God's action would not violate the laws He had established. Thus, the development of the world would depend both on the laws imposed by the Creator that are of a deterministic character, as well as on occasional divine interventions which man is not capable of recognizing. Assuming a certain interpretation of quantum mechanics, as presented in previous sections of this study, one could suppose that God continuously intervenes at a subatomic level, creating physical circumstances for the realization of His everlasting plan. This would not be acting *contra naturam*.[121]

However, one can ask in this context: do God's actions require His interference in nature in order to realize His intended plans? It seems that divine perfection is also not compatible with the model according to which the Creator, in realizing His plans for creation, has to "prove" that He holds absolute power over each contingent being—from elementary particles to the earthly observer himself. Is not an authentically omnipotent being one who, in order to achieve His goals, does not need to intervene in order to maintain His domination over the world? After all, the world's autonomy in relation to the Creator, as well as the great possibilities for "experimentation" within nature itself grant it such a fertility as results in the diversity and wealth of creation. Human freedom also cannot be illusory if it is to resemble the image of God who does not hold individual people "on a lead" and allows them to take part in the creative potential of their minds. These arguments enable us to discern at least some of the reasons for the recent appearance of many continuators of D. J. Bartholomew's thought.[122] In this context, the problems characteristic of theism, as well as of the development of the natural sciences concerning the issue of indeterministic processes, are of great significance.

Timing chance

The metaphysics of chance stresses that the gathering of individual events, which on a lower level of the world's structure remain indeterministic, generates the order present on a higher level. The phenomenon of nature is to derive regularities and order from original chaos. Such a specificity can be discovered through reflection on the many processes which take place in the development of nature and in the history of humanity. Cosmic evolution, filled with many random events, has resulted in the emergence of carbon which was the condition for the genesis of life as we know it. At every stage of the development of nature there were many possible paths of evolution. The most significant moments in history were frequently determined by chance occurrences that seem to be incompatible with the divine scenario of creation. The collision of an asteroid with the Earth, which determined the fate of the dinosaurs, can hardly be seen as an expression of divine providence. Nevertheless, this allowed for an evolutionary niche which enabled the emergence of a completely new species that, in the course of a long process, gave origin to *Homo sapiens*. On the winding paths of evolution arose the complicated structures whose most special example is the human brain. This formed the physical basis for the functioning of beings that can reason, are sensitive, are self-aware, and are seen from the theistic perspective as the "crown of creation."[123]

Theologians of chance claim that the randomness of natural processes on the microscale does not enforce chaos on the macro-scale. It was not God's intention to create a chaotic world devoid of life and self-awareness. However, it was in God's power to bring about the genesis of complex beings equipped with a real freedom to choose from the bank of existing possibilities. Nonetheless, the indeterminism of the human will does not entail an irrational character of events. Freedom (which allows for mistakes) is not blind force acting beyond the possibility of any mental control. In the process of making a decision, we consider the appropriate reasons that do not determine our choice but rather support it. Probabilistic theism, which underlines the role of indeterminism, highlights human sapience understood as the ability to balance the "pros" and "cons" of a given situation. Nevertheless, even the most sophisticated deliberations carried out in order to make a rational decision do not eliminate a certain dose of risk. This is also embedded in God's relationship with the world, the development of which takes place with the contribution of necessary as well as contingent processes.[124]

The ideas presented above are alien to the mechanistic mentality which rules out the presence of chance in the development of the world. For several hundred years, the system of mechanics elaborated by Newton was gradually consolidating the thesis of the rationality of nature, the functioning of which, sooner or later, was to be fully explained by deterministic laws. This seemed to be compatible with the concept of God as the *Logos* who controls the development of the world without leaving space for random processes. They were usually thought to form a breach in the rationality of creation and a threat to the view of divine perfection.

The situation changed at the beginning of the twentieth century in the context of the distinction between the ontological and the epistemological aspects of a system's non-determination. The expansion of the natural sciences produced many new enigmas that revealed such spaces in which the question concerning the specificity of processes could not be answered with reference to the category of physical necessity. In spite of this, it was often thought that the problem resides in the limited character of human cognition which does not cover all of the nuances necessary to explain the specificity of events. From this perspective, forecasting the weather for the days to come was deemed difficult mainly on account of the limitations of human cognitive powers. Man was thought of as being incapable of grasping all of the factors. The components of natural processes which slip away from human perception would supposedly determine the difficulties present in predicting the successive states of a system, the functioning of which was believed to be ultimately a manifestation of deterministic conditionings.

The development of science resulted in the emergence of an essential novelty in the question. It transpired that the randomness of the course of physical phenomena is an integral trait of many systems both on the level of the macro-world and in the micro-world. In classical mechanics there are many unstable processes, the explanation of which requires reference to the theory of probability, as exemplified by the framework of the theory of deterministic chaos.[125] One can deliberate whether strict determinism is concealed at a very basic level. However, the fact that there are fluctuations ("attacking" an examined system "from the outside"), which basically make it impossible to precisely determine the course of a given phenomenon, seems to reveal the truth of nature itself, let alone the earthly observer.

The situation becomes even more complicated when taking into consideration nature's action on the quantum level. Quantum indeterminacies place essential constraints on the possibility of knowing the specificity of the course of a given system and its initial conditions. Even more, quantum equations do not predetermine the evolution of a system's properties, but merely enable one to predict the distributions of probability. Certain traits of the micro-world remain essentially different from the specificity of the macroscopic world, as when we consider the strong non-locality of quantum systems.

Contemporary science leaves open the question of explaining phenomena on the fundamental level. It cannot be ruled out that the much-awaited quantum theory of gravity will reveal the presence of determinism in these areas of research. It transpires, however, that in attempting to elaborate such a theory scholars employ the methods appropriate to the theory of probability. This is why one can put forward the thesis that the existence of chance in the functioning of the world is a natural component thereof. The objective and subjective interpretative factors often co-occur in descriptions of phenomena which, both on account of the complicated character of their course and their intrinsic features, remain beyond the scope of statements specific to classical physics.[126]

Necessity and chance are integral constituents in the network of the laws of nature. Even more, a single system can reveal indeterministic as well as deterministic traits. Even relatively uncomplicated examples demonstrate how disappointing commonsense intuitions can be, in accordance with which the world is divided into a part subject to Newton's laws and an area governed by chance. A throw of the dice, which is associated with randomness, is subject to the law of probability that indicates that, with the use of classical dice, the statistical probability of throwing a desired six is one in six. Nevertheless, the entire trajectory of the flight of a dice, including the moment it rests, is the subject of research in the field of classical physics with its deterministic laws of object behavior.

A seemingly simple analysis of the course of a physical process becomes even more complicated when we take into account the many components of conducted research. A long enough observation of the results of dice throwing makes the observer realize that it is governed by relatively simple regularities, e.g. that with an increase of attempts, the relative frequency of results tends to achieve a certain constant.[127] There are regularities in random events which meet the conditions of certain mathematical theorems. The laws of nature disclose an important feature of the world not only in games of chance but also in the statistics of death, e.g. during the times of a pandemic within a given environment.[128]

The specificity of nature in which random events coexist with deterministic events is revealed during analysis of the two-dimensional character of phenomena. This emerges both in the macro- and micro-world. The property of nature which is still unexplained in its entirety is the fact that natural phenomena are being depicted in the categories of classical mechanics, while simultaneously, on an elementary level, serving as an example of the operation of indeterministic forces that allow one to predict only the approximate position of a particle. Many philosophy-oriented scientists approach this phenomenon as analogous to the nature of light. Despite Newton having dissimilar intuitions, already at the turn of the twentieth century physicists were convinced that light is only an electromagnetic wave. Quantum mechanics has refuted this idea, stressing that light can behave both as a particle and as a wave. In 1905, on the basis of theoretical reflection, it was ascertained that there are portions of light, i.e., quanta.[129] In the course of time, the hypothesis of the wave-particle nature of light has been experimentally proved.

An equally significant expression of the discussion on the interaction between necessity and chance in nature are the debates concerning the biological theory of evolution. From the time of Darwin, scholars have started to perceive the transformations of living organisms as a two-stage process. First, due to mutations, genetic variability emerges. Subsequently, selection starts to operate, thanks to which rises the frequency of modifications that increase the probability of survival. Less beneficial or harmful changes are eliminated in successive generations.

Randomness is an integral component of the evolutionary process. Mutations, which are the source of genetic variability, appear randomly,[130] without purposeful connection to the potential effects which pertain to an organism's capability of survival and reproduction. Without hereditary mutations, evolution would not be able to take place since there would be no variability passed down from generation to generation. Many mutations are harmful, hence the expression of mutated genes might lead to the disorganization or death of a cell (organism).[131] In the process of organic transformations, a non-random selection also operates which possesses the trait of directionality and can generate a certain order. Selection does not function according to a precise plan for the future but is a natural (opportunistic) process that results from the mutual interaction of the physical, chemical, and biological properties of a given system. Selection is sometimes perceived solely as a process which eliminates harmful mutations. Meanwhile, as the result of an operating selection, new evolutionary "paths" emerge that increase the possibility of the occurrence of unlikely gene combinations.[132]

Dangerous adjectives

Many mistakes made while interpreting random events are the consequence of an inappropriate application of terminology and a colloquial understanding thereof. This fact often diverts scholarly attention from substantive discourse and is the cause of various fears. A telling example thereof is the fear of the evolutionary interpretation of the genesis of man that allegedly forms an alternative to the concept of creation as an intentional and planned act of God. The biological theory of evolution is treated as a threat to Christian theism mostly because of the role of chance in the functioning of nature.[133] This is granted a suggestive, though non-substantive expression when the processes of nature are claimed to be "blind."[134]

The excessive use of adjectives in the course of the debate not only leads to misunderstandings in terms of the interpretation of natural phenomena and potential philosophical and theological implications, but this also distracts academic attention from the essence of the matter, as well as entering into the territory of ideological conflict. In this context, one can give the example of the document issued on November 27, 2006 by the Council for Science of the Polish Bishops' Conference. On the one hand, many sections of the text titled *The Church on Evolution* contain statements of great significance, critically assessing fundamentalist creationism and indicating the value of science and religion as complementary cognitive perspectives. On the other hand—while legitimately criticizing materialist evolutionism—the authors duplicate stereotypical patterns of thought by underlining that the world is not in the clutches of blind forces, nor is it victim to brutal determinisms.[135]

The representatives of new atheism "juggle with words" in an analogical manner. Richard Dawkins, famous for many provocative speeches, already in the titles of his books refers to the selfish gene,[136] the blind watchmaker, and the unintentional process of evolution.[137] Apart from understandable criticism of Paley's concept, one can easily observe a conscious juxtaposition of the words "blind" and "intentional" which are perceived, in the evolutionary context, as a disjunction. Such an opposition ceases to function when we adopt a complementary explanation of natural phenomena in the categories of determinism and randomness without resorting to rhetorical figures of speech.[138]

While voicing the doctrine of creation and the development of the world and humankind, it is sometimes stressed in Christian circles that apart from the laws of nature, one needs more to explain the specificity of the course of analyzed phenomena, especially when, at a certain stage, genuine novelty appears and is treated as ontological discontinuity. Such an intellectual attitude resembles vitalistic concepts, according to which there is a need for a certain additional force so that nature can manifest its ability to be creative.[139] The concept of the laws of nature is granted a narrow scope if seen in this way, and the possibility of the God–world interaction that takes place through the actualization of potentialities encoded in nature itself is programmatically rejected. Meanwhile, the cooperation of the many factors that make up the complicated network of the principles that govern nature constitutes its great wealth, the ultimate source of which, for theism, is the Creator.

Randomness in the hands of God

Valuable publications rarely view the randomness of the processes of nature as an argument against God's action in the world. On the contrary, randomness is at times treated as an "instrument in the hands of the Creator."[140] The unceasing novelty of creation stems from the fact that the successive stages of evolution are not a duplication of previous stages and assume the indeterministic character of the evolution of the universe. The actual state of the development thereof is not a simple consequence of the realization of hidden possibilities that have been inscribed into nature once and for all. There are phenomena which are unpredictable, and the course of history remains open. Divine interaction with nature becomes an intermediate influence that is the ultimate cause of the appearance of order in the world and of its tendency "to self-organize into a richer variety of ever more complex forms."[141]

Thus, in contemporary times the following question is being posed anew: how can the omnipotent God effectively act in the world and realize His goals when a given physical system is governed by statistical laws, and the essential role is played by the indeterministic processes or fluctuations which are characteristic of nonlinear thermodynamic evolution? This question, analyzed in light of the natural sciences, should be addressed complementarily in reference to inanimate nature and reflection on biotic systems. In the past, scholars stressed the difficulties in reconciling the evolution of individual elements of a bio-system with the principles of thermodynamics, on account of their allegedly opposing specificity.[142] In revealing emergent traits, biotic systems adopt increasingly "higher" forms of organization. On the other hand, the second law of thermodynamics indicates that physical systems strive to attain the maximum level of entropy and dispersion. As of today, there are no visible grounds for justifying a programmatic opposition of the theory of biological evolution and nonlinear thermodynamics. After all, as is emphasized, life evolves not against the laws of thermodynamics but thanks to them in states that are far from equilibrium. On the grounds of theism, as practiced in light of science, a new problem arises: can the omnipotent God arrive at a given result in the evolution of a thermodynamic system in which the so-called bifurcations occur, thus designating a landmark state of evolution?

The specificity of nonlinear physical systems has already partly been the object of reflection in the section of the book devoted to the laws of nature. However, it is worth stressing here that comprehension of how nature functions is essential to the question of divine action, specifically at the most critical stages of the world's development, e.g. the genesis of life. The moment a system is put off course (by a fluctuation derived from a system's surroundings) from its existing evolutionary path, the principle of aiming to minimize entropy "forces" this system to return to its original route of development. It has transpired, however, that, in light of available knowledge, there is no physical law which may ensure a system's resilience to such perturbations. Fluctuations can become strengthened or even dominate the entire course of a system's development, which had previously seemed in practice to be improbable. This determines the instability of a nonlinear system that goes through a certain chain of states which move this same system further away from equilibrium. At a certain stage of evolution, the system becomes less sensitive to fluctuations; however, it subsequently arrives at the so-called stability threshold. When this is attained, practically any fluctuation can upset a system's current evolutionary rhythm, and the laws of statistics begin to dominate over deterministic conditionings. It is exactly this critical point of evolution that is called bifurcation, after the occurrence of which a system returns to its relatively stable development. Such a process can be repeated and this allows one to conclude that what matters in the thermodynamic evolution of systems is probabilistic laws, as well as physical necessity.[143]

The above statement is important because the nonlinear character of the evolutionary processes changes the existing idea of there being only a small probability of the occurrence of certain natural phenomena. In circumstances favorable for nonlinear evolution, when structures begin to organize themselves in states far from equilibrium, the probability of the emergence of life significantly increases. When conditions for nonlinear evolution had arisen on Earth, the emergence ("bifurcation") of life had become very probable. This does not entail a physical necessity, but simultaneously affects the theistic interpretation of biogenesis. The role of God in this respect does not have to be connected with interventionist action.[144]

The self-organization of nonlinear systems is based on the mutual interaction of fluctuations and deterministic laws. In the development of a system, what is of essential significance between states of bifurcation is the physical necessity of the occurrence of particular states, whereas during the periods of bifurcation—the fluctuations that are difficult to predict. Comprehension of the natural complexity of evolutionary processes requires taking into account both of the enumerated components. In the theistic context, one can focus on the indeterministic factor and ask: can God predict a scenario of development that is subject to bifurcation? In light of contemporary nonlinear thermodynamics, the answer to this question seems to be open. If we assume that the omnipotent God possesses knowledge of future events, there are no reasons for divine knowledge to be programmatically confined merely to events of a deterministic character. On the one hand, it seems that God does not act similarly to Laplace's demon who determines the course of evolutionary processes in detail. On the other hand, nature's openness to different scenarios of development does not have to predetermine God as a helpless being devoid of an effective influence on the fate of the world.[145]

In the light of the above reflection, it is clear that probabilistic theism is not a variety of deism. In having created primordial matter in a specific state and in introducing the set of laws which would govern primordial matter's development, the Creator did not cease to be active and interested in the world. God not only created the world, but He also sustains all beings in existence and affects their development. Without such action neither the stable laws of nature nor the particular components of the continuously evolving physical world would be able to exist.[146]

The theology of chance does not reject the idea of the divine *conservatio mundi* but puts greater emphasis on the autonomy of the world and on human freedom. God endowed His creation with a relative power of self-preservation and self-determination. The actions of the Creator in creation are mostly revealed on the level of the human spirit. However, God's action is always free of any form of physical or metaphysical violence. God accompanies man and the world in a subtle way, all the while wielding real influence on the development of the world, but not by means of completely determining everything and everyone.

Probabilistic theism is not a form of occasionalism. Without rejecting the theory of creating from nothing, as do the processualists, probabilistic theists attempt a coherent presentation of the complicated network of the laws of nature and take the world's specificity into account during the formulation of the concept of divine action. Such a presentation complementarily includes the individual components of evolution: necessity, chance, and the time needed for the genesis of complex structures.[147]

One of the essential issues of the program of probabilistic theism is to address the question of whether the divine presence in the world, as viewed in light of this same system, seems too minimal or insufficient. Will God, acting in this manner, attain all of the goals designed for creation? Does He appear to risk failure too much? If the course of nature's evolution on the cosmic and biological level, as well as the history of mankind, are dependent on such a great number of factors and random circumstances outside of anyone's control, is not the probability of God "losing" too great?

Even though theology of chance is sometimes given the name of theology of risk, its representatives do not share any of these fears. The nature of the world, to a sufficiently high degree, guarantees that the goals intended by God for His creation will be achieved. This is why the intervention of God is not necessary. Assuming an appropriate amount of time and an adequate size of the universe, not only biogenesis, but also anthropogenesis, both have a highly probable chance of development. What is conducive to these things are biochemical mechanisms, as well as the long-term and innumerable processes of mutation and adaptation. At a certain stage of evolution, the arrival of humans on one of the planets of the universe was highly probable, almost inevitable. Nature, not being confined in the restricted, fixed framework of determinism, provides space for the operation of chance and is simultaneously highly creative itself.[148] We observe flexibility in the evolution of nature (when one path of development fails, others appear), the organisms' ability to survive in harsh conditions (owing to random mutations, among other things), as well as in the countless ways of regeneration after all kinds of natural disasters (with a particular overabundance in this regard).[149]

Another problem that is intensely examined is the price paid for the evolutionary (indeterministic and probabilistic) mechanism of the world by sensitive and sentient beings. This specifically concerns those manifestations of pain, suffering, and evil which seem undeserved, extremely unjust, and pointless (and hence, according to one of the previously given definitions, random). Apart from the immediate context of the theology of chance, this issue was discussed in detail in the second section of the previous chapter of this book. The immensity of pain, suffering, and evil seems to lie outside the reach of divine omnipotence and is hard to inscribe in the everlasting design for the world.[150] It is worth noticing at this point that this question poses an equal challenge to theism accentuating the role of God's meticulously designed plan for the world. On the other hand, probabilistic theists underline that the Creator had taken the risk of creating the world. In providing the world with a maximally probable field for autonomous and simultaneously creative functioning, God knew that the price of freedom would be the existence of evil that is difficult to justify. Nevertheless, it is not the Creator who is the author of such events. He did not bestow any meaning on evil regardless its kind.[151]

New Manicheism

Contrasting chance with the intended action of the Divine Designer is characteristic of the Intelligent Design theory. Its proponents strive to minimize the role of chance in biological and cosmic evolution. In this area, two American scholars are particularly notable: M. Behe and W. A. Dembski. The latter, in elaborating an original version of the argument from design, rules out the possibility of explaining the genesis of life by reference to the mechanisms described by contemporary natural sciences. A significant position in his interpretation is taken up by the so-called law of conservation of information according to which information cannot arise as a result of the cooperation between chance and the laws of nature.[152] The information embedded in the universe has to be generated by other means, which are the essence of intelligent design.

In attempting a critical analysis of the above view one needs to bear in mind that the law of conservation of information is a modified version of the entropy conservation principle. It is a special case of the second law of thermodynamics when in a given system no dissipative processes take place, e.g., friction. The emergence of any form of friction results in the loss of information, which can still be generated as a consequence of the functioning of natural processes. Open systems, in interacting with other systems, create more organized structures. The Earth generates novelty thanks to the energy provided by the Sun that assists in the proper functioning of living organisms. When a drop of water changes into an icicle, the organization of the resultant system does not require reference to any special law of conservation of information.[153] Recalling the specificity of such processes demands a distanced attitude towards the strong theses of the Intelligent Design theory which have become the object of much criticism in scientific circles.[154] Moreover, this concept paradoxically does not provide any substantive support for a defense of Christian theism.[155]

One of the known propagators of intelligent design, Philip Johnson, rejects the Darwinian theory of natural selection since, he claims, from its perspective the following theses could be formulated: (a) God does not exist; (b) natural selection can only take place randomly; (c) whatever happens randomly cannot be ascribed to the actions of God. The problem is, however, that the above theses are not an expression of professional scientific knowledge in discussing the presence of God in the world. As I have mentioned before, natural selection is not a random process, but a directional one. It would also be erroneous to postulate this disjunction: either natural selection works, or there is an intelligent Creator. Postulating atheism as a consequence of accepting the basics of the biological theory of evolution is characteristic of the opinion presented by Dawkins. There is no reason to copy his mental schemata on the grounds of the theistic interpretation of life processes.[156]

Chance is sometimes perceived in the categories of a quasi-metaphysical being which is a kind of rival to God. Meanwhile, the functioning of chance on the level of biological evolution is not essentially different from the role it serves in other scientific theories. Physicists who refer to randomness conclude that the final state of a given system cannot be fully foreseen only on the basis of knowledge of initial conditions. In quantum mechanics, chance functions as a component of a theory designed to determine the probable outcome of measurement. Classical mechanics, in turn, speaks of such a dependence of the final state of chaotic systems on initial conditions that, in research practice, one cannot precisely predict the course of events. What is at the most possible is a delineation of the scale of expected probability. Neither of the above concepts of chance justify the absolutization of the calculus of probability. A small probability is not a type of anti-absolute contrary to God but is rather a component of His creative strategy.[157]

In light of biology, a random process is understood as impossible to explained causally only on the basis of the interactions which take place in an organism, and unpredictable from the perspective of knowledge concerning a given biological system. Making use of the word "chance" does not have to lead to stating a lack of causality but rather our lack of knowledge of causality, or our difficulty in the precise explanation of how the final state of a given state was achieved.[158] God's knowledge is different, especially if we assume that He obtains knowledge "via observation." God can act by means of events deemed random, affecting their course and having a full knowledge thereof. The randomness discovered in the laws of nature does not provide grounds for negating the divine presence in biological as well as physical processes.[159]

It is worth stressing that the concept of Christian theism which takes account of the scientific worldview becomes more easily formulated with the justifiable assumption that the role of chance in natural processes is strictly connected to actions defined as necessary.[160] Random events often take place in systems which, to some extent, enforce a particular course while also leaving open various paths of development. The unpredictable (to a great extent) interaction of molecules in prebiotic organisms occurs within systems governed by specific laws. DNA structures have also not emerged by "pure accident." Their genesis should be searched for in the connection between chance combinations and the processes which stem from deterministic physical laws. Without the participation of these laws, ten billion years would not suffice for life to arrive at the proteinaceous form familiar to us. Nuclear energy appeared to be necessary for the protons and neutrons in the atom nucleus; electromagnetic phenomena helped to hold atoms and molecules together; gravity allowed the produced components to give origin to the living organisms emerging on the surface of the Earth.[161]

The problem of the proponents of the Intelligent Design project, who place chance against God's action, is also based on the fact that despite declarations of their argumentation being independent of theological premises, they frequently blur the boundary between science and religion. On the one hand Dembski claims that intelligent design has nothing in common with Christianity, or even theism, but is a purely scientific research program. He stresses that the scholars participating in the project demonstrate the "indisputable" merits of this theory without referring to a religious authority. On the other hand, in a peculiar manifesto of the Intelligent Design project, published in 1999, we can read that the "view of the sciences that leaves Christ out of the picture must be seen as fundamentally deficient ... the conceptual soundness of the theory can in the end only be located in Christ ... as the completion of our scientific theories."[162]

Chance, discredited by the proponents of intelligent design, is not a destructive force that violates or destroys the structure of the universe encoded in the laws of nature. Chance is an irremovable component of the structure of the universe, incorporated into it in a nonlinear way. Random events are also not a fracture in the mathematical order of the world since they are of a statistical character and remain an important aspect of nature's mathematicality.[163] Presuming, after Einstein, that the mathematical structure of the universe is the realization of God's creative design, one can assume that random events are an important component thereof. In this context, Heller states that the theory of Intelligent Design is an ideology, not a science, and is a contemporary version of Manichaeism, the heresy from the first centuries of Christian history that saw matter as the principle of evil and a force opposing God.[164]

Claiming that nature has no traits of creativity undermines the possibility of a rational demonstration of the Creator's immanent presence in creation and places the world of nature, with its allegedly blind forces, in opposition to God who acts in a designed and intentional way. Such theses are to a great extent a consequence of the Manichaean approach, the principal feature of which is to identify matter with everything that is evil and devoid of the values appropriate to the spiritual world. Meanwhile, Christian theism perceives the entirety of the creation as the work of God. The philosophical statement concerning God sustaining the world in existence is connected with the idea of *creatio continua* that presupposes the Creator's incessant activity in creation, as well as creation's goodness which is a reflection of God's perfection. Thus, there are no grounds for contrasting the Creator, who is distant from His creation, with a nature that does not possess any of the auto-creative properties which would generate novelty. The condition for the emergence of novelty lies in the openness of nature, the functioning of which is inextricably linked to chance.

In search of unity and the means for its expression

Unity in diversity

The development of the natural sciences has undoubtedly contributed to placing greater emphasis on the unity of the universe.[165] In this context, Collins underlines the role of interconnections in the world, and distinguishes their several types.[166] Within one of them it is stressed that humans should not be contrasted with "the rest of nature." After all, biological evolution demonstrates our connection with other species that have "intermediated on the way" to our genesis. The idea that we derive from common ancestors highlights the bonds that exist in animate nature. On the other hand, explaining the emergence of the first living organisms takes into consideration the theory of the natural continuity between inanimate and animate beings. In light of contemporary science, we know that the compounds of carbon which appeared billions of years ago were necessary for the arrival of life as we know it, the evolution of which has resulted in the genesis of humankind, but not until life generally had reached a very advanced stage. In presenting the various assets of "interconnectivism," Łukasiewicz writes that it attempts to address the problem of the suffering of animals to a greater degree, and expressly articulates the fact that our consciousness and freedom, understood in a libertarian way, are grounded in the structure and mechanisms of the entirety of nature, and even of the entire universe. After all, if freedom of the will is a phenomenon which results from natural processes, this would mean that indeterminism is, as it were, inscribed in the deepest structures of nature, including quantum reality.[167]

Similarly, what is being stressed today is the unity of the spiritual (vel the psychic or the mental) and the corporeal in the construction of the *animal rationale*. This is important since the residues of Cartesian thought, frequently present in Christian anthropological reflection, hinder the presentation of psycho-physical unity.[168] This is also significant when constructing models of divine action in the world.[169]

The reason for the rejection of the dualistic concept of the human being stems from the conviction that mind and matter make up an integral whole. However, this does not have to entail the propagation of panpsychism, according to which even the most basic forms of matter are equipped with some kind of cognition that develops gradually until it arrives at the emergence of consciousness. The adherents of such solutions were processualists who introduced the idea that events go through a quasi-subjective phase after which objectivization occurs, with this leading to the integration of matter and thought. Panpsychism was the object of criticism which stressed that there is a fundamental ontic difference between such objects of the inanimate world as a stone or grains of sand, and beings endowed with life evolving through an interaction with its surroundings, up to reflective forms, including those of the lowest level of awareness.[170]

On the other hand, analysis of the relationship between matter and thought demonstrates that the complexity of the physical system has an essential significance for the specificity of systems whose traits become emergent in relation to their material background. In this context, many authors claim that there are no two kinds of substance with two different natures existing in the world (like the Cartesian *res cogitans* and *res extensa*), and recommend a monistic ontology, but not being identified with panpsychism or extreme reductionism (physicalism). A classic expression of anti-dualistic reasoning comes with the idea of the so-called emergentist monism which highlights the unity of nature in which there are different levels of the organization of structures. The relations between the physical substrate and the consciousness that emerges at a specific stage of development are viewed as hierarchic and temporal.[171]

Emergentist monism distances itself from the anthropological concept in accordance with which in explaining the functioning of the human being it is sufficient to refer only to physical causes. What is not postulated, however, is the existence of a hidden entity, e.g., the Cartesian substance of the soul, opposite to the body. A person is a complex structure and possesses diverse properties, the description and interpretation of which call for reference to different scientific disciplines. The particular levels of the human structure are not reducible to themselves; hence, what is required is a plurality of explanations that would enable one to grasp the specificity of being endowed with exceptional complexity. In emergentism understood in this vein causal reductionism is rejected, and what is adopted is the real existence of mental causes.[172]

The pivotal statement of the supporters of emergentist monism refers to the specificity of the universe's development and the emergence of structures in the course of its evolution.[173] At each stage of history, there is a specific order giving rise to new properties. In this way, newly emergent traits are not reducible to previously existing ones, with this simultaneously demonstrating the continuity of evolutionary development. The world appears to be much more complex than is claimed by the propagators of strong physicalism who obliterate the boundary between the research method and metaphysical statements. The creativity of nature, the wealth of its structures and emerging properties are not given an appropriate explanation within extremely reductionist research programs.[174]

Within the emergentist concept of nature it is presupposed that there is a real and two-way causal relationship between the brain and the mind.[175] This is not synonymous with promoting dualism because what is being stressed in this situation is the existence of many types of properties within one substance of the human being. Acknowledging the hierarchic structure of the physical world enables one to arrive at such a philosophical interpretation that is not confined to choosing between dualism and physicalism. The latter interpretation, on the grounds of anthropology, negates the irreducible character of man's first-person experience and his ontic distinction in the world.[176]

The richness and limits of language

The above statements form the context for developing the analogical and metaphorical means of conveying the content of various aspects of theism that accentuate the Creator's closeness to creation. The concept of psycho-physical unity has become a point of reference for the formulation of the thesis concerning the analogy found between the mind–body union and God's relation to the world. A condition necessary for constructing such a comparison is the rejection of the anthropological dualism in which the casual relationship between the mental level and the physical substrate is viewed as parallel to the way a bodily machine is steered by the human mind. From such a perspective, the "initiative" of action is seen as taken solely by the mind.

Viewing God's union with the world as analogous to the psycho-physical unity risks rendering the Creator dependent on His creation.[177] Thus, a question arises if, in this context, God would remain a perfect being. The reasons for such fears are not acknowledged by the authors who adopt the idea of the *kenosis* of God who does not become isolated from the world, and who experiences, in some sense, the various forms of creation's imperfection.[178]

One of the most ardent defenders of the strong view of the God–world union is Grace Jantzen. According to her, the entirety of the universe appears as the body of God. In this model, the Creator's activity that concerns the world is not limited only to one part of creation. The world in relation to God is treated as a specific whole, the functioning of which is presented analogously to the functioning of a living organism.[179] There are interactions between the specific parts of the world that result in the particular homeostatic regulation of the whole. This is at times compared to the workings of the human brain and its complexity as expressed in the huge number (10^{14}) of neural connections.[180] Nevertheless, Polkinghorne points out that, despite their complexity, cosmic processes have a diverse and much less coherent character when compared to the biochemical dynamism of the components of a single living cell.[181]

Authors who emphasize the need for revising the classical model of the God–world interaction make use of the image that demonstrates the biological characteristics of mammals' reproductive process. In this context it is stressed that in classical theism, the divine influence on the world is presented in terms of an external activity analogous to the way one specimen inseminates its partner. What was given insufficient attention was the aspect of creation, which in the world of mammals corresponds to the specificity of the fetal phase, as well as the help pregnant females provide to offspring during their development at this stage of life. In making use of this analogy, panentheism assumes that God creates in Himself, not outside of Himself, a world that is different from Him.[182]

Panentheists criticize the sharp opposition between the Creator and the creation found in certain positions and claim that if God is viewed in substantial categories, He can affect the world only from "the outside" on an interventionism. Nevertheless, such concepts generate serious problems, especially in light of the scientific view of the chain of phenomena which occur in the causally closed world. In the context of evolution, it is increasingly difficult to present the Creator–creation interaction as a substantial influence. *Ex definitione*, substances cannot be contained in one another without losing their ontological identities.[183]

Striving not to obliterate the difference between the necessary being and contingent beings, the adherents of panentheism discern the need for a renewed elaboration of models to express God's presence in events, individuals, structures, and the processes of nature. For panentheists, assistance on the way to comprehending the Creator-creation interaction comes with the theory of the whole affecting its parts (detectable in the complex systems of nature), as well as with the metaphor of "the world's immersion in God." Such an idea has been present in several currents of the Christian tradition for some time,[184] but this has not been sufficiently understood, even though, according to Peacocke, it has a certain advantage over classical presentations of the God–world relationship.[185]

Panentheists claim that the specificity of God's existence and action can be better comprehended under the assumption that He embraces everything that is in existence, and acts in and through everything, while at the same time surpassing the entirety of the world. Everything that is not God has its existence in Him. Divine infinity embraces all finite individuals, structures, events, and processes. Hence, there is no "room" for creation other than in the infinite God who creates in Him everything that exists.[186]

If God contains individual parts as well as the systems, including the entirety of the world's system, His interaction with creation takes place on all levels of nature "from the inside." God is immanently and creatively present in the whole and in its parts, not only in terms of sustaining an entity's existence. There is no need for separate interventions in the specific areas of the world's structure. A special culmination of one of the branches of increasing natural complexity is human being whose construction and functioning are viewed as a point of reference for elaborating the model of divine action in the world. Human intentions and goals go beyond the bodily structure but remain integrally connected with the processes taking place in the brain and can be realized only with the intermediation of the body. In a sense, as reasonable and conscious beings we surpass our bodies but are also contained in them. The concept of a person's psychosomatic unity helps panentheists to create a model of the relationship between God and the world. In light of this model, God is presented as acting "from the inside" on all levels of the world's structure similar to the way we are present in and act through our own bodies.[187]

The analogy between God's relation to the world and a human being's relation to their body raises certain doubts. First of all, God creates the world in granting it existence, but also infinitely surpasses the world. Humans, on the other hand, do not create their own bodies. Secondly, people are not aware of the many processes that take place inside their bodies, such as breathing, digesting, or metabolizing. God, by contrast, possesses knowledge of all the "patterns" that exist in the world of events, both those that pertain to universal providence (giving and sustaining the existence of individuals, structures, and world processes), as well as those that result from His particular intentions. Third, the comparison between the actions of a human being and the way the Creator interacts with creation does not signify that God is a person in the meaning of the word that we are familiar with. God should be rather viewed as "more than personal." God is "suprapersonal" in the sense that certain important aspects of His nature move beyond the notion of a human person. One of the fundamental challenges to this concept is the significance of creation's changeability in defining the nature of the Creator. Is God, at least in a way, dependent on a continuously evolving nature? A positive answer to this question is given by processualists.[188]

The above remarks can be treated as serious objections to the metaphor of the world as being God's body. On the other hand, however, the model to some extent provides a better solution to the problem of evil than the externalist solution. After all, viewing God as existing outside the world implies His separation from it. God understood in this manner can solve the problem of evil only via an external intervention. On the basis of some classical presentations of this issue, it seems that God is a witness to the suffering of the world without participating in it—even when He "takes an interest in it." Meanwhile, God as viewed in the Christian tradition (even without reference to revelation) should to a greater degree reveal the traits of a person who co-suffers in the face of all kinds of evil, pain, and death. Assuming that the world resides "in God" allows for the formulation of a thesis that the tragedy of suffering takes place "inside the divine being." In this sense, God experiences nature. This experience includes all of the events which make up the entirety of evil in the world, both the one intended and realized by man as well as that which happens as a consequence of natural processes.[189]

Presenting the Creator–creation interaction as analogical to the relationship between the mind and the body calls for great insight during the formulation of particular solutions. One of the less frequently noticed, albeit significant, aspects of the question is the analysis of the phenomenon of human freedom conducted in reference to the theory of divine action. Even though we are convinced that the causal interconnections which integrate physical processes are inextricably entwined, the experience of free will does not seem fictitious to us. If in a world thus understood there is still room for our free activity then, all the more so, we can assume that the laws of nature do not hinder God's action.

Polkinghorne focuses additional attention on two other important issues pertaining to the problem under discussion. On the one hand, it cannot be ruled out that the development of physics might bring forth another view of the laws of nature. Hence, it can transpire that the narrow concept of the miracle as God's action performed *contra naturam* will altogether cease to be of use when we take into consideration the previously unknown interpretations of natural phenomena. On the other hand, the specificity of the functioning of the world which we are already familiar with suggests that many processes are of a more "open" character than was previously thought.[190] Thus, there is still room in the physical world for the free activity of a subjective agent: both humans and, all the more so, God.[191]

The flexibility of natural processes undermines the thesis—which is still supported in some circles—that inert and shapeless matter cannot evolve into the universe as we know it.[192] Contemporary scientific theories elaborated on in disciplines such as cosmology, genetics, and evolutionary biology demonstrate the immense potential matter is equipped with. Matter's flexibility and fertility allow new properties to emerge at successive stages of development, including the emergence of personal traits. The concept of the world constituting an integral entity leads to a new comprehension of matter which is not opposed to the psyche, the mind, and the spirit.[193]

The artist replaces the watchmaker

The trait of nature's auto-creativity is currently highlighted by many authors. They are often critical of the metaphor of the God-watchmaker who meticulously designed the history of the world, only to make sure that the "clock of creation" never ceases to work.

Within Paley's view of divine action, it was presupposed that at the stage of cosmogenesis, God pre-set all details that are to be revealed in subsequent phases of the world's development. New interpretative propositions accentuate that the evolving universe is not subject to one fixed plan. In the process of the transformations which the world of nature is undergoing, one should discern an element of auto-creativity and a particular kind of art, the specificity of which cannot be confined to the strict framework of algorithmic predictions since this is being actualized in the non-linear course of physical systems and their unpredictable bifurcations. The evolutionary scenario is not only dependent on the decision of the divine constructor, but also on the autonomous and auto-creative development of creation which aims at ultimate fulfillment.[194]

The relationship between the Creator and creation gains a more comprehensive explanation in reference to the categories of the possibilities and inclinations encoded in nature by God. He is often compared to a composer who gradually reveals the potentialities hidden in creation. When we listen to a musical piece, there are moments when the music engages us to the extent that we begin to identify with its author and admire his talent. The composer is, in some sense, identified with his music and can be detected in it. On an ontological level, the composer surpasses his works, but communicates with us via his music, and to some extent is contained and represented by it. The composer remains immanently present in his work. Hence, there is no need to look for him anywhere else to experience his creative role. The processes of nature discovered by science are an analogous manifestation of God's action and there are no visible reasons to search for His presence in any additional actions or factors apart from the world He created.[195]

God is sometimes compared to an improvising artist who demonstrates his genius through the creation of beauty at the different stages of the realization of his composition. The Creator can be viewed both as a composer and as an orchestra director. In relation to ourselves, the Creator not only defines the "patterns of harmony" that can be realized in life, but also helps us to actualize them. All the same, we remain free as far as the performance of the "musical piece" is concerned. As a result, the components of life are not solely those which constitute its beauty. A natural ingredient of life is also the occurring disharmony of existence.[196]

Peacocke also sees God as a creative discoverer of the beauty embedded in nature. The element of improvisation which he introduces to the way in which God acts in the world enables one to put stronger emphasis on the aspect of the open adaptivity of nature. The world's development is not entirely determined and relies both on the influence of factors which allow future states of the system to be predicted, as well as on the random sequence of events. However, the potentialities hidden in nature by God do not have an equal distribution of probability. In the process of evolution, those traits are favored which are conducive to the genesis of life and the emergence of consciousness.[197]

God acting through the laws of nature, which form a complicated network of necessary and contingent events, is also sometimes compared to a painter working on a canvas or a writer creating a poem in their mind, which in time assumes a particular form. Such ideas enable one to underline that divine action is revelatory, creative, and connected to improvisation. Nonetheless, an artist creates with the use of natural means with their inherent possibilities and limitations. The novelty which emerges in the course of the universe's development "comes from the interplay of creativity and respect for what is already there."[198]

The metaphor of the artist enables one to demonstrate the way in which God acts in the world in a way better than that of the concept of the engineer-designer. Instead of the model included in Paley's natural theology, today a much more expressive comparison is the one which refers to the painter who creates a painting by means of blending and spreading paints on a canvas. In respecting the autonomy of paint and canvas, a painter can creatively use them and match particular colors and shapes in such a way that the final version of a painting becomes a masterpiece of art.[199]

The above solution is an example of the influence of the philosophy practiced by Whitehead, who himself presents God as the Poet of the world. What is attempted in this manner is the combination of the belief in the real influence which the Creator has on creation with an appreciation for the freedom of the world. God is the creator of the canons of nature's development but does not enforce them. Divine action is portrayed in the categories of persuasion or attraction, not coercion. In respecting the autonomy of nature, God creates the possibilities of its evolutionary development.[200]

Bearing in mind the risk of overusing anthropomorphisms while speaking of persuasion and auto-creativity, Życiński suggests a more extensive employment of the analogy to nonlinear thermodynamics which would enable comparing God's action to the role of an attractor. The non-linear development of physical systems at a certain stage reaches a state referred to as the "attractor." This is because during the entire evolution of the system it behaves as if it were attracting individual levels of dynamic growth.[201] God, appearing to be the cosmic attractor in relation to the processes of evolution, directs the course of a given system's development towards as yet unactualized goals and includes them in His design. The concept of cosmic directionality is a more sophisticated form of defining the Creator–creation interaction than the classic argument from design. "In the explanatory framework of Christian theism, God understood as an evolutionary attractor shares with all creatures their own openness to a future that is not fully determined."[202]

Despite numerous problems with clarifying the sense of the particular parallels and metaphors, it is worth stressing that they have long been an inseparable component of the language used in discourse pertaining to God and His relation to the world. Christian doctrine has a wide range of presentations at its disposal, which assist in the expression of the essential elements of religious faith. The comparisons known from biblical texts in which God is referred to as a commander-in-chief or a shepherd are a resonant component of reflection for those people for whom military categories or associations with caring for the fate of a herd are still held close. What is additionally helpful on the way to elaborating an image of God is knowledge of nature and its functioning. The specificity of the Creator–creation interaction can be presented both by means of natural metaphors that are well-consolidated in the Christian tradition, as well as through the possibilities which have arisen as a result of the development of contemporary science. Metaphorical statements are not to be taken literally, but this, however, does not deny their value for theistic analysis.

*   *   *

Apart from the ones suggested above, one might also elaborate upon other threats and challenges for theists in attempting to tackle the problem of divine action in the world. The postulates presented in the present chapter seem specifically crucial because theistic reflection constantly has to face manifestations of the indiscriminate application of the "God of the gaps" strategy, practices of naive teleology, and the absolutization of ideas which, in their dogmatized version, stall the development of valuable analysis. On the other hand, an opportunity to enrich the thought concerning the Creator-creation interaction comes with including the scientific worldview, presenting events deemed as random as being the possible "ways" in which providence functions, and in searching for unity in areas that have been for years (often unfoundedly) dominated by dualistic interpretations. The realization of the last task is supported by the development of the linguistic level of discourse, with particular attention being given to metaphors.

Conclusion

The entirety of the analyses conducted in the present study clearly proves that the question of divine action in the world is of essential significance to theism. This is understandable considering that the problem pertains to the most fundamental ontological relationship. For this reason, one would be hard pressed to find philosophers of God who maintain that the issue of the Creator–creation interaction is merely a marginal component of research. Despite the widely voiced declarations stressing the weight of reflection in this area, it is still not appropriately represented in the literature of the subject. One can indicate many publications on the individual aspects of the problem. However, there is no substantial number of monographs highlighting this field of theism, and thus distinguishing it from other comprehensive studies. This state of affairs has become one of the main reasons for my research, the main incentive of which was to feature and appreciate this important subject matter.

At successive stages of the realization of the task which I have undertaken, I was increasingly convinced that the structure of the monograph I proposed, as well as the sources I used, allowed for the discerning of the fundamental components of the questions and problems which arise. In the course of my analysis, many initial hypotheses were confirmed. This was manifested both by the theses formulated in the concluding sections of the first three chapters, as well as by the postulates introduced in the fourth chapter. Laborious study allowed me to arrive at conclusions which are summarized below. It begins with general statements connected to the theme of the book, leading to a presentation of more detailed research outcomes, and ends with assertions concerning contemporary theism.

Giving thought to the complicated question of divine action in the world requires taking into consideration the diverse forms of theistic reflection. One needs to include many philosophical traditions and their mutual openness, as well as various inter-systemic analyses. Instead of simply contrasting the solutions proposed within specific theisms, we need to make use of all valuable ideas since they are not necessarily mutually exclusive. On the basis of research conducted as part of the present study, I can safely state that there are substantive reasons for a partial revision of the main branch of Christian theism, which does not *ipso facto* signify a refutation of the fundamental thereof, but serves to place more emphasis on the possible ways in which the Creator can influence creation.

In highlighting the problem of action in the first chapter of the book, I demonstrated that insightful analysis carried out in the context of the God–world relationship should not stop at accentuating the important division between primary cause and secondary causes. After all, many of the contemporary models of the Creator–creation interaction refer to the uniqueness of nature's functioning. Scientific-philosophical presentations of causality become a greater intellectual support for theistic discourse the more it is stressed that the principal way God influences the world is not of an interventionist character. Detailed demonstration of the complexity of the interactions present in nature can be creatively employed, especially when the rationality of the world is comprehended as the work of a Creator who does not treat creation as does a watchmaker who intervenes every now and then to prevent the mechanism of a clock from stopping. Thanks to inspiration provided by reflection on the interactions which exist between the particular levels of the structures of nature, today we can construct such theories of divine action that serve as valuable examples of the development of the discussed area. In this way, one can discover the wealth of potential "paths" of providence found in the processes of nature, its laws, regularities and random events, boundary conditions, chaotic systems, the self-organization of structures, and human activity.

The second chapter of this book discusses the idea of God and the contemporary ways of its presentation on the grounds of philosophy. Nonetheless, what is mainly identified and analyzed are those attributes of God without which reflection on His action in the world would be incomplete. Certain questions connected with the nature of the Creator as examined in light of His interaction with creation have appeared in different sections of this part of the book. After all, such problems as God's relationship to time, His immutability and impassibility, and the "tension" between immanence and transcendence had to be reflected upon in several sections. As a result of the analyses, it should be stressed that the solution to one of the specific problems concerning the nature of God caring for the world essentially affects the solutions from another particular field of the same area of research. Mutual correlation between concepts can be discerned within the following pairs of issues:

> God's simplicity :: the freedom of God's action and His personal existence;
> God's omniscience :: the freedom of man and the indeterminism of the processes of nature;
> the Creator's omnipotence :: evil in the world.

Moreover, it is difficult to argue in support of unlimited divine omnipotence when stressing God's immanence in the world, as well as while strongly emphasizing creation's autonomy from the Creator. Additionally, the question arises of how God existing outside of time can affect the course of events in the reality which is characterized by the difference between the past and the future. Finally, there are doubts concerning the idea of the immutability of the simple God who, in this way, appears as an abstract entity and not a being who is close to us and the world.

I have presented these problems not only in light of solutions formulated by particular currents of theism. Reflecting on the nature of the necessary being has led me to the fundamental conviction that to absolutize the solutions elaborated upon at certain stages of the history of the philosophy of God is not conducive to the development of this field of knowledge and at times can even stall the possibility of conducting any creative research. Scholars have been aware of this for centuries when attempting to examine the question of divine omnipotence, with this finding its expression in the reflection concerning the moral perfection of God and His indispensable obligation to respect the principle of non-contradiction. Today, certain conditions can also be more strongly formulated during the analysis of other divine attributes such as omniscience, immutability, and simplicity. This is of great significance since the image of God created within the field of philosophical theology should not seem contrary to fundamental Christian ideas, especially to the idea of the Creator's providence embracing creation. An additional argument in this regard is provided by the scientific worldview. This does not mean that we should elaborate the concept of God on the grounds of the natural sciences. Nevertheless, the justified autonomy of philosophical inquiry should not result in the elaboration of such a theory of divine action in the perspective of which the functioning of creation seems to be a particular kind of competition with the Creator. If the world is the work of God, why would He act *contra naturam*?

A detailed reflection on the world in the context of its relationship with God was the subject of the analyses carried out in the third chapter of the present study. I attempted to demonstrate that the autonomous development of the world does not signify creation's independence from the Creator and that the laws of nature can be interpreted as a manifestation of divine design. Theists see these laws as the source of the rationality of the world that remains a contingent being different from the necessary being. The ontic or moral imperfection of the world is not proof of God not acting within it. Evil does not falsify the idea of providence, especially when—instead of stressing the role of selective interventions in the structure of the world—divine custody manifests itself in providing people with a stable environment for moral growth. Reflecting on the presence of evil and suffering in the world enables one to formulate the thesis that God suspends the possibility of an interventionist manifestation of His omnipotence. Such a conviction has been effectively mirrored by the concept of divine *kenosis* which conveys the specificity of crucial Christian intuitions and does not force one to search for the selective expressions of God's action in the world. The specificity of the continuous and simultaneously strong relationship between creation and the Creator is stressed in panentheism. Even though one might comprehend some of the reasons for finding the theory of "the world's immersion in God" interesting, this still calls for a more elaborate study since panentheism is frequently combined with an unclear means of expression and solutions which risk obliterating the boundary between the Creator and creation.

Meticulous investigation of the area delineated by the theme of my book helped me to formulate the several fundamental postulates that I have introduced in the fourth chapter. In particular sections of this chapter I discuss issues that can be deemed to be threats and challenges that need to be tackled by theists who examine the problem of divine action in the world. I attempted to highlight the questions which, in my mind, should become the subject of animated discussion in research on this particular problem. Clarifying the significant areas of this field required taking into consideration a wider theistic and historical perspective. In this context, I have conducted a critical analysis of the "God of the gaps" strategy, as well as a critique of the naive version of teleology which leads to the formulation of the concept of the Creator controlling every detail of evolving creation. However, nowadays teleology is also presented in a rational way that enables a complementary application of both teleological and deterministic interpretations during analysis of the potential ways of the Creator–creation interaction.

Reflecting on the problem of God's relation to the world should not be connected with dogmatizing ideas and particular theistic systems. Their creative evolution provides an opportunity to enliven theism. Appreciating the value of the classical philosophy of God and the thought elaborated by this system's renowned representatives should not be identified with treating their solutions as demarcating the path of theism and all of its nuances once and for all. I do not mean to merely stress that the concepts elaborated upon by Augustine, Anselm, Thomas Aquinas, and Duns Scotus are in some aspects fundamentally different from one another. What I wish to underline is the necessity of noticing the signs of philosophical development in all epochs, including the present day.

An attempt at enriching reflection on the problem of God's action in the world has come in the form of the recently undertaken analyses of events that are deemed random. In this area, thanks to references to currently developed scientific theories, an important reconstruction of ideas has been accomplished. This stems from the conviction that chance is not a "fracture in the rationality of creation," nor is it a kind of "rival to the Creator, fighting for a proper place in the world." The scientific worldview has also contributed to the fact that the academics involved in theistic reflection have moved away from contrasting human beings with "the rest of nature" and now pay stronger attention to the unity present at the various levels of world's structure. In the context of characterizing the God–human relationship, this unity has been given expression in the new terminological solutions that cover many analogies and metaphors. Irrespective of the numerous valuable presentations of the discussed question, one of the most fundamental and simultaneously difficult problems for theism is pushing the issue of God's action centered on human beings to the margins of discussion. This is why research in this field should place more emphasis on the personalistic aspect of the problem.

Nonetheless, the above postulate does not entail the necessity of assuming the hypothesis of divine interventionism with regard to the creation of human beings, in terms of phylogenesis as well as ontogenesis. The idea of our transcendence in the world is given a rational presentation also in those currents of theism which accentuate the significance of the non-interventionist model of God's action, for example by means of including the emergent character of the processes of nature. Thus, the concept of the potential ways of the Creator's influence on creation should take into account a maximally wide range of ways to generate novelty in the world. It seems particularly paradoxical in this context that for some theists the long-appreciated idea of *creatio continua* does not form the basis for the formulation of the theory of God's creative action in relation to humankind. Meanwhile, there are no visible impediments to a complementary presentation of the continuity of the processes of nature with the ontological "leap" which, within anthropological reflection, underlines our unique status in the world.

Reluctance to combine scientific theories with theistic issues is manifested by anti-scientific creationists. They contrast the pre-designed character of God's influence on man and the world with the "blind forces" of nature that randomly affect the course of subsequent stages of evolutionary history. Such a way of reasoning as presented by Christian fundamentalists is an expression of their selective treatment of scientific theories and remains close to the narration proposed by new atheists. The latter, while profusely using (in the context of the specificity of evolutionary processes) expressions like the "selfish gene" or the "blind watchmaker," distract academic attention from substantive aspects of the problem attempting to prove (and sometimes persuade) that the natural sciences have to result in an atheistic interpretation of reality. A thesis posed in this way moves beyond the competence of scientists and cannot be rationally justified. All the same, some theists seem to share the conviction that the development of empirical sciences poses a threat to the Christian doctrine of the Creator–creation interaction. Consequently, these theists shun interdisciplinary research and/or treat the potential weaknesses inherent in scientific theories as particular confirmation of the value of theism. Contrary to such intellectual attitudes, many contemporary theists who undertake reflection on the question of divine action in the world are able to make creative use of inspiration provided by the natural sciences. I have given numerous examples of this at successive stages of the present book.

From among the many diverse components of the issues, I have extracted their most important aspects. I have also presented particular problems which often lack straightforward solutions. Irrespective of the difficulties in the formulation of a final conclusion, I have tried to systematize contemporary approaches to the issue and stress the fact that many of them can become an extremely interesting object of further analysis. The theory of God's action in the world should be enriched with new ways of justifying the proposed theses. In the course of discussing the problem, I have often had to refer to fundamental issues like causality, the laws of nature, and evil. This proves the complexity and significance of this research that should be continued not only by academics interested in natural theology.

Laborious analysis has made me increasingly aware of the fact that elaborating upon a coherent concept of the Creator–creation interaction is a huge intellectual challenge. It is probably for this very reason that the problem is currently of too little appeal to theologians. This needs to be noticed with all the greater alarm since addressing the question of whether (and how) God acts in the world seems to be one of the most important religious queries. Many of the themes examined in the present book resonate with the principal formulas of Christian doctrine. However, this fact is not sufficiently mirrored in theological thought.[1]

Nevertheless, what has been recently more noticeable is the increased interest expressed by philosophers in problems from the field of natural theology. Many diverse forms of research include valuable manifestations of insightful and creative reflection on such issues as divine *kenosis*, God's relationship to time, His ways of acting in nature, and the problem of evil. Assuming openness to criticism of formulated concepts, as well as to the value of the discussion, I am convinced that the examples of theistic solutions which I have enumerated in this book will provide assistance in capturing the specificity of God's interaction with the world.

Anselm's maxim *fides quaerens intellectum* can be understood in many different ways. Its fundamental meaning puts stress on the fact that faith seeks understanding, while reason is necessary on the path to creating an idea of the absolute being. It is true that excessive intellectualization of religious faith frequently leads to an exaggerated focus being given to the justification of statements which—despite referring to the question of God and His relation to the world—do not arrive at the crux of the matter. No kind of philosophical inquiry, even that which takes into account the role of human subjectivity as well as the most recent scientific findings, can exhaust religious discussion and—all the more so—serve as a substitute for the experience of a personal relationship with God. Such experience is inexpressible either through mathematical and physical parameters or by means of terminology governed by the strict principles of logic.

An equally significant threat comes in the form of attempts at depriving religion of its intellectual roots. Such attempts result not only in believers limiting themselves merely to the practical dimension of religious activity, but also in more dangerous manifestations of religious doctrines shutting themselves off from critical analysis. The extreme expression of this is given by religious fundamentalism, both in the shape of various theories as well as in the form of direct human behaviors. This is why it is so important to keep accentuating the fact that religion is a rational phenomenon, with the integral part being its theoretical level that moves beyond narrowly understood dogmatic formulas. Even if the message of the idea *philosophia ancilla theologiae* used to be incorrectly understood (for example as removing the autonomy of philosophical inquiry), it is worth retrieving its proper sense anew, appreciating such disciplines as the philosophy of God, philosophical theology, and the philosophy of religion.

In deeming the above-mentioned fields of cognitive involvement to be at least anachronistic, the representatives of new atheism place strong emphasis on the fact that they have managed to find a way to "disenchant" religion which, as they claim, is a natural phenomenon.[2] It needs to be noted, however, that Christian doctrine had long been submitted to a conscious and programmatic process of "naturalization," understood as choosing between various components of reflection on God and His relationship with the world and especially human beings. In this respect, reliable forms of searching for truth do not weaken the significance of religion, but only serve to strengthen it. This also includes those manifestations of substantive criticism which pose a challenge irrespective of whether they come from "the outside" or from "the inside" of the religious sphere. It is better to give up theories of a dubious quality, than to maintain them at all cost,[3] for instance finding consolation in the fact that the representatives of other religions do not pay much attention to justifying the theses they proclaim. Such a defense strategy is very short-sighted. In the long term, however, the harmful effects of dogmatizing irrational concepts become evident.

Partial reinterpretation of theism can help to elaborate a rational approach to the question of the Creator–creation interaction. It should not merely come down to rejecting the elements of reflection which do not respect the basics of logical reasoning or blatantly contradict contemporary science and hence impede interdisciplinary dialogue. Moreover, it is essential to avoid mental inflexibility manifested in excessively abstract forms of expression, hermetic language, and a choice of terminology that has an entirely different (and at times contrary) meaning outside of Christian culture. A perception of theism renewed in the light of the above would allow a greater approximation of the content of discussions to the fundamental religious dilemmas, while at the same time ensuring that the image of God contains His essential traits included in the Christian message.[4]

A coherent presentation of the biblical and philosophical image of God is one of the most difficult problems of theism. Certain reserve in this respect seems unavoidable and is easier to understand thanks to contemporary theological hermeneutics. This stresses the necessity of taking into consideration cultural conditions characteristic of the subsequent stages of the creation of the Judeo-Christian tradition subjected to various types of conditioning. Despite the differences which stem from the autonomous research perspectives assumed by philosophy and theology, what is of utmost importance is the idea of the Creator looking after creation, but also granting it a real autonomy of development, the culmination of which being human freedom. Such should be the image of God delineated within philosophical discourse. This has a specificity of its own in embracing both the language employed and the method of searching for the solutions to particular theistic issues.

Academic circles critical of theism often object to the allegedly imprecise language used in reference to God and His action in the world, as well as to the lack of objective criteria with which to assess potentially valuable concepts. Nevertheless, the theistic system can be treated as one that meets the criteria of verifiability if this is not perceived as a conclusive procedure but as a confirmation by means of rational argumentation.[5] In the past half century, the latter has become the domain of many ambitious philosophical approaches. Cooperation between the representatives of various academic centers helped to clarify the concepts important to the dialogue between religion and science (e.g., causality and the laws of nature), and facilitated the uncovering of new, cognitively interesting concepts of God's interaction with nature, as exemplified by inspiration provided by the findings of the fields of quantum mechanics and chaos theory.

Examples which enable a fuller comprehension of the challenges faced by contemporary thought on God's action in the world can be found in Życiński's works. What proves them exemplary in this respect is that their author remains open to the natural sciences, assumes an original approach, enriches the terminological level of discourse, stresses the value of the rationality of thought, and attempts to coherently present the philosophical and theological perspective of a problem. What also needs to be highlighted is the conviction, voiced by the author of *God and Evolution*, that the conducted analyses have to take into account the questions that stem from man's existential dilemmas. One of the most essential reasons for doubting religious faith is an experience of evil and suffering that puts into question God's existence in the world and especially in the life of man. A theistic system constructed in the light of the above, should be open to new solutions, both regarding the content and the means of conveying it.

The development of theism can, to some extent, be perceived as analogous to the progress achieved in other disciplines of knowledge. Such progress is necessarily conditioned by an openness to conceptual evolution. Just as contemporary physics should not be practiced with the employment of language characteristic of the scientific research done by Galileo and Kepler, theistic reflection should not be undertaken on the basis of a limited set of terms that were elaborated upon in the past.[6] Solving problems with the help of a small and simultaneously absolutized collection of universal philosophical categories may result in the repetition of generalizing clichés. Admittedly, no linguistic procedures are capable of facilitating the creation of a non-contradictory and comprehensive concept of God in relation to the world but remaining lexically receptive is an indispensable component of developing valuable theories.[7]

An unrestrained realization of the above postulate might transform philosophical inquiry into literary reflection, thus making it impossible to define the content of particular arguments. That is why the efforts to analyze the meaning of the terms used by various philosophical schools remain valuable. Such research methods can be compared to the procedures employed in exact sciences, in the framework of which a given description is never treated as an absolute and unique means of expression. Linguistic relativity is of no substantive character, but is of a formal one, i.e., pertaining to means and not to content. The latter is also subject to modification, but this does not entail the undermining of the classical concept of truth.

An inter-systemic philosophical openness is not a goal of theistic research, but does provide tools that enable the improvement of conceptual instruments by means of a maximally extensive inclusion of the achievements of many currents of reflection on the question of divine action in the world. This is supposed to result in a more complete use of comparative analyses in the revision of the assumptions and lexicon of a given system. As a consequence of employing such a methodology, we may not only eliminate some of the fundamental difficulties that exist in the philosophy of God, but also create monographs that take into consideration the output of authors who belong to diverse theistic traditions. This is not a forced merger of different theistic currents for the sake of producing one eclectic system. All the same, nothing stands in the way of combining the philosophy of big questions with analytic studies.[8]

Developing theism, as situated in a wide context of issues, does not entail a radical rejection of the classical elements of Christian thought. Nevertheless, being faithful to tradition has to be coupled with an awareness of its wealth. After all, a valuable heritage is not limited to a small area of the most well-known theories but embraces diverse ways of reflecting on the problem of God's nature and action. Even if there are moments when, while conducting our research, we have to resort to searching "in the dark," and the language we use is not able to express the specificity of providence, our sincere desire to find the truth is reason enough to derive intellectual and spiritual satisfaction from following in the footsteps of the householder who "brings out of his storeroom new treasures as well as old."[9]

Notes

Introduction

1 Walter Kasper, *The God of Jesus Christ* (New Edition) (London–New York: Continuum, 2012), 24.
2 The manifesto of open theism can be found in a book edited by the forerunners of this approach: Clark H. Pinnock et al., *The Openness of God. A Biblical Challenge to the Traditional Understanding of God* (Downers Grove, IL: InterVarsity Press, 1994).
3 A crucial point of reference for probabilistic theism is the scientific worldview. There are several similar ways to practice theism, with naturalistic theism and evolutionary theism being examples thereof. Theistic (or Christian) naturalism is mentioned in this context as well.
4 Ian G. Barbour, *Issues in Science and Religion* (Englewood Cliffs, NJ: Prentice-Hall, 1966).
5 The abbreviation index contains a list of post-conference volumes. A tangible proof that the DAP has been realized is, among other things, the project-concluding publication titled *Scientific Perspectives on Divine Action. Twenty Years of Challenge and Progress*, by Robert J. Russell, Nancey Murphy, and William R. Stoeger, eds. (Vatican City State: Vatican Observatory Publications, Berkeley, CA: The Center for Theology and the Natural Sciences, 2008).
6 John Paul II, *Letter of His Holiness John Paul II to Reverend George V. Coyne, S.J. Director of the Vatican Observatory* (June 1, 1988), accessed April 29, 2020, http://www.vatican.va/content/john-paul-ii/en/letters/1988/documents/hf_jp-ii_let_19880601_padre-coyne.html.
7 In some sections of my analyses, phrases like "God's influence on the world" or "God's interaction with the world" seem to be more adequate. However, the phrasing which remains fundamental to my study is: "God's action in the world."
8 See, e.g., John F. Haught, *Resting on the Future. Catholic Theology for an Unfinished Universe* (New York: Bloomsbury, 2015), 193.
9 Józef Życiński, *Teizm i filozofia analityczna*, vol. 1 (Cracow: Znak, 1985), and vol. 2 (1988).
10 Dariusz Łukasiewicz, *Opatrzność Boża, wolność, przypadek. Studium z analitycznej filozofii religii* (Cracow: Dominikańskie Studium Filozofii i Teologii, Poznań: W drodze, 2014). The discussion upon this book has been published in *Roczniki Filozoficzne* 68, no. 3 (2020).
11 David R. Griffin, *Reenchantment without Supernaturalism. A Process Philosophy of Religion* (London– Ithaca, NY: Cornell University Press, 2001), 7; Peter van Inwagen, *The Problem of Evil. The Gifford Lectures Delivered in the University of St Andrews in 2003* (Oxford: Clarendon Press, 2008), 2.
12 I am well aware of the evolution of the detailed solutions provided by Karl Popper's philosophy of science.

13 Even though the problem of demarcation has not been definitively settled yet, we can point to many indicators of a fundamental distinction between rational scientific thought and irrational discourse, with the latter lying outside the domain of science. Later in my study I will provide examples of this.
14 Willem B. Drees, *Creation. From Nothing Until Now* (London–New York: Routledge, 2002), 65–67. See also Robert J. Berry, *God and the Biologist. Faith at the Frontiers of Science* (Leicester: Apollos/InterVarsity Press, 1996), 23–24.
15 Richard Dawkins, *The God Delusion* (New York: Houghton Mifflin Company, 2006). See also Alister McGrath and Joanna Collicutt McGrath, *The Dawkins Delusion? Atheism Fundamentalism and the Denial of the Divine* (Downers Grove, IL: IVP Books, 2007).
16 Michael J. Dodds, *Unlocking Divine Action. Contemporary Science and Thomas Aquinas* (Washington, DC: The Catholic University of America Press, 2012), 5.
17 The question of miracles is outside the scope of the present study. However, I refer to this problem when necessary.
18 I assume that a contingent world cannot even for a moment exist without its relationship with God. Here, however, I find it worthwhile to look at the actions of the Creator which are not limited to merely sustaining creation in existence. The Latin word *conservatio* used in this context points to the passive dimension of the God–world relationship. This, in turn, is one of the reasons why we look for other ways of demonstrating the Creator's influence on creation.
19 A Biblical manifestation of such conviction is found in the statement that the attributes of God can be recognized by the work of His creation (Romans 1:20). See also William R. Stoeger, "Key Developments in Physics Challenging Philosophy and Theology," in *Religion and Science. History, Method, Dialogue*, ed. W. Mark Richardson and Wesley J. Wildman (New York: Routledge, 1996), 194.
20 In the light of certain traumatic events the following question may arise: Where was God? This was posed, among others, by Benedict XVI during a speech delivered in the former German Nazi concentration camp Auschwitz-Birkenau on May 28, 2006. The speech is available at https://www.ewtn.com/catholicism/library/auschwitz-visit-to-concentration-camp-6836 (accessed January 18, 2020). The very act of posing such a question like this is not equal to stating that God is inactive, but rather liberates an open reflection on an extremely important issue. See also James A. Keller, *Problems of Evil and the Power of God* (Aldershot: Ashgate, 2007).
21 Exodus 3:14, NIV.

1 On the Action

1 In the strict sense, the theory of action refers exclusively to persons. Statements concerning, for example, the activity of nature make use of the language of analogy and metaphor. Serving as a significant reference point for reflection on divine action, classical philosophical thought on human action originates mainly from the analysis practiced on the grounds of ethics. That is why, within traditional approaches, action was thought of as those forms of human activity which are undertaken in the name of the ethical good. In contemporary reflection, the ethical aspect, as directing action to what is right, has been moved to the background, while attention has been given to the very analysis of acting. On the one hand, attempts are being made to answer the question: What is action and what differentiates action from human agents' other

behaviors? On the other hand, what is being analyzed are the ways of explaining action, with scholars posing the questions: What is the reason for human action? Why do humans undertake a given action? What inclines humans to take action? The paradigmatic examples of action are thought to be deliberate and intentional acts. It is stressed that actions are events for which the agent (the cause of an action) can be deemed responsible. Detailed analyses also include questions regarding renunciations, habitual actions, mannerisms, spontaneous actions, mistakes, and irrational behaviors. The conventionally enumerated conditions for action are rationality, intention, voluntariness, awareness of value, and subjective identity. An insightful analysis of this issue can be found, for instance, in Lilian O'Brien, *Philosophy of Action* (Basingstoke: Palgrave, 2014); Rowland Stout, *Action* (Chesham: Acumen, 2005); Timothy O'Connor and Constantine Sandis, eds., *A Companion to the Philosophy of Action* (Oxford: Wiley-Blackwell, 2010); Constantine Sandis, ed., *New Essays on the Explanation of Action* (Basingstoke: Palgrave, 2009); and Jonathan Dancy and Constantine Sandis, eds., *Philosophy of Action. An Anthology* (Oxford: Wiley-Blackwell, 2015). In the context of the above remarks, it needs to be noted that the authors of studies concerning divine action take an approach closer to classical propositions, and do not undertake detailed analyses of action as such.

2   No doubt, the notions of action (or acting) and causality are not identical, but I assume that the question of divine action in the world can be efficiently examined in the context of reflection on causality. This stems, among other things, from a well-established practice in the tradition of theism that draws on the notion of cause (primary-secondary) during analysis of the potential ways in which the Creator influences His creation. Apart from that, contemporary research in this area, by way of analogy, makes use of the notion of causation that is typical of natural processes interpretations. In general, in the currently prevailing English-language works concerning the issues of causality, there is an affirmed distinction between *event causation* and *agent causation*; on this, see Michael Brent, "Agent Causation as a Solution to the Problem of Action," *Canadian Journal of Philosophy* 47, no. 5 (2017): 656–73; John Bishop, "Causal Pluralism and the Problem of Natural Agency," *Res Philosophica* 91, no. 3 (2014): 527–36; Randolph Clarke, "Agent Causation and Event Causation in the Production of Free Action," *Philosophical Topics* 24, no. 2 (1996): 19–48.

3   Robert J. Russell, *Cosmology from Alpha to Omega. The Creative Mutual Interaction of Theology and Science* (Minneapolis: Fortress Press, 2008), 124.

4   Damian Mrugalski, "Stwarzanie wieczne i poza czasem. Filozoficzne źródła koncepcji 'generatio aeterna' Orygenesa," *Verbum Vitae* 35 (2019): 367–412.

5   Jonathan L. Kvanvig and Hugh J. McCann, "Divine Conservation and the Persistence of the World," in *Divine and Human Action. Essays in the Metaphysics of Theism*, ed. Thomas V. Morris (Ithaca, NY: Cornell University Press, 1988), 13–49.

6   Robert J. Russell, "Introduction," in *CC*, 10.

7   Alvin C. Plantinga, "What is 'Intervention'?" *Theology and Science* 6, no. 4 (2008): 369–401.

8   Russell, "Introduction," 10.

9   John C. Polkinghorne, "The Metaphysics of Divine Action," in *CC*, 150–51; see also Russell, "Introduction," 12; Stephen Happel, "Divine Providence and Instrumentality. Metaphors for Time in Self-Organizing Systems and Divine Action," in *CC*, 197–99.

10 Dariusz Łukasiewicz, "O założeniach filozoficznych opatrzności kwantowej i jej niektórych konsekwencjach," *Filo-Sofija* 31, no. 4/1 (2015): 206.

11 The models of the Creator–creation interaction can differ, for instance depending on the object of influence. That is why a separate study could be devoted to a detailed examination of the problem of the differences between the concepts of God's influence on inanimate and animate nature (with the latter mainly including conscious beings).
12 *God's Activity in the World. The Contemporary Problem*, ed. Owen C. Thomas (Chico, CA: Scholars Press, 1983).
13 Russell, "Introduction," 7–9.
14 See, e.g., Maurice F. Wiles, *God's Action in the World. The Bampton Lectures for 1986* (London: SCM Press, 1986).
15 William P. Alston, "Divine Action, Human Freedom, and the Laws of Nature," in *QC*, 187–91.
16 See, e.g., Arthur R. Peacocke, "God's Interaction with the World. The Implications of Deterministic 'Chaos' and of Interconnected and Interdependent Complexity," in *CC*, 263–88.
17 Grace Jantzen, *God's World, God's Body* (London: Darton; Longman & Todd, 1984).
18 Sallie McFague, "Models of God for an Ecological, Evolutionary Era. God as Mother of the Universe," in *Physics, Philosophy, and Theology. A Common Quest for Understanding*, ed. Robert J. Russell, William R. Stoeger, and George V. Coyne (Vatican City State: Vatican Observatory Publications, 1988), 249–72.
19 Thomas F. Tracy, *God, Action, and Embodiment* (Grand Rapids, MI: Eerdmans, 1984).
20 Russell, "Introduction," 9; see also John C. Polkinghorne, "The Laws of Nature and the Laws of Physics," in *QC*, 429–40.
21 David R. Griffin, *Unsnarling the World-Knot. Consciousness, Freedom, and the Mind-Body Problem* (Eugene, OR: Wipf & Stock Publishers, 2007), 35.
22 George F. R. Ellis, "Quantum Theory and the Macroscopic World," in *QM*, 259.
23 Ian G. Barbour, "Indeterminacy, Holism and God's Action," in *God's Action in Nature's World. Essays in Honour of Robert John Russell*, ed. Ted Peters and Nathan Hallanger (Aldershot: Ashgate, 2006), 113.
24 Steven Weinberg, "Reductionism redux," *The New York Review of Books* 42, no. 15 (1995): 39–42.
25 John C. Polkinghorne, *One World. The Interaction of Science and Theology* (London–Philadelphia, PA: Templeton Foundation Press, 2007), 58; see also Niels H. Gregersen, "Special Divine Action and the Quilt of Laws. Why the Distinction between Special and General Divine Cannot Be Maintained," in *SPDA*, 187–89.
26 William G. Pollard, *Chance and Providence. God's Action in the World Governed by Scientific Laws* (London: Faber and Faber, 1958); see also Alvin Plantinga, *Where the Conflict Really Lies. Science, Religion and Naturalism* (Oxford: Oxford University Press, 2011), 113–21.
27 Bradley Monton, "God Acts in the Quantum World," in *Oxford Studies in Philosophy of Religion*, ed. Jonathan L. Kvanvig (Oxford: Clarendon Press, 2012), 5:133–46.
28 The basic equation of quantum mechanics (Schrödinger's equation) is deterministic in its mathematical structure. The indeterministic nature of wave function is derived from the interpretation provided by quantum mechanics, see Kitty Ferguson, *The Fire in the Equations. Science, Religion, and the Search for God* (West Conshohocken, PA: Templeton Press, 2004), 195–203.
29 Nancey Murphy, "Divine Action in the Natural Order. Buridan's Ass and Schrödinger's Cat," in *CC*, 325–57; see also George F. R. Ellis, "Ordinary and Extraordinary Divine Action. The Nexus of Interaction," in *CC*, 360–95.
30 John C. Polkinghorne, "The Metaphysics of Divine Action," 147–56.

31 Ernan McMullin, "Formalism and Ontology in Early Astronomy," in *QM*, 55–56.
32 Michał Heller, *Sens życia i sens wszechświata. Studia teologii współczesnej* (Tarnów: Biblos, 2002), 122–26; see also Nicolas T. Saunders, "Does God Cheat at Dice? Divine Action and Quantum Possibilities," *Zygon* 35, no. 3 (2000): 517–44.
33 Łukasiewicz, "O założeniach filozoficznych," 216.
34 Griffin, *Unsnarling the World-Knot*, 37.
35 Józef Bremer, "Przyczynowość skierowana ku dołowi i jej rozumienie w biologii," in *Aktywność poznawcza podmiotu w perspektywie badań kognitywistycznych*, Poznańskie Studia z Filozofii Nauki, vol. 24, no. 1, ed. Piotr Przybysz (Poznań: Wydawnictwo Fundacji Uniwersytetu im. A. Mickiewicza, 2015), 93–103. See also Fulvio Mazzocchi, "Complexity and the Reductionism-Holism Debate in Systems Biology," *WIREs Systems Biology and Medicine* 4 (2012): 413–27.
36 Donald T. Campbell, "'Downward Causation' in Hierarchically Organized Biological Systems," in *Studies in the Philosophy of Biology*, ed. Francisco J. Ayala and Theodosius Dobzhansky (Berkeley–Los Angeles, CA: University of California Press, 1974), 179–86; see also Donald T. Campbell, "Levels of Organization, Downward Causation, and the Selection-Theory Approach to Evolutionary Epistemology," in *Theories of the Evolution of Knowing*, ed. Gary Greenberg and Ethel Tobach (Hillsdale, NJ: Lawrence Erlbaum, 1990), 1–17; James M. Marcum, *The Conceptual Foundations of Systems Biology. An Introduction* (New York: Nova Science Publishers, 2009), for example, p. 50.
37 Christophe Malaterre, "Life as an Emergent Phenomenon. From an Alternative to Vitalism to an Alternative to Reductionism," in *Vitalism and the Scientific Image in Post-Enlightenment Life Science, 1800–2010*, ed. S. Normandin and Charles T. Wolfe (Dordrecht–Heidelberg–London–New York: Springer, 2013), 155–78.
38 Bremer, "Przyczynowość skierowana ku dołowi," 104–6; see also Józef Bremmer, *Downward Causation. Minds, Bodies and Matter*, ed. Peter B. Andersen, Claus Emmeche, Niels Finnemmann, and Peder Christiansen (Aarhus: Aarhus University Press, 2000).
39 Arthur R. Peacocke, "God's Interaction with the World. The Implications of Deterministic 'Chaos' and of Interconnected and Interdependent Complexity," in *CC*, 272–73.
40 Bremer, "Przyczynowość skierowana ku dołowi," 107.
41 Russell, "Introduction," 12.
42 Keith Ward, *Divine Action. Examining God's Role in an Open and Emergent Universe* (West Conshohocken, PA: Templeton Foundation Press, 2007), 74–102.
43 Polkinghorne, *The Metaphysics of Divine Action*, 153.
44 Arthur R. Peacocke, "God's Interaction with the World," 286, and his *Paths from Science Towards God. The End of All Our Exploring* (Oxford: Oneworld Publications, 2002), 108–14.
45 John C. Polkinghorne, *Science and Providence. God's Interaction with the World* (West Conshohocken, PA: Templeton Foundation Press, 2005), 35.
46 1 Kings 19.
47 Arthur R. Peacocke, "The Sound of Sheer Silence. How Does God Communicate with Humanity?" in *NAP*, 215–47.
48 William R. Stoeger, "Describing God's Action in the World in Light of Scientific Knowledge of Reality," in *CC*, 246–50. See also Dodds, *Unlocking Divine Action*, 190–204.
49 Tadeusz Pabjan, "Nieinterwencjonistyczny model działania Boga w świecie przyrody," *Tarnowskie Studia Teologiczne* 35, no. 1 (2016): 42.

50 Ignacio Silva, "Revisiting Aquinas on Providence and Rising to the Challenge of Divine Action in Nature," *Journal of Religion* 94, no. 3 (2014): 277–91.
51 Pabjan, "*Nieinterwencjonistyczny model*," 43.
52 Thomas Aquinas, *Summa Theologiae* (*The One God*, 1.22.3), http://www.newadvent.org/summa/1022.htm (accessed April 28, 2020).
53 Aquinas, *Summa Theologiae* (*The Government of Creatures*, 1.105.5), http://www.newadvent.org/summa/1105.htm (accessed February 4, 2020).
54 Stoeger, "Describing God's Action," 254; see also Dodds, *Unlocking Divine Action*, 11–44.
55 Stoeger, "Describing God's Action," 255.
56 Griffin, *Unsnarling the World-Knot*, 30.
57 Heller, *Sens życia i sens wszechświata*, 127.
58 Józef Życiński, "The Laws of Nature and the Immanence of God in the Evolving Universe," *Studies in Science and Theology* 5 (1997): 15.
59 Michał Heller, "Chrześcijański naturalizm," *Roczniki Filozoficzne* 51, no. 3 (2003): 52.

2 On God

1 Richard Swinburne, *The Coherence of Theism* (2nd ed.) (Oxford: Oxford University Press, 2016), 1. The unique character of some theories justifies why some theists put a greater emphasis on the significance of particular religious doctrines for philosophical thought. The theory of *kenosis*, as elaborated in some intellectual circles, was born in the context set by the depiction of the Incarnation found in the second chapter of the Letter of St. Paul to the Philippians. Concepts more independent from theology were formulated at an advanced stage of reflection upon God's *kenosis*.
2 Griffin, *Reenchantment without Supernaturalism*, 8.
3 Michał Heller, "Naukowy obraz świata a zadanie teologa," in *Obrazy świata w teologii i naukach przyrodniczych*, ed. Michał Heller, Stanisław Budzik, and Stanisław Wszołek (Tarnów: Biblos, 1996), 14–27.
4 Van Inwagen, *The Problem of Evil*, 18.
5 Dariusz Łukasiewicz, "Atrybuty Boga," in *Przewodnik po filozofii religii. Nurt analityczny*, ed. Janusz Salamon (Cracow: WAM 2016), 11.
6 Attempts at specifying the nature of this relationship come in a variety of forms. A consistent Thomistic scholar would say that this relationship is not a real relation but rather a mental one. This ensues from the way in which God exists; Robert Sokolowski, *God of Faith and Reason. Foundations of Christian Theology* (Washington, DC: The Catholic University of America Press, 1998), 34; see also Jacek Wojtysiak, *Wprowadzenie do teologii naturalnej* (Cracow: Dominikańskie Studium Filozofii i Teologii, 2013), 48.
7 Griffin, *Reenchantment without Supernaturalism*, 11–12.
8 Peacocke, *Paths from Science*, 56–57.
9 Phillip Clayton, "Tracing the Lines. Constraint and Freedom in the Movement from Quantum Physics to Theology," in *QM*, 230–31.
10 Alvin Plantinga, *The Nature of Necessity* (New York: Oxford University Press, 1974), 44–87.
11 Thomas V. Morris, "Properties, Modalities, and God," in *Anselmian Explorations. Essays in Philosophical Theology*, by Thomas V. Morris (Notre Dame, IN: University of Notre Dame Press, 1987), 76–77.

12 Alvin Plantinga, *Does God Have a Nature?* (Milwaukee, WI: Marquette University Press, 1980).
13 David Blumenfeld, "On the Compossibility of the Divine Attributes," *Philosophical Studies* 34 (1978): 91–103.
14 Norman Kretzmann, "Omniscience and Immutability," *The Journal of Philosophy* 63 (1966): 409–21; Nelson Pike, "Omnipotence and God's Ability to Sin," *American Philosophical Quarterly* 6, no. 3 (1969): 208–16.
15 Dariusz Łukasiewicz, "O spójności teizmu," in *Filozofia Boga*, vol. 1, *Poszukiwanie Boga* (Lublin: KUL, 2017), 531.
16 Thomas M. Crisp, "Presentism, Eternalism and Relativity Physics," in *Einstein, Relativity and Absolute Simultaneity*, ed. William L. Craig and Quentin Smith (London–New York: Routledge, 2007), 262–78; Paul C. W. Davies, "That Mysterious Flow," *Scientific American* 287, no. 3 (2002): 40–47; Katherin Rogers, "Back to Eternalism," *Faith and Philosophy* 26, no. 3 (2009): 320–38.
17 Ryszard, Mordarski, "Spójność (jedność) atrybutów Boga," *Przegląd Filozoficzny – Nowa Seria* 25, no. 2 (2016): 339–41.
18 Łukasiewicz, *Opatrzność Boża, wolność, przypadek*, 29.
19 Philip L. Quinn and Charles Taliaferro, eds., *A Companion to Philosophy of Religion* (Oxford: Blackwell Publishing, 1997), 221–319; William E. Mann, ed., *The Blackwell Guide to the Philosophy of Religion* (Oxford: Blackwell Publishing, 2005), 1–77; William J. Wainwright, ed., *The Oxford Handbook of Philosophy of Religion* (New York: Oxford University Press, 2005), 15–58; Charles Taliaferro and Chad V. Meister, *The Cambridge Companion to Christian Philosophical Theology* (New York: Cambridge University Press, 2010), 15–91; Thomas P. Flint and Michael C. Rea, eds., *The Oxford Handbook of Philosophical Theology*, vol. 2 (Oxford: Oxford University Press, 2012), 103–238; Anthony C. Thiselton, *A Concise Encyclopedia of the Philosophy of Religion* (Oxford: Oneworld, 2002), 118–23.
20 For example, Stephen T. Davis, *Logic and the Nature of God* (Grand Rapids, MI: William B. Eerdmans Publishing Company, 1983); Edward R. Wierenga, *The Nature of God. An Inquiry into Divine Attributes* (Ithaca, NY: Cornell University Press, 1989); Joshua Hoffman and Gary S. Rosenkrantz, *The Divine Attributes* (Oxford: Blackwell Publishing, 2002); Katherin Rogers, *Perfect Being Theology* (Edinburgh: Edinburgh University Press, 2002).
21 Mordarski, "Spójność (jedność) atrybutów Boga," 344; see also Brian Davies, *The Thought of Thomas Aquinas* (Oxford: Clarendon Press, 1992); Brian J. Shanley, *The Thomist Tradition* (Dordrecht–London–Boston, MA: Kluwer Academic Publishers, 2002), 179–207.
22 Some modifications move so far away from their origins that one might wonder whether they are still a type of theism, at least in its Christian form. However, it is also true that providing a precise definition of Christian theism is not an easy task when God's attributes themselves are being thoroughly examined.
23 Łukasiewicz, *Opatrzność Boża, wolność, przypadek*, 30–31.
24 Mordarski, "Spójność (jedność) atrybutów Boga," 345; see also William J. Wainwright, "Omnipotence, Omniscience, and Omnipresence," in *The Cambridge Companion to Christian Philosophical Theology*, ed. Charles Taliaferro and Chad V. Meister (Cambridge: Cambridge University Press, 2010), 46–65.
25 Sokolowski, *God of Faith and Reason*, 12–13.
26 Robert Wright, *The Evolution of God* (New York–Boston–London: Little, Brown, and Company, 2009), 216–44.

27 This way of reasoning is meaningfully expressed in the *Letter to Diognetus*, a Christian apology written by an anonymous author (earlier identified as Justin) at the end of the second century, probably in Alexandria: "To speak in general terms, we may say that the Christian is to the world what the soul is to the body. As the soul is present in every part of the body, while remaining distinct from it, so Christians are found in all the cities of the world, but cannot be identified with the world. As the visible body contains the invisible soul, so Christians are seen living in the world, but their religious life remains unseen. The body hates the soul and wars against it, not because of any injury the soul has done it, but because of the restriction the soul places on its pleasures. Similarly, the world hates the Christians, not because they have done it any wrong, but because they are opposed to its enjoyments. Christians love those who hate them just as the soul loves the body and all its members despite the body's hatred. It is by the soul, enclosed within the body, that the body is held together, and similarly, it is by the Christians, detained in the world as in a prison, that the world is held together. The soul, though immortal, has a mortal dwelling place; and Christians also live for a time amidst perishable things, while awaiting the freedom from change and decay that will be theirs in heaven." http://www.vatican.va/spirit/documents/spirit_20010522_diogneto_en.html (accessed February 5, 2020).
28 Maurice F. Wiles, *Christian Fathers* (London: SCM Press, 1966), 27.
29 Augustine, *Tractates on the Gospel of John* (29, 6), http://www.newadvent.org/fathers/1701029.htm (accessed February 6, 2020). Polkinghorne draws attention to a significant paradox: the quoted plea was formulated by St. Augustine whose reflection on God is a manifestation of an extraordinary precision of rational thinking and an insightful "bottom–up" analysis; John Polkinghorne, *Science and Creation. The Search for Understanding* (Philadelphia–London: Templeton Foundation Press, 2006), 15.
30 Mordarski, "Spójność (jedność) atrybutów Boga," 341.
31 William E. Mann, "The Divine Attributes," *American Philosophical Quarterly* 12, no. 2 (1975): 151–59.
32 Mordarski, "Spójność (jedność) atrybutów Boga," 342.
33 There have been known cases of medieval condemnations formulated against many aspects of Aristotelian philosophy, as exemplified by Pope Innocent IV and S. Tempier, the bishop of Paris; Michał Heller, *Nowa fizyka i nowa teologia* (Tarnów: Biblos, 1992), 42; Hans Thijssen, "Condemnation of 1277," in *The Stanford Encyclopedia of Philosophy* (Fall 2008 Edition), ed. Edward N. Zalta, https://plato.stanford.edu/archives/fall2008/entries/condemnation (accessed February 7, 2020).
34 Mordarski, *Spójność (jedność) atrybutów Boga*, 343.
35 In Aquinas's model, human freedom is compatible with the determination of the will. Nevertheless, as rightly observed by one of the anonymous reviewers of this book to whom I'm very thankful, Aquinas's position on the relation between the divine will and human freedom is quite different from what has become known today as the "compatibilist" position. According to contemporary compatibilism our will is actually determined either by natural causes or by God. Human "freedom" consists in the fact that we do not know that our will is so determined. This ignorance on our part is thought to make the actual determinism of our will "compatible" with freedom. There is, however, a contradiction in referring to human action as free, while simultaneously viewing it as determined. Aquinas's account of human freedom in relation to divine causality is essentially different. God is the primary cause of both our action and the mode of that action (as free). The free character of our action does not arise from our ignorance of the fact that God has really produced some necessary action in us.

Instead, it arises from God's very intention that our act be produced freely (and not by necessity or by chance). In compatibilism, apart from our cognitive ignorance, we could not say that we act freely. See Aquinas's *In meta.* VI, lect. 3 [§1218–22] and *In peri herm.* I, lect. 14, no. 22; see also: Dodds, *Unlocking Divine Action*, 225–28; Brian J. Shanley, "Beyond Libertarianism and Compatibilism. Thomas Aquinas on Created Freedom," in *Freedom and the Human Person*, ed. Richard Velkley (Washington, DC: The Catholic University of America Press, 2007), 70–89. The classical conception of the Creator–creation interaction also has an indeterministic version: God knows the world from an atemporal perspective, without determining events taking place in the world. According to some scholars, such an approach can be found in St. Anselm's metaphysics; Dariusz Łukasiewicz, "Przypadek i prawdopodobieństwo a zagadnienie opatrzności Bożej w filozofii przypadku Michała Hellera," *Filo-Sofija* 25, no. 2 (2014): 197–98.

36 Mordarski, *Spójność (jedność) atrybutów Boga*, 343.
37 William J. Abraham, *Divine Agency and Divine Action*, vol. 1, *Exploring and Evaluating the Debate* (Oxford: Oxford University Press, 2017), 165–86.
38 Stoeger, "Describing God's Action," 246–50; Ernan McMullin, "Natural Science and Belief in a Creator. Historical Notes," in *Physics, Philosophy, and Theology. A Common Quest for Understanding*, ed. Robert J. Russell, William R. Stoeger, and George V. Coyne (Vatican City State: Vatican Observatory Publications, 1988), 58–59; see also Russell, "Introduction," 7.
39 The primordial and consequent natures of God are sometimes described as aspects (or dimensions) of one divine nature. I discuss this further in the next part of this book. I am well aware of the multiplicity of interpretations concerning Whitehead's philosophy. One of its crucial problems is: How can God affect the world? In processualism this issue is even more complex than the problem of the world's influence on God. Basic issues of the processual philosophy of religion are well presented by Griffin in his *Reenchantment without Supernaturalism*, 1–7.
40 Acts 17:28; see also Joseph A. Bracken, *Does God Roll Dice? Divine Providence for a World in the Making* (Collegeville, MN: Liturgical Press, 2012): 31–45.
41 Tadeusz Szubka, "Analityczna filozofia religii Richarda Swinburne'a," translator's introduction to *Spójność teizmu*, by Richard G. Swinburne (Cracow: Znak, 1995), 7–25.
42 Mordarski, *Spójność (jedność) atrybutów Boga*, 346.
43 William Hasker, "Analytic Philosophy of Religion," in *The Oxford Handbook of Philosophy of Religion*, ed. William J. Wainwright (Oxford: Oxford University Press, 2005), 428.
44 Mordarski, *Spójność (jedność) atrybutów Boga*, 347.
45 Peter Vardy, *The Puzzle of God* (London–New York: Routledge, 2015), 39.
46 Vardy, *The Puzzle of God*, 40–44.
47 Heller, *Nowa fizyka*, 39–41.
48 Pedersen, *The Two Books: Historical Notes on Some Interactions between Natural Science and Theology*, ed. George V. Coyne and Tadeusz Sierotowicz (Notre Dame, IN: University of Notre Dame Press, 2007), 172–81.
49 The Church had even more reasons for being critical of Aristotelian thought, for example, in the context of Aristotle's reflection on God's omnipotence; Neil Lewis, "Space and Time," in *The Cambridge Companion to John Duns Scotus*, ed. Thomas Williams (Cambridge: Cambridge University Press, 2002), 69.
50 Heller, *Nowa fizyka*, 42.
51 Alexandre Koyré, *Études d'histoire de la pensée scientifique* (Paris: Gallimard, 1973), 39.

52 Heller, *Nowa fizyka i nowa teologia*, 43. Contemporary solutions to this problem are elaborated upon in great detail by Robert J. Russell; see his "Finite Creation without a Beginning. The Doctrine of Creation in Relation to Big Bang and Quantum Cosmologies," in *QC*, 292–93.
53 Michał Heller and Tadeusz Pabjan, *Stworzenie i początek wszechświata. Teologia – Filozofia – Kosmologia* (Cracow: Copernicus Center Press, 2013), 44–46; see also Ernan McMullin, "Introduction. Evolution and Creation," in *Evolution and Creation*, ed. Ernan McMullin (Notre Dame, IN: University of Notre Dame Press, 1985), 8–20.
54 For Aquinas this was an object of faith. Reason is unable to prove that the universe is eternal or not. By means of reason, however, we can prove that the world was created. Swinburne, *The Coherence of Theism*, 126–30.
55 Thomas Aquinas, *Summa Contra Gentiles*, 1.2.21, http://www.documentacatholicaomnia.eu/03d/1225-1274,_Thomas_Aquinas,_Summa_Contra_Gentiles,_EN.pdf (accessed February 8, 2020). See also Heller and Pabjan, *Stworzenie i początek wszechświata*, 79–81.
56 Thomas Aquinas, *On the Eternity of the World*, https://isidore.co/aquinas/DeEternitateMundi.htm (accessed February 8, 2020).
57 Aquinas, *On the Eternity*, https://isidore.co/aquinas/DeEternitateMundi.htm; see also Heller and Pabjan, *Stworzenie i początek wszechświata*, 82. When analyzing the Thomistic approach, one can claim that as far as the question of creation is concerned, the problem of time does not exist. God is atemporal and his act of creation does not mean initiating an event.
58 Augustine, *The Literal Meaning of Genesis*, Book 5, 20(40), in Augustine *On Genesis. A Refutation of the Manichees. Unfinished Literal Commentary on Genesis. The Literal Meaning of Genesis* (1/13), trans. Edmund Hill and John E. Rotelle (New Hyde, NY: New City Press, 2002), 297; see also ibid, Book 4, 12(22), p. 253.
59 Aquinas, *On the Eternity of the World*, https://isidore.co/aquinas/DeEternitateMundi.htm; see also Heller and Pabjan, *Stworzenie i początek wszechświata*, 84.
60 Łukasiewicz, *O założeniach filozoficznych*, 205–6. Assuming a Thomistic concept of divine action, it can be said that these distinctions are of an entirely formal character. Ultimately, all forms of divine action in the world are one simple act.
61 It could appear this way, especially when the concept of *creatio continua* was thought to refer to God "adding" something to the world every now and then. However, *creatio continua* signifies a continuous ontic dependence.
62 Russell, "Introduction," in *QC*, 5.
63 David J. Bartholomew, *Uncertain Belief. Is it Rational to be a Christian?* (Oxford: Clarendon Press, 1996), 79–99.
64 Russell, "Introduction," 6.
65 In this context, slightly different dating methods can be indicated. Pedersen, *The Two Books*, 277.
66 Peacocke, *Paths from Science Towards God*, 135.
67 See, e.g., Stoeger, "Describing God's Action," 248.
68 William R. Stoeger, "The Origin of the Universe in Science and Religion," in *Cosmos, Bios, Theos. Scientists Reflect on Science, God, and the Origins of the Universe, Life, and Homo Sapiens*, ed. Henry Margenau and Roy A. Varghese (La Salle, IL: Open Court, 1992), 254–69.
69 Stoeger, "Describing God's Action," 247.
70 Jürgen Moltmann, *The Trinity and the Kingdom of God* (London: SCM Press, 1981), 109–10. Some theists criticize the idea of "God withdrawing Himself" to make room for

the world. Even when it is assumed that what is meant is not the physical but the metaphysical sense, it is stressed that creation takes place through giving and multiplying rather than through God's specific "withdrawal" (Jacek Wojtysiak, "Panenteizm. W związku z poglądami Józefa Życińskiego, Charlesa Hartshorne'a i innych przedstawicieli 'zwrotu panenteistycznego'," *Roczniki Filozoficzne* 60, no. 4 [2012]: 323).

71 Elisabeth A. Johnson, *She Who Is. The Mystery of God in Feminist Theological Discourse* (New York: Crossroad, 1992), 234–35.
72 Denis Edwards, *The God of Evolution. A Trinitarian Theology* (Mahwah, NY: Paulist Press, 1999), 28–34.
73 Stanisław Judycki, *Bóg i inne osoby. Próba z zakresu teologii filozoficznej* (Poznań: W drodze, 2010), 94.
74 Swinburne, *The Coherence of Theism*, 127.
75 See ibid., 128–29.
76 I analyze this question in Marek Słomka, *Ewolucjonizm chrześcijański o pochodzeniu człowieka* (Lublin: Gaudium, 2004), 71–86; see also Swinburne, *The Coherence of Theism*, 130.
77 Mateusz Przanowski, "Wprowadzenie do kwestii VII. O prostocie Bożej istoty." In *Kwestie dyskutowane o mocy Boga*, vol. 4, *O prostocie Bożej istoty. O tym, co odwiecznie relacyjnie orzeka się o Bogu*, ed. Mateusz Przanowski and Jan Kiełbasa (Kęty–Warsaw: Wydawnictwo Marek Derewiecki; Instytut Tomistyczny, 2010), 5; see also: Vardy, *The Puzzle of God*, 37.
78 Origen, *Contra Celsum*, IV, 14; SC 136, 216; see also Przanowski, "Wprowadzenie do kwestii VII," 16.
79 Origen, *De principiis*, I, 1, 6; SC 252, 100.
80 Przanowski, "Wprowadzenie do kwestii VII," 17.
81 Martyna Koszkało and Marek Pepliński, "Prostota", in *Przewodnik po filozofii religii*, 89.
82 Christopher Hughes, *On a Complex Theory of a Simple God. An Investigation in Aquinas' Philosophical Theology* (London–Ithaca, NY: Cornell University Press, 1989), 60–62. See also Przanowski, "Wprowadzenie do kwestii VII," 18–19.
83 Eleonore Stump, "Simplicity," in *A Companion to Philosophy of Religion* (2nd ed.), ed. Charles Taliaferro, Paul Draper, and Philip L. Quinn (Oxford–Malden, MA: Wiley-Blackwell, 2010), 273.
84 Scott MacDonald, "The Divine Nature," in *The Cambridge Companion to Augustine*, ed. Eleonore Stump and Norman Kretzmann (Cambridge: Cambridge University Press, 2001), 84–86.
85 Przanowski, "Wprowadzenie do kwestii VII," 20.
86 Ibid., 21; see also James E. Dolezal, *God without Parts. Divine Simplicity and the Metaphysics of God's Absoluteness* (Eugene, OR: Pickwick Publications, 2011), 4–5.
87 Richard La Croix, "Augustine on the Simplicity of God," *The New Scholasticism* 51, no. 4 (1977): 453–68. See also Przanowski, "Wprowadzenie do kwestii VII," 22.
88 Katherin Rogers, *Anselm on Freedom* (Oxford: Oxford University Press, 2008), 108; see also Przanowski, "Wprowadzenie do kwestii VII," 26; Steven J. Duby, *Divine Simplicity. A Dogmatic Account* (London–New York: Bloomsbury; T. & T. Clark, 2016), 9–10.
89 Dolezal, *God without Parts*, 6; see also Przanowski, "Wprowadzenie do kwestii VII," 27; Stump, "Simplicity," 273.
90 Przanowski, "Wprowadzenie do kwestii VII," 30.
91 Eleonore Stump, "God's Simplicity," in *The Oxford Handbook of Aquinas*, ed. Brian Davies and Eleonore Stump (Oxford–New York: Oxford University Press, 2012), 135–46.

92 Przanowski, "Wprowadzenie do kwestii VII," 24.
93 Koszkało and Pepliński, "Prostota", 88–89.
94 Przanowski, "Wprowadzenie do kwestii VII," 25.
95 Ibid., 8; see also Stanisław Kowalczyk, "Próba opisu jedności transcendentalnej," *Roczniki Filozoficzne* 10, no. 1 (1962): 124; Zofia J. Zdybicka, *Partycypacja bytu. Próba wyjaśnienia relacji między światem a Bogiem* (Lublin: Polskie Towarzystwo Tomasza z Akwinu, 2017), 190–202.
96 Przanowski, "Wprowadzenie do kwestii VII," 10; see also Stefan Swieżawski, *Byt. Zagadnienia metafizyki tomistycznej* (Cracow: Znak, 1999), 148.
97 James A. Weisheipl, *Friar Thomas d'Aquino. His Life, Thought, and Work* (Garden City, NY: Doubleday, 1974), 195–215; Jean-Pierre Torrell, *Initiation à saint Thomas d'Aquin. Sa personne et son oeuvre* (Fribourg: Cerf, 2002), 236–37; Przanowski, "Wprowadzenie do kwestii VII," 14.
98 Vardy, *The Puzzle of God*, 38.
99 Judycki, *Bóg i inne osoby*, 196.
100 Stanisław Kowalczyk, *Filozofia Boga* (Lublin: Wydawnictwo KUL, 2001), 323–24; see also Koszkało and Pepliński, "Prostota," 91–92; Peter J. Weigel, *Aquinas on Simplicity. An Investigation into the Foundations of his Philosophical Theology* (Oxford: Peter Lang, 2008), 23–90.
101 Kowalczyk, *Filozofia Boga*, 325; see also Duby, *Divine Simplicity*, 11–17.
102 Przanowski, "Wprowadzenie do kwestii VII," 213–15.
103 Gerard J. Hughes, *The Nature of God. An Introduction to the Philosophy of Religion* (London–New York: Routledge, 1995), 53–54; see also Przanowski, "Wprowadzenie do kwestii VII," 53.
104 Koszkało and Pepliński, "Prostota," 93–94.
105 Przanowski, "Wprowadzenie do kwestii VII," 51–52; see also Thomas G. Weinandy, *Does God Suffer?* (Edinburgh: T&T Clark, 2000), 2–6; Dariusz Oko, "Doskonale obojętny? Zarys współczesnej krytyki Tomaszowego pojmowania niezmienności Boga," *Analecta Cracoviensia* 37 (2005): 61–71.
106 Koszkało and Pepliński, "Prostota," 94.
107 Ibid., 95.
108 Ibid.
109 Piotr Gutowski, *Filozofia procesu i jej metafilozofia. Studium metafizyki Ch. Hartshorne'a* (Lublin: RW KUL, 1995), 96.
110 Alvin C. Plantinga, *Does God Have a Nature?* (Milwaukee, WI: Marquette University Press, 1980).
111 Eleonore Stump and Norman Kretzmann, "Absolute Simplicity," *Faith and Philosophy* 2, no. 4 (1985): 353–91.
112 Plantinga, *Does God Have a Nature?* 46–47; see also Przanowski, "Wprowadzenie do kwestii VII," 54–55; Brian Davies, "Classical Theism and the Doctrine of Divine Simplicity," in *Language, Meaning and God. Essays in Honour of Herbert McCabe*, ed. Brian Davies (London: Geoffrey Chapman, 1987), 53.
113 Brian Leftow, "Is God an Abstract Object?" *Noûs* 24, no. 4 (1990): 593; see also Brian Leftow, "Divine Simplicity," *Faith and Philosophy* 23, no. 4 (2006): 365–80; Przanowski, "Wprowadzenie do kwestii VII," 55.
114 Eleonore Stump, *Aquinas* (London–New York: Routledge, 2005), 99–100.
115 Przanowski, "Wprowadzenie do kwestii VII," 56; see also: Barry D. Smith, *The Oneness and Simplicity of God* (Eugene, OR: Pickwick Publications, 2014), 92–93.
116 Davies, *Classical Theism and the Doctrine of Divine Simplicity*, 59.

117 Katherin Rogers, "The Traditional Doctrine of Divine Simplicity," *Religious Studies* 32, no. 2 (1996): 171. See also Przanowski, "Wprowadzenie do kwestii VII," 57; Jeffrey Brower, "Making Sense of Divine Simplicity," *Faith and Philosophy* 25 (2008): 3–30.
118 M. Piwowarczyk claims that this question cannot be reasonably posed because we do not know how God's simple freedom is realized. See Marek Piwowarczyk, "Prostota Boga," in *Filozofia Boga*, vol. 2, *Odkrywanie Boga*, ed. Stanisław Janeczek and Anna Starościc (Lublin: Wydawnictwo KUL, 2017), 392.
119 Jay W. Richards, *The Untamed God. A Philosophical Exploration of Divine Perfection, Simplicity, and Immutability* (Downers Grove, IL: InterVarsity Press, 2003), 168–71.
120 Stump, "Simplicity," 250–56; see also Stanisław Judycki, "Wszechmoc i istnienie," *Diametros* 21 (2009): 52.
121 Stump, *Aquinas*, 96–97; see also: Koszkało and Pepliński, "Prostota," 96.
122 Hughes, *The Nature of God*, 39.
123 Przanowski, "Wprowadzenie do kwestii VII," 60–61 and "Dodatek II."
124 Koszkało and Pepliński, "Prostota," 98.
125 Ibid., 99; see also Timothy O'Connor, "Simplicity and Creation," *Faith and Philosophy* 16 (1999): 405–12; Alexander R. Pruss, "On Two Problems of Divine Simplicity," *Oxford Studies in Philosophy of Religion* 1 (2008): 150–67.
126 Stanisław Judycki, "Personalistyczny teizm i pojęcie osoby," in *Teologia filozoficzna. Wokół książki Stanisława Judyckiego "Bóg i inne osoby"*, ed. Janusz Pyda (Poznań-Cracow: W drodze, 2013), 278.
127 Van Inwagen, *The Problem of Evil*, 20. See also Judycki, "Personalistyczny teizm," 277.
128 Judycki, "Personalistyczny teizm," 279.
129 Wojtysiak, "Osobowość," 178.
130 Anselm, *Proslogium*, chapter V, https://sourcebooks.fordham.edu/basis/anselm-proslogium.asp#CHAPTER%20V (accessed February 9, 2020).
131 Rene Descartes, *Meditations on First Philosophy* (Meditation 3 & 5). See also Wojtysiak, "Osobowość," 178.
132 Alvin C. Plantinga, *God, Freedom, and Evil* (Grand Rapids, MI: Eerdmans, 2002), 111.
133 Wojtysiak, "Osobowość," 179–80.
134 William Craig, *The Kalam Cosmological Argument* (Eugene, OR: Pickwick Publications, 2016).
135 Antoni B. Stępień, *Wstęp do filozofii*, 5th ed. (Lublin: TN KUL, 2007), 207; see also: Wojtysiak, "Osobowość," 181.
136 Swinburne, *The Existence of God*, chapters 2–3, 5–8, and 14. In the scientific explanation of events, one points to preceding events or states of things, as well as the laws of nature, particularly as a set of such laws or certain generalizations. This type of explanation is used in an everyday context (e.g., the phenomenon of boiling water is explained by describing the conditions in which this process takes place and refers to a generalization according to which heated water boils in suitable conditions). In the light of this explanatory method, specific reasons (laws of nature) guarantee an effect (its occurrence). In the personal kind of explanation (irreducible to the scientific one) a given event is explained as caused by a person who has an intention to cause this event. It is the intention and abilities of this person that result in the occurrence of an effect. Speaking of God's actions, theists usually refer to the personal type of explanation.
137 Wojtysiak, "Osobowość," 182–84.

138 Gottfried W. Leibniz, *Theodicy. Essays on the Goodness of God, the Freedom of Man and the Origin of Evil*, trans. Eveleen M. Huggard (La Salle, IL: Open Court, 1996), 127–28.
139 Johann Dorschner, "Kosmologie und Schöpfungsglaube zwischen Konfrontation und Konsonanz," in *Der Kosmos als Schöpfung. Zum Stand des Gesprächs zwischen Naturwissenschaft und Theologie*, ed. Johann Dorschner (Regensburg: Verlag Friedrich Pustet, 1998), 96–100.
140 Kenneth T. Gallagher, "Remarks on the Argument from Design," *Review of Metaphysics* 48, no. 1 (1994): 1, 30.
141 Słomka, *Ewolucjonizm chrześcijański*, 153; see also Judycki, "Personalistyczny teizm," 280; John Leslie, *Universes* (New York: Routledge, 1989), 165–74.
142 Judycki, *Bóg i inne osoby*, 47–55.
143 Judycki, "Personalistyczny teizm," 281.
144 See, e.g., George F. Ellis, "The Theology of the Anthropic Principle," in *QC*, 378–79; Peacocke, *Paths from Science Towards God*, 114–15.
145 Peacocke, *Paths from Science Towards God*, 43.
146 John R. Lucas, "The Temporality of God," in *QC*, 235, 243.
147 Keith Ward, "God as a Principle of Cosmological Explanation," in *QC*, 248–49; Ted Peters, "The Trinity in and Beyond Time," in *QC*, 284.
148 Ward, "God as a Principle," 250.
149 Peters, "The Trinity," 285.
150 Boethius, *Consolation of Philosophy*, Book V, 6, https://web.archive.org/web/20070526065426/http://etext.library.adelaide.edu.au/b/boethius/consolation/book5.html (accessed February 9, 2020).
151 Łukasiewicz, *Opatrzność Boża, wolność, przypadek*, 17.
152 Thomas D. Senor, "The Real Presence of an Eternal God," in *Metaphysics and God. Essays in Honor of Eleonore Stump*, ed. Kevin Timpe (London–New York: Routledge, 2008), 39–60.
153 Mordarski, "Wszechwiedza a wieczność," *Filo-Sofija* 19, no. 4 (2012): 102.
154 Ibid., 103.
155 Peacocke, *Paths from Science Towards God*, 46.
156 Ibid., 114.
157 There are many heterogeneous opinions on the scope and nature of such influence; e.g., Michael J. Dodds, *The One Creator God in Thomas Aquinas and Contemporary Theology* (Washington, DC: The Catholic University of America Press, 2020), 14-5; Paul L. Gavrilyuk, *The Suffering of the Impassible God. The Dialectics of Patristic Thought* (New York: Oxford University Press, 2004); R. Hübner, *Der Gott der Kirchenväter und der Gott der Bibel. Zur Frage der Hellenisierung des Christentums* (München: Minerva Publikation, 1979).
158 Weinandy, *Does God Suffer?* ,19.
159 Richard E. Creel, "Immutability and Impassibility," in *A Companion to Philosophy of Religion*, 2nd ed., 322–28. See also Donald A. Carson, *The Difficult Doctrine of the Love of God* (Leicester: Inter-Varsity Press, 2000), 55.
160 Weinandy, *Does God Suffer?*, 19.
161 Bauckham, "'Only the Suffering God Can Help'. Divine Passibility in Modern Theology," *Themelios* 9 (1984): 7–8; Kevin J. Vanhoozer, *Remythologizing Theology. Divine Action, Passion, and Authorship* (Cambridge: Cambridge University Press, 2010), 387–415.
162 Wolfhart Pannenberg, *Basic Questions in Theology*, trans. George H. Kehm (London: SCM Press, 1971), 1:162. See also Weinandy, *Does God Suffer?* 20–21; Jung Y. Lee, *God*

Suffers for Us. A Systematic Inquiry into a Concept of Divine Passibility (Den Haag: Nijhoff, 1974), 40.
163 Weinandy, *Does God Suffer?* 2–3. See also Hans Jonas, "The Concept of God after Auschwitz. A Jewish Voice," *The Journal of Religion* 67, no. 1 (1987): 1–13.
164 Weinandy, *Does God Suffer?* 24. He himself argues in support of impassibility, invoking both the philosophical concept of the immutable *Actus Purus* as well as the theological truth of the Holy Trinity's complete love.
165 Stanisław Judycki, "Wszechmoc i istnienie," *Diametros* 21 (2009): 35.
166 When discussing the concept of omnipotence as formulated by Pietro Damiani, scholars stress considerable divergence in interpretations concerning his statements. Ryszard Kleszcz, "Logika, Wszechmoc, Bóg," *Filo-Sofija* 19, no. 4 (2012): 39–40.
167 Judycki, *Bóg i inne osoby*, 187.
168 Ryszard Kleszcz, "O filozofii religii, wszechmocy Boga oraz ograniczoności naszego języka," *Filo-Sofija* 30, no. 3 (2015): 204–6.
169 Judycki, "Wszechmoc i istnienie," 36.
170 In the strict sense, the principle of non-contradiction does not limit God's omnipotence. Aquinas claims that "it is better to say that such things cannot be done, than that God cannot do them". *Summa Theologiae* (*The Government of Creatures*, 1.25.3), https://www.newadvent.org/summa/1025.htm (accessed February 10, 2020).
171 Vardy, *The Puzzle of God*, 112–20; see also Judycki, "Wszechmoc i istnienie," 37.
172 Aquinas, *Summa contra gentiles*, 1.2.25. See also Kleszcz, "Logika, Wszechmoc, Bóg," 41–42; Leo J. Elders, *The Philosophical Theology of St. Thomas Aquinas* (Leiden: Brill, 1990), 268–74.
173 Aquinas, *Summa contra gentiles*, 1.1.95.
174 "To sin is to fall short of a perfect action; hence to be able to sin is to be able to fall short in action, which is repugnant to omnipotence. Therefore it is that God cannot sin, because of His omnipotence". Aquinas, *Summa Theologiae* (*The Government of Creatures*, 1.25.3), https://www.newadvent.org/summa/1025.htm.
175 Kleszcz, *O filozofii religii,* 209.
176 William J. Courtenay, *Capacity and Volition. A History of the Distinction of Absolute and Ordained Power* (Bergamo: Pierluigi Lubriana Editore, 1990), 101–2; see also Judycki, "Wszechmoc i istnienie," 37.
177 Martyna Koszkało, "Wszechmoc, wola Boża i struktura świata. Stanowisko Jana Dunsa Szkota," *Filo-Sofija* 30, no. 3 (2015): 85.
178 Ibid., 86.
179 Koszkało and Pepliński, "Wszechmoc," in *Przewodnik po filozofii religii*, 43.
180 Koszkało, "Wszechmoc, wola Boża," 86.
181 Ibid., 87.
182 Marek Pepliński, "Problematyka wszechmocy Boga – rzeczy nowe i stare," *Filo-Sofija* 30, no. 3 (2015): 23.
183 Koszkało, "Wszechmoc, wola Boża," 89.
184 Ibid., 92.
185 Henri Veldhuis, "Ordained and Absolute Power in Scotus' Ordinatio I 44," *Vivarium* 38, no. 2 (2000): 229.
186 Koszkało, "Wszechmoc, wola Boża," 93.
187 Vardy, *The Puzzle of God*, 110–11.
188 Kleszcz, "Logika, Wszechmoc, Bóg," 40–41.
189 Judycki, "Wszechmoc i istnienie," 39.

190 Leibniz, *Theodicy. Essays on the Goodness of God, the Freedom of Man and the Origin of Evil*, trans. Eveleen M. Huggard (La Salle, IL: Open Court, 1996), 377.
191 Marcin Trepczyński, "Sens pytania o Bożą wszechmoc," *Filo-Sofija* 30, no. 3 (2015): 248.
192 David Hume, *Dialogues Concerning Natural Religion* (London: Robinson, 1779), 186.
193 Trepczyński, "Sens pytania," 249.
194 Hume, *Dialogues*, 194.
195 Trepczyński, "Sens pytania," 250.
196 Charles Hartshorne, *Omnipotence and Other Theological Mistakes* (Albany, NY: State University of New York Press, 1984), 18.
197 John L. Mackie, *The Miracle of Theism. Arguments for and Against the Existence of God* (Oxford: Oxford University Press, 1982), 160–62; John L. Mackie, "Evil and Omnipotence," *Mind* 64 (1955): 200–212. See also Judycki, "Wszechmoc i istnienie," 40; William E. Mann, "Paradoxes of Omnipotence," in *Cambridge Dictionary of Philosophy*, ed. Robert Audi (Cambridge: Cambridge University Press, 1998), 559; Joshua Hoffman and Gary Rosenkrantz, "Omnipotence," in *The Routledge Companion to Philosophy of Religion*, ed. Chad V. Meister and Paul Copan (London–New York: Routledge, 2010): 271–80. Brian Leftow, "Omnipotence," in *The Oxford Handbook of Philosophical Theology*, ed. Thomas P. Flint and Michael C. Rea (Oxford–New York: Oxford University Press, 2009), 167–98; Moti Mizrahi, "New Puzzles about Divine Attributes," *European Journal for Philosophy of Religion* 5, no. 2 (2013): 147–57.
198 Pike, "Omnipotence," 208–16; Marek Pepliński, "Czy Bóg jest w mocy działać moralnie źle? *Filo-Sofija* 30, no. 3 (2015): 261–84.
199 Ryszard Kleszcz, "O filozofii religii, wszechmocy Boga oraz ograniczoności naszego języka," *Filo-Sofija* 30, no. 3 (2015): 206.
200 Swinburne, *The Coherence of Theism*, 144; see also Kleszcz, "O filozofii religii," 207.
201 Peter T. Geach, "Omnipotence," *Philosophy* 43 (1973): 7–20, and his "Omnipotence," in *Providence and Evil* by Peter T. Geach (Cambridge: Cambridge University Press, 1977), 3–28. See also Judycki, „Bóg i inne osoby," 186; Kleszcz, "O filozofii religii," 210.
202 Gijsbert van den Brink, *Almighty God. A Study of the Doctrine of Divine Omnipotence* (Kampen: Kok Pharos Publishing House, 1993), 184–203; see also Judycki, "Wszechmoc i istnienie," 43.
203 Swinburne, *The Coherence of Theism* (Oxford: Oxford University Press, 2016), 150–51.
204 Kleszcz, "Logika, Wszechmoc, Bóg," 43.
205 Łukowski, *Paradoksy*, Łódź: Wydawnictwo Uniwersytetu Łódzkiego 2006, 138–139.
206 Kleszcz, *Logika, Wszechmoc, Bóg*, 44.
207 Swinburne, *The Coherence of Theism*, 152–53.
208 Kleszcz, "Logika, Wszechmoc, Bóg," 44.
209 Edward R. Wierenga, "Divine Attributes," in *The Cambridge Dictionary of Philosophy*, ed. Robert Audi (Cambridge: Cambridge University Press, 1995), 207.
210 Kleszcz, "Logika, Wszechmoc, Bóg," 45–46. The question of the paradox of the stone was elaborated on in many insightful studies, e.g., George I. Mavrodes, "Some Puzzles Concerning Omnipotence," *The Philosophical Review* 72, no. 2 (1963): 221–23; C. Wade Savage, "The Paradox of the Stone," *Philosophical Review* 76, no. (1967): 74–79; David E. Schrader, "A Solution to the Stone Paradox," *Synthese* 42, no. 2 (1979): 255–64; M. P. Smith, "The New Paradox of the Stone," *Faith and Philosophy* 5, no. 3 (1988): 283–90; Erik J. Wielenberg, "The New Paradox of the Stone Revisited," *Faith and Philosophy* 18, no. 2 (2001): 261–68; Ryszard Mordarski, "Paradoksy

omnipotencji," *Filo-Sofija* 30, no. 3 (2015): 221–37 (the whole issue is devoted to the problem of omnipotence, also from the historical perspective).
211 Swinburne, *The Coherence of Theism*, 168–74; see also Kleszcz, "O filozofii religii," 211.
212 Judycki, *Bóg i inne osoby*, 189–90.
213 Judycki, "Wszechmoc i istnienie," 44–45.
214 Kleszcz, "O filozofii religii," 208–10.
215 Judycki, *Bóg i inne osoby*, 191–92.
216 Vardy, *The Puzzle of God*, 120.
217 Phil. 2:7, NIV.
218 Phil. 2:8, NIV.
219 Edwards, *The God of Evolution*, 36–45.
220 Edward Schillebeeckx, *Church. The Human Story of God*, trans. John Bowden (New York: Crossroad, 1990), 90.
221 John Haught, "Darwin's Gift to Theology," in *EMB*, 400.
222 Sallie McFague, *Models of God. Theology for a Nuclear Age* (Philadelphia, PA: Fortress Press, 1987), 16. See also Karl K. Rahner, *Grundkurs des Glaubens. Einführung in den Begriff des Christentums* (Freiburg im Breisgau: Herder Verlag, 2008), 73–76.
223 John Macquarrie, *The Humility of God* (Philadelphia, PA: The Westminster Press, 1978), 34.
224 Haught, "Darwin's Gift to Theology," 401.
225 Peacocke, *Paths from Science Towards God*, 58–59.
226 Vardy, *The Puzzle of God*, 121–22. See also Dariusz Łukasiewicz, "Wszechmoc Boga a teologia przypadku," *Filo-Sofija* 30, no. 3 (2015): 169.
227 Vardy, *The Puzzle of God*, 124.
228 Hughes, *The Nature of God*, 54–60.
229 Vardy, *The Puzzle of God*, 125.
230 Piotr Kaszkowiak, "Teizm otwarty. Poszukiwanie drogi środka w filozofii religii," *Diametros* 18 (2008): 22.
231 Vardy, *The Puzzle of God*, 126.
232 Hasker, *God, Time and Knowledge* (London–Ithaca, NY: Cornell University Press, 1989), 73. See also Dariusz Łukasiewicz, "O wiedzy Boga i wolności człowieka," *Filozofuj* 6 (2015): 15.
233 John Polkinghorne, "The Laws of Nature and the Laws of Physics," 439; see also Christopher J. Isham and John C. Polkinghorne, "The Debate over the Block Universe," in *QC*, 144.
234 Vardy, *The Puzzle of God*, 127.
235 Geach, *Providence and Evil*, 58.
236 Vardy, *The Puzzle of God*, 128; see also Ward, "God as a Principle," in *QC*, 254.
237 Ellis, "The Theology of the Anthropic Principle," 388.
238 Vardy, *The Puzzle of God*, 130.
239 Paul C. Davies, *God and the New Physics* (New York: Simon & Schuster, 1984), 133.
240 Evan Fales, *Divine Intervention. Metaphysical and Epistemological Puzzles* (New York–London: Routledge, 2010), 43–56 and 70–88. See also Alan Pagdett, *God, Time, and the Nature of Time* (Eugene, OR: Pickwick Publications, 2000); William L. Craig, *Time and Eternity. Exploring God's Relationship to Time* (Wheaton, IL: Crossway Books, 2001).
241 Davies, *God and the New Physics*, 134.

242 Mordarski, "Wszechwiedza a wieczność," 104–5. See also Paul C. Davies, *About Time. Einstein's Unfinished Revolution* (New York–London–Toronto–Sydney: Simon & Schuster, 1995).
243 Mordarski, "Wszechwiedza a wieczność," 106.
244 Peacocke, *Paths from Science Towards God*, 58.
245 James Bradley, "Randomness and God's Nature," *Perspectives on Science and Christian Faith* 64, no. 2 (2012): 75–89.
246 Peacocke, *Paths from Science Towards God*, 59.
247 Griffin, *Reenchantment without Supernaturalism*, 2.
248 Charles Hartshorne, *The Divine Relativity. A Social Conception of God* (New Haven, CT: Yale University Press–London: Cumberlege, 1948), 121.
249 Rafał S. Niziński, *Między teizmem a panteizmem. Charlesa Hartshorne'a procesualna filozofia Boga* (Lublin: KUL, 2002), 152–53.
250 Santiago Sia, *God in Process Thought. A Study in Charles Hartshorne's Concept of God* (Dordrecht–Lancaster–Boston, MA: Martinus Nijhoff, 1985), 59–61.
251 Charles Hartshorne, Introduction to *Philosophers of Process*, ed. Douglas Browning (New York: Random House, 1965), viii–x.
252 Donald W. Viney, *Charles Hartshorne and The Existence of God* (Albany, NY: State University of New York Press, 1985), 29–30; John C. Moskop, *Divine Omniscience and Human Freedom. Thomas Aquinas and Charles Hartshorne* (Macon, GA: Mercer University Press, 1984), 74–75.
253 Timothy L. Sprigge, "Hartshorne's Conception of the Past," in *The Philosophy of Charles Hartshorne*, ed. Lewis E. Hahn (La Salle, IL: Open Court, 1991), 409; Rafał S. Niziński, *Między teizmem a panteizmem*, 154–55.
254 Charles Hartshorne, *Omnipotence and Other Theological Mistakes* (Albany, NY: State University of New York Press, 1985): 26–27; Piotr Gutowski, *Filozofia procesu i jej metafilozofia. Studium metafizyki Ch. Hartshorne'a* (Lublin: KUL, 1995), 103.
255 Niziński, *Między teizmem a panteizmem*, 156. See also Richard E. Creel, *Divine Impassibility. An Essay in Philosophical Theology* (Cambridge: Cambridge University Press, 1986), 35–42.
256 Hartshorne, *The Divine Relativity*, 121. See also Charles Hartshorne, *Creative Synthesis and Philosophic Method* (Lanham, MD: University Press of America, 1983), 122–27; Niziński, *Między teizmem a panteizmem*, 157; Józef Życiński, *Teizm i filozofia analityczna* (Cracow: Znak, 1988), 2:172–173.
257 Gutowski, *Filozofia procesu i jej metafilozofia*, 104. Processualists also presented an unclassical theory concerning God's knowledge of past events. Detailed analysis of this theory goes beyond the scope of my study. One can read more in Donald W. Viney, "God Only Knows? Hartshorne and the Mechanics of Omniscience," in *Hartshorne, Process Philosophy and Theology*, ed. Robert Kane and Stephen H. Phillips (Albany, NY: State University of New York Press, 1989), 71–90.
258 Mordarski, "Wszechwiedza a wieczność," 106–7. See also Stump, *Aquinas*, 131–58, and the articles she coauthored with N. Kretzmann: "Eternity," *Journal of Philosophy* 78 (1981): 429–58; "Eternity, Awareness, and Action," *Faith and Philosophy* 9 (1992): 463–82; "Eternity and God's Knowledge. A Reply to Shanley," *The American Catholic Philosophical Quarterly* 72 (1998): 439–45.
259 Mordarski, "Wszechwiedza a wieczność," 109–10.
260 Ibid., 111.
261 William Hasker, *God, Time, and Knowledge* (Ithaca, NY: Cornell University Press, 1989), 158–70. See also Mordarski, "Wszechwiedza a wieczność," 111.

262 Stump and Kretzmann, *Eternity*, 456-57. See also Mordarski, "Wszechwiedza a wieczność," 111.
263 Mordarski, "Wszechwiedza a wieczność," 113.
264 Ibid., 114.
265 Peter Simons, "Questions of freedom" (foreword) in *Free Will and Modern Science*, ed. Richard Swinburne (Oxford–New York: Oxford University, Press 2011), vii–xv.
266 Stanisław Judycki, "Kuszenie i wolna wola," in *Teologia filozoficzna*, 319.
267 Przemysław Gut and Arkadiusz Gut, "Kompatybilizm a problem wolności człowieka," in *Veritas in caritate. Księga pamiątkowa ku czci Księdza Profesora Andrzeja Szostka MIC*, ed. Marcin Tkaczyk, Marzena Krupa, and Krzysztof Jaworski (Lublin: Wydawnictwo KUL, 2016), 165-74.
268 Judycki, "Kuszenie i wolna wola," 320. See also Roderick M. Chisholm, *Human Freedom and the Self. The Lindley Lecture* (Lawrence, KS: University of Kansas Press, 1964).
269 Łukasiewicz, *Opatrzność Boża, wolność, przypadek*, 179-87.
270 Judycki, "Kuszenie i wolna wola," 321.
271 Hasker, *God, Time, and Knowledge*, 73. See also Adam Świeżyński, "Miejsce koncepcji ograniczonej wiedzy Boga w strukturze 'teizmu otwartego,'" *Filo-Sofija* 19, no. 4 (2012): 131-42.
272 Judycki, "Kuszenie i wolna wola," 322.
273 Łukasiewicz, "O wiedzy Boga," 15. See also Ted A. Warfield, "Ockhamism and Molinism. Foreknowledge and Prophecy," in *Oxford Studies in Philosophy of Religion*, ed. Jonathan L. Kvanvig (Oxford: Oxford University Press, 2009), 2:317-32.
274 Broadening the Molinist idea of "would-counterfactuals," open theism also introduces the concept of "might-counterfactuals." Gregory A. Boyd, "An Open-Theism Response." In *Divine Foreknowledge. Four Views*, ed. James K. Beilby and Paul R. Eddy (Downers Grove, IL: Inter Varsity Press, 2001), 147.
275 Łukasiewicz, "Wszechwiedza Boża a problem zła z perspektywy teizmu otwartego," *Filo*-Sofija 19, no. 4 (2012): 119-20.
276 See ibid., 123.
277 William L. Rowe, "Evil and the Theistic Hypothesis. A Response to Wykstra," in *The Problem of Evil*, ed. Marylin McCord Adams and Robert M. Adams (Oxford: Oxford University Press, 1990), 161-67.
278 William Hasker, *Providence, Evil and the Openness of God* (London–New York: Routledge, 2004), 58-79.
279 Łukasiewicz, "Wszechwiedza Boża," 127.
280 Gregory A. Boyd, "Two Ancient (and Modern) Motivations for Ascribing Exhaustively Definite Foreknowledge to God. A Historic Overview and Critical Assessment," *RelS* 46, no. 1 (2010): 41-59.
281 William Hasker, "Why Simple Foreknowledge Is Still Useless (In Spite of David Hunt and Alex Pruss)," *JETS* 52, no. 3 (2009): 537-44.
282 Łukasiewicz, "Wszechwiedza Boża," 69.
283 Peter Helm, "The Augustinian-Calvinist View," *Divine Foreknowledge*, 181; see also his *The Providence of Go*d (Leicester, IL: InterVarsity Press, 1993).
284 Łukasiewicz, "Wszechwiedza Boża," 70. See also *Calvinism and the Problem of Evil*, ed. David E. Alexander and Daniel M. Johnson (Eugene, OR: Pickwick Publications, 2016).
285 Łukasiewicz, "Wszechwiedza," 70.
286 Marcin Tkaczyk, *Futura contingentia* (Lublin: KUL, 2015), 215-17.

287 William L. Craig and David P. Hunt, "Perils of the Open Road," *Faith and Philosophy* 30, no. 1 (2013): 49–71; Linda Zagzebski, "Recent Work on Divine Foreknowledge and Free Will," in *The Oxford Handbook of Free Will*, ed. Robert Kane (Oxford: Oxford University Press, 2002), 45–64; Peter van Inwagen, "What Does an Omniscient Being Know about the Future?" in *Oxford Studies in Philosophy of Religion*, ed. Jonathan L. Kvanvig (Oxford: Oxford University Press, 2008), 1:216–30; John M. Fischer and Patric Todd, eds., *Freedom, Fatalism, and Foreknowledge* (Oxford: Oxford University Press, 2012).
288 Łukasiewicz, "Wszechwiedza," 71.

3 On the World

1 Łukasiewicz, *O założeniach filozoficznych*, 207.
2 Robin Collins, "Divine Action and Evolution," in *The Oxford Handbook of Philosophical Theology*, ed. Thomas P. Flint and Michael C. Rea (Oxford: Oxford University Press, 2011), 241–61.
3 Łukasiewicz, *O założeniach filozoficznych*, 208.
4 In the context of God's relationship with man, it would be more appropriate to use pedagogical rather than physical or biological models, and to refer to the categories of encouragement or inspiration rather than pressure. In this way, theists develop a concept of the Creator's "soft" influence on His creation, e.g., by means of forming certain ideals or defining goals, just as parents do in relation to their children. The educational ideal seems to be a combination of effectiveness with which a given system of values is fostered in pupils and a gradual extension of their freedom.
5 Karl Rahner, *Natural Science and Reasonable Faith*, vol. 21 of *Theological Investigations* by Karl Rahner, trans. Hugh M. Riley (New York: Crossroad, 1988), 37; see also Denis Edwards, *How God Acts. Creation, Redemption, and Special Divine Action* (Minneapolis, MN: Fortress Press, 2010), 43.
6 Karl Rahner, *Christology in the Setting of Modern Man's Understanding of Himself and His World*, vol. 11 of *Theological Investigations* by Karl Rahner, trans. David Bourke (New York: Seabury, 1974), 223–26; see also Edwards, *How God Acts*, 44–45.
7 Karl Rahner, *Grundkurs des Glaubens*, 77–81; see also Edwards, *How God Acts*, 47–48.
8 Herbert McCabe, *God Matters* (London: Mowbray, 1987), 11–13.
9 Edwards, *How God Acts*, 49; see also Herbert McCabe, *God Still Matters* (London: Continuum 2002, 11–12).
10 The notion of *autopoiesis* initially appeared in reflection on the self-organization of biotic systems; see, e.g., Pablo Razeto-Barr, "Autopoiesis 40 years Later," *Origins of Life and Evolution of Biospheres* 42, no. 6 (2012): 543–67
11 Elisabeth A. Johnson, "Does God Play Dice? Divine Providence and Chance," *Theological Studies* 57 (1996): 17.
12 Irenaeus of Lyons, *Contra Haereses*, bk. 3, chap. 34, sec. 7.
13 Edwards, *How God Acts*, 51–52.
14 See, e.g., Walter Thirring, *Kosmische Impressionen. Gottes Spuren in den Naturgesetzen* (Vienna: Molden, 2004).
15 Nicholas Saunders, *Divine Action and Modern Science* (Cambridge: Cambridge University Press, 2002), 60–71.

16 Józef Życiński, "The Rationality Field and the Laws of Nature," in *Wyzwania racjonalności. Księdzu Michałowi Hellerowi współpracownicy i uczniowie*, ed. Stanisław Wszołek and Robert Janusz (Cracow: WAM, 2006), 88.
17 Simon C. Morris, *Life's Solution. Inevitable Humans in a Lonely Universe* (Cambridge: Cambridge University Press, 2003), 33.
18 Życiński, "The Rationality Field," 89.
19 Życiński, "The Rationality Field," 90.
20 William R. Stoeger, "The Immanent Directionality of the Evolutionary Process, and Its Relationship to Teleology," in *EMB*, 163–90.
21 Życiński, "The Rationality Field," 94; see also Michael A. Arbib, "Towards a Neuroscience of the Person," in *NAP*, 100.
22 Paul C. W. Davies, "Physics and the Mind of God. The Templeton Prize Address," https://www.firstthings.com/article/1995/08/003-physics-and-the-mind-of-god-the-templeton-prize-address-24 (accessed February 10, 2020).
23 A classic example of this being the model of the origin of the universe as the result of a quantum fluctuation of the vacuum: Edward Tryon, "Is the universe a vacuum fluctuation?" *Nature* 246 (1973): 396–97.
24 Davies, "Physics and the Mind."
25 Ibid.
26 Davies, *Cosmic Jackpot. Why Our Universe is Just Right for Life* (New York: Orion Productions, 2007).
27 Davies, "Physics and the Mind."
28 To become familiar with the intellectual output of Freeman Dyson, it is worth reading chapter 16 of the book *The Faith of Scientists. In Their Own Words*, ed. Nancy K. Frankenberry (Oxford–Princeton, NJ: Princeton University Press, 2008).
29 Davies, "Physics and the Mind."
30 Melanie Mitchell, Peter T. Hraber, and James P. Crutchfield, "Revisiting the Edge of Chaos. Evolving Cellular Automata to Perform Computations," *Complex Systems* 7 (1993): 89–130; Roger Lewin, *Complexity. Life at the Edge of Chaos* (Chicago: University of Chicago Press 1999); *Complex Systems. Science on the Edge of Chaos*, ed. Heikki Hyötyniemi (Espoo: Helsinki University of Technology, 2004).
31 Davies, "Physics and the Mind."
32 Some experts in the problem of chaos and complexity disagree with this conclusion. However, this position is often formulated by many biologists, including those who are critical of theism. Ferguson, *Fire in the Equations*, 161–63.
33 Paul C. W. Davies, *The Mind of God. The Scientific Basis for a Rational World* (New York: Simon & Schuster Paperbacks, 2005), 231–32.
34 Davies, "Physics and the Mind."
35 Thomas Tracy, "Evolution, Divine Action, and the Problem of Evil," in *EMB*, 517.
36 Życiński, "The Rationality Field," 95.
37 Józef Życiński, "Alternatywne wersje ewolucji a problem wszechmocy Boga," *Roczniki Filozoficzne* 56, no. 1 (2008): 373.
38 See Józef Życiński, "God, Freedom and Evil. Perspectives from Religion and Science," *Zygon* 35, no. 3 (2000): 653–64. Some DAP participants distance themselves from the concept of God who acts as an attractor, emphasizing that a sufficient theistic explanation of creative evolution until the stage of anthropogenesis is to assume that the Creator "has given and continues to give existence to entities that, given time under the appropriate conditions, have the inherent capacity to become alive and to

evolve and eventually to manifest the qualities of self-conscious, thinking persons" (Peacocke, *Paths from Science Towards God*, 75).
39 Życiński, *Alternatywne wersje ewolucji*, 374.
40 Ibid.
41 Tracy, "Evolution, Divine Action," 518
42 Życiński, "The Rationality Field," 95.
43 Paul C. W. Davies, *Cosmic Blueprint. New Discoveries in Nature's Creative Ability to Order the Universe* (Philadelphia–London: Templeton Foundation Press, 2004), 29–31.
44 Stoeger, "Describing God's Action," 243–44; see also Tracy, "Evolution, Divine Action," 514–15.
45 John Byl, "Indeterminacy, Divine Action and Human Freedom," *Science and Christian Belief* 15, no. 2 (2003):101–5. However, there are also opponents of this view, being exemplified by Heller's argumentation as discussed in the first chapter of the present study.
46 Alston, *Divine Action, Human Freedom*, 187–91.
47 Paul C. W. Davies, "The Intelligibility of Nature," in *QC*, 155.
48 Edwards, *The God of Evolution*, 121; see also Stephen M. Barr, "The Concept of Randomness in Science and Divine Providence," in *Divine Action and Natural Selection. Science, Faith and Evolution*, ed. Joseph Seckbach and Richard Gordon (New Jersey: World Scientific, 2009), 465–81.
49 Stoeger, "Describing God's Action," 249.
50 Polkinghorne, *The Laws of Nature*, 428–29.
51 This metaphorical expression often appears in the context of reflection on ontological discontinuities found in nature's development.
52 Polkinghorne, *The Laws of Nature*, 430.
53 Willem B. Drees, *Religion and Science in Context. A Guide to the Debates* (London: Routledge, 2009), 39–41.
54 John C. Polkinghorne, *Reason and Reality. The Relationship between Science and Theology* (London: SPCK, 1991), 34–35.
55 Polkinghorne, *The Laws of Nature*, 431
56 Ian G. Barbour, "Neuroscience, Artificial Intelligence, and Human Nature. Theological and Philosophical Reflections," in *NAP*, 268.
57 Polkinghorne, *The Laws of Nature*, 433.
58 Davies, *Cosmic Blueprint*, 199–204.
59 Polkinghorne, *The Laws of Nature*, 433.
60 Davies, "The Intelligibility of Nature," 152; see also Polkinghorne, *The Laws of Nature and the Laws of Physics*, 434.
61 Tracy, "Evolution, Divine Action," 515.
62 Polkinghorne, *The Laws of Nature*, 435.
63 William R. Stoeger, "Contemporary Physics and the Ontological Status of the Laws of Nature," in *QC*, 207.
64 Tracy, "Evolution, Divine Action," 516.
65 Polkinghorne, *The Laws of Nature*, 437
66 Ibid., 438.
67 Tracy, "Evolution, Divine Action," 517.
68 Polkinghorne, *The Laws of Nature*, 438.
69 Stoeger, "Contemporary Physics," 209–31.
70 Eleonore Stump, "The Problem of Suffering. A Thomistic Approach," in *Thomas Aquinas. Teacher and Scholar*, ed. James McEvoy, Michael Dunne, and Julia Hynes (Dublin: Four Courts Press, 2012), 101–3.

71 Michael A. Arbib, "Crusoe's Brain. Of Solitude and Society," in *NAP*, 447.
72 Tracy, "Evolution, Divine Action," 519-20.
73 Ian Wilks, "The Structure of the Contemporary Debate on the Problem of Evil," *Religious Studies* 40, no. 3 (2004): 310.
74 Nelson Pike, "Hume on Evil," in *The Problem of Evil*, 38-52; Plantinga, *God, Freedom, and Evil*, 5-64. See also Krzysztof Hubaczek, *Bóg a zło. Problematyka teodycealna w filozofii analitycznej* (Wrocław: Wydawnictwo Uniwersytetu Wrocławskiego, 2010), 60-131; Michael L. Peterson, "The Logical Problem of Evil," in *A Companion to Philosophy of Religion*, 2nd ed., 491-98.
75 Krzysztof Hubaczek, "Teodycea bez 'unde malum'? Marilyn McCord Adams odpowiedź na problem zła," *Roczniki Filozoficzne* 55, no. 1 (2007), 71. See also Richard Otte, "Evidential Arguments from Evil," *International Journal for Philosophy of Religion* 48 (2000): 1; Graham Oppy, "The Evidential Problem of Evil," in *A Companion to Philosophy of Religion* (2nd ed.), 500-508.
76 Keith E. Yandell, "The Greater Good Defense," *Sophia* 13 (1974): 1-16; Keith E. Yandell, "The Problem of Evil and the Content of Morality, *International Journal for Philosophy of Religion* 17, no. 3 (1985): 139-65.
77 Rowe, "The Problem of Evil," 126-37. See also Hubaczek, "Teodycea bez 'unde malum'?" 72 and his "Williama Rowe'a bayesiański argument ze zła przeciwko istnieniu Boga. Próba analizy i oceny," *Diametros* 14 (2007): 32-52.
78 Paul Draper, "Pain and Pleasure. An Evidential Problem for Theists," *Noûs* 23, no. 3 (1989): 332-33. See also Hubaczek, "Teodycea bez 'unde malum'?" 73.
79 Dariusz Łukasiewicz, "Metafizyczne podstawy chrześcijańskiej wizji cierpienia," in *Rozumieć cierpienie? Wokół myśli Jana Pawła II i pytań o przyszłość chrześcijaństwa*, ed. Dariusz Łukasiewicz, Marek Siwiec, and Sylwester Warzyński (Bydgoszcz: Wydawnictwo Uniwersytetu Kazimierza Wielkiego, 2010), 93.
80 The Spinozian concept is close to some contemporary processualists. What is more, Griffin claims that classical theism is pantheism in disguise. Since God is simple and eternal, His will is necessary. If nothing can stop God from fulfilling His will, everything necessarily stems from the divine nature. Thus, the world transpires to be a necessary creation of God, and all beings are part of God or His "ways." Everything is contained in the simple God. God does not differ from the world: David R. Griffin, *God, Power and Evil. A Process Theodicy* (Philadelphia, PA: The Westminster Press, 1976, 98). In this context, Łukasiewicz stresses that even if we manage to avoid the pantheistic conclusion through the use of certain distinctions (as does Aquinas), then, assuming that God is simple, we reach the conclusion that He wants evil and causes it (Łukasiewicz, "Metafizyczne podstawy," 94).
81 Helm, "The Augustinian-Calvinist view," 171. See also Dariusz Łukasiewicz, "Racjonalizacje cierpienia i zła w filozofii religii," *Studia Religiologica* 48, no. 3 (2015): 192-93.
82 Eleonore Stump, "Aquinas on the Sufferings of Job," in *Reasoned Faith*, ed. Eleonore Stump (Ithaca, NY: Cornell University Press, 1993), 340-44, and her *Faith and the Problem of Evil* (Grand Rapids, MI: Calvin College, 1999). See also Łukasiewicz, "Metafizyczne podstawy," 95.
83 Łukasiewicz, "Metafizyczne podstawy," 96.
84 Stump, "Aquinas on the Sufferings," 345.
85 Łukasiewicz, "Metafizyczne podstawy," 97.
86 Ibid.
87 William Hasker, "God the Creator of Good and Evil?" in *The God Who Acts*, ed. Thomas F. Tracy (University Park, PA: Pennsylvania University Press, 1994), 137-46.

88 Hugh J. McCann, "Divine Providence," in *The Stanford Encyclopedia of Philosophy*, ed. Edward N. Zalta (Stanford, CA: Stanford University Press, 2006), 4.
89 Łukasiewicz, "Metafizyczne podstawy," 98.
90 Ibid., 99.
91 Ibid, 100.
92 Krzysztof Hubaczek, "Molinizm a problem zła moralnego," *Filo-Sofija* 19, no. 4 (2012): 144.
93 Ibid., 145.
94 Thomas P. Flint, *Divine Providence. The Molinist Account* (Ithaca, NY: Cornell University Press, 2006), 41–45.
95 Hubaczek, *Molinizm*, 146.
96 Józef Piórczyński, *Spór o panteizm. Droga Spinozy do filozofii i kultury niemieckiej* (Warsaw–Toruń: Fundacja na Rzecz Nauki Polskiej, 2016), 185.
97 Hubaczek, *Molinizm*, 147.
98 Plantinga, *God, Freedom, and Evil*, 47–48. See also Hubaczek, *Molinizm*, 148.
99 Alvin C. Plantinga, *God and Other Minds* (Ithaca, NY: Cornell University Press, 1967), 146. See also Hubaczek, *Bóg a zło*, 114.
100 One of de Molina's first and main opponents was Domingo Báñez, a Spanish Dominican and Scholastic theologian; see, for example, Robert J. Matava, *Divine Causality and Human Free Choice. Domingo Báñez, Physical Premotion and the Controversy de Auxiliis Revisited* (Leiden: Brill, 2016).
101 Hubaczek, *Molinizm*, 148–49.
102 For example, Robert M. Adams, "Middle Knowledge and the Problem of Evil," *American Philosophical Quarterly* 14, no. 2 (1977): 109–17; Hasker, *God, Time, and Knowledge*.
103 Hubaczek, *Molinizm*, 152.
104 Linda Zagzebski, *The Dilemma of Freedom and Foreknowledge* (Oxford: Oxford University Press, 1991), chap. 1.
105 Hubaczek, *Molinizm*, 152.
106 Ibid., 152–53.
107 Bernard Williams, *Making Sense of Humanity and Other Philosophical Papers 1982-1993* (Cambridge: Cambridge University Press, 1995), 241–47.
108 Hubaczek, *Bóg a zło*, 110–11.
109 Hubaczek, *Molinizm*, 153.
110 Ibid., 154.
111 Ibid.
112 See, e.g., Flint, *Divine Providence*; Eef Dekker, *Middle Knowledge* (Leuven: Peeters, 2000).
113 Hubaczek, *Molinizm*, 155. See also Linda Zagzebski, "Foreknowledge and Free Will (2.3 The Ockhamist solutions)," https://plato.stanford.edu/entries/free-will-foreknowledge/ (accessed February 11, 2020).
114 Robert Swinburne is a representative of this kind of reasoning; see, for example, his *Providence and the Problem of Evil* (Oxford: Clarendon Press, 1998).
115 Tracy, "Evolution, Divine Action," 523.
116 Richard Swinburne, "Problem zła—ujęcie analityczne," (lecture delivered at the Department of Theology at the Adam Mickiewicz University in Poznań, Poland, on October 19, 2000), trans. Małgorzata Wiertlewska, *Poznańskie Studia Teologiczne* 14 (2003): 93–94.
117 Ibid., 95–96.

118 Ibid., 97.
119 Ibid., 98.
120 Richard Swinburne, "The Problem of Evil," in *Richard Swinburne. Christian Philosophy in a Modern World*, ed. Nicola Mössner, Sebastian Schmoranzer, and Christian Weidemann (Frankfurt: Ontos Verlag, 2008), 25.
121 Swinburne, "Problem zła—ujęcie analityczne," 100.
122 Ibid., 101.
123 This issue is also addressed by John Hick, e.g., in his *Evil and the God of Love* (London: Macmillan, 1977), 281.
124 Tracy, "Evolution, Divine Action," 521.
125 Hick, *Evil and the God of Love*, 256–57.
126 Krzysztof Hubaczek, "Teodycea braku teodycei. Problem zła w koncepcji Johna Hicka," *Diametros* 7 (2006): 6–8.
127 Hick, *Evil and the God of Love*, 325.
128 Peacocke, *Paths from Science Towards God*, 84.
129 Edward Madden and Peter Hare, "Critique of Hick's Theodicy," in *Philosophy of Religion. An Anthology*, ed. Louis P. Pojman (Belmont, CA: Wadsworth Publishing Company, 2003), 156–59; see also William Rowe, "Evil and Theodicy," *Philosophical Topics* 16 (1988), 119–32.
130 Tracy, "Evolution, Divine Action," 523.
131 Peter van Inwagen, *The Problem of Evil. The Gifford Lectures Delivered in the University of St. Andrews in 2003* (Oxford: Calderon Press, 2008), 68.
132 Tracy, "Evolution, Divine Action," 524.
133 Such a logic of reasoning is close to many representatives of analytic philosophy; see Jakub Gomułka, "Krótka historia analitycznej filozofii religii," in *Anglosaska filozofia religii wobec wyzwań współczesności*, ed. Jowita Guja and Jakub Gomułka (Cracow: Libron, 2011), 28–31.
134 Tracy, "Evolution, Divine Action," 524.
135 William Hasker, "The Necessity of Gratuitous Evil," *Faith and Philosophy* 9, no. 1 (1992): 23–44. See also Eleonore Stump, "The Problem of Evil," *Faith and Philosophy* 4, no. 2 (1985): 392–423.
136 Tracy, "Evolution, Divine Action," 525.
137 Rom. 8:22, NIV.
138 Rom. 8:21, NIV.
139 Peacocke, *Paths from Science Towards God*, 83–84.
140 Tracy, "Evolution, Divine Action," 526.
141 Ibid., 528.
142 Michał Tempczyk, *Teoria chaosu a filozofia* (Warsaw: CIS, 1998).
143 Tracy, "Evolution, Divine Action," 529.
144 Peter van Inwagen, "The Problem of Evil," in *The Oxford Handbook of Philosophy of Religion*, ed. William J. Wainwright (Oxford: Oxford University Press, 2005), part 1.
145 John S. Mill, *Three Essays on Religion* (London: Longmans, Green, Reader, and Dyer, 1875), 183.
146 Van Inwagen, "The Problem of Evil," part 2.
147 Ibid, parts 3 and 4.
148 Ibid., part 5.
149 Łukasiewicz, "Racjonalizacje cierpienia i zła," 190.
150 Van Inwagen, "The Problem of Evil," 65–67.
151 Ibid., part 6.

152 Van Inwagen, "The Problem of Evil," 73–74.
153 Here we mean incompatibilism in the libertarian sense. This concept proclaims the existence of freedom on the assumption that the freedom of will and universal determinism are mutually exclusive. The same assumption is linked to undermining freedom in so-called hard incompatibilism. Robert Kane, *A Contemporary Introduction to Free Will* (New York: Oxford University Press, 2005), 1–11; see also Dariusz Łukasiewicz, "Teizm a twardy inkompatybilizm," *Roczniki Filozoficzne* 65, no. 3 (2017): 191–202.
154 Van Inwagen, "The Problem of Evil," parts 8 and 9.
155 Ibid. 84–85.
156 Ibid., part 11.
157 William L. Rowe, "The Problem of Evil and Some Varieties of Atheism," *American Philosophical Quarterly* 16 (1979): 337.
158 Van Inwagen, "The Problem of Evil," part 12.
159 Ibid., 100–101.
160 Ibid., part 13.
161 Peter van Inwagen, "The Problem of Evil, the Problem of Air, and the Problem of Silence," *Philosophical Perspectives* 5 (1991): 135–65.
162 Van Inwagen, "The Problem of Evil" (part 14) and his "The Magnitude, Duration, and Distribution of Evil. A Theodicy," *Philosophical Topics* 16, no. 2 (1988): 161–87, and his "The Argument from Particular Horrendous Evils," *Proceedings of the American Catholic Philosophical Association* 74 (2000): 65–80.
163 Łukasiewicz, "Racjonalizacje cierpienia i zła," 194.
164 Ibid., 195.
165 Ibid. See also David J. Bartholomew, *God, Chance and Purpose. Can God Have It Both Ways?* (Cambridge: Cambridge University Press, 2008).
166 Henri Bergson, *The Two Sources of Morality and Religion*, trans. R. Ashley Audra, Cloudesley Brereton, and William H. Carter (London: Macmillan, 1935), 224.
167 Marilyn McCord Adams, *Horrendous Evils and the Goodness of God* (Ithaca, NY: Cornell University Press, 1999), 8–9, and her "Problems of Evil. More Advice to Christian Philosophers," *Faith and Philosophy* 5, no. 2 (1988): 121–43. See also Philip L. Quinn, "Marilyn McCord Adams, Horrendous Evils and the Goodness of God," *The Philosophical Review* 110, no. 3 (2001): 478; Hubaczek, "Teodycea bez 'unde malum'?" 73.
168 Marilyn McCord Adams, "Duns Scotus on the Goodness of God," *Faith and Philosophy* 4, no. 4 (1987): 486–505, and her *Horrendous Evils*, 54–55. See also Hubaczek, "Teodycea bez 'unde malum'?" 74.
169 Adams, *Horrendous Evils*, 17–29. See also Hubaczek, "Teodycea bez 'unde malum'?" 75.
170 Adams, *Horrendous Evils*, 25–26. It is also here that Adams provides, in her opinion, paradigmatic examples of horrendous evil.
171 See ibid., 187. See also Hubaczek, "Teodycea bez 'unde malum'?" 76.
172 Adams, *Horrendous Evils*, 52.
173 Ibid., 13.
174 Hubaczek, "Teodycea bez 'unde malum'?" 78. See also Adams, *Horrendous Evils*, 3.
175 Adams, *Horrendous Evils*, 103.
176 Hubaczek, "Teodycea bez 'unde malum'?" 79
177 Marilyn McCord Adams, "Divine Justice, Divine Love and Life to Come," *Crux* 13 (1976–77): 13–28.

178 Marilyn McCord Adams, "Theodicy without Blame," *Philosophical Topics* 16 (1988): 215–45.
179 Adams, *Horrendous Evils*, 52–53.
180 Hubaczek, "Teodycea bez 'unde malum'?" 79; McCord Adams, *Horrendous Evils*, 103. See also Łukasiewicz, "Racjonalizacje cierpienia i zła," 192.
181 McCord Adams, *Horrendous Evils*, 155.
182 Hubaczek, "Teodycea bez 'unde malum'?" 80–81; see also McCord Adams, *Horrendous Evils*, 172–73.
183 See, e.g., van Inwagen, "The Problem of Evil," 217n2.
184 Charles C. Hefling, "Christ and Evils. Assessing an Aspect of Marilyn McCord Adams's Theodicy," *Anglican Theological Review* 83, no. 4 (2001): 869–82.
185 Hubaczek, "Teodycea bez 'unde malum'?" 82. See also Ian Wilks, "The Structure of the Contemporary Debate on the Problem of Evil," *Religious Studies* 40 (2004): 307–21.
186 Hubaczek, "Teodycea bez 'unde malum'?" 86.
187 In some contemporary approaches, the problem of the Incarnation is examined as an element of philosophical theology. This is done, for instance by Stanisław Judycki (see his *Bóg i inne osoby*, 76–77). See also Tracy, "Evolution, Divine Action," 530; Peacocke, *Paths from Science Towards God*, 86–88.
188 Moltmann, *The Trinity*, 109.
189 Polkinghorne, *Science and Creation*, 77.
190 Józef Życiński, *God and Evolution. Fundamental Questions of Christian Evolutionism*, trans. Kenneth W. Kemp and Zuzanna Maślanka (Washington, DC: The Catholic University of America Press, 2006), 171–72.
191 Życiński, *Teizm i filozofia analityczna*, 2:149.
192 Aquinas, *Suma teologiczna*, 1.3.8 (*responsio*), and his *Summa contra gentiles*, 1.17 and 1.26.
193 Życiński, *God and Evolution*, 167–69.
194 Pseudo-Dionysius, *Celestial Hierarchy*, 4. The entire work is available in *The Complete Works*, trans. Colm Luibheid (New York: The Paulist Press, 1987).
195 Aquinas, *Summa contra gentiles*, 1.26.10.
196 Dermot Moran, "Pantheism from John Scottus Eriugena to Nicholas of Cusa," *American Catholic Philosophical Quarterly* 64, no. 1 (1990): 131–52.
197 Cusanus, *On the Gift of the Father of Lights*, 2, 97. His entire work is available in *Complete Philosophical and Theological Treatises of Nicholas of Cusa*, trans. Jasper Hopkins (Minneapolis, MN: The Arthur J. Banning Press, 2001).
198 Cusanus, *De docta ignorantia* (*On Learned Ignorance*), II, 9, 150.
199 Życiński, *God and Evolution*, 172.
200 Cusanus, *De docta ignorantia*, II, 4, 115.
201 The echo of such an understanding of the God–world relationship can be found in many twentieth-century studies that stress that without the Creator, creation would disappear. Such an enunciation is explicitly present in one of the most important documents of the Vatican II. What is interesting is that the context for introducing such a formulation is the emphasis put on the autonomy of nature and the freedom of scientific research which, in the past, had been at times unjustly opposed to faith. "For by the very circumstance of their having been created, all things are endowed with their own stability, truth, goodness, proper laws and order. Man must respect these as he isolates them by the appropriate methods of the individual sciences or arts. Therefore if methodical investigation within every branch of learning is carried out in a genuinely scientific manner and in accord with moral norms, it never truly

conflicts with faith, for earthly matters and the concerns of faith derive from the same God. Indeed whoever labors to penetrate the secrets of reality with a humble and steady mind, even though he is unaware of the fact, is nevertheless being led by the hand of God, who holds all things in existence, and gives them their identity. Consequently, we cannot but deplore certain habits of mind, which are sometimes found too among Christians, which do not sufficiently attend to the rightful independence of science and which, from the arguments and controversies they spark, lead many minds to conclude that faith and science are mutually opposed." Vatican Council II, Pastoral Constitution on the Church in the Modern World *Gaudium Et Spes*, no. 36 (Vatican, December 7, 1965), http://www.vatican.va/archive/hist_councils/ii_vatican_council/documents/vat-ii_const_19651207_gaudium-et-spes_en.html (accessed February 12, 2020). See also Życiński, *God and Evolution*, 173–74.

202 *De possest* (*On Actualized Possibility*), 8, 19–22; see also 8, 13.
203 Aquinas, *Summa contra gentiles*, 1.29.5.
204 Życiński, *God and Evolution*, 175.
205 A. N. Whitehead, *Process and Reality* (New York: Macmillan, 1957), 60.
206 Heinz R. Pagels, *Perfect Symmetry. The Search for the Beginning of Time* (Toronto: Bantam Books, 1986), 187.
207 George V. Coyne, "Anche la teologia deve cambiare?" in *La Favola dell'Universo*, ed. George V. Coyne, Giulio Giorello, and Elio Sindoni (Piemme: Casale Monferrato, 1997), 116f. See also Życiński, *God and Evolution*, 176.
208 A. R. Peacocke, *God and the New Biology* (San Francisco, CA: Harper & Row: 1986), 96f.
209 Peacocke, *Paths from Science towards God*, 109.
210 Ibid., 110.
211 Keith Ward, *God. A Guide for the Perplexed* (London: Oneworld, 2013), 161.
212 Augustine, *Confessions*, book VII, 5. See also Peacocke, *Paths from Science Towards God*, 112–13.
213 Arthur R. Peacocke, *Science and the Christian Experiment* (London–New York–Toronto: Oxford University Press, 1971), 84.
214 Arthur R. Peacocke, "Articulating God's Presence in and to the World Unveiled by the Sciences," in *In Whom We Live and Move and Have Our Being. Panentheistic Reflections on God's Presence in a Scientific World*, ed. Philip Clayton and Arthur R. Peacocke (Cambridge–Grand Rapids, MI: William B. Eerdmans Publishing Company, 2004), 137–54. See also Wojtysiak, "Panenteizm," 323–24.
215 G. F. R. Ellis, "Intimations of Transcendence. Relations of the Mind and God," in *NAP*, 454. See also Józef Życiński, "Pluralistyczna ontologia przyrody w ujęciu George'a F. R. Ellisa," *Studia Philosophiae Christianae* 40, no. 2 (2004): 132–34; Kevin M. Cronin, *Kenosis* (New York: Continuum, 1992); John Schellenberg, *Divine Hiddenness and Human Reason* (London–Ithaca, CA: Cornell University Press, 2006); Kathryn Tanner, *God and Creation in Christian Theology. Tyranny and Empowerment?* (Minneapolis, MN: Fortress Press, 2005).
216 Karl Ch. F. Krause, *Vorlesungen über die Grundwahrheiten der Wissenschaft, zugleich in ihrer Beziehung zu dem Leben* (Göttingen: Dieterich,1829).
217 Wojtysiak, "Panenteizm," 315. See also Philip Clayton, "Panentheism in Metaphysical and Scientific Perspective," in *In Whom We Live and Move and Have Our Being*, 81.
218 Charles Hartshorne and William L. Reese, *Philosophers Speak of God* (Chicago, IL: The University of Chicago Press, 1953); see also Wojtysiak, "Panenteizm," 317.

219 Wojtysiak, "Panenteizm," 319; see also Ch. Hartshorne, *From Aquinas to Whitehead. Seven Centuries of Metaphysics of Religion (The Aquinas Lecture)* (Milwaukee, WI: Marquette University Publications, 1976), 18–19.
220 Życiński, *Teizm i filozofia analityczna*, 2:146.
221 Ibid., 140; see also Wojtysiak, "Panenteizm," 325.
222 Życiński, *Teizm i filozofia analityczna*, 2:152–53; see also Wojtysiak, "Panenteizm," 325.
223 Józef Życiński, *Świat matematyki i jej materialnych cieni. Elementy platonizmu w podstawach matematyki* (Cracow: Copernicus Center Press, 2011), 100.
224 I discuss this in more detail in the section devoted to the scientific worldview.
225 Życiński, *Teizm i filozofia analityczna*, 2:187; see also Wojtysiak, "Panenteizm," 329.
226 Życiński, *Teizm i filozofia analityczna*, 2:151.
227 Wojtysiak, "Panenteizm," in *Filozofia Boga*, 2:520–22.
228 While demonstrating the specificity of the God–world relationship, such an approach might give more attention to the classical theory of the participation of being. A different proposition is presented by Ruth Page: see her "Panentheism and Pansyntheism. God in Relation," in *God and Evolution. A Reader*, ed. Mary K. Cunningham (London–New York: Routledge, 2007), 349–59. A panorama of the various panentheisms present in the history of theistic thought can be found in John W. Cooper, *Panentheism. The Other God of the Philosophers: From Plato to the Present* (Grand Rapids, MI: Baker Academic, 2006). Some of the most recent research in this area is available in *International Journal for Philosophy of Religion* 85, no. 1 (February 2019), Special Issue on Pantheism and Panentheism.

4 Threats and Challenges

1 Heller, *Sens życia i sens wszechświata*, 124. See also Tracy, "Particular Providence and the God of Gaps," in *CC*, 289–324.
2 Aubrey L. Moore, "The Christian Doctrine of God," in *Lux Mundi* (12th ed.), ed. Charles Gore (London: John Murray, 1891), 73, accessed January 28, 2020, https://www.gutenberg.org/files/46478/46478-h/46478-h.htm#Page_68 (10th ed.), page 99.
3 Ibid. (10th ed.), 100.
4 Aubrey L. Moore, *Science and the Faith. Essays on Apologetic Subjects* (London: Kegan Paul, 1889), 226–32.
5 Życiński, *God and Evolution*, 27–28.
6 Henry Drummond, *The Lowell Lectures on the Assent of Man* (London: Hodder & Stoughton 1894), 428; See also Polkinghorne, *Beyond Science. The Wider Human Context* (Cambridge: Cambridge University Press, 1998), 77.
7 Peacocke, *Paths from Science Towards God*, 136–37.
8 Polkinghorne, "The Laws of Nature," 438.
9 Willem Drees, "Gaps for God?" in *CC*, 228, accessed January 28, 2020, https://openaccess.leidenuniv.nl/bitstream/handle/1887/10274/909_063.pdf?sequence=1
10 There is no need to introduce this here in detail. What matters is that such a theory exists. For further investigation see, e.g., Klaus Mainzer, *Poznawanie złożoności. Obliczeniowa dynamika materii umysłu i ludzkości*, trans. Marek Hetmański et al. (Lublin: Wydawnictwo UMCS, 2007), 9–16; Michał Tempczyk, *Teoria chaosu dla odważnych* (Warsawa: PWN, 2002).
11 Drees, "Gaps for God?" 228.

12 Davies, *Cosmic Blueprint*, 51–52.
13 Drees, "Gaps for God?" 230.
14 Ibid., 231–32.
15 Peacocke, *Paths from Science Towards God*, 99–103.
16 Ibid., 104.
17 Ibid., 105.
18 Ibid., 106.
19 N. T. Saunders suggests that we imagine God planning to destroy dinosaurs by means of an asteroid colliding with the Earth. If the natural trajectory of the asteroid was to run close to the Earth then God would be able to cause an impact by means of manipulation conducted on the quantum level. In accordance with physical laws, such a navigation would have lasted for approximately three million years. Thus, to do so, God would have had to begin His intervention a long time before dinosaurs themselves had appeared on the Earth. Such a mental experiment makes us realize the scale of God's potential action, with this action simultaneously having to be effective and undetectable by man (Saunders, "Does God Cheat at Dice?" 517–44).
20 Peacocke, *Paths from Science Towards God*, 107.
21 Michał Heller, "Chaos, Probability, and the Comprehensibility of the World," in *CC*, 120.
22 Stephen Hawking, *A Brief History of Time. From the Big Bang to Black Holes* (New York: Bantam Books, 1998), 174; Peacocke, *Paths from Science Towards God*, 39.
23 Heller, "Chaos, Probability," 121.
24 Stoeger, "Describing God's Action," 242.
25 Peters, "The Trinity in and Beyond Time," 281–82.
26 Stoeger, "Describing God's Action," 243.
27 Ibid., 247.
28 Ellis, "The Theology of the Anthropic Principle," 392–93.
29 Stoeger, "Describing God's Action," 248.
30 Ibid., 249.
31 Życiński, "Kategorie przyczynowości i celowości w filozoficznej interpretacji przyrody," *Analecta Cracoviensia* 33 (2001): 283.
32 Słomka, *Ewolucjonizm chrześcijański*, 54.
33 Marian Morawski, *Celowość w naturze. Studium przyrodniczo-filozoficzne* (Cracow: Nakładem Przeglądu Powszechnego, 1887), 31; see also Życiński, "Kategorie przyczynowości i celowości," 284.
34 James P. Joule, *Matter, Living Force and Heat (The Scientific Papers of James Prescott Joule)* (London: Taylor & Francis, 1884), 1:273.
35 Józef Życiński, *Ułaskawianie natury* (Cracow: Znak, 1992), 31f. See also Pedersen, *The Two Books*, 277–80.
36 Słomka, *Ewolucjonizm chrześcijański*, 53.
37 William Paley, *Natural Theology or Evidences of the Existence and Attributes of the Deity* (London: R. Faulder, 1802).
38 Słomka, *Ewolucjonizm chrześcijański*, 150.
39 Charles Darwin, *More Letters*, ed. Francis Darwin and Albert C. Seward (London: John Murray, 1903), 1:321, accessed December 10, 2019, http://darwin-online.org.uk/content/frameset?itemID=F1548.1&viewtype=text&pageseq=1.
40 Charles Darwin, "A Letter to Asa Gray (22 May 1860)," in *The Correspondence of Charles Darwin*, vol. 8, *1860*, ed. Frederick Burkhardt, Janet Browne, Duncan M. Porter, and Marsha Richmond (Cambridge: Cambridge University Press, 1993), 224. See also

online at: https://www.darwinproject.ac.uk/letter/DCP-LETT-2814.xml (accessed February 12, 2020).
41 Hugh Miller, *Foot-prints of the Creator, Or, The Asterolepis of Stromness* (London: Johnstone and Hunter, 1849), 279–313. See also Życiński, "Kategorie przyczynowości i celowości," 285.
42 John W. Clark and Thomas M. Hughes, *The Life and Letters of the Reverend Adam Sedgwick* (Cambridge: Cambridge University Press, 1890), 2:357–358. See also Życiński, *God and Evolution*, 25–26.
43 James Iverach, *Christianity and Evolution* (London: Hodder 1894), 175–76, accessed December 10, 2019, https://archive.org/details/christianityevol00iver/page/174; James Iverach, *Theism in the Light of Present Science and Philosophy* (London: Hodder, 1899).
44 Iverach, *Christianity and Evolution*, 128f. See also Życiński, "Naturalistyczne a chrześcijańskie interpretacje ewolucji," *Forum Teologiczne* 9 (2008): 47.
45 Francisco J. Ayala, "Darwin's Devolution. Design without Designer," in *EMB*, 105.
46 Słomka, *Chrześcijański ewolucjonizm*, 150–51.
47 Langdon Gilkey, "The God of Nature," in *CC*, 219.
48 Davies, "The Intelligibility of Nature," 160.
49 Peacocke, *Paths from Science Towards God*, 75–77.
50 Davies, "The Intelligibility of Nature," 161.
51 Examples of rehabilitated teleological categories are provided by the variational principles found in classical mechanics – for more on this topic, see Christopher G. Gray, Gabriel Karl, and Viktor A. Novikov, "Progress in Classical and Quantum Variational Principles," *Reports on Progress in Physics* 67 (2004): 159–208 – as well as Maxwell's differential and integral formulation of equations, about which you can find information, for instance, in Pavel Šolín, *Partial Differential Equations and the Finite Element Method* (Hoboken, NJ: John Wiley & Sons, 2006).
52 John D. Barrow and Frank J. Tipler, *The Anthropic Cosmological Principle* (Oxford: Clarendon Press, 1986), 152. Some of the theses put forward in their monograph are fairly controversial. Nevertheless, it continues to be a frequent reference point in reflection on anthropic principles.
53 Życiński, "Alternatywne wersje ewolucji," 372.
54 This theorem states that "if the properties of a physical system are invariant during certain transformations, then there is a corresponding conservation law. Thus, to the invariance of action in relation to displacement in time (homogeneity of time) corresponds the law of the conservation of energy; from the homogeneity of space results the law of the conservation of momentum; from the isotropy of space, the law of the conservation of angular momentum; etc. These dependencies show the deep connection between principles of conservation and symmetries which have a dynamic character and therefore go beyond local connections, thus showing the influence of global causation" (Życiński, *God and Evolution*, 105)
55 Ibid.
56 Jacques Monod, *Leçon inaugurale* (Paris: Collège de France, 1968), 9.
57 Życiński, *God and Evolution*, 126–27.
58 Stoeger, "The Immanent Directionality," 163–90.
59 Życiński, *God and Evolution*, 101–4.
60 "The structure of the system is not the result of an a priori design, nor is it determined directly by external conditions. It is a result of the interaction between the system and its environment." Paul Cilliers, *Complexity and Postmodernism. Understanding Complex Systems* (London: Routledge 1998), 91.

61 Clayton, "The Emergence of Spirit," *CTNS Bulletin* 20, no. 4 (2000): 9.
62 Życiński, *God and Evolution*, 107.
63 Słomka, "Fides et ratio – Jan Paweł II i Abp Józef Życiński," in *Relacja nauka – wiara. Nowe ujęcie dawnego problemu*, ed. Jacek Golbiak and Monika Hereć (Lublin: Wydawnictwo KUL, 2014), 173.
64 Edwards, *How God Acts*, 1–2.
65 Heller, "Naukowy obraz świata," 25–26.
66 See, e.g., Stoeger, "Contemporary Cosmology and Its Implications for the Contemporary Science-Religion Dialogue," in *Physics, Philosophy and Theology. A Common Quest for Understanding*, ed. Robert Russell, William Stoeger, and George Coyne (Vatican City State: Vatican Observatory, 1988), 219–47.
67 In this context, Peacocke puts forward an interesting suggestion as to what the first chapters of *Genesis* might have looked like if they were written from the perspective of current scientific awareness; see his *Paths from Science Towards God*, 1–2.
68 Edwards, *How God Acts*, 4–5.
69 See, e.g., Francis Collins, *The Language of God. A Scientist Presents Evidence for Belief* (New York: Free Press, 2007), 199–200.
70 Janusz Mączka and Piotr Urbańczyk, eds., *Teologia nauki* (Cracow: Copernicus Center Press, 2015). The discipline which still awaits greater scholarly interest and calls for autonomous development is the theology of nature.
71 Nonetheless, this does not mean that the Catholic Church accepted Teilhard de Chardin's ideas. On the contrary, Church representatives addressed the intellectual output of the French Jesuit with criticism, particularly his views concerning the theory of evolution. Teilhard de Chardin was forbidden to publish soon after the release of his first studies on this topic. Seven years after his death the Vatican issued a statement in which Teilhard de Chardin's theological and philosophical texts were said to have contained serious errors as far as Catholic teachings are concerned. However, the authors of the document did not name any of his specific studies or particular statements. The Congregation of the Holy Office (now Congregation for the Doctrine of the Faith) warned the public against reading Teilhard de Chardin's texts and banned the studying of them in Catholic educational institutions. The change of the stance of the Church was gradual during the pontificates of John Paul II, Benedict XVI, and Francis. On November 23, 2017 the Pontifical Council for Culture announced that it was planning to ask Pope Francis to rehabilitate Teihard de Chardin (https://www.americamagazine.org/faith/2017/11/21/will-pope-francis-remove-vaticans-warning-teilhard-de-chardins-writings accessed April 29, 2020).
72 Jakub Dziadkowiec, "Tworzenie świata – stwarzaniem Boga. Metafizyka Samuela Alexandra i Alfreda Northa Whiteheada," in *Finding Design in Nature? Interdyscyplinarna dyskusja wokół ewolucji*, ed. Monika Czarnuch and Jan Oko (Katowice: Emmanuel, 2007), 15–27.
73 Słomka, *Ewolucjonizm chrześcijański*, 12.
74 Daniel C. Dennett, *Darwin's Dangerous Idea. Evolution and the Meanings of Life* (New York: Simon & Schuster, 1995), 310.
75 Haught, "Darwin's Gift to Theology," 395.
76 Ibid.
77 Ibid., 396.
78 Ibid., 401.
79 Daniel C. Dennett, *Breaking the Spell. Religion as a Natural Phenomenon* (New York: Viking, 2006).

80 Józef Życiński, *Na zachód od domu niewoli* (Poznań: W drodze, 1997, 165); see also Willem B. Drees, "Creazionismo e evoluzione", *Concilium* 36, no. 1 (2000): 66.
81 Haught, *Darwin's Gift to Theology*, 395.
82 Francisco Ayala, "Address by Doctor Honoris Causa Professor Francisco J. Ayala," in *Francisco J. Ayala doktorem honoris causa Uniwersytetu Warszawskiego* (Warsaw: Biuro Promocji UW, 2009), 74. https://www.uw.edu.pl/wp-content/uploads/2018/01/prof.francisco_j._ayala_publikacja_dhc.pdf (accessed February 13, 2020).
83 Haught, *Darwin's Gift to Theology*, 400.
84 Macquarrie, *The Humility of God*, 34.
85 Haught, *Darwin's Gift to Theology*, 401.
86 Pabjan, *Anatomia konfliktu. Między nowym ateizmem a teologią nauki* (Cracow: Copernicus Center Press, 2016), 48.
87 Haught, *Darwin's Gift to Theology*, 404. See also Polkinghorne, *The Work of Love. Creation as Kenosis* (Grand Rapids, MI: Eerdmans, 2001), 21f.
88 George S. Johnston, *Did Darwin Get it Right? Catholics and the Theory of Evolution* (Huntington, IN: Our Sunday Visitor Publishing Division, 1998), 12.
89 John Gribbin, *In the Beginning. After COBE and Before the Big Bang* (Boston, MA: Little, Brown and Company, 1993).
90 Haught, *Darwin's Gift to Theology*, 402.
91 Griffin, *Reenchantment without Supernaturalism*, 17–18
92 Słomka, *Ewolucjonizm chrześcijański*, 48–49.
93 Dennett, *Darwin's Dangerous Idea*, 73–80.
94 Haught, *Darwin's Gift to Theology*, 402.
95 Mieszko Tałasiewicz, "Naturalizm ontologiczny a naturalizm metodologiczny (na marginesie artykułu Marcina Miłkowskiego *Naturalizm ontologiczny a argument Hume'a przeciwko wiarygodności cudów*)," *Przegląd Filozoficzno-Literacki* 17, no. 2 (2007): 403–8.
96 In the context of the science-religion relationship, D. R. Griffin introduces a distinction between the minimum and maximum version of naturalism. According to Griffin, science requires the assumption of the first version only. In adopting the maximum version of naturalism, although widespread in scientific circles, means going beyond the limits of scientific methodology and unavoidably leads to a conflict between science and religion (see his *Religion and Scientific Naturalism*, xv–xvi).
97 Haught, *Darwin's Gift to Theology*, 403.
98 See, e.g., Życiński, "The Rationality Field," 87–101.
99 Haught, *Darwin's Gift to Theology*, 404.
100 Gavin de Beer, "Evolution," in *The New Encyclopedia Britannica*, 15th ed. (London: Encyclopedia Britannica 1973-1974), 7:23. See also: Holmes Rolston III, *Science and Religion. A Critical Survey* (New York: Random House, 1987), 106.
101 Haught, *Darwin's Gift to Theology*, 414.
102 See, e.g., John Bowker, *Is God a Virus? Genes, Culture and Religion* (London: SPCK, 1995).
103 Dennett, *Darwin's Dangerous Idea*, 180–81; see also Haught, *Darwin's Gift to Theology*, 415.
104 Idem, 415–16. It is also a cognitively interesting fact that the randomness of the events which take place in the macro-world is frequently interpreted by religious people as a sign of God's action. Meeting someone after years of separation, which is a consequence of a combination of random conditions, is often seen as providence. Obviously, this cannot lead to the statement that God does not act within the

non-random circumstances of life. However, to perceive God's presence when events of little probability are at play (*nomen omen*) is a certain contradiction to the intuition that randomness excludes the rationality of an event or Divine activity.
105 Życiński, "The Laws of Nature," 3–19; see also Kenneth R. Miller, *Finding Darwin's God. A Scientist's Search for Common Ground Between God and Evolution* (New York: Harper/Collins Publishers, 1999).
106 John C. Polkinghorne, *The Faith of a Physicist* (Princeton, NJ: Princeton University Press, 1994), 25–26, 75–87.
107 Haught, *Darwin's Gift to Theology*, 416.
108 Richard Dawkins, *The Blind Watchmaker. Why the Evidence of Evolution Reveals a Universe without Design* (New York–London: W. W. Norton & Company, 1987), 14.
109 Haught, *Darwin's Gift to Theology*, 416.
110 Ibid., 417.
111 Jeffrey S. Wicken, *Evolution, Thermodynamics, and Information* (New York: Oxford University Press, 1987), 59f.
112 Haught, *Darwin's Gift to Theology*, 417.
113 Ibid., 418.
114 Pabjan, *Anatomia konfliktu*, 54.
115 Stoeger, "Describing God's Action," 241.
116 Peter van Inwagen, "The Place of Chance in a World Sustained by God," in *God, Knowledge, and Mystery*, (Ithaca, NY: Cornell University Press, 1988), 42–65.
117 Łukasiewicz, "Wszechmoc Boga," 169–70. The author of the above-quoted book titled *Opatrzność Boża, wolność, przypadek*, in addition to his primary reflection, also provides a more detailed presentation of the semantics of chance (363–93). See also Grzegorz Bugajak, "Pojęcie przypadku i jego zastosowanie w analizach teorii naukowych," in *Filozofia przyrody współcześnie*, ed. Mariola Kuszyk-Bytniewska and Andrzej Łukasik (Cracow: Universitas, 2010), 235–46.
118 Łukasiewicz, "Wszechmoc Boga," 171.
119 Mark I. T. Robson, *Ontology and Providence in Creation. Taking "Ex Nihilo" Seriously* (London–New York: Continuum, 2008), 146.
120 Łukasiewicz, "Wszechmoc Boga," 172.
121 Ibid., 173.
122 See, e.g., David J. Bartholomew, *God of Chance* (London: SCM Press, 1984).
123 Łukasiewicz, "Wszechmoc Boga," 174.
124 Ibid., 175.
125 Ian Stewart, *Does God Play Dice? The New Mathematics of Chaos*, 2nd ed. (Malden, MA: Blackwell Publishers, 2002), 282.
126 Heller, *Filozofia przypadku. Kosmiczna fuga z preludium i kodą* (Cracow: Copernicus Center Press, 2011), 125–26.
127 In probability calculus this is defined as "the law of large numbers."
128 Heller, *Filozofia przypadku*, 68.
129 Albert Einstein received the 1921 Nobel Prize for explaining this photoelectric effect.
130 Keith Ward, *God, Chance and Necessity* (Oxford: One World, 1996), 119.
131 Apart from genetic mutations, the change in the frequency of alleles, as well as the modifications of the genetic composition of a population (genetic drift) are also of a random character. Random factors can rule the death of well-assimilated organisms, or even the course of large-scale evolutionary changes, as in global catastrophes that result in the so-called large extinction events. See also Paweł Polak, "Teizm i

ewolucja," in *Przewodnik po filozofii religii. Nurt analityczny*, ed. Janusz Salamon (Cracow: WAM, 2016), 427.
132 Here I refer to the text already been cited (see note 674) of the lecture delivered by Francisco Ayala at the University of Warsaw on May 15, 2009. Ayala distinctly differentiates between the randomness of mutation and the determinism of selection (p. 75). Publications by other academics are in accordance: see, e.g., Mateusz S. Konczal, "Genomika adaptacji," *Kosmos. Problemy nauk biologicznych* 62, no. 1 (2013): 13; or Kazimierz Jodkowski, *Spór ewolucjonizmu z kreacjonizmem. Podstawowe pojęcia i poglądy*, Biblioteka Filozoficznych Aspektów Genezy 1 (Warsaw: MEGAS, 2007), 46.
133 Józef F. Krawczyk, *Człowiek nie zaistniał przez przypadek – przegrałeś Darwinie!* (Sandomierz: Wydawnictwo Diecezjalne 2003), 111.
134 Słomka, "Antynaukowy kreacjonizm jako negacja teistycznego ewolucjonizmu," in *Naukowy a religijny obraz początku wszechświata i człowieka. Perspektywy dialogu*, ed. Jacek Golbiak, Karol Jasiński, and Wojciech Kotowicz (Olsztyn: Wydział Teologii UWM, 2015), 119.
135 Council for Science of the Polish Bishops' Conference, "Kościół wobec ewolucji" (Nov 27, 2006), no. 9, accessed January 31, 2018, https://opoka.org.pl/biblioteka/W/WE/kep/kosciol_ewolucja_27112006.html.
136 Richard Dawkins, *The Selfish Gene* (Oxford: Oxford University Press, 1976).
137 Dawkins, *The Blind Watchmaker*.
138 Słomka, "Antynaukowy kreacjonizm," 120.
139 Polkinghorne, *The Laws of Nature and the Laws of Physics*, 431.
140 Bartholomew, *God, Chance, and Purpose. Can God Have It Both Ways?* (Cambridge: Cambridge University Press, 2008).
141 Davies, *The Mind of God*, 183. See also Heller, "Chaos, prawdopodobieństwo i pojmowalność świata," 270; Bartholomew, *Uncertain Belief*, 56; Peacocke, "God as the Creator of the World of Science," in *Interpreting the Universe as Creation. A Dialogue of Science and Religion*, ed. Vincent Brümmer (Kampen: Kok Pharos Pub. House, 1991), 110–11.
142 Michał Heller, introduction to *Ewolucja i stworzenie*, by Ernan McMullin, transl. Jacek Rodzeń (Cracow-Tarnów: OBI – Biblos 2006), xxiii.
143 Życiński, "Alternatywne wersje ewolucji a problem wszechmocy Boga," *Roczniki Filozoficzne* 56, no. 1 (2008): 370.
144 Ibid., 371.
145 Ibid., 372.
146 Łukasiewicz, "Wszechmoc Boga a teologia przypadku," 176.
147 Ibid., 177.
148 Mariano Artigas, *The Mind of the Universe. Understanding Science and Religion* (Philadelphia-London: Templeton Foundation Press, 2000), 148.
149 Łukasiewicz, "Wszechmoc Boga a teologia przypadku," 178.
150 Steve Stewart-Williams, *Darwin, God, and the Meaning of Life. How Evolutionary Theory Undermines Everything You Thought You Knew* (Cambridge: Cambridge University Press, 2010), 103–27.
151 Łukasiewicz, "Wszechmoc Boga a teologia przypadku," 178.
152 William A. Dembski, *Intelligent Design. The Bridge Between Science & Theology* (Downers Grove, IL: InterVarsity Press, 1999), 168.
153 Marek Słomka, "Argument Bożego planu ('intelligent design') a ewolucjonizm chrześcijański," *Logos i Ethos* 18, no. 1 (2005): 73

154 See, e.g., *Intelligent Design Creationism and Its Critics. Philosophical, Theological, and Scientific Perspectives*, ed. Robert T. Pennock (Cambridge, MA: MIT Press, 2001); *Intelligent Thought. Science versus the Intelligent Design Movement*, ed. John Brockman (New York: Vintage Books, 2006); Robert T. Carroll, "Intelligent Design," *The Skeptic's Dictionary*, accessed July 14, 2017, http://skepdic.com/intelligentdesign.html.
155 Michał Heller, *Ostateczne wyjaśnienia wszechświata* (Cracow: Universitas, 2008), 216.
156 Słomka, "Argument Bożego planu," 76. See also Philip E. Johnson, "Creator or Blind Watchmaker?" *First Things*, no. 29 (1993): 8–22.
157 Heller, *Ostateczne wyjaśnienia wszechświata*, 221; see also Słomka, "Argument Bożego planu," 77.
158 Michał Heller, "Konieczność i przypadek w ewolucji Wszechświata," *Studia Philosophiae Christianae* 46, no. 1 (2010): 22.
159 Haught states that "the 'chance' character of the variations which natural selection chooses for survival may just as easily be accounted for as the product of human ignorance. The apparent randomness of what we today call genetic mutations could be a mere illusion resulting from the limitedness of our perspective. Religions claim, after all, that any purely human angle of vision is always exceedingly narrow. Hence, what appears to be absurd chance from a purely scientific perspective could be quite rational and coherent from that of an infinite Wisdom" (John F. Haught, *Science and Religion. From Conflict to Conversation* [Mahwah, NY: Paulist Press, 1995], 59). See also Słomka, "Argument Bożego planu," 77; Loren Haarsma, "Chance from a Theistic Perspective," *The TalkOrigins Archive*, accessed July 14, 2017, http://www.talkorigins.org/faqs/chance/chance-theistic.html.
160 Heller, "Konieczność i przypadek," 21.
161 Słomka, "Argument Bożego planu," 77. In the same context Polkinghorne writes: "Necessity is the regular ground of possibility, expressed in scientific law. Chance, in this context, is the means for the exploration and realization of inherent possibility, through continually changing (and therefore at any time contingent) individual circumstances. It is important to realize that chance is being used in this 'tame' sense, meaning the shuffling operations by which what is potential is made actual. It is not a synonym for chaotic randomness, nor does it signify just a lucky fluke … I am still deeply impressed by the anthropic potentiality of the laws of nature which enable the small-step explorations of tamed chance to result in systems of such wonderful complexity as ourselves" (*Science and Providence*, 46). See also Victor J. Stenger, "Intelligent Design. Humans, Cockroaches, and the Laws of Physics," *The TalkOrigins Archive*, accessed July 14, 2017, http://www.talkorigins.org/faqs/cosmo.html, and his *Not by Design. The Origin of the Universe* (Buffalo, NY: Prometheus Books, 1995).
162 Dembski, *Intelligent Design*, 206, 210. See also Heller, *Ostateczne wyjaśnienia wszechświata*, 220.
163 Życiński, "Jak rozumieć matematyczność przyrody?" in *Matematyczność przyrody*, ed. Michał Heller and Józef Życiński (Cracow: Petrus 2010), 19–36.
164 Heller, "Konieczność i przypadek," 24.
165 Artigas, *The Mind of the Universe*, 89.
166 Collins, "Divine Action and Evolution," 247–53. See also Peacocke, *Theology for a Scientific Age. Being and Becoming – Natural and Divine* (Oxford: Basil Blackwell, 1990), 41–43.
167 Łukasiewicz, *O założeniach filozoficznych*, 210. See also David Hodgson, "Quantum Physics, Consciousness, and Free Will," in *The Oxford Handbook of Free Will*, ed. Robert Kane (Oxford: Oxford University Press, 2011), 80–83; Gregory Bateson, *Mind and Nature. A Necessary Unity* (New York: Dutton, 1979).

168 Griffin, *Unsnarling the World-Knot*, 49–51.
169 Polkinghorne, *Science and Providence*, 23; Peters, "Resurrection of the Very Embodied Soul," in *NAP*, 310–11.
170 Polkinghorne, *Science and Creation*, 88.
171 Philip Clayton, "Neuroscience, the Person, and God. An Emergentist Account," in *EMB*, 209.
172 Ibid., 210.
173 Słomka, *Ewolucjonizm chrześcijański*, 77.
174 Clayton, "Neuroscience, the Person, and God," 211.
175 On the one hand, a positive attitude and a patient's will to fight an illness are an important component of effective treatment. On the other hand, however, the human psyche is affected by the changes which occur in the structure of brain tissue. This can be manifested in mental impairment, as exemplified in the development of Alzheimer's disease. Polkinghorne, *Science and Providence*, 24.
176 Clayton, "Neuroscience, the Person, and God," 212.
177 Fraser Watts, "Cognitive Neuroscience and Religious Consciousness," in *NAP*, 340–41.
178 Polkinghorne, *Science and Providence*, 25.
179 Jantzen, *God's World, God's Body*, 80.
180 Clayton, "Neuroscience, the Person, and God," 210.
181 Polkinghorne, *Science and Providence*, 29.
182 Peacocke, *Paths from Science Towards God*, 139.
183 Ibid., 138.
184 Heller, *Sens życia i sens wszechświata*, 134.
185 Peacocke, *Paths from Science Towards God*, 139.
186 Ibid.
187 Ibid., 140.
188 Ibid., 141.
189 Ibid., 142.
190 Davies, *Cosmic Blueprint*, 56.
191 Polkinghorne, *Science and Providence*, 30–31.
192 John Macquarrie, *In Search of Deity. An Essay in Dialectical Theism* (London: SCM Press, 1984), 49.
193 Peacocke, *God and the New Biology*, 123.
194 Życiński, "The Rationality Field," 95.
195 Peacocke, *Paths from Science Towards God*, 77, 137–38.
196 Życiński, "The Rationality Field," 95; see also Peacocke, "Biological Evolution—A Positive Theological Appraisal," in *EMB*, 357–76.
197 Peacocke, *Theology for a Scientific Age*, 174–77.
198 Edwards, *The God of Evolution*, 55.
199 Słomka, "Argument Bożego planu," 82.
200 Życiński, "The Rationality Field," 95.
201 We can characterize the behaviors of certain biotic systems in the same way: Emmeche et al., "Levels, Emergence and Three Versions of Downward Causation," in *Downward Causation, Minds, Bodies and Matter*, ed. Peter B. Andersen and Claus Emmeche (Aarhus: Aarhus University Press, 2000), 27–28. See also Bremer, *Przyczynowość skierowana ku dołowi*, 108–10.
202 Życiński, "The Rationality Field," 96.

Conclusion

1 The *Credo* begins with the statement: "I believe in God . . . Almighty, Creator . . .," and many liturgical prayers are often initiated with the words: "Almighty, eternal God . . ." One can also point to many other examples of formulas used in Christian doctrine which contain reference to God's attributes or His manner of acting in the world.
2 Dennett, *Breaking the Spell.*
3 Drees, *Religion and Science in Context*, 47.
4 Miłosz Hołda, "Pasja łączenia. Katolicka teologia naturalna Józefa Życińskiego," *Roczniki Filozoficzne* 60, no. 4 (2012): 214–15.
5 Szubka, "Analityczna filozofia religii," 11.
6 NB: theistic terminology has often been transplanted to philosophical grounds from other disciplines of knowledge (most frequently from the natural sciences) at a specific stage of their development.
7 Michał Heller, *Filozofia przyrody. Zarys historyczny* (Cracow: Znak, 2004), 23.
8 Życiński, *Teizm i filozofia analityczna* (vol. 2), 42–46.
9 Matt. 13:52, NIV.

Select Bibliography

Abraham, William J. *Divine Agency and Divine Action.* Vol. 1, *Exploring and Evaluating the Debate,* 165–86. Oxford: Oxford University Press, 2017.
Alexander, David E., and Daniel M. Johnson, eds. *Calvinism and the Problem of Evil.* Eugene, OR: Pickwick Publications, 2016.
Alston, William P. "Divine Action, Human Freedom, and the Laws of Nature." In *QC,* 185–206.
Andersen, Peter B., Claus Emmeche, Niels Finnemmann, and Peder Christiansen, eds. *Downward Causation. Minds, Bodies and Matter.* Aarhus: Aarhus University Press 2000.
Arbib, Michael A. "Towards a Neuroscience of the Person." In *NP,* 77–100.
Artigas, Mariano. *The Mind of the Universe. Understanding Science and Religion.* Philadelphia & London: Templeton Foundation Press, 2000.
Ayala, Francisco J. *Darwin's Gift to Science and Religion.* Washington, DC: Joseph Henry Press, 2007.
Ayala, Francisco J. "Darwin's Devolution. Design without Designer." In *EMB,* s. 101–116.
Barbour, Ian G. "Indeterminacy, Holism and God's Action." In *God's Action in Nature's World. Essays in Honour of Robert John Russell,* edited by Ted Peters, Nathan Hallanger, 113–28. Aldershot: Ashgate, 2006.
Barbour, Ian G. "Neuroscience, Artificial Intelligence, and Human Nature. Theological and Philosophical Reflections." In *NP,* 249–80.
Barr, Stephen M. "The Concept of Randomness in Science and Divine Providence." In *Divine Action and Natural Selection. Science, Faith and Evolution,* edited by Joseph Seckbach and Richard Gordon, 465–81. New Jersey–London–Singapore–Beijing–Shanghai–Taipei–Chennai–Hong Kong: World Scientific, 2009.
Bartholomew, David J. *God, Chance and Purpose. Can God Have It Both Ways?* Cambridge: Cambridge University Press, 2008.
Bishop, John. "Causal Pluralism and the Problem of Natural Agency." *Res Philosophica* 91, no. 3 (2014): 527–36.
Boyd, Gregory A. "An Open-Theism Response." In *Divine Foreknowledge. Four Views,* edited by James K. Beilby and Paul R. Eddy, 144–48. Downers Grove, IL: Inter Varsity Press, 2001.
Boyd, Gregory A. "Two Ancient (and Modern) Motivations for Ascribing Exhaustively Definite Foreknowledge to God. A Historic Overview and Critical Assessment." *Religious Studies* 46, no. 1 (2010): 41–59.
Bracken, Joseph. *Does God Roll Dice? Divine Providence for a World in the Making,* 31–45. Collegeville, MN: Liturgical Press, 2012.
Bradley, James. "Randomness and God's Nature." *Perspectives on Science and Christian Faith* 64, no. 2 (2012): 75–89.
Brent, Michael. "Agent Causation as a Solution to the Problem of Action." *Canadian Journal of Philosophy* 47, no. 5 (2017): 656–73.
Brower, Jeffrey. "Making Sense of Divine Simplicity." *Faith and Philosophy* 25 (2008): 3–30.

Byl, John. "Indeterminacy, Divine Action and Human Freedom." *Science and Christian Belief* 15, no. 2 (2003): 101–15.

Carson, Donald A. *The Difficult Doctrine of the Love of God*. Leicester: Inter-Varsity Press, 2000.

Clayton, Philip. "Panentheism in Metaphysical and Scientific Perspective." In *In Whom We Live and Move and Have Our Being. Panentheistic Reflections on God's Presence in a Scientific World*, edited by Philip Clayton and Arthur Peacocke, 73–91. Cambridge-Grand Rapids, MI: William B. Eerdmans Publishing Company, 2004.

Clayton, Philip. "Neuroscience, the Person, and God. An Emergentist Account." In *EMB*, 181–214.

Clayton, Philip. "Tracing the Lines. Constraint and Freedom in the Movement from Quantum Physics to Theology." In *QM*, 211–34.

Clayton, Philip. "The Emergence of Spirit." *CTNS Bulletin* 20, no. 4 (2000): 3–20.

Collins, Francis. *The Language of God. A Scientist Presents Evidence for Belief*. New York–London–Toronto–Sydney: Free Press, 2007.

Collins, Robin. "Divine Action and Evolution." In *The Oxford Handbook of Philosophical Theology*, edited by Thomas P. Flint and Michael C. Rea, 241–61. Oxford: Oxford University Press, 2011.

Cooper, John W. *Panentheism. The Other God of the Philosophers. From Plato to the Present*. Grand Rapids, MI: Baker Academic, 2006.

Craig, William L., and David P. Hunt. "Perils of the Open Road." *Faith and Philosophy* 30, no. 1 (2013): 49–71.

Craig, William L. *The Kalam Cosmological Argument*. Eugene, OR: Pickwick Publications, 2016.

Craig, William L. *Time and Eternity. Exploring God's Relationship to Time*. Wheaton, IL: Crossway Books, 2001.

Crisp, Thomas M. "Presentism, Eternalism and Relativity Physics." In *Einstein, Relativity and Absolute Simultaneity*, edited by William L. Craig and Quentin Smith, 262–78. London–New York: Routledge, 2007.

Dancy, Jonathan, and Constantine Sandis, eds. *Philosophy of Action. An Anthology*. Oxford: Wiley-Blackwell, 2015.

Davies, Paul C. *Cosmic Jackpot. Why Our Universe is Just Right for Life*. New York: Orion Productions, 2007.

Davies, Paul C. *Cosmic Blueprint. New Discoveries in Nature's Creative Ability to Order the Universe*. Philadelphia–London: Templeton Foundation Press, 2004.

Davies, Paul C. *The Mind of God. The Scientific Basis for a Rational World*. New York: Simon & Schuster Paperbacks, 2005.

Davies, Paul C. "The Intelligibility of Nature." In *QC*, 149–64.

Davies, Paul C. "That Mysterious Flow." *Scientific American* 287, no. 3 (2002): 40–47.

Dekker, Eef. *Middle Knowledge*. Leuven: Peeters, 2000.

Dennett, Daniel C. *Breaking the Spell. Religion as a Natural Phenomenon*. New York: Viking, 2006.

Dodds, Michael J. *Unlocking Divine Action. Contemporary Science and Thomas Aquinas*. Washington DC: The Catholic University of America Press, 2012.

Dolezal, James E. *God without Parts. Divine Simplicity and the Metaphysics of God's Absoluteness*. Eugene, OR: Pickwick Publications, 2011.

Drees, Willem B. "Gaps for God?" in *CC*, 223–37.

Drees, Willem B. *Religion and Science in Context. A Guide to the Debates*. London: Routledge, 2009.

Duby, Steven J. *Divine Simplicity. A Dogmatic Account.* London–New York: Bloomsbury T. & T. Clark, 2016.
Edwards, Denis. *How God Acts. Creation, Redemption, and Special Divine Action.* Minneapolis, MN: Fortress Press, 2010.
Ellis, George F. "Intimations of Transcendence. Relations of the Mind and God." In *NP*, 447–74.
Ellis, George F. "Ordinary and Extraordinary Divine Action. The Nexus of Interaction." In *CC*, 359–95.
Ellis, George F. "Quantum Theory and the Macroscopic World." In *QM*, 259–91.
Ellis, George F. "*The Theology of the Anthropic Principle*." In *QC*, 363–99.
Emmeche, Claus, Simo Køppe, and **Frederik Stjernfelt.** "Levels, Emergence and Three Versions of Downward Causation." In *Downward Causation, Minds, Bodies and Matter*, edited by Peter B. Andersen, Claus Emmeche, Niels O. Finnemann, and Peder Voetmann Christiansen, 13–34. Aarhus: Aarhus University Press, 2000.
Everitt, Nicholas. *The Non-Existence of God.* London–New York: Routledge, 2004.
Fales, Evan. *Divine Intervention. Metaphysical and Epistemological Puzzles.* New York–London: Routledge, 2010.
Ferguson, Kitty. *The Fire in the Equations. Science, Religion, and Search for God.* West Conshohocken, PA: Templeton Press, 2004.
Fischer, John M., and **Patrick Todd, eds.** *Freedom, Fatalism, and Foreknowledge.* Oxford: Oxford University Press, 2012.
Flint, Thomas P. *Divine Providence. The Molinist Account.* Ithaca, NY: Cornell University Press, 2006.
Flint, Thomas P., and **Michael C. Rea,** eds. *The Oxford Handbook of Philosophical Theology.* Vol. 2. Oxford University Press, 2012.
Frankenberry, Nancy, ed. *The Faith of Scientists. In Their Own Words.* Oxford–Princeton, NJ: Princeton University Press, 2008.
Gilkey, Langdon. "The God of Nature." In *CC*, 211–20.
Gołosz, Jerzy. "Presentism, Eternalism, and the Triviality Problem." *Logic and Logical Philosophy* 22 (2013): 45–61.
Gregersen, Niels H., "Special Divine Action and the Quilt of Laws. Why the Distinction between Special and General Divine Cannot be Maintained." In *SPDA*, 179–99.
Grib, Andrej A. "Quantum Cosmology, Observer, Logic." In *QC*, 165–84.
Griffin, David R. *Religion and Scientific Naturalism. Overcoming the Conflicts.* Albany, NY: State University of New York Press, 2000.
Griffin, David R. *Reenchantment without Supernaturalism. A Process Philosophy of Religion.* London–Ithaca, NY: Cornell University Press, 2001.
Griffin, David R. *Unsnarling the World-Knot. Consciousness, Freedom, and the Mind–Body Problem.* Eugene, OR: Wipf & Stock Publishers, 2007.
Haarsma, Loren. *Chance from a Theistic Perspective.* Accessed July 14, 2017. http://www.talkorigins.org/faqs/chance/chance-theistic.html.
Happel, Stephen. "Divine Providence and Instrumentality. Metaphors for Time in Self-Organizing Systems and Divine Action." In *CC*, 177–203.
Hasker, William. "Analytic Philosophy of Religion." In *The Oxford Handbook of Philosophy of Religion*, edited by William J. Wainwright, 421–46. Oxford: Oxford University Press, 2005.
Hasker, William. *Providence, Evil and the Openness of God.* London–New York: Routledge, 2004.

Hasker, William. "Why Simple Foreknowledge Is Still Useless (In Spite of David Hunt and Alex Pruss)." *JETS* 52, no. 3 (2009): 537–44.
Haught, John F. "Darwin's Gift to Theology." In *EMB*, 393–418.
Hefling, Charles. "Christ and Evils. Assessing an Aspect of Marilyn McCord Adams's Theodicy." *ATR* 83, no. 4 (2001): 869–82.
Heller, Michał. "Chaos, Probability, and the Comprehensibility of the World." In *CC*, 107–21.
Hodgson, David. "Quantum Physics, Consciousness, and Free Will." In *The Oxford Handbook of Free Will*, edited Robert Kane, 86–110. Oxford: Oxford University Press, 2011.
Hoffman, Joshua, and Gary S. Rosenkrantz. "Omnipotence." In *A Companion to Philosophy of Religion*, ed. Philip L. Quinna and Charles Taliaferro, 229–35. Cambridge, MA: Blackwell, 1997.
Hoffman, Joshua, and Gary S. Rosenkrantz. "*Omnipotence.*" In *The Routledge Companion to Philosophy of Religion*, edited by Chad V. Meister and Paul Copan, 271–80. London–New York: Routledge, 2010.
Hoffman, Joshua, and Gary S. Rosenkrantz. *The Divine Attributes*. Oxford: Blackwell Publishing, 2002.
Hyötyniemi, Heikki, ed. *Complex Systems. Science on the Edge of Chaos*. Espoo: Helsinki University of Technology, 2004.
Isham, Chris, and John C. Polkinghorne. "The Debate over the Block Universe." In *QC*, 139–47.
Kane, Robert. *A Contemporary Introduction to Free Will*. New York: Oxford University Press, 2005.
Keller, James A. *Problems of Evil and the Power of God*. Aldershot: Ashgate 2007.
Leftow, Brian. "Divine Simplicity." *Faith and Philosophy* 23, no. 4 (2006): 365–80.
Leftow, Brian. "Omnipotence." In *The Oxford Handbook of Philosophical Theology*, edited by Thomas P. Flint and Michael C. Rea, 167–98. Oxford–New York: Oxford University Press 2009.
Lewis, Neil. "Space and Time." In *The Cambridge Companion to John Duns Scotus*, edited by Thomas Williams, 69–99. Cambridge: Cambridge University Press, 2002.
Lucas, John R. "The Temporality of God." In *QC*, 235–46.
MacDonald, Scott. "The Divine Nature." In *The Cambridge Companion to Augustine*, edited by Eleonore Stump and Norman Kretzmann, 71–90. Cambridge: Cambridge University Press, 2001.
Mackie, John L. "Evil and Omnipotence." *Mind* 64 (1955): 200–212.
Madden, Edward, and Peter Hare. "Critique of Hick's Theodicy." In *Philosophy of Religion. An Anthology*, edited by Louis P. Pojman, 156–59. Belmont, CA: Wadsworth Publishing Company, 2003.
Malaterre, Christophe. "Life as an Emergent Phenomenon. From an Alternative to Vitalism to an Alternative to Reductionism." In *Vitalism and the Scientific Image in Post-Enlightenment Life Science, 1800–2010*, edited by Sebastian Normandin and Charles T. Wolfe, 155–78. Dordrecht–Heildelberg–London–New York: Springer, 2013.
Mann, William E., ed. *The Blackwell Guide to the Philosophy of Religion*. Oxford: Blackwell Publishing, 2005.
Mann, William E. "The Divine Attributes." *American Philosophical Quarterly* 12, no. 2 (1975): 151–59.
Mavrodes, George I. "Some Puzzles Concerning Omnipotence." *The Philosophical Review* 72, no. 2 (1963): 221–23.

Mazzocchi, Fulvio. "Complexity and the Reductionism-Holism Debate in Systems Biology." WIREs Systems Biology and Medicine 4 (2012): 413–27.

McCabe, Herbert. *God Still Matters*. London: Continuum, 2002.

McCann, Hugh J., and Daniel M. Johnson. "Divine Providence." In *The Stanford Encyclopedia of Philosophy* (Spring 2017 Edition), edited by Edward N. Zalta. Accessed February 20, 2018. https://plato.stanford.edu/entries/providence-divine/.

McGrath, Alister, and Joanna Collicutt McGrath. *The Dawkins Delusion? Atheist Fundamentalism and the Denial of the Divine*. Downers Grove, IL: IVP Books, 2007.

Mizrahi, Moti. "New Puzzles about Divine Attributes." *European Journal for Philosophy of Religion* 5, no. 2 (2013): 147–57.

Monton, Bradley. "God Acts in the Quantum World." In *Oxford Studies in Philosophy of Religion*, edited by Jonathan L. Kvanvig, 5:133–146. Oxford: Clarendon Press, 2012.

Morris, Simon C. *Life's Solution. Inevitable Humans in a Lonely Universe*. Cambridge: Cambridge University Press, 2003.

Murphy, Nancey. "Divine Action in the Natural Order. Buridan's Ass and Schrödinger's Cat." In *CC*, 325–57.

O'Brien, Lilian. *Philosophy of Action*. Basingstoke: Palgrave, 2014.

O'Connor, Timothy, and Constantine Sandis, eds. *A Companion to the Philosophy of Action*. Oxford: Wiley-Blackwell, 2010.

Otte, Richard. "Evidential Arguments from Evil." *International Journal for Philosophy of Religion*" 48 (2000): 1–10.

Pagdett, Alan G. *God, Time, and the Nature of Time*. Eugene, OR: Pickwick Publications, 2000.

Page, Ruth. "Panentheism and Pansyntheism. *God in Relation*." In *God and Evolution. A Reader*, edited by Mary K. Cunningham, 349–59. London–New York: Routledge, 2007.

Peacocke, Arthur R. "Articulating God's Presence in and to the World Unveiled by the Science." In *In Whom We Live and Move and Have Our Being. Panentheistic Reflections on God's Presence in a Scientific World*, edited by Philip Clayton and Arthur Peacocke, 137–54. Cambridge–Grand Rapids, MI: William B. Eerdmans Publishing Company, 2004.

Peacocke, Arthur R. "Biological Evolution—A Positive Theological Appraisal." In *EMB*, 357–76.

Peacocke, Arthur R. *Paths from Science Towards God. The End of All Our Exploring*. Oxford: Oneworld Publications, 2002.

Peacocke, Arthur R. "God's Interaction with the World. The Implications of Deterministic "Chaos" and of Interconnected and Interdependent Complexity." In *CC*, 263–88.

Peacocke, Arthur R. "God's Interaction with the World. The Implications of Deterministic "Chaos" and of Interconnected and Interdependent Complexity." In *CC*, 272–73.

Peacocke, Arthur R. "The Sound of Sheer Silence. How Does God Communicate with Humanity?" In *NAP*, 215–47.

Pedersen, Olaf. *The Two Books. Historical Notes on Some Interactions between Natural Science and Theology*. Edited by George V. Coyne and Tadeusz Sierotowicz. Notre Dame, IN: University of Notre Dame Press, 2007.

Peters, Ted. "Resurrection of the Very Embodied Soul." In *NAP*, 305–26.

Peters, Ted. "The Trinity in and Beyond Time." In *QC*, 264–89.

Plantinga, Alvin C. *God, Freedom, and Evil*. Grand Rapids, MI: Eerdmans, 2002.

Plantinga, Alvin C. "What is 'Intervention'?" *Theology and Science* 6, no. 4 (2008): 369–401.

Plantinga, Alvin C. *Where the Conflict Really Lies. Science, Religion and Naturalism.* Oxford: Oxford University Press, 2011.
Polkinghorne, John C., *Science and Creation. The Search for Understanding*, Philadelphia – London: Templeton Foundation Press 2006.
Polkinghorne, John C., *One World. The Interaction of Science and Theology.* London–Philadelphia, PA: Templeton Foundation Press, 2007.
Polkinghorne, John C. "The Laws of Nature and the Laws of Physics." In *QC*, 429–40.
Polkinghorne, John C. "The Metaphysic of Divine Action." In *CC*, 147–56.
Polkinghorne, John C. *The Work of Love. Creation as Kenosis.* Grand Rapids, MI: Eerdmans, 2001.
Pruss, Alexander R. "On Two Problems of Divine Simplicity." *Oxford Studies in Philosophy of Religion* 1 (2008): 150–67.
Quinn, Philip L. "Marilyn McCord Adams, Horrendous Evils and the Goodness of God." *The Philosophical Review* 110, no. 3 (2001): 476–79.
Razeto-Barry, Pablo. "Autopoiesis 40 years Later." *Origins of Life and Evolution of Biospheres* 42, no. 6 (2012): 543–67.
Richards, Jay W. *The Untamed God. A Philosophical Exploration of Divine Perfection, Simplicity, and Immutability.* Downers Grove, IL: InterVarsity Press, 2003.
Robson, Mark I. *Ontology and Providence in Creation. Taking "Ex Nihilo" Seriously.* London–New York: Continuum, 2008.
Rogers, Katherin. "Back to Eternalism." *Faith and Philosophy* 26, no. 3 (2009): 320–38.
Rogers, Katherin. *Anselm on Freedom.* Oxford: Oxford University Press, 2008.
Rogers, Katherin. *Perfect Being Theology.* Edinburgh: Edinburgh University Press, 2002.
Russell, Robert J. "Introduction." In *CC*, 1–31.
Russell, Robert J. "Introduction." In *QC*, 1–31.
Russell, Robert J. *Cosmology from Alpha to Omega. The Creative Mutual Interaction of Theology and Science.* Minneapolis: Fortress Press, 2008.
Russell, Robert J. "Finite Creation without a Beginning. The Doctrine of Creation in Relation to Big Bang and Quantum Cosmologies." In *QC*, 291–325.
Russell, Robert J., Nancey Murphy, and **William R. Stoeger,** eds. *Scientific Perspectives on Divine Action. Twenty Years of Challenge and Progress.* Vatican City State: Vatican Observatory Publications; Berkeley, CA: The Center for Theology and the Natural Sciences, 2008.
Sandis, Constantine, ed. *New Essays on the Explanation of Action.* Basingstoke: Palgrave, 2009.
Saunders, Nicholas T. *Divine Action and Modern Science.* Cambridge: Cambridge University Press, 2002.
Saunders, Nicholas T. "Does God Cheat at Dice? Divine Action and Quantum Possibilities." *Zygon* 35, no. 3 (2000): 517–44.
Schellenberg, John. *Divine Hiddenness and Human Reason.* London–Ithaca, CA: Cornell University Press, 2006.
Senor, Thomas. "The Real Presence of an Eternal God." In *Metaphysics and God. Essays in Honor of Eleonore Stump*, edited by Kevin Timpe, 39–60. London–New York: Routledge, 2008.
Shanley, Brian J. *The Thomist Tradition.* Dordrecht–London–Boston, MA: Kluwer Academic Publishers, 2002.
Silva, Ignacio. "Revisiting Aquinas on Providence and Rising to the Challenge of Divine Action in Nature." *JR* 94, no. 3 (2014): 277–91.

Simons, P. "Questions of freedom (Foreword)." In *Free Will and Modern Science*, edited by Richard Swinburne, 1–15. Oxford–New York: Oxford University Press, 2011.

Smith, Barry D. *The Oneness and Simplicity of God.* Eugene, OR: Pickwick Publications, 2014.

Stenger, Victor J. "Intelligent Design. Humans, Cockroaches, and the Laws of Physics." Accessed July 14, 2017. http://www.talkorigins.org/faqs/cosmo.html.

Stewart, Ian. *Does God Play Dice? The New Mathematics of Chaos.* 2nd ed. Malden, MA: Blackwell Publishers, 2002.

Stewart-Williams, Steve. *Darwin, God, and the Meaning of Life. How Evolutionary Theory Undermines Everything You Thought You Knew.* Cambridge: Cambridge University Press, 2010.

Stoeger, William R. "Contemporary Physics and the Ontological Status of the Laws of Nature." In *QC*, 209–31.

Stoeger, William R. "*Describing God's Action in the World in Light of Scientific Knowledge of Reality*." In *CC*, 239–61.

Stoeger, William R. "Describing God's Action in the World in Light of Scientific Knowledge of Reality." In *CC*, 239–69.

Stoeger, William R. "The Immanent Directionality of the Evolutionary Process, and Its Relationship to Teleology." In *EMB*, 163–90.

Stout, Rowland. *Action.* Chesham: Acumen, 2005.

Stump, Eleonore. "*God's Simplicity*." In *The Oxford Handbook of Aquinas*, edited by Brian Davies and Eleonore Stump, 135–46. Oxford–New York: Oxford University Press, 2012.

Stump, Eleonore. "The Problem of Suffering. A Thomistic Approach." In *Thomas Aquinas. Teacher and Scholar*, edited by James McEvoy, Michael Dunne, and Julia Hynes, 101–19. Dublin: Four Courts Press, 2012.

Stump, Eleonore. "Simplicity." In *A Companion to Philosophy of Religion* (2nd ed.), edited by Charles Taliaferro, Paul Draper, Phillip L. Quinn, 270–77. Oxford–Malden, MA: Wiley–Blackwell, 2010.

Swinburne, Richard G. *The Coherence of Theism.* Oxford: Oxford University Press, 2016.

Taliaferro, Charles, and Chad Meister, eds. *The Cambridge Companion to Christian Philosophical Theology.* New York: Cambridge University Press, 2010.

Tanner, Kathryn. *God and Creation in Christian Theology. Tyranny and Empowerment?* Minneapolis, MN: Fortress Press, 2005.

Thirring, Walter. *Kosmische Impressionen. Gottes Spuren in den Naturgesetzen.* Vienna: Molden, 2004.

Thiselton, Anthony C. *A Concise Encyclopedia of the Philosophy of Religion.* Oxford: Oneworld, 2002.

Torrell, Jean-Pierre. *Initiation à saint Thomas d'Aquin. Sa personne et son oeuvre.* Fribourg: Cerf, 2002.

Tracy, Thomas F. "Evolution, Divine Action, and the Problem of Evil." In *EMB*, 511–30.

Tracy, Thomas F. *God, Action, and Embodiment.* Grand Rapids, MI: Eerdmans, 1984.

Tracy, Thomas F. *Particular Providence and the God of Gaps.* In *CC*, 289–324.

van Inwagen, Peter. *The Problem of Evil. The Gifford Lectures Delivered in the University of St. Andrews in 2003.* Oxford: Calderon Press, 2008.

van Inwagen, Peter. "The Argument from Particular Horrendous Evils." *Proceedings of the American Catholic Philosophical Association* 74 (2000): 65–80.

van Inwagen, Peter. *What Does an Omniscient Being Know about the Future?*, w: *Oxford Studies in Philosophy of Religion* (vol. 1), red. J.L. Kvanvig, Oxford: Oxford University Press 2008, s. 216–230.

Wainwright, William J., ed. *The Oxford Handbook of Philosophy of Religion*. New York: Oxford University Press, 2005.

Wainwright, William J. "Omnipotence, Omniscience, and Omnipresence." In *The Cambridge Companion to Christian Philosophical Theology*, edited by Charles Taliaferro and Chad V. Meister, 46–65. Cambridge: Cambridge University Press, 2010.

Ward, Keith. *Divine Action. Examining God's Role in an Open and Emergent Universe*. West Conshohocken, PA: Templeton Foundation Press, 2007.

Ward, Keith. "God as a Principle of Cosmological Explanation." In *QC*, 247–61.

Warfield, Ted A. "Ockhamism and Molinism. Foreknowledge and Prophecy." In *Oxford Studies in Philosophy of Religion*, edited by Jonathan L. Kvanvig, 2:317–32. Oxford: Oxford University Press, 2009.

Watts, Fraser. "Cognitive Neuroscience and Religious Consciousness." In *NAP*, 327–46.

Weigel, Peter J. *Aquinas on Simplicity. An Investigation into the Foundations of his Philosophical Theology*. Oxford: Peter Lang, 2008.

Weinandy, Thomas G. *Does God Suffer?* Edinburgh: T&T Clark, 2000.

Wielenberg, Erik J. "The New Paradox of the Stone Revisited." *Faith and Philosophy* 18, no. 2 (2001): 261–68.

Wildman, Wesley J. "Evaluating the Teleological Argument for Divine Action." In *EMB*, 117–50.

Wilks, Ian. "The Structure of the Contemporary Debate on the Problem of Evil." *RelS* 40 (2004): 307–21.

Wright, Robert. *The Evolution of God*. New York–Boston–London: Little, Brown, and Company, 2009.

Zagzebski, Linda. "Foreknowledge and Free Will ." Accessed July 17, 2017. https://plato.stanford.edu/entries/free-will-foreknowledge/.

Zagzebski, Linda. "Recent Work on Divine Foreknowledge and Free Will." In *The Oxford Handbook of Free Will*, edited by Robert Kane, 45–64. Oxford: Oxford University Press, 2002.

Życiński, Józef. *God and Evolution. Fundamental Questions of Christian Evolutionism*. Translated by Kenneth W. Kemp and Zuzanna Maślanka. Washington, DC: The Catholic University of America Press, 2006.

Życiński, Józef. "God, Freedom and Evil. Perspectives from Religion and Science." *Zygon* 35, no. 3 (2000): 653–64.

Życiński, Józef. "The Rationality Field and the Laws of Nature." In *Wyzwania racjonalności. Księdzu Michałowi Hellerowi współpracownicy i uczniowie*, edited by Stanisław Wszołek and Robert Janusz, 87–101. Cracow: WAM, 2006.

Index

Abraham, W.J. 183 n.37
Adams, R.M. 28, 193 n. 277, 198 n.102
Alexander, D.E. 193 n. 284
Alexander of Hales, 116
Alston, W.P. 11, 28, 85, 178 n.15, 196 n.46
Andersen, P.B. 179 n.38, 211 n.201
Anselm, St. 5, 25–6, 32, 37, 45, 52, 170–1, 183 n.35, 185 n. 88, 187 n. 130
Aquinas, Thomas St. 5, 17–18, 26–9, 31–2, 38–9, 42, 52–3, 55, 63, 67, 74, 92–3, 116–17, 170, 176 n.16, 180 n.50, 180 nn.52–3, 181 n.21, 182 n.35, 184 nn.54–7, 184 n.59, 197 n.80, 197 n.82, 197 n.84, 185 n.82, 185 n. 91, 186 n.100, 186 n.114, 187 n.121, 188 n.157, 189 n.170, 189 nn.172–4, 192 n.252, 192 n.258, 196 n.70, 197 n.80, 197 n.82, 197 n.84, 201 n.192, 201 n.195, 202 n.203, 203 n.219
Arbib, M.A. xi, 195 n.21, 197 n.71
Aristotle 26, 30–2, 39, 183 n.49
Artigas, M. 209 n.148, 210 n.165
Audi, R. 190 n.197
Audra, R.A. 200 n.166
Augustine, St. 5, 25–6, 32, 36–7, 49, 51–2, 55, 82, 118, 170, 182 n.29, 184 n.58, 185 n.84, 185 n.87, 202 n.212
Ayala, F.J. 3, 205 n.45, 207 n.82, 209 n.132

Báñez, D. 198 n.100
Barbour, I.G. 2, 3, 175 n.4, 178 n.23, 196 n.56
Barr, S.M. 196 n.48
Barrow, J.D. 134, 205 n.52
Bartholomew, D.J. 148, 184 n.63, 200 n.165, 208 n.122, 209 nn.140–1
Bateson, G. 210, n.167
Bauckham, R. 188 n.161
Behe, M. 155
Beilby, J.K. 193 n.274
Bénard, H.C. 15

Benedict XVI, Pope 176 n.20, 206 n.71
Bergson, H. 111, 200 n.166
Berry, R.J. 176 n.14
Bishop, J. 177 n.2
Blumenfeld, D. 23, 181 n.13
Boethius 38, 48–9, 68, 74, 188 n.150
Bohm, D. 14
Bohr, N. 14
Bourke, D. 194 n.6
Bowden, J. 191 n.220
Bowker, J. 207 n.102
Boyd, G.A. 193 n.274, 193 n.280
Bracken, J.A. 183 n.40
Bradley, J. 192 n.245
Bremer, J. 179 n.35, 179 n.38, 179 n.40, 211 n.201
Brent, M. 177
Brereton, C. 200 n.166
Brockman, J. 210 n.154
Brower, J. 187 n.117
Browne, J. 204 n.40
Brümmer, V. 209 n.141
Budzik, S. 180 n.3
Bugajak, G. 208 n.117
Burkhardt, F. 204 n.40
Byl, J. 196 n.45

Campbell, D.T. 179 n.36
Carroll, R.T. 210 n.154
Carson, D.A. 188 n.159
Carter, W.H. 200 n.166
Chisholm, R.M. 193 n.268
Christiansen, P. 179 n.38
Cilliers, P. 205 n.60
Clark, J.W. 205 n.42
Clarke, R. 177 n.2
Clarke, W.N. 27
Clayton, P. 2, 136, 180 n.9, 202 n.214, 202 n.217, 206 n.61, 211 n.171, 211 n.174, 211 n.176, 211 n.180

Cobb, J. 28
Collicutt McGrath, J. 176 n.15
Collins, F. 206 n.69
Collins, R. 158, 194 n.2, 210 n.166
Cooper, J.W. 203 n.228
Copan, P. 190 n.197
Copernicus, N. 136
Courtenay, W.J. 189 n.176
Coyne, G.V. 3, 175 n.6, 178 n.18, 183 n.38, 183 n. 48, 202 n. 207, 206 n.66
Craig, W.L. 181 n.16, 187 n.134, 191 n.240, 194 n.287
Creel, R.E. 188 n.159, 192 n.255
Crick, F. 136
Crisp, T.M. 181 n.16
Cronin, K.M. 202, n.215
Crutchfield, J.P. 195 n.30
Cunningham, M.K. 203 n.228
Cusanus, see Nicholas of Cusa
Czarnuch, M. 206 n.72

Damiani, P. 52, 189 n.166
Darwin, C. 131–2, 136, 140, 151, 191 n.221, 191 n.224, 204 nn.39–40, 205 n.45, 206 n.74–5, 207 n.81, 207 n.83, 207 n.85, 207 n.87–8, 207 n.90, 207 n.93–4, 207 n.97, 207 n.99, 207 n.101, 207 n.103, 208 n.105, 208 n.107, 208 n.109, 208 n.112, 209 n.133, 209 n.150
Darwin, F. 204 n.39
Davies, B. 42, 181 n.21, 185 n.91, 186 n.112, 186 n.116
Davies, P.C. 3, 64, 65, 81–3, 181 n.16, 191 n.239, 191 n.241, 192 n.242, 195 n.22, 195 n.24, 195 nn.26–7, 195 n.29, 195 n.31, 195 nn.33–4, 196 n.43, 196 n.47, 196 n.58, 196 n.60, 204 n.12, 205 n.48, 205 n.50, 209 n.141, 211 n.190
Davis, S.T. 181 n.20
Dawkins, R. 139, 142, 152, 156, 176 n.15, 208 n.108, 209 nn.136–7
de Beer, G. 207 n.100
de Molina, L. 72, 95–6, 198 n.100
Dekker, E. 198 n.112
Dembski, W.A. 155, 157, 209 n.152, 210 n.162
Dennett, D.C. 139, 143–4, 206 n.74, 206 n.79, 207 n.93, 207 n.103, 212 n.2

Descartes, R. 45, 55, 187 n.131
Dobzhansky, T. 179 n.36
Dodds, M.J. 2, 176 n.16, 179 n.48, 180 n.54, 183 n.35, 188 n. 157
Dolezal, J.E. 185 n.86, 185 n.89
Dorschner, J. 188 n.139
Draper, P. 91, 197 n.78
Drees, W.B. 2, 125, 176 n.14, 196 n.53, 203 n.9, 203 n.11, 204 n.13, 207 n.80, 212 n.3
Drummond, H. 124, 203 n.6
Duby, S.J. 185 n.88, 186 n.101
Dunne, M. 196 n.70
Duns Scotus, J. 53–5, 116, 170, 183 n.49, 189 n.177, 189 n.185, 200 n.168
Dyson, F. 83, 195 n.28
Dziadkowiec, J. 206 n.72

Eddy, P.R. 193 n.274
Edwards, D. 2, 34, 86, 185 n.72, 191 n.219, 194 nn.5–7, 194 n.9, 194 n.13, 196 n.48, 206 n.64, 206 n.68, 211 n.198
Einstein, A. 136, 157, 181 n.16, 192 n.242, 208 n.129
Elders, L.J., 189 n.172
Ellis, G.F.R. 3, 14, 119, 178 n.22, 178 n.29, 188 n.144, 191 n.237, 202 n.215, 204 n.28
Emmeche, C. 179 n.38, 211 n.201

Fales, E. 191 n.240
Ferguson, K. 178 n.28, 195 n.32
Finnemmann, N. 179 n.38
Fischer, J.M. 194 n.287
Flint, T.P. 181 n.19, 190 n.197, 194 n.2, 198 n.94, 198 n.112

Galileo Galilei, 136, 173
Gallagher, K.T. 188 n.140
Gavrilyuk, P.L. 188 n.157
Geach, P. 57, 64, 190 n.201, 191 n.235
Gilkey, L. 205 n.47
Giorello, G. 202 n.207
Golbiak, J. 206 n.63, 209 n.134
Gomułka, J. 199 n.133
Gray, A. 204 n.40
Gray, C.G. 205 n.51
Greenberg, G. 179 n.36
Gregersen, N.H. 2, 178 n.25

Gribbin, J. 207 n.89
Griffin, D.R. 2, 28, 175 n.11, 178 n.21, 179 n.34, 180 n.56, 180 n.2, 180 n.7, 183 n.39, 192 n.247, 197 n.80, 207 n.91, 207 n.96, 211 n.168
Gut, A. 193 n.267
Gut, P. 193 n.267
Gutowski, P. 3, 186 n.109, 192 n.254, 192 n.257

Haarsma, L. 210 n.159
Hahn, L.E. 192 n.253
Happel, S. 177 n.9
Hare, P. 199 n.129
Hartshorne, C. 28, 41, 56, 66–8, 120, 185 n.70, 186 n.109, 190 n.196, 192 n.248–57, 202 n.218, 203 n.219
Hasker, W. 69, 73, 183 n.43, 191 n.232, 192 n.261, 193 n.271, 193 n.278, 193 n.281, 197 n.87, 198 n.102, 199 n.135
Haught, J.F. 2–3, 62, 140–1, 175 n.8, 191 n.221, 191 n.224, 206 n.75, 207 n.81, 207 n.83, 207 n.85, 207 n.87, 207 n.90, 207 n.94, 207 n.97, 207 n.99, 207 n.101, 207 n.103, 208 n.107, 208 n.109, 208 n.112, 210 n.159
Hawking, S. 204 n.22
Hefling, C. 201 n.184
Hegel, G.W.F. 40
Heller, M. 3, 14, 127, 157, 179 n.32, 180 n.57, 180 n.59, 180 n.3, 182 n.33, 183 n.47, 183 n.50, 184 nn.52–3, 184 n.55, 184 n.57, 184 n.59, 196 n.45, 203 n.1, 204 n.21, 204 n.23, 206 n.65, 208 n.126, 208 n.128, 209 nn.141–2, 210 n.155, 210 nn.157–8, 210 n.160, 210 n.162, 210 n.164, 211 n.184, 212 n.7
Helm, P. 193 n.283, 197 n.81
Heraclitus, 47
Hereć, M. 206 n.63
Hetmański, M. 203 n.10
Hick, J. 98, 102, 113, 199 n.123, 199 n.125–7, 199 n.129
Hill, E. 184 n.58
Hodgson, D. 210 n.167
Hoffman, J. 181 n.20, 190 n.197
Hołda, M. 212 n.4
Hopkins, J. 201 n.197

Hraber, P.T. 195 n.30
Hubaczek, K. 197 nn.74–5, 197 nn.77–8, 198 n.92, 198 n.95, 198 nn.97–9, 198 n.101, 198 n.103, 198 n.105, 198 nn.108–9, 198 n.113, 199 n.126, 200 nn.167–9, 200 n.171, 200 n.174, 200 n.176, 200 n.180, 201 n.182, 201 nn.185–6
Hübner, R. 188 n.157
Huggard, E.M. 188 n.138, 190 n.190
Hughes, C. 185 n.82
Hughes G.J. 186 n.103, 187 n.122, 181 n.228
Hughes, T.M. 205 n.42
Hume, D. 33, 39, 41, 55–6, 80, 112, 190 n.192, 190 n.194, 197 n.74, 207 n.95
Hunt, D.P. 194 n.287
Hynes, J. 196 n.70

Innocent IV, Pope 31, 182 n.33
Irenaeus of Lyons, St. 194 n.12
Isham, C.J. 191 n.233
Iverach, J. 133, 205 n.43, 205 n.44

James, W. 40
Janeczek, S. 187 n.118
Jantzen, G. 11–12, 160, 178 n.17, 211 n.179
Janusz, R. 195 n.16
Jasiński, K. 209 n.134
Jaworski, K. 193 n.267
Jodkowski, K. 209 n.132
John Paul II, St. Pope 2–3, 175 n.6, 206 n.71
Johnson, D.M. 193 n.284
Johnson, E. 34, 185 n.71, 194 n.11
Johnson, P.E. 156, 210 n.156
Johnston, G.S. 142, 207 n.88
Jonas, H. 189 n.163
Joule, J.P. 131, 204 n.34
Judycki, S. 3, 47, 185 n.73, 186 n.99, 187 n.120, 187 nn.126–8, 188 nn.141–3, 189 n.165, 189 n.167, 189 n.169, 189 n.171, 189 n.176, 189 n.189, 190 n.197, 190 nn.201–2, 191 nn.212–13, 191 n.215, 193 n.266, 193 n.268, 193 n.270, 193 n.272, 201 n.187
Justin, St. 182 n.27

Kane, R. 192 n.257, 194 n.287, 200 n.153
Kant, I. 27, 33
Karl, G. 205 n. 51
Kasper, W. 175 n.1
Kaszkowiak, P. 191 n.230
Kaufman, G. 11
Kehm, G.H. 188 n.162
Keller, J.A. 176 n.20
Kemp, K.W. 201 n.190
Kepler, J. 130, 173
Kiełbasa, J. 185 n.77
Kleszcz, R. 189 n.166, 189 n.168,
    189 n.172, 189 n.175, 189 n.188,
    190 n.199, 190 nn.200–1, 190 n.204,
    190 n.206, 190 n.208, 190 n.210,
    191 n.211, 191 n.214
Kłósak, K. 27
Konczal, M.S. 209 n.132
Koszkało, M. 185 n.81, 186 n.93, 186 n.100,
    186 n.104, 186 n.106, 187 n.121,
    187 n.124, 189 n.177, 189 nn.179–80,
    189 n.183, 189 n.186
Kotowicz, W. 209 n.134
Kowalczyk, S. 186 n.95, 186 n.100,
    186 n.101
Koyré, A. 31, 183 n.51
Krause, K.C.F. 119, 202 n.216
Krawczyk, J.F. 209 n.133
Kretzmann, N. 23, 41–2, 68, 70, 181 n.14,
    185 n.84, 186 n.111, 192 n.258,
    193 n.262
Krupa, M. 193 n.267
Kuszyk-Bytniewska, M. 208 n.117
Kvanvig, J.L. 177 n.5, 177 n.27, 193 n.273,
    194 n.287

La Croix, R.R. 185 n.87
Laplace, P.-S. 13, 154
Lee, J.Y. 188 n.162
Leftow, B. 41, 186 n.113, 190 n.197
Leibniz, G.W. 40, 46, 55, 95, 111–12, 114,
    188 n.138, 190 n.190
Lewin, R. 195 n.30
Lewis, n. 183 n.49
Lucas, J.R. 48, 188 n.146
Luibheid, C. 201 n.194
Łukasiewicz, D. 3, 11, 72, 93, 158, 175 n.10,
    177 n.10, 179 n.33, 180 n.5, 181 n.15,
    181 n.18, 181 n.23, 182 n.35, 184 n.60,
    188 n.151, 191 n.226, 191 n.232,
    193 n.269, 193 n.273, 193 n.275,
    193 n.279, 193 n.282, 193 nn.284–5,
    194 n.288, 194 n.1, 194 n.3,
    197 nn.79–83, 197 n.85, 198 n.89,
    199 n.149, 200 n.153, 200 n.163,
    201 n.180, 208 nn.117–18, 208 n.120,
    208 n.123, 209 n.146, 209 n.149,
    209 n.151, 210 n.167
Łukasik, A. 208 n.117
Łukowski, P. 190 n.205

McCabe, H. 194 nn.8–9
McCann, H.J. 93, 177 n.5, 198 n.88
McCord Adams, M. 112–14, 193 n.277,
    197 n.75, 200 nn.167–70, 200 n.72, 200
    nn.174–5, 200 nn.177–3, 200 nn.168–
    73, 200 n.175, 200 nn.177–82, 200
    n.184
MacDonald, S. 185 n.84
McEvoy, J. 196 n.70
McFague, S. 12, 178 n.18, 191 n.222
McGrath, A. 176 n.15
Mackie, J.L. 56, 190 n.197
McMullin, E. 27, 179 n.31, 183 n.38,
    184 n.53, 209 n.142
Macquarrie, J. 191 n.223, 207 n.84,
    211 n.192
Mączka, J. 206 n.70
Madden, E. 199 n.129
Mainzer, K. 203 n.10
Malaterre, C. 179 n.37
Mann, W.E. 181 n.19, 182 n.31, 190 n.197
Marcum, J.M. 179 n.36
Maślanka, Z. 201 n.190
Matava, R.J. 198 n.100
Mavrodes, G.I. 190 n.210
Mazierski, S. 27
Mazzocchi, F. 179 n.35
Meister, C.V. 181 n.19, 181 n.24,
    190 n.197
Meister Eckhart, 116
Mendel G.J., 136
Mercier, D. 27
Mill, J.S. 106, 199 n.145
Miller, H. 132, 205 n.41
Miller, K.R. 208 n.105
Mitchell, M. 195 n.30
Mizrahi, M. 190 n.197

Moltmann, J. 34, 115, 184 n.70, 201 n.188
Monod, J. 135, 205 n.56
Monton, B. 178 n.27
Moore, A.L. 124, 203 n.2, 203 n.4
Moran, D. 201 n.196
Morawski, M. 204 n.33
Mordarski, R. 3, 26, 181 n.17, 181 n.21,
    181 n.24, 182 n.30, 182 n.32, 182 n.34,
    183 n.36, 183 n.42, 183 n.44, 188 n.153,
    190 n.210, 192 n.242, 192 n.243,
    192 nn.258–9, 192 n.261, 193 nn.262–3
Morris, S.C. 195 n.17
Morris, T.V. 23, 180 n.11
Moskop, J.C. 192 n.252
Mössner, N. 199 n.120
Mrugalski, D. 177 n.4
Murphy, N. 2, 14, 175 n.5, 178 n.29

Newton, I. 2, 16, 33, 63, 85, 87, 136, 149–51
Nicholas of Cusa, 116–17, 201 n.196–8,
    201 n.200
Niziński, R.S. 192 n.249, 192 n.253,
    192 nn.255–6
Normandin, S. 179 n.37
Novikov, V.A. 205 n.51

O'Brien, L. 176 n.1
O'Connor, T. 43, 177 n.1, 187 n.125
Oko, D. 186 n.105
Oko, J. 206 n.72
Oppy, G. 197 n.75
Origen 36, 185 nn. 78–9
Otte, R. 197 n.75

Pabjan, T. 179 n.49, 180 n.51, 184 n.53,
    184 n.55, 184 n.57, 184 n.59, 207 n.86,
    208 n.114, 179 n.49
Pagdett, A.G. 191 n.240
Page, R. 203 n.228
Pagels, H.R. 202 n.206
Paley, W. 81, 84, 131–3, 152, 163–4, 204 n.37
Pannenberg, W. 188 n.162
Pasteur, L. 130
Paul, St. 28, 180 n.1
Peacocke, A.R. 3, 16, 48–50, 118–19, 127,
    161, 163, 178 n.16, 179 n.39, 179 n.44,
    179 n.47, 180 n.8, 184 n.66, 188 nn.144–
    5, 188 n.155, 191 n.225, 192 n.244,
    192 n.246, 195 n.38, 199 n.128,

199 n.139, 201 n.187, 202 nn.208–9,
    202 nn.212–14, 203 n.7, 204 n.15,
    204 n.20, 204 n.22, 205 n.49, 206 n.67,
    209 n.141, 210 n.166, 211 n.182,
    211 n.185, 211 n.193, 211 nn.195–7
Pedersen, O. 183 n.48, 184 n.65, 204 n.35
Pennock, R.T. 210 n.154
Pepliński, M. 185 n.81, 186 n.93, 186 n.100,
    186 n.104, 186 n.106, 187 n.121,
    187 n.124, 189 n.179, 189 n.182,
    190 n.198
Peters, T. 48, 178 n.23, 188 n.147,
    188 n.149, 204 n.25, 211 n.169
Peterson, M.L. 197 n.74
Phillips, S.H. 192 n.257
Philo, 50
Pike, N. 23, 90, 181 n.14, 190 n.198,
    197 n.74
Pinnock, C.H. 175 n.2
Piórczyński, J. 198 n.96
Piwowarczyk, M. 187 n.118
Planck, M. 82
Plantinga, A.C. 2–3, 28, 41–2, 45, 90, 95,
    97–8, 177 n.7, 178 n.26, 180 n.10,
    181 n.12, 186 n.110, 186 n.112,
    187 n.132, 197 n.74, 198 nn.98–9
Plato 30, 50, 203 n.228
Polak, P. 208 n.131
Polkinghorne, J.C. 3, 12, 14, 16, 63, 86–8,
    125, 160, 162, 177 n.9, 178 n.20,
    178 n.25, 178 n.30, 179 n.43, 179 n.45,
    182 n.29, 191 n.233, 196 n.50, 196 n.52,
    196 nn.54–5, 196 n.57, 196 nn.59–60,
    196 n.62, 196 n.65, 196 n.68, 201 n.189,
    203 n.6, 203 n.8, 207 n.87, 208 n.106,
    209 n.139, 210 n.161, 211 n.169,
    211 n.170, 211 n.175, 211 n.178,
    211 n.181, 211 n.191
Pollard, W.G. 13, 178 n.26
Popper, K.R. 4, 87, 175 n.12
Porter, D.M. 204 n.40
Pruss, A.R. 187 n.125, 193 n.281
Przanowski, M. 38, 43, 185 n.77, 185 n.78,
    185 n.80, 185 n.82, 185 n.85, 185 nn.87–
    90, 186 n.92, 186 n.94, 186 nn.96–7,
    186 nn.102–3, 186 n.105, 186 nn.112–13,
    186 n.115, 187 n.117, 187 n.123
Pseudo-Dionysius the Areopagite, 116, 201
    n.194

Quinn, P.L. 181 n.19, 185 n.83, 200 n.167

Radziszewski, I. 27
Rahner, K. 78-9, 191 n.222, 194 nn.5-7
Razeto-Barr, P. 194 n.10
Rea, M. C. 181 n.19, 190 n.197, 194 n.2
Richards, J.W. 187 n.119
Richardson, W.M. 176 n.19
Richmond M. 204 n.40
Riley, H.M. 195 n.5
Robson, M.I.T. 208 n.119
Rodzeń, J. 209 n.142
Rogers, K. 42, 181 n.16, 181 n.20, 185 n.88, 187 n.117
Rolston III, H. 207 n.100
Rosenkrantz, G.S. 181 n.20, 190 n.197
Rotelle J.E. 184 n.58
Rowe, W.L. 73, 91, 108, 193 n.277, 197 n.77, 199 n.129, 200 n.157
Russell, R.J. 3, 12, 175 n.5, 177 n.3, 177 n.6, 177 nn.8-9, 178 n.13, 178 n.18, 178 n.20, 178 n.23, 179 n.41, 183 n.38, 184 n.52, 184 n.62, 184 n.64, 206 n.66

Sagan, C.E. 139
Salamon, J. 180 n.5, 209 n.131
Sandis, C. 177 n.1
Saunders, N.T. 179 n.32, 194 n.15, 204 n.19
Savage, C. Wade 190 n.210
Schellenberg, J. 202 n.215
Schillebeeckx, E. 61, 191 n.220
Schleiermacher, F. 33
Schrader, D.E. 190 n.210
Scopes, J. 140
Scotus Eriugena, J. 116, 201 n.196
Sedgwick, A. 132, 205 n.42
Senor, T.D. 188 n.152
Seward, A.C. 204 n.39
Shanley, B.J. 181 n.21, 183 n.35, 192 n.258
Sia, S. 192 n.250
Sierotowicz, T. 183
Silva, I. 180 n.50
Simons, P. 193 n.265
Sindoni, E. 202 n.207
Słomka, M. 185 n.76, 188 n.141, 204 n.32, 204 n.36, 204 n.38, 205 n.46, 206 n.63, 206 n.73, 207 n.92, 209 n.134, 209 n.138, 209 n.153, 210 nn.156-7,
210 n.159, 210 n.161, 211 n.173, 211 n.199
Smith, B.D. 186 n.115
Smith, M.P. 210 n.210
Smith, Q. 181 n.16
Sokolowski, R. 180 n.6, 181 n.25
Šolín, P. 205 n.51
Spinoza, B. 91, 198 n.96
Sprigge, T.L. 192 n.253
Stagirite, see Aristotle
Starościc, A. 187 n.118
Stenger, V.J. 210 n.161
Stewart, I. 208 n.125
Stewart-Williams, S. 209 n.150
Stępień, A.B. 45-6, 187 n.135
Stoeger, W.R. 3, 18, 27, 34, 86, 89, 128, 135, 137, 175 n.5, 176 n.19, 178 n.18, 179 n.48, 180 nn.54-5, 183 n.38, 184 nn.67-9, 195 n.20, 196 n.44, 196 n.49, 196 n.63, 196 n.69, 204 n.24, 204 n.26, 204 n.29, 205 n.58, 206 n.66, 208 n.115
Stout, R. 176 n.1
Stump, E. 41-2, 68, 70, 89, 92-3, 185 nn.83-4, 185 n.89, 185 n.91, 186 n.111, 186 n.114, 187 nn.120-1, 188 n.152, 192 n.258, 193 n.262, 196 n.70, 197 n.82, 197 n.84, 199 n.135
Swieżawski, S. 186 n.96
Świeżyński, A. 193 n.271
Swinburne, R. 2-3, 35, 46, 57-8, 98-9, 101, 180 n.1, 183 n.41, 184 n.54, 185 n.74, 185 n.76, 187 n.136, 190 n.200, 190 n.203, 190 n.207, 191 n.211, 193 n.265, 198 n.114, 198 n.116, 199 nn.120-1
Szubka, T. 183 n.41, 212 n.5

Tałasiewicz, M. 207 n.95
Taliaferro, C. 181 n.19, 181 n.24, 185 n.83
Tanner, K. 202 n.215
Teihard de Chardin, P. 81, 84, 138, 206 n.71
Tempczyk, M. 199 n.142, 203 n.10
Tempier, S. 182 n.33
Thijssen, H. 182 n.33
Thirring, W. 194 n.14
Thiselton, A.C. 181 n.19
Thomas Aquinas, St. see Aquinas

Thomas, O.C. 11
Tipler, F.J. 134, 205 n.52
Tkaczyk, M. 193 n.286
Tobach, E. 179 n.36
Todd, P. 194 n.287
Torrell, J.P. 186 n.97
Tracy, T.F. 2, 12, 178 n.19, 195 n.35,
    196 n.41, 196 n.44, 196 n.61, 196 n.64,
    196 n.67, 197 n.72, 198 n.115,
    199 n.124, 199 n.130, 199 n.132,
    199 n.134, 199 n.136, 199 n.140,
    199 n.143, 201 n.187, 203 n.1
Trepczyński, M. 190 n.191, 190 n.193,
    190 n.195
Tryon, E. 195 n.23

Urbańczyk, P. 206 n.70
Ussher, J. 33

van den Brink, G. 57, 190 n.202
van der Veken, J. 27
van Inwagen, P. 2, 28, 98, 105-8, 110,
    175 n.11, 180 n.4, 187 n.127, 194 n.287,
    199 n.131, 199 n.144, 199 n.146,
    199 n.150, 200 n.152, 200 n.154,
    200 n.158, 200 nn.161-2, 201 n.183,
    208 n.116
Vanhoozer, K.J., 188 n.161
Vardy, P. 64, 183 nn.45-6, 185 n.77,
    186 n.98, 189 n.171, 189 n.187,
    191 n.216, 191 nn.226-7, 191 n.229,
    191 n.231, 191 n.234, 191 n.236,
    191 n.238
Veldhuis, H. 189 n.185
Velkley, R. 183 n.35
Viney, D.W. 192 n.252, 192 n.257

Wainwright, W.J. 181 n.19, 181 n.24, 183
    n.43, 199 n.144
Ward, K. 2, 179 n.42, 188 nn.147-8,
    191 n.236, 202 n.211, 208 n.130
Warfield, T.A. 193 n.273
Watson, J. 136
Watts, F. 211 n.177
Weidemann, C. 199 n.120

Weigel, P.J. 186 n.100
Weinandy, T.G. 186 n.105, 188 n.158,
    188 n.160, 188 nn.162-4
Weinberg, S. 13, 178 n.24
Weisheipl, J.A. 186 n.97
Whitehead, A.N. 27, 61, 81, 117, 120, 138,
    164, 183 n.39, 202 n.205, 203 n.219, 206
    n.72
Wicken, J.S. 208 n.111
Wielenberg, E.J. 190 n.210
Wierenga, E.R. 181 n.20, 190 n.209
Wildman, W.J. 176 n.19
Wiles, M.F. 11, 178 n.14, 182 n.28
Wilks, I. 197 n.73, 201 n.185
Williams, B. 198 n.107
Williams, T. 183 n.49
Wojtysiak, J. 3, 45-6, 121, 180 n.6, 184
    n.70, 185 n.70, 187 n.129, 187 n.131,
    187 n.133, 187 n.135, 187 n.137,
    202 n.214, 202 nn.217-19, 203
    nn.221-2, 203 n.225, 203 n.227
Wolfe, C.T.. 179 n.37
Wright, R. 181 n.26
Wszołek, S. 180 n.3, 195 n.16

Yandell, K.E. 197 n.76

Zagzebski, L. 194 n.287, 198 n.104,
    198 n.113
Zalta, E.N. 182 n.33, 198 n.88
Zdybicka, Z.J. 186 n.95
Życiński, J. 3, 84, 120, 164, 173, 175 n.9,
    180 n.58, 185 n.70, 192 n.256, 195
    n.16, 195 nn.18,-19, 195 n.21,
    195 nn.36-9, 196 n.42, 201 nn.190-1,
    201 n.193, 201 n.199, 202 n.201,
    202 n.204, 202 n.207, 202 n.215,
    203 n.220, 203 nn.222-3, 203 n.225,
    203 n.226, 203 n.5, 204 n.31, 204 n.33,
    204 n.35, 205 nn.41-2, 205 n.44,
    205 nn.53-4, 205 n.57, 205 n.59,
    206 n.62-3, 207 n.80, 207 n.98,
    208 n.105, 209 n.143, 210 n.163,
    211 n.194, 211 n.196, 211 n.200,
    211 n.202, 212 n.4, 212 n.8

www.ingramcontent.com/pod-product-compliance
Lightning Source LLC
Chambersburg PA
CBHW072231290426
44111CB00012B/2043